JOURNAL FOR THE STUDY OF THE NEW TESTAMENT
SUPPLEMENT SERIES

271

The Educated Elite in 1 Corinthians

Education and Community Conflict in Graeco-Roman Context

Robert S. Dutch

T & T CLARK INTERNATIONAL
A Continuum imprint
LONDON • NEW YORK

A Continuum imprint

Published by T&T Clark International
The Tower Building,
11 York Road,
London SE1 7NX

15 East 26th Street,
Suite 1703,
New York, NY 10010

www.tandtclark.com

British Library Cataloguing-in-Publication Data
A catalogue record for this book is available from the British Library

ISBN 0826470882 (hardback)

Typeset by Tradespools, Frome, Somerset
Printed on acid-free paper in Great Britain by CPI Bath

Contents

Acknowledgments

This book is a revision and update of my PhD completed at the University of Bristol (1995–98) and funded throughout by the University of Bristol with a Postgraduate Research Scholarship. My adviser Dr Diane Treacy-Cole provided guidance, encouragement, and comments to ensure that my work remained focused and came to fruition within the required period. I gratefully acknowledge her support in both this and my successful application for funding.

While pursuing my inter-disciplinary research in the Department of Theology and Religious Studies I attended classes in the Department of Classics and Ancient History. Thanks are due to the scholars who welcomed me to their classes and staff who facilitated the arrangements. Particular recognition goes to Onno M. van Nijf while he was a Teaching Fellow at Bristol. His course 'Rome in the East: Culture and Imperialism' was the most relevant to my research. Moreover, his understanding and enthusiasm for the Greek East under the impact of Rome was most helpful and enjoyable. His suggestion that I examine education in Corinth through the Greek gymnasium is gratefully acknowledged.

I also thank my external and internal examiners Francis Young (University of Birmingham) and Neville Morley (University of Bristol) who discussed my PhD and supported publication.

Thanks are due to Sally Knights and Gill Greef (Filton College) who taught me Classical Civilisation and Latin and facilitated study tours to ancient sites in Greece and Turkey. In addition, I thank Susan Brown, the Librarian at Trinity College (Bristol), for her help.

I gladly acknowledge the assistance of the following scholars: Elizabeth R. Gebhard (Director of the University of Chicago Excavations at Isthmia), David G. Horrell (University of Exeter), Kathleen Krattenmaker (Editor of *Hesperia*), Onno M. van Nijf (Universities of Bristol and Cambridge, now the University of Groningen), Richard Oster (Harding University Graduate School of Religion), Guy D.R. Sanders (Director of Corinth Excavations, Athens), Antony J.S. Spawforth (University of Newcastle upon Tyne), and James Wiseman (Boston University). Onno M. van Nijf, while Research Fellow in the Department of Classics at

Cambridge University, gave valuable comments on my chapter 'The Greek Gymnasium and the Corinthian Christians'. Thanks are due also to Dr Diane Treacy-Cole and Revd. Peter Kay for reading my draft PhD. Finally, I am grateful to Stephen Paynter, a fellow worshipper at Cairns Road Baptist Church, for reading my revised work before submission and the editorial staff at Continuum who ensured its publication.

In a study on education it would be an oversight if I neglected acknowledgments to my own family. In contrast to the ancient elite who had wealth, influence and noble birth, I grew up in a working-class family in Liverpool where I attended a secondary modern school. While many parents wanted their children to leave school and earn their own wages, my parents, Stanley and Lilian Dutch, encouraged me to transfer to a grammar school at sixteen. I studied there before entering the University of Salford to read Physics. Following their sacrifices I have worked for many years in industry as a physicist and tutor.

Now I must again thank my family for supporting my theological education. To my wife, Susan, and our children, Laura, Jessica and Timothy, I gratefully admit their continued help and patience. It has not always been easy with a 'perpetual student' at home but the outcome has made it worthwhile. Since completing my PhD I have worked as a scientific consultant, lectured in Biblical Studies and completed continuing professional development. However, to revise my PhD for this book I used summer 2004 for writing to take account of the many new scholarly works. I feel honoured and privileged for two generations of 'family endurance' in the face of advancing my education. Finally, thanks be to God for support in all this work.

I dedicate this work to two generations of my family who have supported my education.

ὁ καυχώμενος ἐν κυρίῳ καυχάσθω (1 Cor. 1.31)
'Let the one who boasts, boast in the Lord' (NRSV)

List of Illustrations

Figure

Abbreviations

ABSA	*Annual of the British School at Athens*
ABSR	*Annual of the British School at Rome*
AGJU	Arbeiten zur Geschichte des antiken Judentums und des Urchristentums
AJA	*American Journal of Archaeology*
AJAH	*American Journal of Ancient History*
AJP	*American Journal of Philology*
AnBib	Analecta biblica
ANRW	Hildegard Temporini and Wolfgang Haase (eds.), *Aufstieg und Niedergang der römischen Welt: Geschichte und Kultur Roms im Spiegel der neueren Forschung* (Berlin: W. de Gruyter, 1972–)
Ath. Mitt.	*Mitteilungen des deutschen archäologischen Instituts, Athenische Abteilung*
ASCSA	American School of Classical Studies at Athens
ASMA	Aarhus Studies in Mediterranean Antiquity
BA	*Biblical Archaeologist*
BAGD	Walter Bauer, William F. Arndt, F. William Gingrich and Frederick W. Danker, *A Greek–English Lexicon of the New Testament and Other Early Christian Literature* (Chicago: University of Chicago Press, 2nd edn, 1958)
BARev	*Biblical Archaeology Review*
BCH	*Bulletin de Correspondance Hellénique*
BE	*Bulletin épigraphique* (in *Revue des études grecques*)
BEFAR	Bibliothèque des Écoles Françaises d'Athènes et de Rome
BETL	Bibliotheca ephemeridum theologicarum lovaniensium
BibInt	*Biblical Interpretation: A Journal of Contemporary Approaches*
BJRL	*Bulletin of the John Rylands University Library of Manchester*
BM CAT	British Museum Catalogue

BTB	*Biblical Theology Bulletin*
CBC	The Cambridge Bible Commentary
CBQ	*Catholic Biblical Quarterly*
Cicero	
De Or.	*De Oratore*
CIG	*Corpus inscriptionum graecarum*
CIL	*Corpus inscriptionum latinarum*
ClAnt	*Classical Antiquity*
CPJ	*Corpus papyrorum judaicarum*
CJ	*Classical Journal*
CPhil	*Classical Philology*
ClQ	*Classical Quarterly*
CR	*Classical Review*
CW	*Classical World*
Diog. Laert.	Diogenes Laertius
DHA	*Dialogues d'histoire ancienne*
EMC	*Echoes du Monde Classique*
Ep.	*epistulae*, letters
Epict.,	Epictetus
Diss.	*Discourses*
EvQ	*Evangelical Quarterly*
ExpTim	*Expository Times*
Galen	*Protrept.*
GD	*Guide de Délos*, 2nd ed. Paris: E. de Boccard, 1965. P. Bruneau and G. Daux
GR	*Greece and Rome*
GRBS	*Greek, Roman, and Byzantine Studies*
HeyJ	*Heythrop Journal*
Hesp	*Hesperia*
Hierocles	
Stob.	*Stobaeus*
HNT	Handbuch zum Neuen Testament
HSCP	*Harvard Studies in Classical Philology*
HTR	*Harvard Theological Review*
Iamblichus	
Vit. Pyth.	*Vita Pythagorae*
IBS	*Irish Biblical Studies*
ICC	International Critical Commentary
ID	*Inscriptions de Délos*, 7 vols. Paris: Librairie ancienne Honoré, Champion, 1926–1973. F. Durrbach, P. Roussel, M. Launey, A. Plassart, and J. Coupry
IG	*Inscriptiones Graecae* (1873-)

IGR	*Inscriptiones graecae ad res romanas pertinentes* (4 vols.; ed. René L. Cagnat,. *et al.*, Paris: E. Leroux, 1901–27)
IGRom	*Inscriptiones Graecae ad res Romanas pertinentes* (1906–)
I.Eph.	*Die Inschriften von Ephesos*
I.Kyme	*Inschriften griechischer Städte aus Kleinasien* V. *Die Inschriften von Kyme*, (ed. H. Engelmann, 1976)
I.Priene	*Die Inschriften von Priene*
Int	*Interpretation*
I.Sestos	*Die Inschriften von Sestos und der Thrakischen Chersones* (J. Krauss, 1980)
IVO	*Die Inschriften von Olympia* ed. W. Dittenberger and K. Purgold (1896)
JAAR	*Journal of the American Academy of Religion*
JBL	*Journal of Biblical Literature*
JCE	*Journal of Christian Education*
JETS	*Journal of the Evangelical Theological Society*
JFSR	*Journal of Feminist Studies in Religion*
JNSL	*Journal of Northwest Semitic Languages*
Josephus	
Ant.	*Antiquities of the Jews*
War	*De Bello Judaico/The Jewish War*
JRA	*Journal of Roman Archaeology*
JRA Supp.	*JRA* Supplementary Series
JRS	*Journal of Roman Studies*
JSH	*Journal of Sport History*
JSJ	*Journal for the Study of Judaism in the Persian, Hellenistic and Roman Period*
JSNT	*Journal for the Study of the New Testament*
JSNTSup	*Journal for the Study of the New Testament*, Supplement Series
JSOT	*Journal for the Study of the Old Testament*
JTS	*Journal of Theological Studies*
KJV	King James Version
LCL	Loeb Classical Library
LSJ	H.G. Liddell, Robert Scott and H. Stuart Jones, *Greek–English Lexicon* (Oxford: Clarendon Press, 9th edn, 1968)
LXX	The Septuagint
MAMA	*Monumenta Asiae Minoris Antiquae* (Manchester/London, 1928-)
MM	J.H. Moulton and G. Milligan, *The Vocabulary of the Greek Testament*

NCB	New Century Bible
NEB	New English Bible
NICNT	New International Commentary on the New Testament
NIGTC	The New International Greek Testament Commentary
NIV	New International Version
NovT	*Novum Testamentum*
NovTSup	*Novum Testamentum*, Supplements
NRSV	New Revised Standard Version
NT	New Testament
NTS	*New Testament Studies*
OGIS	*Orientis Graeci Inscriptiones Selectae* I-II (ed. W. Dittenberger, 1903–1905)
Or.	Oration
OT	Old Testament
PBSR	Papers of the British School at Rome
PCPS	Proceedings of the Cambridge Philological Society
Philo	Philo Judaeus
Abr.	*De Abrahamo*
Agr.	*De agricultura*
Cher.	*De cherubim*
Congr.	*De congressu eruditionis gratia*
Dec.	*De decalogo*
Det. Pot. Ins.	*Quod deterius potiori insidiari soleat*
Deus Imn. Quod	*Deus sit immutabilis*
Ebr.	*De ebrietate*
Fug.	*De fuga et inventione*
Jos.	*De Josepho*
L.A.	*Legum Allegoriae*
Migr. Abr.	*De migratione Abrahami*
Mut. Nom.	*De mutatione nominum*
Plant.	*De plantatione*
Poster. C.	*De posteritate Caini*
Omn. Prob. Lib.	*Quod omnis probus liber sit*
Prov.	*De Providentia*
Somn.	*De somniis*
Spec. Leg.	*De specialibus legibus*
Vit. Mos.	*De vita Mosis*
PIR	*Prosopographia Imperii Romani Saeculi I, II, III* 1st. edn. by E. Klebs and H. Dessau (1897–8); 2nd. edn. by E. Groag, A. Stein, and others (1933-)

Plato	
Grg.	*Gorgias*
Prt.	*Protagoras*
Pliny	*Naturalis historia*
P.Lond	Greek Papyri in the London (British) Museum
P.Mich	Papyri in the University of Michigan Collection
P.Oxy	The Oxyrhynchus Papyri
Plutarch	
Mor.	*Moralia*
Amat.	*Amatorius*
De Lib. Ed.	*De liberis educandis*
Vit.	*Vitae Parrallelae*
Ant.	*Antonius*
Quaest. Rom.	*Quastiones Romanae*
Quint.	Quintilian
Inst.	*Institutio Oratoria*
REG	*Revue des études grecques*
RSV	Revised Standard Version
Salvian	Salvianus
Gub. Dei	*De Gubernatione Dei*
Seneca	
Contra	*Controversiae*
Ep.	*Epistulae*
SBL	Society of Biblical Literature
SBLDS	SBL Dissertation Series
SBLSP	SBL Seminar Papers
SBLSS	SBL Semeia Studies
SEG	*Supplementum Epigraphicum Graecum* (ed. J.J.E. Hondius *et al.*, 1923-)
SIG^3	*Sylloge Inscriptionum Graecarum* (ed. W. Dittenberger *et al*, 3rd edn, 1915–24)
SJT	*Scottish Journal of Theology*
SNTS	Society for New Testament Studies
SNTSMS	Society for New Testament Studies Monograph Series
SRHE	The Society for Research into Higher Education
Soranus	
Gyn.	*Gynaecia*
TAPA	*Transactions of the American Philological Association*
TEV	Today's English Version
THKNT	Theologischer Kommentar zum Neuen Testament
TNTC	Tyndale New Testament Commentaries
TynBul	*Tyndale Bulletin*

Vitr. *De arch*	Vitruvius, *De architectura*
WBC	Word Biblical Commentary
WUNT	Wissenschaftliche Untersuchungen zum Neuen Testament
ZNW	*Zeitschrift für die neutestamentliche Wissenschaft*
ZPE	*Zeitschrift für Papyrologie und Epigraphik*

Introduction

1. *Rationale*

First Corinthians is a fascinating New Testament letter because it reveals, in some detail, a first-century church in which the early believers are learning to live together in community within the Graeco-Roman world. In their particular situation there are many pressing issues requiring answers. Indeed, James Dunn captures this importance of 1 Corinthians when he discusses the various views straining their community.[1] Within the letter we see Paul handling these tensions. Yet these are not just merely theoretical theological tensions, but tensions threatening the unity of this first-century church. This apostolic letter deals with practical situations and this very practical value means that the letter has been extensively studied. Victor Paul Furnish rightly observes the practical aspects of the letter and the pastoral problems that Paul addressed.[2] Moreover, Paul may be seen as an apologist to the Corinthians.[3] His letter also speaks to the twenty-first century postmodern viewpoint as Anthony Thiselton demonstrates in his comprehensive commentary.[4] He notes that the many issues Paul confronts in his pluralist culture look remarkably similar to issues people face today.

1. James D.G. Dunn, *1 Corinthians* (New Testament Guides; Sheffield: Sheffield Academic Press, 1995), p. 9.

2. Victor Paul Furnish, *The Theology of the First Letter to the Corinthians* (New Testament Theology; Cambridge: Cambridge University Press, 1999), p. 18. Furnish sees Paul as a theologian addressing the Corinthians' misunderstanding of the gospel and hence dealing with the pastoral needs in their situation.

3. Paul Barnett, 'Paul, Apologist to the Corinthians', in Burke and Elliott (eds.), *Paul and the Corinthians: Studies on a Community in Conflict* (NovTSup, 109; Leiden: Brill, 2003), pp. 313–26. For the wider relationship of Paul with his Corinthian converts he cites V.P. Furnish, 'Paul and the Corinthians', *Int* 52 (1998), pp. 229–45.

4. Anthony C. Thiselton, *The First Epistle to the Corinthians: A Commentary on the Greek Text* (NIGTC; Grand Rapids: Eerdmans; Carlisle: Paternoster, 2000), pp. 16–17.

This epistle continues to be relevant in our time. Consequently, there is a wide scholarly interest in 1 Corinthians, which has generated a considerable amount of useful secondary literature.

Over the years various approaches have been applied to enhance our understanding of Paul's letter, and more recently scholars have used ideas and perspectives from the social sciences to address this letter.[5] My interest in social-scientific interpretation of the New Testament developed while I completed my MA (Biblical Studies), and in my dissertation 'Pupils, Pedagogues and Paul: Education in the Greco-Roman World' I applied such an approach to examine Paul's education language in 1 Cor. 1–4.[6] My interest further developed into doctoral work and the publication of this study.

When we read 1 Corinthians we see that slogans used within the church indicate that there were divisions (1.12).[7] The significance of these slogans has caught the attention of scholars who have attempted to identify the parties or groups within the church. Indeed, Dunn notes that this debate has run for over 150 years.[8] Recent scholarship continues to address this area.[9] Nevertheless, many scholars now see not parties, but social divisions in the church.[10] Yet church conflict continues to be an issue as Bruce

5. The appropriate terminology is clarified by Philip F. Esler, 'Review of David G. Horrell, *The Social Ethos of the Corinthian Correspondence. Interests and Ideology from 1 Corinthians to 1 Clement*', *JTS* 49 (1998), pp. 253–60. He states, 'Many New Testament critics now use ideas and perspectives from the social sciences in their work. The best description of this approach is social-scientific interpretation (or criticism), because its primary focus is on making historical sense of biblical texts, with the social sciences having an adjunct role in that task. Since various social sciences are employed, not just sociology, but also anthropology, social psychology and economics, it is inappropriate to refer to this enterprise as "sociological"' (p. 253). Nevertheless, many New Testament scholars use 'sociological' for this enterprise. Where they do this I use their terminology, rather than attempting to harmonise terms.

6. R.S. Dutch, 'Pupils, Pedagogues and Paul: Education in the Greco-Roman World' (unpublished masters dissertation, University of Bristol, 1994).

7. Gordon D. Fee, *The First Epistle to the Corinthians* (NICNT; Grand Rapids: Eerdmans, 1987), p. 55, remarks on 1.12, 'This verse is a crux in terms of how one is going to understand 1 Corinthians as a whole and especially the historical situation of the church to which Paul is writing'. In 3.4 two of the slogans are repeated: 'I belong to/follow Paul' and 'I belong to/follow Apollos'. Other slogans are evident in the letter, for example, in 6.12, 'Everything is permissible for me', which is repeated in 10.23, and in 6.13, 'Food for the stomach and the stomach for food'. See also 8.1-6.

8. Dunn, *1 Corinthians*, p. 27.

9. See, for example, C.K. Barrett, 'Sectarian Diversity at Corinth' in Burke and Elliott (eds.), *Paul and the Corinthians*, pp. 287–302.

10. For example, see the discussion in Dunn, *1 Corinthians*, pp. 46–50.

Winter has recently shown.[11] My interest is in social-status issues with a particular focus on the elite.

Theissen's groundbreaking work on 1 Corinthians sought to identify the elite as converts in conflict with Paul.[12] Indeed, it can be argued that the identity, and behaviour, of the elite are of considerable importance to Paul and the Corinthian Christians. In particular, the identity of these members as *educated* merits further study within the social locus of Paul and his converts. I believe that our understanding of the identity of the elite, and Paul's interaction with them in 1 Corinthians, will be enhanced by the approach of constructing and applying an ancient education model. With this in mind I now turn to outline the aims of my study.

2. *Aims*

The aims of this study are to examine the 'educated elite' in 1 Corinthians through constructing, and applying, an ancient education model.[13] The research does not construct the model from the text alone. Rather, it engages with the social world of the Corinthian Christians. Moreover, my application of the research model examines a number of verses in 1 Cor. 1–4; 7 and 9. I examine the historical question of what the texts meant to Paul and his original audience. I do not deny the importance of what the texts might mean for a modern audience, but I concur with Philip Esler, who comments, 'Whether this latter issue can ever be properly addressed, however, without attending to the former seems to me highly doubtful.'[14] If we fail to investigate the texts within the social dimension of the first-century Mediterranean world then our understanding of what the texts meant to Paul's readers will be impaired and on such a faulty foundation it is a risky business to build a meaning for a modern readership.[15]

11. Bruce W. Winter, 'The "Underlays" of Conflict and Compromise in 1 Corinthians', in Burke and Elliott (eds.), *Paul and the Corinthians*, pp. 139–55. Winter notes Paul's family language for his converts (p. 154).

12. Gerd Theissen, *The Social Setting of Pauline Christianity* (trans. John H. Schütz; Edinburgh: T. & T. Clark, 1982). I outline his work in chapter 1 including challenges made to his position, e.g. whether there were any elite in the Corinthian church.

13. I discuss the use of models in chapter 1.

14. Philip F. Esler, *The First Christians in their Social Worlds: Social-Scientific Approaches to New Testament Interpretation* (London: Routledge, 1994), p. 2.

15. I use the term 'readers' although, given the absence of a universal free education system in the ancient world, it is highly likely that very many Corinthian Christians would not be able to read Paul's letter. They would be hearers, listeners or auditors. Where 'readers' is used in my research this should be understood as 'readers and/or hearers'. New Testament critics can omit this important point. See, for example, G.H.R. Horsley, 'Review of Sjef van Tilborg, *Reading John in Ephesus*,' *JTS* 49 (1998), pp. 265–73, in which Horsley criticises Tilborg's assumption throughout the book 'that reading was a widespread skill in antiquity,'

The model is intentionally an *ancient* education model. By this I attempt to avoid reading, explicitly or implicitly, a modern Western educational system, or philosophy, into the first-century eastern Mediterranean world where Paul is engaging with his readers in a culture quite different to ours. For this important distinction Philip Esler comments on the New Testament texts:

> They are written in a social script which reflects their cultural contexts and which is, inevitably, quite different from ours. If we make no allowance for these divergences we risk the twin perils of ethnocentrism, of assuming the values of another society are the same as ours, . . . , and of anachronism, of assuming that another society remote in time from us shares our culture and perspectives.[16]

Moreover, my ancient education model is not a model proposed by an ancient author, such as is set forth in Plato's *Republic*. Philo of Alexandria used this, as Alan Mendelson notes:

> From a philosophical point of view, Philo appropriates the elitism of Platonic educational theory with little modification. For Philo's sage, as for Plato's guardian, the arts and sciences are merely the first propaedeutic step toward understanding the truth. Hence there are striking similarities between Philo's Moses and Plato's philosopher-king, not the least of which is the curriculum which they followed. In the careers of both, encyclical studies occupy a subordinate position compared with the final goal of sophia.[17]

Philo's theological perspective, however, departs from Plato's elitism. The model I construct is designed to describe an education system used in antiquity. In this I follow the modern social-scientific methodology of constructing models that are appropriate for the New Testament world. Historians of education also use such models. For example, Teresa Morgan in her book *Literate Education in the Hellenistic and Roman Worlds* argues that a 'core and periphery' model should replace a 'curricular' model for the structure of Graeco-Roman education.[18]

and comments, 'Moreover, only a very tiny percentage of people in antiquity were readers with any fluency; most were hearers' (p. 266). For a discussion on the Corinthian factions and a modern readership see Clive Marsh, '"Who are you for?" 1 Corinthians 1:10–17 as Christian Scripture in the Context of Diverse Methods of Reading', in Burke and Elliott (eds.), *Paul and the Corinthians*, pp. 157–76.

16. Esler, *The First Christians in their Social Worlds*, p. 22.

17. Alan Mendelson, *Secular Education in Philo of Alexandria* (Monographs of the Hebrew Union College, 7; Cincinnati: Hebrew Union College Press, 1982), p. 81.

18. Teresa Morgan, *Literate Education in the Hellenistic and Roman Worlds* (Cambridge Classical Studies; Cambridge: Cambridge University Press, 1998), pp. 67–73. See my chapter 2 for a further discussion.

My study first surveys the scholarship and then develops the ancient education model before applying it to selected texts. In chapter 1, 'Survey of the Scholarship', I lay the foundation for my research by surveying the contribution of scholarship to the study of 1 Corinthians. I outline the history of interpretation of the community divisions and demonstrate developments, from assuming theological disputes were behind the situation, to recognition of the significant role a socially stratified community played in the problems Paul encountered. Next, I show how the identification of social-status issues has considerably enhanced the understanding of certain sections in Paul's letter. The central place of the status issues between the educated elite and the non-elite is identified. My chapter includes the current debate on the 'new consensus'. Finally, I consider the nature of first-century Corinth as a Roman colony.

Chapter 2, 'First Corinthians and Ancient Education Models', focuses on the educated elite in 1 Corinthians. I describe, and evaluate, the ancient education models that New Testament scholars use for examining the elite in the church. By ancient education models I mean those models that critics use to reconstruct the education of these elite in antiquity. I consider scholarship on the Corinthian correspondence that primarily addresses research in 1 Corinthians. Their models are evaluated against education models for the Graeco-Roman world described by biblical and classical scholarship. Finally, I address the understanding gained through recent works by historians of education. This chapter highlights the significant omission of the Greek gymnasium from education models employed for interpreting Paul's letter.

This serious oversight is addressed in chapter 3, 'The Greek Gymnasium and the Corinthian Christians', where I survey the Greek gymnasium. I examine the development, and typical features, of the gymnasium to locate it historically in the New Testament world. A section considers gymnasiarchs (γυμνασίαρχοι), ephebes (ἔφηβοι) and *neoi* (νέοι). Furthermore, I investigate routes by which residents at Corinth, and Corinthian Christians, may have received an education in the gymnasium. Here, I examine the literary, epigraphic and archaeological evidence for gymnasia in Corinth. Then I describe two further routes, based on mobility in the Roman empire, by which a gymnasium education might be received and people thus educated could be resident in Corinth. Finally, my chapter uses the analytical tools developed by John Barclay to investigate the Greek gymnasium, education and the Diaspora Jews.[19] I demonstrate that the gymnasium was an important education institution primarily for the male social elite and was frequented by Greeks, Romans and Jews. This chapter

19. As given in John M.G. Barclay, *Jews in the Mediterranean Diaspora: From Alexander to Trajan (323 BCE – 117 CE)* (Edinburgh: T. & T. Clark, 1996).

demonstrates the relevance of the Greek gymnasium model for understanding 1 Corinthians, and fills the lacuna in biblical scholarship.

My education model is developed further in chapter 4 'Education, Family and Society in the Graeco-Roman World'. The study of families in antiquity is fairly recent, yet it is an important topic in early Christianity.[20] This lack of interest also prevailed in Graeco-Roman studies until comparatively recently. The failure to examine education, with its relationship to family and society, has been a defect in education models used by New Testament scholars for interpreting 1 Corinthians. This chapter addresses the deficiency. I introduce Paul's family language together with associated studies. Next, I investigate literacy in ancient society, and the relationships between education and parental responsibilities, genealogy and status. Moreover, I examine child education and labour, infant prodigies, and youth in politics. This analysis more fully locates the Greek gymnasium within its social setting and lays the foundation for the essential application of the model to 1 Corinthians.

Chapters 5 and 6 examine selected texts in 1 Corinthians through the insights of the model. Eight topics are investigated: Paul's Corinthian Household, Ancient Athletes (1 Cor. 9.24–27), Nurses, Nutrition and Nurture (1 Cor. 3.1–4), Agriculture and Education (1 Cor. 3.5–9), Disciplining with the Rod (1 Cor. 4.21), The *Grammateus* (1 Cor. 1.20), Ancient Writing (1 Cor. 4.6) and Circumcision (1 Cor. 7.18–24). These chapters provide an enhanced understanding of Paul's interaction with the Corinthian church, and particularly the educated elite. Esler remarks that, 'The model is neither valid nor invalid; it is useful or not'.[21] However, I am willing for my model to be measured against the text and if found wanting then to be modified or merged with other models.[22] I believe that the reader's understanding of 1 Corinthians is enhanced through this useful model. Its application yields a more nuanced interpretation of the educated elite among the Corinthian Christians than previous models have accomplished.

20. For recent works on the family see: Stephen C. Barton (ed.), *The Family in Theological Perspective* (Edinburgh: T. & T. Clark, 1996), Halvor Moxnes (ed.), *Constructing Early Christian Families: Family as Social Reality and Metaphor* (London and New York: Routledge, 1997) and Trevor J. Burke, *Family Matters: A Socio-Historical Study of Kinship Metaphors in 1 Thessalonians* (JSNTSup, 247; London and New York: T & T Clark International, 2003).

21. Esler, 'Review of David G. Horrell', pp. 256–57. He cites Stanley R. Barrett, *A Student's Guide to Theory and Method* (Toronto: University of Toronto Press, 1996), p. 216, who is a writer on anthropological theory.

22. For models see Kenneth Berding, 'The Hermeneutical Framework of Social-Scientific Criticism: How much can Evangelicals get involved?' *EvQ* 75 (2003), pp. 3–22. His principles for evangelicals using social-scientific criticism include the need to let the model be subservient to Scripture (pp. 20–21). I am willing to 'abandon or alter the model instead of altering the text' (p. 20). See below for my discussion of social-scientific criticism.

The Conclusion summarises the outcome of applying my social-scientific methodology. Many Pauline scholars attribute the conflict evident in 1 Corinthians to the socially stratified community within the church. Two main divisions are evident in the distinction between the elite and non-elite. The educated elite are described by New Testament critics using various approaches to explain their education. However, a notable oversight by scholarship has been the omission of education in the Greek gymnasium. The ancient education model of the Greek gymnasium, and its relationship to family and society, provides a model that fills the oversight of New Testament scholarship on this educational institution for the social elite. In reading selected texts from 1 Corinthians, the construction and application of this ancient education model, within the context of first-century eastern Mediterranean society, shows that it is a useful way forward in investigating Paul's interaction with the educated elite. The merits of the model are summarised. Further texts in 1 Corinthians, 2 Corinthians and throughout the Pauline corpus, can be investigated using this model.[23] Elsewhere in the Pauline writings evidence for the relevance of the Greek gymnasia as an educational institution should be sought in the local social and historical contexts.

By now I hope that the aims of the project are clear to my readers and the structure of my work is evident. To achieve my aims I adopt the methodology of social-scientific criticism to which I now turn, together with a discussion on reading theory.

3. *Methodology*

a. *Reading Theory Perspective*

Bruce Malina clearly demonstrates the importance of reading theory perspective in interpreting ancient texts.[24] He states, 'People use language to have an effect on others in terms of the meanings of the social system. And people learn those meanings along with the language of their society in the process of growing up'.[25] He notes two dimensions of reading: the

23. My study is restricted to 1 Corinthians to provide some bounds on the size of the enterprise.

24. Bruce J. Malina, 'Reading Theory Perspective: Reading Luke-Acts', in Neyrey (ed.), *The Social World of Luke-Acts: Models for Interpretation* (Peabody, MA: Hendrickson Publishers, 1991), pp. 3–23.

25. Malina, 'Reading Theory', pp. 5–6. Moreover, Malina explains, 'Social system refers to the general ways in which a society provides its members with a socially meaningful way of living. The social system includes: (1) culture, i.e. the accepted ways of interpreting the world and everything in it; (2) social structures, e.g. the accepted ways of marrying, having children, working, governing, worshipping, and understanding God; and the accepted ways of being a person (including self-understanding)' (p. 5).

'intrapersonal (individual)' and the 'interpersonal (social)'. Within the intrapersonal dimension Malina discusses two models of reading comprehension: the *propositional model* and the *scenario model.*

The propositional model attends to how texts are worded in sentences, while the scenario model concentrates on meaning. Malina argues for the scenario model (which has supporting empirical evidence) as the basis for the models in the book, *The Social World of Luke-Acts: Models for Interpretation.* Thus Malina remarks:

> This [scenario] model considers the text as setting forth a succession of explicit and implicit mental representations of scenes or schemes. These, in turn, evoke corresponding scenes or schemes in the mind of the reader. Such scenes or schemes are composed of a series of settings, episodes, or models. These latter derive directly from the mind of the reader, who carries out appropriate alterations to the settings, episodes, or models as directed by the text.[26]

This model 'presupposes that every reader has a full and verifiable grasp of how the world works'[27]. Ancient texts, such as 1 Corinthians, were written to first-century readers and not modern readers, so Malina rightfully remarks, 'Hence if we seek to be fair to the biblical authors, we must endeavor to be considerate readers. Considerate readers of documents from the past will obviously make the effort to bring to their reading a set of scenarios proper to the time, place, and culture of the biblical author'.[28]

Besides the intrapersonal dimension of reading in which an individual establishes a meaning for the text Malina observes that 'readers rarely, if ever, read alone, for reading is anchored in the social or interpersonal world of the reader and writer'.[29] The interpersonal dimension considers how reading is organised in a society or in the social setting. One significant feature is the language 'context' of the society. *Low context* societies use detailed texts with little to be imagined, in contrast *high context* societies have texts that are 'sketchy and impressionistic'.[30] More imagination is required of the reader or hearer. But these texts function because, as Malina remarks, 'people have been socialized into shared ways of perceiving and acting' therefore more is assumed.[31] First Corinthians, fits into this *high* context profile. Although Malina separates, for

26. Malina, 'Reading Theory', pp. 14–15.
27. Malina, 'Reading Theory', p. 15.
28. Malina, 'Reading Theory', p. 16.
29. Malina, 'Reading Theory', p. 17.
30. Malina, 'Reading Theory', pp. 19–20. The U.S. and northern European countries are low context societies. Malina draws on Edward Hall's terminology.
31. Malina, 'Reading Theory', p. 20.

discussion, the intrapersonal and interpersonal dimensions he warns that they should be kept together.[32]

In conclusion, my research shares the view that the *scenario model* for reading is appropriate for readers. Moreover, 1 Corinthians is a *high* context document. Within the reading process there are intrapersonal and interpersonal dimensions for the first-century reader. For the modern reader, Malina helpfully summarises the first step as:

> *To strive to understand what the author says and means to say to his Mediterranean hearers in terms of their culture and within their social setting*. Theirs was a high context society, with much of what they intended to communicate totally absent from the text, yet rather firmly in place in the common social system into which they were socialized. The considerate reader needs to fill in the social system in order not to be mystified.[33]

The importance of reading theory is recognised by John Nolland in his favourable review of *The Social World of Luke-Acts*.[34] He considers Malina's chapter 'a compelling defense' for reading ancient texts within their original cultures.[35] So now let us turn to the methodology of social-scientific criticism.

b. *Social-Scientific Criticism*

The primary methodology used in my research is social-scientific criticism, also called social-scientific interpretation. Dale Martin in his 'Social-Scientific Criticism' usefully comments on the wide terminology that has been employed by scholars. He notes that scholars have preference for various terms to describe their approaches, e.g. sociologists, social historians, while others call their work cultural anthropology, ethnography or social-scientific.[36] I follow Martin, and John Elliott, in using the term social-scientific criticism.[37]

The use of social-scientific criticism is not meant to exclude other approaches that explore social aspects of biblical issues. My research

32. Malina, 'Reading Theory', pp. 21–22.

33. Malina, 'Reading Theory', p. 22. Emphasis in original.

34. John Nolland, 'Review of *The Social World of Luke-Acts: Models for Interpretation*, edited by Jerome H. Neyrey', *EvQ* 66 (1994), pp. 81–87. While Nolland is critical of some conclusions he regards the work as offering, 'an important and accessible set of studies which provide an excellent introduction to the potential fruitfulness of Social Sciences perspectives' (p. 87).

35. Nolland, 'Review of *The Social World of Luke-Acts*', p. 82.

36. Dale B. Martin, 'Social-Scientific Criticism,' in McKenzie and Haynes (eds.), *To Each Its Own Meaning*, pp. 103–19 (103). He notes the chapter title will not please all scholars whose work comes within it.

37. John Elliott, *Social-Scientific Criticism of the New Testament* (London: SPCK, 1995).

adheres to the approach expounded by John Elliott who defines social-scientific criticism as:

> That phase of the exegetical task which analyzes the social and cultural dimensions of the text and of its environmental context through the utilization of the perspectives, theory, models, and research of the social sciences. As a component of the historical-critical method of exegesis, social-scientific criticism investigates biblical texts as meaningful configurations of language intended to communicate between composers and audiences.[38]

Consequently, social-scientific criticism is a '*sub-discipline of exegesis*' complementing, rather than replacing, other modes of critical analysis that examine the biblical texts. Elliott clearly states, 'Its aim is the determination of the meaning(s) explicit and implicit in the text, meanings made possible and shaped by the social and cultural systems inhabited by both authors and intended audiences'.[39]

Even though the discipline is now well established in New Testament studies, any methodology has presuppositions and social-scientific criticism is no exception. The chief presuppositions that guide the research of most, if not all, social-scientific critics are identified, discussed and illustrated by Elliott.[40] Two important points should be made. First, many of the presuppositions relate to the central requirement of the method, 'to clarify as clearly and comprehensively as possible the social and cultural differences that separate ancient and modern worlds and to discover adequate bridges for facilitating conversation between these worlds'.[41]

Second, the presuppositions address the use of models. Elliott defines a 'model' as 'a symbolic representation of selected aspects of the behaviour of a complex system for particular purposes'.[42] He also cites Malina for a more comprehensive definition, 'an abstract simplified representation of some real world object, event, or interaction constructed for the purpose of understanding, control, or prediction'.[43] Moreover, Elliott notes, 'The difference between a model and an analogy or metaphor lies in the fact that the model is consciously structured and systematically arranged in order to serve as a speculative instrument for the purpose of organizing,

38. Elliott, *Social-Scientific Criticism*, p. 7.

39. Elliott, *Social-Scientific Criticism*, p. 8.

40. Elliott, *Social-Scientific Criticism*, pp. 36–59.

41. Elliott, *Social-Scientific Criticism*, p. 59.

42. Elliott, *Social-Scientific Criticism*, p. 41. He cites Ian G. Barbour, *Myths, Models, and Paradigms: A Comparative Study in Science and Religion* (New York: Harper & Row, 1974), p. 6.

43. Elliott, *Social-Scientific Criticism*, p. 41. He cites Bruce J. Malina, 'The Social Sciences and Biblical Interpretation', in Gottwald (ed.), *The Bible and Liberation: Political and Social Hermeneutics* (Maryknoll, NY: Orbis Books, 1983), pp. 11–25 (14).

profiling, and interpreting a complex welter of raw material'.[44] This presupposition requires further consideration because it is a contested area in New Testament scholarship.

c. *Models: Explicit, Implicit or Absent?*

In my methodology, I consider that an explicit statement of theory and models is helpful on three accounts. These follow Elliott who states:

1. explicit presentation of the theory and models that guide the analysis makes it possible for the reader to follow an investigation and to evaluate its conclusions;
2. when theory and models are set out clearly at the outset, the fit of the data to the models can be more easily ascertained and the model's interpretive capacity more easily assessed;
3. clearly exposed theory, models, and research design make it possible for other researchers to employ and experiment with the method and the models for themselves rather than submit to the impressive but inimitable inspirations of the 'great teacher'.[45]

Nevertheless, the presupposition of models, implicit or explicit, as essential to all social-scientific critics is not universally held. For example, David Horrell has developed his work on the Corinthian correspondence out of an interest in sociological approaches to the New Testament.[46] Yet, notably, he has criticised the use of models although he notes New Testament scholars often see a sociological approach as one that uses sociological models.[47] Following a detailed critical discussion on their use Horrell remarks:

> In summary: models, correctly understood, are not an ubiquitous feature of sociological analysis, although they may sometimes be valid and useful tools. Models are the result of empirical study and not its

44. Elliott, S*ocial-Scientific Criticism*, p. 41. Elliott's glossary states that a social model is, 'An abstract selective representation of the relationships among social phenomena used to conceptualize, analyze, and interpret patterns of social relations, and to compare and contrast one system of social relations with another. Models are heuristic constructs that operationalize particular theories and that range in scope and complexity according to the phenomena to be analyzed' (p. 132).

45. Elliott, S*ocial-Scientific Criticism*, p. 48.

46. David G. Horrell, *The Social Ethos of the Corinthian Correspondence. Interests and Ideology from 1 Corinthians to 1 Clement* (Studies of the New Testament and Its World; Edinburgh: T. & T. Clark, 1996), p. 1. See Esler, 'Review of David G. Horrell', p. 255, for his criticism of Horrell's use of the term 'sociological'.

47. Horrell, *Social Ethos*, p. 9.

> precursor, though once models have been developed their main use is to facilitate further research and comparative investigation.[48]

Horrell's criticism does not reject models entirely but here he is unsympathetic to them. He discusses their uses and possible weaknesses. Thus he prefers to present 'a theoretical basis and a research framework' instead of a model but maintains that his work is still 'sociological'. Another 'social-historical' investigation is the one by Peter Gooch, who states:

> Commentary on 1 Corinthians 8–10 shows a lack of scholarly concern over the concrete social contexts addressed by Paul: meals in temples (8:10), tables of demons (10:21), food sold in markets (10:25) and invitations from those outside the Christian group (10:27). Almost without exception, scholars are uninterested in the concrete social contexts which Paul's instructions addressed or are satisfied with superficial and ill-evidenced assumptions.[49]

He clearly states his interest in the social contexts Paul addresses (although I consider that he overstates his contention with the scholars' performance). To remedy the situation Gooch, therefore, provides an extended attempt to read the chapters 'against the specific and concrete social context of the letter'. He asserts that his method is 'social-historical,' yet states:

> I do not attempt to apply any specific sociological or anthropological model or method to the historical data investigated, both because this would be beyond my expertise and because of my conviction that the data available to us from the texts of earliest Christianity (and Greco-Roman society) are not sufficient to allow legitimate conclusions from such applications.[50]

This is clearly an outright rejection of models from a scholar proclaiming his 'social-historical' method. On this approach Horrell comments, 'Gooch describes his method as 'social-historical', though he (unfortunately) eschews the use of specific sociological or anthropological models or methods'.[51] Thus, the use of models is not a presupposition shared by all scholars who follow a sociological methodology.

48. Horrell, *Social Ethos*, pp. 17–18.

49. Peter D. Gooch, *Dangerous Food: 1 Corinthians 8–10 in Its Context* (Studies in Christianity and Judaism, 5; Waterloo, ON: Wilfrid Laurier University Press, 1993), p. xvii.

50. Gooch, *Dangerous Food*, p. xviii.

51. David G. Horrell, 'Review of Peter D. Gooch, *Dangerous Food: 1 Corinthians 8–10 in Its Context*', *JTS* 46 (1995), pp. 279–82 (280).

Nevertheless, Esler provided a critical review of Horrell's eschewal of model-use, stating:

> The use of *cross-cultural* models, moreover, is virtually essential if we are to break free from our taken-for-granted notions of social reality, derived from a North Atlantic individualistic culture which is very unusual in a world where most cultures are group-orientated. The ancient Mediterranean world was strongly group-orientated and unless we employ explicit means for identifying the extent of its strangeness from us we risk imposing anachronistic and ethnocentric ideas upon it.[52]

In an exchange of views, Horrell has responded to Esler's review and this produced a further response from Esler.[53] Their discussions remain detailed, informed and incisive. Nevertheless, my research does not aim to enter into this debate and establish that *all* social-scientific methodology should use models. Rather, I wish to bring the reader's attention to this contested area and establish my approach in this particular study. I shall produce a particular model based on ancient sources.[54]

Further discussion on social-scientific criticism, and the debate over models, is covered in the literature.[55] But I wish to draw attention to one recent discussion on social-scientific criticism. Kenneth Berding has examined its main authors, their hermeneutical framework and asked about the involvement of evangelicals.[56] His detailed article helpfully scrutinises social-scientific criticism with its presuppositions, understanding of 'meaning' and method before offering a balanced appraisal. He is rightly concerned that evangelicals read/use the output of social-scientific exegetes without unknowingly falling foul of their 'assumptions and overstatements'.[57] His appraisal identifies valuable fundamental and non-fundamental disagreements before offering suggestions for reading their

52. Esler, 'Review of David G. Horrell', p. 257.

53. David G. Horrell, 'Models and Methods in Social-Scientific Interpretation: A Response to Philip Esler', *JSNT* 78 (2000), pp. 83–105. Philip F. Esler, 'Models in New Testament Interpretation: A Reply to David Horrell', *JSNT* 78 (2000), pp. 107–13.

54. However, if scholars wish to disagree with me and argue that my approach is not a model but really a social description I shall not be offended.

55. For example, see Susan R. Garrett, 'Sociology (Early Christianity)', in Freedman, (ed.), *The Anchor Bible Dictionary*, Vol. 6, pp. 89–99; Martin, 'Social-Scientific Criticism'; Philip F. Esler, 'Introduction: Models, Context and Kerygma in New Testament Interpretation', in Esler (ed.), *Modelling Early Christianity: Social-Scientific Studies of the New Testament in its Context* (London and New York: Routledge, 1995), pp. 1–20; Pieter F. Craffert, 'Relationships Between Social-Scientific, Literary, and Rhetorical Interpretations of Texts', *BTB* 26 (1996), pp. 45–55, and Richard L. Rohrbaugh, 'Introduction', in Rohrbaugh (ed.), *The Social Sciences and New Testament Interpretation* (Peabody, MA: Hendrickson Publishers, 1996), pp. 1–15 (8–10).

56. Berding, 'The Hermeneutical Framework', pp. 3–22.

57. Berding, 'The Hermeneutical Framework', p. 12.

books, principles for evangelicals, and a positive example in David A. deSilva's work.[58] Berding's positive article should help calm concerns over social-scientific criticism as he highlights the benefits to evangelical scholars of this dynamic way of approaching Scripture. I hope that my contribution to social-scientific criticism will be of benefit to New Testament scholarship.

4. *Summary*

This introduction has highlighted my fascination with 1 Corinthians as an important letter to the first-century Corinthian church learning to live in its pluralistic society. I have given my rationale for the study and its aims together with a discussion on my use of social-scientific criticism with its contested issues, e.g. the use of models. I have also indicated that my study is meant to engage with the range of New Testament scholarship. Hopefully, it will be of interest to classical scholars engaged in interdisciplinary study.

My aims are to construct, and apply, an ancient education model relevant for first-century Corinth. In my interpretation of 1 Corinthians and examination of the educated elite I adhere to an explicit use of models as a tool in my social-scientific methodology of reading Paul's letter through the insights of an ancient education model.

Finally, at the first T & T Clark annual lecture the Right Revd. Tom Wright (Bishop of Durham) gave an enthralling presentation on 'The State of the Art in Pauline Studies'.[59] He encouraged his listeners to engage in more research on the social world for understanding Paul's letters. This book is my contribution to that exciting investigation. Scholarship has been deeply involved with 1 Corinthians so I turn now to chapter 1 for a survey of that scholarship in which my own particular study is located.

58. David A. deSilva, *Honor, Patronage, Kinship & Purity: Unlocking New Testament Culture* (Downers Grove, IL: InterVarsity Press, 2000).

59. Delivered on 18th November 2003 in the chapel at King's College on the Strand (London).

Part I

Scholarship: Social Issues, the Elite and Education

Chapter 1

Survey of The Scholarship

1. *Introduction*

In my Introduction I explained the rationale, aims and methodology for my study of the educated elite in 1 Corinthians. This chapter locates my work within New Testament scholarship on Paul's letter. I examine aspects of the history of interpretation of 1 Corinthians and the community divisions evident in the letter. I demonstrate the developments in scholarship from early twentieth-century assumptions that theological disputes were behind the situation to a recognition of the significant role a socially stratified community played in the problems Paul encountered. The important contribution of social-scientific studies in providing a fresh approach to this letter is highlighted. I show how the identification of social-status issues has considerably enhanced the understanding of selected sections in Paul's letter. The central place of the status issues between the educated elite and the non-elite are identified. I also consider the so-called 'new consensus' with associated claims and challenges. Finally, I consider the nature of first-century Corinth as a Roman colony.

My analysis is not exhaustive but necessarily selective. My main focus is on the divisions within the Corinthian church, as indicated in 1 Corinthians, and the tensions related to social-status issues. This focus falls on the elite and non-elite Corinthian Christians, and community conflict.

2. *Parties: Four, Two or None?*

James Dunn comments that in the modern period the meaning of the slogans in 1 Cor. 1.12 has been 'The longest running critical question'.[1] The slogans appear connected to the schisms in 1.10 and a plausible conclusion has been that 1.12 shows four parties. Thus Dunn asks how

1. Dunn, *1 Corinthians*, p. 27. 1 Cor. 1.12 states, 'What I mean is this: One of you says, "I follow Paul"; another, "I follow Apollos"; another, "I follow Cephas"; still another, "I follow

many parties existed, who they were and the degree, and nature, of disagreement with Paul.[2] He provides a short discussion on this apparently straightforward conclusion of four parties and demonstrates how identifying and describing these parties has been problematic. In fact this difficulty has encouraged scholars to look for other solutions.

A new era in New Testament scholarship is generally considered to derive from Ferdinand Christian Baur's 1831 essay 'The Christ-party in the Corinthian Church'.[3] Baur argued that in 1 Cor. 1.12, despite the four slogans, there were only two parties involved in the strife. The adherents of Paul and Apollos stood against Cephas' adherents, who claimed to belong to Christ. Nils Dahl notes that Baur tied the situation in Corinth to his view of early Christianity and divisions 'between Paulinists and Petrine Judaizers'.[4] However, as Dahl notes, this was an arbitrary reduction of the slogans to two parties, and since Baur no one has identified any 'Judaizers' in the time of 1 Corinthians'.[5]

Other scholars saw Gnostics at work in Corinth. Wisdom was interpreted in the light of Gnostic mythological themes by Walter Schmithals and Ulrich Wilckens.[6] They tried to reconstruct the doctrines of the Gnostics and saw Paul's references to wisdom and knowledge as belonging in the context of early Hellenistic gnosticism. Gnostic pneumatics who voided the significance of the cross were opposing Paul. He writes to counteract this influence.

Dahl noted that outside Germany scholars had not assumed that Paul's polemic is directed against Judaizers or Gnostics.[7] Johannes Munck's essay 'Menigheden uden Partier' and the title 'The Church without Factions' showed he did not accept 'parties' or 'Judaizers' (or Gnostics).[8] Munck

Christ"' (NIV). For a helpful discussion on the social location of the Corinthian slogans see Dale B. Martin, *Slavery as Salvation: The Metaphor of Slavery in Pauline Christianity* (New Haven and London: Yale University Press, 1990).

2. Dunn, *1 Corinthians*, p. 27.

3. Ferdinand Christian Baur, 'Die Christuspartei in der korinthischen Gemeinde, der Gegensatz des paulinischen und petrinischen Christentums in der ältesten Kirche, der Apostel Petrus in Rom', *Tübinger Zeitschrift für Theologie* 4 (1831), pp. 61–206.

4. Nils A. Dahl, 'Paul and the Church at Corinth according to 1 Corinthians 1:10–4:21', in Farmer, Moule, and Niebuhr (eds.), *Christian History and Interpretation* (Cambridge: Cambridge University Press, 1967), pp. 313–35 (313–14).

5. Dahl, 'Paul', p. 314.

6. Walter Schmithals, *Gnosticism in Corinth: An Investigation of the Letters to the Corinthians* (trans. John E. Steely; Nashville and New York: Abingdon Press, 3rd edn, 1971); Ulrich Wilckens, *Weisheit und Torheit* (Tübingen: Mohr, 1959).

7. Dahl, 'Paul', p. 314.

8. Johannes Munck, 'Menigheden uden Partier', *Danske teologisk Tidsskrift* 15 (1952), pp. 251–53. Incorporated as 'The Church without Factions', in his *Paul and the Salvation of Mankind* (London: SCM Press, 1959).

claimed that the evidence indicated 'cliques' not factions. He argued that from their Greek background the Corinthians misunderstood Christianity as wisdom, and considered the Christian leaders to be teachers of wisdom, like rhetors and sophists. The Corinthian Christians considered themselves to be wise and boasted. But Dunn rightly comments that Munck's reaction probably went too far.[9] Passages in 1 Corinthians (especially 4.3 and 9.3) indicate that Paul was under criticism from some church members.[10]

John Hurd's book *The Origin of 1 Corinthians* argued that Paul's own change of mind between his Corinthian ministry and the 'previous letter' (1 Cor. 5.9–11) caused the difficulties.[11] This change followed the apostolic decree, which Paul had felt obliged to be loyal to in his 'previous letter'.

Thus Dahl's survey showed that while scholars agreed Paul was not opposing Judaizers, there was no consensus on the background and nature of the disputes.[12] He notes the general agreement that in 1 Cor. 1–4 Paul is addressing the whole church and it is not possible to take any one section as referring to any party (if there were parties). However, Dahl observes that no clarity has been reached with regard to the relation between (a) 1 Cor. 1–4 and the rest of the epistle, and (b) the situation reflected in 1 Corinthians and in 2 Corinthians.[13] Dahl notes Hurd's valuable work but he is unhappy with Hurd's handling of 1 Cor. 1–4.[14]

Dahl saw that 1 Cor. 1–4 forms an 'apologetic section' in which Paul justifies his apostolic ministry, but he comments, 'It is a main failure of theories like those of Munck and Hurd that they do not really take account of this'.[15] His solution sees the slogans in 1.12, within the apologetic section 1 Cor. 1–4, as indicating that the strife at Corinth was linked with opposition to Paul.[16] However, Dunn, while recognising the value of Dahl's work, says:

> It is unclear whether Dahl takes sufficient account of 4.18–19, 'But some of you, thinking that I am not coming to you, have become arrogant. But I will come to you soon, if the Lord wills, and I will find out not the talk of these arrogant people, but their power'. This seems to indicate

9. Dunn, *1 Corinthians*, p. 32. He states, 'Munck probably went too far in his reaction to Baur. It seems hard to doubt that Paul was confronted by some sharp criticism if not outright opposition from within the church in Corinth. We need only think of the sharpness of his response in passages like 1.17; 3.1–3; 4.18–21; 8.1–3 and 11.16'.

10. 1 Cor. 4.3 states, 'I care very little if I am judged by you or by any human court; . . .', and 1 Cor. 9.3, 'This is my defence to those who sit in judgment on me' (NIV).

11. John C. Hurd, *The Origin of 1 Corinthians* (London: SPCK, 1965).

12. Dahl, 'Paul', p. 315.

13. Dahl, 'Paul', p. 316.

14. Dahl, 'Paul', p. 316.

15. Dahl, 'Paul', p. 317.

16. Dahl, 'Paul', pp. 322–23.

> that Paul had in mind a particular group, and not just a generalized opposition. Or perhaps we should better say, particular individuals.[17]

Thus scholarly discussion, and solutions, to the identity of the persons associated with the slogans of 1.12 covers the whole range from factions (four parties, two parties, general opposition, particular individuals) to no factions. What is clear, however, is that many scholars found the 'solution' to the slogans of 1.12 of four different parties inadequate, and considering the situation in 1 Corinthians to be more complex, looked elsewhere.[18]

3. *Wisdom: Gnosticism and Hellenistic Judaism*

The slogans in 1.12 have provided one main focus for scholarly interest while the word σοφία (wisdom) has provided another. Three major hypotheses have attempted to explain the language and themes in 1 Cor. 1–4: Gnosticism, Hellenistic Judaism and Rhetoric.

The presence of gnosticism in Corinth was suggested by Richard Reitzenstein (1927) and by Schmithals (1954). Wilckens also argued for a Gnostic hypothesis but other scholars oppose the hypothesis.[19] In the 1960–70s writers explained the situation at Corinth without reference to Gnosticism.[20]

Richard A. Horsley, although he notes that scholars are gradually relinquishing the belief that the Corinthians were Gnostics, suggests 'that it is possible to determine with some degree of precision the nature and

17. Dunn, *1 Corinthians*, p. 33.

18. I am not arguing that modern scholars do not seek to identify parties in 1 Cor 1–4. See, for example, Clive Marsh, '"Who are you for?" 1 Corinthians 1:10–17 as Christian Scripture in the Context of Diverse Methods of Reading', in Burke and Elliott (eds.), *Paul and the Corinthians*, pp. 157–76. He refers to four groups or 'parties'. For a more detailed discussion on groups see Thiselton, *First Epistle*, pp. 123–33, 'The Four So-Called Groups' (1:12) and David R. Hall, *The Unity of the Corinthian Correspondence*, (JSNTSup, 251; London and New York: T. & T. Clark International, 2003), pp. 3–29.

19. Wilckens, *Weitsheit und Torheit*. Dunn, *1 Corinthians*, pp. 36–37, notes that the retreat is partly explained by the terminology. The Messina Colloquium on the Origins of Gnosticism (1966) agreed that Gnosticism (or Gnosis) should be used for the second-century Gnostic systems and 'gnostic' or 'proto-gnosticism' for the earlier period. Any reference to Gnosticism/gnosticism and the Corinthian church may be 'anachronistic and misleading'. Moreover, Dunn notes that terms such as 'gnosis' and 'sophia' were widespread in the Mediterranean world and not restricted to any particular group.

20. Dunn, *1 Corinthians*, p. 37. However, for a recent plea to rethink 'Gnosticism' see Todd E. Klutz, 'Re-Reading 1 Corinthians after *Rethinking "Gnosticism"*', *JSNT* 26 (2003), pp. 193–216.

background of the "proto-Gnosticism" in Corinth: Hellenistic Jewish religiosity focused on *sophia* and *gnosis*'.[21] Thus, Horsley says that Paul does not respond to a Gnostic libertinism as prescribed by some scholars:

> But a Hellenistic Jewish *gnosis* at home precisely in the mission context. Whereas Gnosticism of almost any form was hostile to the creation and the Creator-God, this Hellenistic Jewish *gnosis*, despite its apparent alienation from the body and 'earthly' matters, focused precisely on the knowledge of the One true God as the Creator, in contrast with cosmic forces or idols which are in fact non-existent.[22]

For Horsley, the conflict in 1 Corinthians is rooted in Jewish religious viewpoints, therefore:

> In a pattern of religiosity very similar to that expressed in Wisdom and Philo, some of the Corinthians are caught up into an exalted spiritual status through possession of *sophia*. Their *gnosis* is the theological content (and goal) of this mystical faith. Paul, on the other hand, with his Pharisaic training, maintains an apocalyptic perspective.[23]

Horsley's approach, built upon his previous work, helps us to read 1 Corinthians in the light of contemporary Hellenistic Judaism.[24] But Horsley does not introduce any discussion on Philo's appropriation of Greek culture and education. Philo's position lies between two extremes. He does not reject everything associated with Hellenism but neither does he adopt Greek culture uncritically.

James Davis, in his examination of Jewish sapiential tradition, has identified the strong link in this tradition between Wisdom and Spirit.[25] The hypotheses of the importance played by Hellenistic-Jewish Wisdom seems more suitable than the Gnostic hypothesis. However, Davis' thesis,

21. Richard A. Horsley, 'Gnosis in Corinth: 1 Corinthians 8.1–6', *NTS* 27 (1980), pp. 32–51 (32).

22. Horsley, 'Gnosis in Corinth', pp. 48–49.

23. Horsley, 'Gnosis in Corinth', p. 51.

24. Richard A. Horsley, 'Pneumatikos vs. Psychikos: Distinctions of Spiritual Status among the Corinthians', *HTR* 69 (1976), pp. 269–88; Richard A. Horsley, 'Wisdom of Words and Words of Wisdom in Corinth', *CBQ* 39 (1977), pp. 224–39; Richard A. Horsley, '"How can some of you say that there is no resurrection of the dead?" Spiritual Elitism in Corinth', *NovT* 20 (1978), pp. 203–31.

25. James A. Davis, *Wisdom and Spirit: An Investigation of 1 Corinthians 1.18–3.20 Against the Background of Jewish Sapiential Traditions in the Greco-Roman Period* (Lanham, MD: University Press of America, 1984).

which builds on the work begun by Horsley and Pearson, overlooks the importance of Greek education in Philo.[26] Horsley, for example, notes parallels between Paul and Philo but focuses on spiritual status, ignoring social status and access to education.[27] In his discussion he does not mention that the school subjects Philo refers to are from Greek not Jewish education.[28] Davis also neglects this distinction. When Horsley speaks of Philo addressing a community of devout Jews he notes that these '(like the community Paul addresses in Corinth) contain an elite of exalted spiritual status, in distinction from the ordinary believers'.[29] But this does not address social distinctions. Mendelson clarifies the class divisions in the Jewish population.[30] He observes that the majority of the Jewish population 'were in no economic position to provide their children with the benefits of gymnastic and encyclical training', and, 'Lower-class Jews not only lacked the basic prerequisites for an encyclical education; they also seem to have been opposed to it in principle'.[31] Horsley and Davis do not address these essential distinctions.[32]

Gordon Fee, in his commentary on 1 Corinthians, argues that most likely the key issue, or point of contention, was the Corinthians' assumption that they were *pneumatikoi* ('related to their experience of Spirit inspiration') but were not so sure about Paul.[33] Fee identifies the source of their false spirituality, not in Hurd's suggestion that most of the problems stem from Paul, or their Hellenistic-Jewish Wisdom tradition, but rather along sociological lines. In this Fee follows Gerd Theissen.[34]

26. Davis, *Wisdom and Spirit*, pp. 4–5. B.A. Pearson, *The Pneumatikos-Psychikos Terminology in 1 Corinthians* (SBLDS, 12; Missoula, MT: Scholars Press, 1973).

27. Horsley, 'Pneumatikos vs. Psychikos', p. 283. He sees, as with *teleios* in the *teleios-nepios* contrast, the designations of 'wise', 'nobly born', 'king' as referring to a spiritual elite.

28. Horsley, 'Pneumatikos vs. Psychikos', p. 282. This is in marked contrast to Mendelson, *Secular Education*, pp. 28–33, who asks whether Jewish youths undertook their secular training in Greek or Jewish institutions, and notes that, 'The consensus of contemporary scholarly opinion is that Alexandrian Jews had access to Greek education as offered in the gymnasium' (p. 29). He summarises, 'And since there is no evidence that synagogue schools were open on weekdays, we may conclude that if the Jews encountered secular studies in an institutional setting, it would have been in the Greek gymnasium' (p. 33).

29. Horsley, 'Pneumatikos vs. Psychikos', p. 279.

30. Mendelson, *Secular Education*, pp. 28–33,

31. Mendelson, *Secular Education*, pp. 29, 33.

32. Although Horsley, 'Spiritual Elitism in Corinth', p. 215, for example, mentions the '"milk-like" teachings of the "school studies" in contrast with the true knowledge and wisdom employed by the perfect', he does not discuss the nature of these studies or social access to them. His emphasis on spiritual, or religious, status and elitism, although valid, is weakened by his neglect of social status.

33. Fee, *First Epistle*, pp. 10–15.

34. Fee, *First Epistle*, pp. 13–15. Theissen, *Social Setting*.

Fee's commentary proceeds from the perspective of rivalry between patrons and Paul.[35] His position is only briefly explained in his Introduction but, fortunately, it is addressed in other sections of his commentary

4. *Wisdom and Rhetoric*

The rhetorical dimension of 1 Cor. 1–4 was recognised at the beginning of the twentieth century but its study was overshadowed by other approaches. In the 1990s three major studies, by Stephen Pogoloff, Duane Litfin, and Michael Bullmore, addressed the role Graeco-Roman rhetoric played in the problems at Corinth.[36] However, there was little interaction between them.[37] The Pauline scholar Litfin remarks on these studies:

> Oddly, until these three studies no one had attempted to explore in depth this traditional understanding of 1 Corinthians 1–4. As a result, Gnostic and Philonic Wisdom hypotheses had gained prominence, particularly after the publication of Ulrich Wilckens's *Weisheit und Torheit* and Walther Schmithals's *Gnosticism in Corinth*. By examining the full case for the traditional understanding of this important passage, each of these studies was thus bucking what had become dominant trends. All the more significant, then, that each of these efforts arrived at similar conclusions.[38]

Nevertheless, the conclusions are not identical. Bullmore, although he affirmed much of Litfin's work attempted to take the discussion further.

35. Fee, *First Epistle*, p. 15.

36. Stephen M. Pogoloff, *Logos and Sophia: The Rhetorical Situation of 1 Corinthians* (SBLDS, 134; Atlanta, GA: Scholars Press, 1992); Duane Litfin, *St. Paul's Theology of Proclamation: 1 Corinthians 1–4 and Greco-Roman Rhetoric* (SNTSMS, 79; Cambridge: Cambridge University Press, 1994); Michael A. Bullmore, *St. Paul's Theology of Rhetorical Style: An Examination of 1 Corinthians 2:1–5 in the Light of First-Century Rhetorical Criticism* (San Francisco: International Scholars Publications, 1995).

37. Duane Litfin, 'Review of Michael A. Bullmore, *St. Paul's Theology of Rhetorical Style: An Examination of 1 Corinthians 2:1–5 in the Light of First-Century Rhetorical Criticism*', *JBL* 116 (1997), pp. 568–70 (568), notes that Pogoloff's monograph shows no awareness of Litfin's dissertation from a decade earlier and when Litfin revised his work he was unaware of Pogoloff's dissertation. Pogoloff's work appeared too late to be included in Litfin's revision. Thus Litfin comments, 'Only Bullmore's book could have synthesized the three studies, but it is one of the weaknesses of his work that Bullmore remained unaware of Pogoloff's 1992 monograph and did not do more to interact with the arguments of mine' (p. 568).

38. Litfin, 'Review of Michael A. Bullmore', p. 568.

According to Bullmore, Paul rejects a particular form of preaching: the flamboyant Asian style of oratory. He does not reject something essential to Graeco-Roman rhetoric. Nevertheless, Litfin points out that Bullmore, rather than taking the argument further argues for something less radical and his 'treatment is vulnerable to the charge that it is reductionistic in that it portrays first-century rhetoric as focusing almost exclusively on matters of style'.[39] Thus Litfin concludes his review:

> Bullmore claims that Paul is rejecting the grand style of speaking in favor of the plain. Stephen Pogoloff's [*sic*] disagrees: 'Paul is not rejecting a "fancy" rhetoric in favor of a "plainer" one.... Paul rejects not rhetoric, but the cultured values wedded to it' (p. 121). I, in turn, argue that ancient rhetoric epitomized the worldly values Paul was forced by his theology to disavow, which is why he limited himself to the role of herald rather than persuader.[40]

He admits that these three theses reflect serious differences, yet they do hold the common conviction that Graeco-Roman rhetoric had a crucial role in the troubles at Corinth.

Litfin clarifies Paul's practice as a preacher by examining 1 Cor. 1–4 and asking, '*How did Paul conceive of his preaching, and in what ways did this conception relate to the basic presuppositions of the Apostle's thought?*'[41] He notes the 'thicket of interpretational questions' regarding 1 Cor. 1–4 with the chief one being the meaning of the word σοφία.

This term was widely used in Paul's time in many contexts. Paul and the Corinthians used the word with ease, but Litfin states, 'the two sides seemed diametrically opposed in their meanings'.[42] The main difficulty in understanding Paul's argument in 1 Cor. 1–4 is knowing what the Corinthians understood by σοφία and only by determining the implica-tions for the Corinthian community can we see what Paul was responding to.

Until recent times, Litfin notes, the phrase σοφία λόγου was consistently interpreted by exegetes 'with primary reference to Greco-Roman rhetoric'.[43] Paul's preaching did not match 'the standards of a culture profoundly influenced by an unparalleled rhetorical heritage'. However, this rhetorical view is almost eclipsed by two approaches to σοφία. One approach interprets wisdom through gnostic themes. The other approach interprets wisdom through Hellenistic Jewish tradition seen in Philo and the *Wisdom of Solomon*. Hence, Litfin notes that, in this view, the Corinthians accepted 'a Philonic type of Heavenly Wisdom' for 'attaining

39. Litfin, 'Review of Michael A. Bullmore', p. 569.
40. Litfin, 'Review of Michael A. Bullmore', p. 569.
41. Litfin, *St. Paul's Theology of Proclamation*, p. 2. Emphasis in original.
42. Litfin, *St. Paul's Theology of Proclamation*, p. 2.
43. Litfin, *St. Paul's Theology of Proclamation*, p. 3.

the highest spiritual status or even salvation itself. These Wisdom enthusiasts considered Paul simply another Wisdom teacher and evaluated him accordingly, finding his wisdom deficient.'[44]

Litfin maintains that these two perspectives (including various mixtures of them) currently seem to dominate in Pauline studies. He agrees that they were active in first-century thought and they help in our insight into Paul's letters. But he rightly asks 'whether either or both of these perspectives provide the best interpretation of 1 Cor. 1.17–2.5. In other words, has the eclipse of the older rhetorical view been justified?'[45]

In an in-depth study, which traces rhetoric from the sophists through Plato, Isocrates, Aristotle and Cicero to Quintilian and other first-century writers, Litfin demonstrates the nature and importance of rhetoric in Roman Corinth.[46] He rightly remarks, 'A failure to appreciate the full dimensions of classical rhetoric has been costly in the exegesis of 1 Cor. 1–4, leading to numerous false leads and much unnecessary confusion'.[47] Litfin summarises his study:

> My work explores the ancient contrast between the role of the persuader and the role of the herald, and portrays Paul in 1 Corinthians 1–4 as repudiating the former and embracing the latter for his own *modus operandi* as an apostle. Thus, according to my argument it is the *quintessence* of Greco-Roman rhetoric, the stance of the persuader itself, that Paul disavows in 1 Corinthians 1–4.[48]

Litfin sees the clash of rhetoric in chapters 1–4 but, as Dunn notes, L.L. Welborn 'had already demonstrated an inescapable social and political dimension to the situation addressed in chs. 1–4'.[49] Welborn noted that Paul's terms were used by Graeco-Roman historians for conflicts in city-

44. Litfin, *St. Paul's Theology of Proclamation*, p. 4.

45. Litfin, *St. Paul's Theology of Proclamation*, p. 4.

46. A recent essay on Isocrates' pedagogy and politics is given by Niall Livingstone, 'The voice of Isocrates and the dissemination of cultural power', in Too and Livingstone (eds.), *Pedagogy and Power: Rhetorics of Classical Learning* (Ideas in Context, 50; Cambridge: Cambridge University Press, 1998), pp. 263–81. For an important discussion on Quintilian see: Teresa Morgan, 'A Good Man Skilled in Politics: Quintilian's Political Theory', in Too and Livingstone (eds.), *Pedagogy and Power*, pp. 245–62. Morgan, p. 245, identifies the two main ways in which Quintilian has been read (a) 'as a type of likeable pedagogue' (by educationalists and historians of education) and (b) as a mine of information (by 'historians of rhetoric and literary theory'). His *Institutio Oratoria* ('Education of the Orator') is our most comprehensive surviving text on ancient education. However, Morgan notes how his educational theory is related to political theory. She shows how questions on his 'political context and purpose of education' demonstrate his 'cogent and original' answer (p. 247).

47. Litfin, *St. Paul's Theology of Proclamation*, pp. 15–16.

48. Litfin, 'Review of Michael A. Bullmore', pp. 568–69.

49. Dunn, *1 Corinthians*, p. 42; L. L. Welborn, 'On the Discord in Corinth: 1 Corinthians 1–4 and Ancient Politics', *JBL* 106 (1987), pp. 85–111.

states. Thus he saw the problem as partisanship, a power struggle rather than a theological controversy. Paul wrote not to refute heresy but to prevent *stasis* (strife, discord). Margaret Mitchell effectively built her thesis on Welborn's conclusions that the letter was against factionalism not particular parties.[50] She argues that 1 Corinthians is a unified deliberative letter which throughout urges unity on the divided church.[51] Paul seeks to persuade the Corinthians to end the factionalism and be reconciled with each other. Mitchell sees the letter in the light of rhetorical forms, and technical terms and phrases, used in ancient discussions on factionalism and concord.

Stephen Pogoloff also interprets 1 Cor. 1–4 as rhetorical and writes a narrative of the rhetorical situation in which he understands rhetoric as primarily functional.[52] He acknowledges that Welborn attempts to determine the rhetorical situation in 1 Cor. 1–4. Although Welborn's conclusions are very close to his, Pogoloff argues that Welborn's focus on form, without sufficient attention to situation, is an error that distorts his argument. Pogoloff notes that Welborn, attracted by a formal parallel, 'fails to notice the obvious *differences* in Paul's situation which dictate different functions for similar forms'.[53] Thus the Corinthian slogans are for teachers and not political leaders. Similarly, Pogoloff criticises Mitchell's work on the rhetorical situation because 'her method is strictly formal'.[54] Mitchell finds parallels in Paul's letter with 'vocabulary and topoi used in political rhetoric' to combat factionalism and thus she assumes that dissension is the issue in all the letter. Yet Pogoloff states, 'this assumption is seriously flawed' because she has not demonstrated that these were used exclusively for this purpose and they were not used in a new metaphorical sense.[55]

50. Margaret M. Mitchell, *Paul and the Rhetoric of Reconciliation: An Exegetical Investigation of the Language and Composition of 1 Corinthians* (Louisville, KY: Westminster/John Knox Press, 1992).

51. Mitchell, *Paul and the Rhetoric of Reconciliation*, p. 296.

52. Pogoloff, *Logos and Sophia*, pp. 87–8. In this he follows Lloyd F. Bitzer, 'Functional Communication: A Situational Perspective', in White (ed.), *Rhetoric in Transition: Studies in the Nature and Uses of Rhetoric* (University Park: Pennsylvania State University, 1980), pp. 21–38 (25), 'Situational rhetoric commences not with attention to speaker intention and artistry, nor with focus on language resources, the argumentation process, or natural psychological processes; rather it commences with the critical relation between persons and environment and the process of interaction leading to harmonious adjustment'.

53. Pogoloff, *Logos and Sophia*, p. 89.

54. Pogoloff, *Logos and Sophia*, pp. 89–90.

55. Pogoloff, *Logos and Sophia*, p. 90.

Pogoloff, after showing the importance of social-status issues at Corinth, concludes:

> Paul is responding to an exigence of division among the Corinthians. These divisions are a result of the Corinthians' competitions for status. As other Hellenists, they compete to be recognized as wise (cultured), well-born, and rich or powerful. When Paul arrived among them, their relationship with him was shaped within the social norms for visiting sophists (i.e. eloquent teachers). They gladly provided the patronage Paul needed to establish a congregation. Paul needed such patronage to give him a legitimate platform to address the gentiles. Among Jews, he could speak in the synagogue, but among gentiles he, as an amateur rhetor, lacked a platform until invited to speak in the homes of his patrons. The Corinthians, in return, gained honor through hosting him, especially at their evening meals followed by cultured discussion.[56]

In his discussion on sophistic and rhetorical studies Bruce Winter notes that Litfin, Mitchell and Pogoloff do not address the sophist movement in the first century AD.[57] Winter notes Pogoloff's reason, 'we have no evidence that sophists who styled themselves as philosophers were present in Corinth'.[58] But in the first century AD the term 'sophist', Winter informs us, 'was used to designate those rhetoricians whose ability in oratory was such that they could both secure a public following and attract students to their schools'. G.W. Bowersock's definition is a 'virtuoso rhetor with a big public reputation'.[59] Winter argues, from first and early second centuries AD, Greek, Jewish and Christian sources, that the sophistic movement accounts for Paul's opponents in both 1 Corinthians and 2 Corinthians 10–13. These sophists were educated in Greek *paideia*. This important work admirably addresses the oversight of the scholars who focus on rhetoric.

56. Pogoloff, *Logos and Sophia*, p. 273. Stanley Kent Stowers, 'Social Status, Public Speaking and Private Teaching: the Circumstances of Paul's Preaching Activity', *NovT* 26 (1984), pp. 59–82, discusses Paul's public speaking in relation to the synagogue and the gymnasium. He concludes, 'It is not surprizing, then, that the gymnasium and synagogue were places of ambiguous status for Paul, but that the private home became the major platform for his preaching activity' (p. 82).

57. Bruce W. Winter, *Philo and Paul Among the Sophists*, (SNTSMS, 96; Cambridge: Cambridge University Press, 1997), pp. 11–13. This is now available in a second edition as: *Philo and Paul Among the Sophists: Alexandrian and Corinthian Responses to a Julio-Claudian Movement* (Grand Rapids and Cambridge, UK: Eerdmans, 2nd edn, 2002). This follows the same layout as the first edition but with a new section on 1 Thess. 1 and 2.1–8 to show that 1 Cor 2.1–5 was not an isolated case for Paul. Other changes are incorporated. My references continue to use the pages in the first edition.

58. Winter, *Philo and Paul*, p. 13; citing Pogoloff, *Logos and Sophia*, p. 65.

59. Winter, *Philo and Paul*, pp. 3–4; citing G.W. Bowersock, *Greek Sophists in the Roman Empire* (Oxford: Clarendon Press, 1969), p. 13.

Finally, Dunn considers that scholars have underplayed certain aspects of 1 Cor. 1–4: Litfin the socio-political and Welborn, Pogoloff and Mitchell the theological.[60] Yet, Dunn recognises that the last three scholars have usefully identified social and political issues.[61] This significant social dimension and debates surrounding it are addressed next.

5. *Social Science Studies*

A fresh approach to the study of 1 Corinthians arose in the mid-1970s with the publication of Gerd Theissen's articles.[62] Dunn summarises the significant influence of Theissen's work: while other scholars had focused virtually exclusively on theological and religious aspects in 1 Corinthians Theissen turned to social factors, and showed that all three factors were intimately intertwined in social reality and needed addressing.[63] Theissen focused attention on the social facts in 1 Cor. 1.26–29. He argues that the majority of members in the Corinthian church were from the lower classes, while a minority were from the upper classes. The minority or 'wise' belonged to the educated classes and their social status would make them a dominant minority. His work pioneered and established the sociological approach to New Testament studies and particularly 1 Corinthians.

Scholars such as Wayne Meeks continued the contribution of Theissen but Meeks' study is much wider than Theissen's, addressing a broad range of social factors that impinged on Paul's churches.[64] Dunn regards it as *the* major work to follow Theissen's approach.[65] In a helpful overview of passages from 1 Cor. 6–10 Dunn summarises how scholars have identified various social issues. Although scholars may take different perspectives on what is happening these studies add value because they make scholars face the social and cultural factors behind Paul's language, and its reception, while recognising that his theology operates in a dynamic historical context.[66] This is a valid point. Social-science studies help us to read Paul

60. Dunn, *1 Corinthians*, p. 43.

61. Dunn, *1 Corinthians*, p. 44. See on politics L.L. Welborn, *Politics and Rhetoric in the Corinthian Epistles* (Macon, GA: Mercer University Press, 1997) and Bruno Blumenfeld, *The Political Paul: Justice, Democracy and Kingship in a Hellenistic Framework* (JSNTSup, 210; Sheffield: Sheffield Academic Press, 2001).

62. These essays were subsequently edited and translated, with an introduction, by John H. Schütz, in Theissen, *Social Setting*.

63. Dunn, *1 Corinthians*, pp. 48–49.

64. Wayne A. Meeks, *The First Urban Christians: The Social World of the Apostle Paul* (New Haven and London: Yale University Press, 1983). This is now available in a second edition (2003).

65. Dunn, *1 Corinthians*, p. 49.

66. Dunn, *1 Corinthians*, p. 65.

more sensitively as considerate readers. Through such studies we see important issues that move us significantly beyond the earlier debate over the number of parties (four, two or none) at Corinth. Now we see social issues and community conflict in the church stemming from social-status structures within the society. 1 Corinthians is a high-context letter and an accurate interpretation must stem from understanding the first-century eastern Mediterranean society in which Paul and his readers lived.[67] Recent scholarship's use of social-scientific approaches has identified many social-status issues in 1 Corinthians. The next section examines some of these issues in which my interest in the educated elite should be located.[68]

6. *Social-Status Issues*

a. *Language, Lifestyle and Leadership (1 Corinthians 1–4)*

Theissen's analysis of 1 Cor. 1.26–29 identifies the majority of the members of the Corinthian church as belonging to the lower classes while a minority belonged to the upper classes. These few were, nevertheless, a dominant minority because they were the 'wise' who belonged to the educated classes, which gave them a disproportionate influence. Theissen remarks, 'If Paul says that there were not many in the Corinthian congregation who were wise, powerful, and wellborn, then this much is certain: there were some'.[69] In this case, Theissen argues that if these people were few in numbers they must have been very influential for Paul to devote so much space to dealing with their 'wisdom'. Moreover, Theissen continues by noting the status issues in 1 Cor. 4.10 where, although the terminology is slightly different, again Paul identifies these people separately using the categories of wise, powerful and esteemed.[70] His argument for social-status divisions in 1 Cor. 1–4 has been widely accepted within Pauline scholarship. Horrell, for example, concludes that social groups led by prominent congregation members makes good

67. On 1 Corinthians as a high-context letter see my Introduction.

68. For an overview on social classes see D.F. Watson, 'Roman Social Classes', in Evans and Porter (eds.), *Dictionary of New Testament Background* (Downers Grove, IL and Leicester, England: InterVarsity Press, 2000), pp. 999–1004. He identifies the three upper classes as first the senatorial order, second the equestrian order and third the decurions ('provincial monied aristocrats'). Above these was the emperor. However, most people were in the lower classes (the *humiliores*, 'of lowly birth and status'). Another helpful article is S.C. Barton, 'Social Values and Structures', in Evans and Porter (eds.), *Dictionary of New Testament Background*, pp. 1127–34. He focuses on their relevance in 1 Corinthians.

69. Theissen, *Social Setting*, p. 72. Referring to 1 Cor. 1.26.

70. Theissen, *Social Setting*, p. 72. Theissen cites 1 Cor. 4:10, 'We are fools for Christ's sake, but you are wise in Christ. We are weak, but you are strong. You are held in honor, but we in disrepute' (RSV).

sense.[71] However, this view has been challenged recently, notably by Justin Meggitt, and I address this below.[72]

In his detailed study, Dale Martin comments on 1 Cor. 1–4, 'Paul's repeated allusions to rhetoric – his own disavowal of it and his allegations that others value it too highly – contribute to the conclusion that rhetoric and its associated status implications constitute a central aspect of the disputes within the Corinthian church'.[73] Martin notes three major themes in Paul's introduction (1.1–10). First, there is the emphasis that 'all' Corinthians experience Christ's blessings. Second, Paul indirectly introduces status by his terminology – he stresses what they *all already* possess. Third, Paul invokes apocalypticism with its imminent eschatology and system of values/status. Martin sees Paul placing two different worlds in opposition: Graeco-Roman rhetoric and status (with its upper-class ideology) and apocalyptic reality in the gospel (with an alternative system of values/status). These opposing realms of reality are seen in 1.18–31. Paul uses status terms (wise, scribe, debater), but then offers an alternative system to the Graeco-Roman ruling class with its dominant ideology. So Martin considers that Paul's rhetoric, with its many status terms, shows most conflict (all?) to focus on status issues.[74]

In 1 Cor. 2.1-16 Martin sees Paul's ministry as an example of the 'other' realm. He shows himself as low status, when judged by the criteria of this age. Then Paul shifts and uses high status terms (redefined with different meanings in this other realm) for himself and other Christians. The Christians in 2.16 have the highest cosmic status position (the mind of Christ) but in 3.1 Paul portrays them as low status (babies needing milk). In 3.1–23 Paul assigns status to the Christians within the different realms. By the end of the chapter they are the owners of all. Finally, Martin examines the ironic contrast between the apostles and 'certain ones' at Corinth in 4.1–11.[75] Paul relativizes the status of the apostles. They are shown as low status but the Corinthians are exalted with high status. Martin observes the juxtaposition in 4.6–13 between the apostles, including Paul, (very low status) and Graeco-Roman society (with high status traditions).[76] Yet Paul, at the end of chapters 1–4 again reverses the

71. Horrell, *Social Ethos* p. 117.

72. Justin J. Meggitt, *Paul, Poverty and Survival* (Studies of the New Testament and Its World; Edinburgh: T. & T. Clark, 1998).

73. Dale B. Martin, *The Corinthian Body* (New Haven and London: Yale University Press, 1995), p. 56.

74. Martin, *Corinthian Body*, p. 61.

75. Martin, *Corinthian Body*, p. 65.

76. Martin, *Corinthian Body*, p. 66. Martin includes popular philosophy with Graeco-Roman society.

status positions. His position is the highest (father) while the Corinthian leaders are pedagogues.[77] At 4.18 Martin argues the reader realizes Paul writes to a 'dual audience' made up of the whole church (shown by his repeated use of 'all') and some others in the church.[78] In chapters 1–4, Martin notes Paul's use of assumptions in Graeco-Roman culture (on hierarchy/status) to claim for himself the highest status (father) and then encourage the high status Christians to imitate his low status position.[79] Social status is a significant reality in these chapters.

Finally, Andrew Clarke's socio-historical and exegetical study shows that in 1 Cor. 1–4 (and 1 Cor. 5–6) Paul addresses issues of leadership among the elite in the Corinthian church. The practices of the Christian leaders corresponded to those of secular leadership and so Paul needed to critique this model of leadership and explain his principles for leadership.[80] Thus chapters 1–4 clearly demonstrate the social-status issues and conflicts evident in the church.

b. *Litigation (1 Corinthians 6.1–11)*

Scholars who use social-scientific approaches to investigate the courts in Corinth include Winter, Chow, Clarke, Mitchell and Kinman.[81] They have identified the central role of social status in the courts and the church.

Bruce Winter's illuminating 1991 article on civil litigation concluded that 'Those in the ἐκκλησία τοῦ θεοῦ who belonged to the class of the wise,

77. See 1 Cor. 4.15.

78. Martin, *Corinthian Body*, p. 67.

79. Martin, *Corinthian Body*, p. 67.

80. Andrew D. Clarke, *Secular and Christian Leadership in Corinth: A Socio-Historical and Exegetical Study of 1 Corinthians 1–6* (AGJU, 18; Leiden: E.J. Brill, 1993), pp. 129–34 for his conclusions.

81. Bruce W. Winter, 'Civil Litigation in Secular Corinth and the Church: The Forensic Background to 1 Corinthians 6.1–8', *NTS* 37 (1991), pp. 559–72; Bruce W. Winter, 'Civil Litigation: 1 Corinthians 6.1–11', in Winter, *Seek the Welfare of the City: Christians as Benefactors and Citizens* (Grand Rapids: Eerdmans; Carlisle: Paternoster, 1994), pp. 105–21; Bruce W. Winter, 'Civil Litigation in Secular Corinth and the Church: The Forensic Background to 1 Corinthians 6.1–8', in Rosner (ed.), *Understanding Paul's Ethics: Twentieth-Century Approaches* (Grand Rapids: Eerdmans; Carlisle: Paternoster, 1995), pp. 85–103; John K. Chow, *Patronage and Power: A Study of Social Networks in Corinth* (JSNTSup, 75; Sheffield: JSOT Press, 1992), pp. 123–30; Clarke, *Secular and Christian Leadership*, pp. 59–71; Alan C. Mitchell, 'Rich and Poor in the Courts of Corinth: Litigiousness and Status in 1 Corinthians 6.1–11', *NTS* 39 (1993), pp. 562–86. Winter's two later articles are based on his article in *NTS* 37 (1991). (Although 'Civil Litigation in Secular Corinth and the Church: The Forensic Background to 1 Corinthians 6:1–8' is dated in Rosner, p. 85, as a 1991 article it is an updated article that includes in the conclusions a critique of Mitchell's 1993 article.) Brent Kinman, '"Appoint the Despised as Judges!" (1 Corinthians 6:4)', *TynBul* 48 (1997), pp. 345–54.

the powerful and the well-born allowed that secular phenomenon to surface in their dealings with one another especially in the area of civil law'.[82] He thus identified elite believers as those involved in litigation. Alan Mitchell, however, argues that the issue of litigation is part of the larger problem of social division but it is the rich, upper status, Christians who were taking the poor, lower status Christians to court.[83] Yet Winter disagrees, concluding, '1 Corinthians 6:1–8 then reflects a typical, first-century struggle for power among the élite'.[84] The struggle was 'between the élite who were social equals or near equals'.[85] Winter, although acknowledging the importance of Mitchell's study, critiques his position and reaffirms his earlier position cited above.[86] More recently, Winter reaffirms that the Corinthian Christians were engaged in civil litigation and this struggle was 'between members of the élite who were social equals (or near equals).'[87] He sees the conflicts in 1 Cor. 1–4 over teachers as linked to the court cases. Thus Winter observes, 'Those few in the "church of God" (ἐκκλησία τοῦ θεοῦ) who belonged to the class of the wise, the powerful, and the well-born allowed the secular phenomenon of vexatious litigation to determine their dealings with one another in the Christian community'.[88] Thus both scholars, despite differences, affirm social status issues in 1 Cor. 6 related to elite believers.

John Chow also considers lawsuits and litigants and identifies status issues. He comments that it is likely that the litigants, or at least the plaintiff, were church members who were 'relatively powerful' and among the wise and strong.[89] Similarly, Andrew Clarke's conclusions on the Roman legal background lead him to suggest that men of 'relatively high social standing' were entering into litigation possibly to ensure that both their reputation and status were protected.[90] Brent Kinman also agrees that elite believers 'were suing one another in order to further their own social status'.[91] Yet he further argues that Paul commands that the 'despised' be appointed as arbiters, those of lower status than the typical litigants. Thus

82. Winter, 'Civil Litigation in Secular Corinth and the Church', pp. 571–72.

83. Mitchell, 'Rich and Poor in the Courts of Corinth'.

84. Winter, 'Civil Litigation: 1 Corinthians 6:1–11', p. 120.

85. Winter, 'Civil Litigation: 1 Corinthians 6:1–11', p. 120.

86. Winter, 'Civil Litigation in Secular Corinth and the Church', in Rosner (ed.), *Understanding Paul's Ethics*, pp. 101–03.

87. Bruce W. Winter, *After Paul Left Corinth: The Influence of Secular Ethics and Social Change* (Grand Rapids, MI and Cambridge, UK: Eerdmans, 2001), pp. 58–75 (74).

88. Winter, *After Paul Left Corinth*, p. 74.

89. Chow, *Patronage and Power*, pp. 123–130 (129).

90. Clarke, *Secular and Christian Leadership*, p. 71.

91. Kinman, '"Appoint the Despised as Judges!" (1 Corinthians 6:4)', p. 353. He identifies these with the wise, powerful and well bred in 1 Cor. 1.26.

Kinman concludes, 'The very appointment of "the despised" as arbiters might do a great deal to discourage lawsuits among the elite, for there would probably be very little to gain in the way of status if a mere "despised one", rather than a socially esteemed magistrate, were to be the arbiter of the dispute.'[92] However, Winter thinks the 'least esteemed' (1 Cor. 6.1) seems to be a reference to 'outsiders', i.e. the judge and jury involved in the courts.[93] Finally, Anthony Thiselton reviews the scholarly discussion of 1 Cor. 6.1-11 and agrees that the socially influential in the congregation could use external social networks to the disadvantage of the 'weak' Christians.[94] Thus recent research clearly demonstrates that conflict in the church, civil litigation and the courts are impregnated with social-status issues related to elite believers. This is not just a matter of justice.

c. *Idol-Food (1 Corinthians 8–10)*

Social-status issues also arise in 1 Cor. 8–10, chapters which deal with idol-food (the 'weak' and 'strong') and 'rights'. Theissen's sociological analysis concludes that probably the strong were among the wise, powerful and those of noble birth in 1.26. Their attitude is associated with the upper classes. These are 'higher social status' Christians.[95] Thus Theissen sees Paul's response as addressed virtually entirely to the strong and a compromise characteristic of the Pauline letters of 'love-patriarchalism', which allowed the continuation of social inequalities but modified by concern and respect.[96]

Dunn observes that Theissen's contribution drew scholars' attention to the social dimensions of 1 Cor. 8–10 when others had almost lost sight of these aspects. Thus Dunn sees obvious social dimensions in the chapters regarding eating idol-food. He follows Theissen's identification of the weak as those of lower social status and the strong/knowledgeable as those of higher social status.[97] Their liberal attitude, according to Dunn, arises because of their 'better education'.[98] Although Dunn agrees in general with Theissen's arguments he does not accept Theissen's solution of love-patriarchalism.

In contrast to Theissen's position on the 'weak' and 'strong', Gooch sees the weak as Paul's construct; a hypothetical group created by

92. Kinman, '"Appoint the Despised as Judges!" (1 Corinthians 6:4)', p. 354.
93. Winter, *After Paul Left Corinth*, pp. 69–70.
94. Thiselton, *First Epistle*, pp. 418–21.
95. Theissen, *Social Setting*, p. 138.
96. Theissen, *Social Setting*, pp. 137–40.
97. Dunn, *1 Corinthians*, pp. 57–59.
98. Dunn, *1 Corinthians*, p. 59.

Paul.[99] Therefore Gooch does not investigate any distinction between the weak and strong, although he states, 'If there were no weak Christians in Corinth when Paul wrote 1 Corinthians, then, there were weak Christians in Corinth after 1 Corinthians had been received – weak not because of intimacy with idols, but because of an anxious eagerness not to violate partnership with their Lord'.[100] He just sees the strong as the Corinthian Christians. The dispute is merely between Paul and the Corinthians. But this will not do. Rather, as Horrell argues, although Gooch takes issue with the 'scholarly consensus' that Paul addresses a divided community this consensus is 'likely still to win the day'.[101]

Three recent specialist studies have addressed 1 Cor. 8–10: Derek Newton's *Deity and Diet*, Alex T. Cheung's, *Idol Food in Corinth* and David Hall's *The Unity of the Corinthian Correspondence*.[102] Newton's study both examines the background of religious pluralism in Corinth and provides an exegesis of the text. He particularly examines the situation from both sides (i.e. Paul's and the Corinthians's) and shows the inherent complexity that needed addressing. He recognises the various social groupings in the congregation (high status, lower status and slave status) complicated the situation.[103] Nevertheless, he argues 'that the idol-food issue was in reality a multi-dimensional problem, not merely a social or economic or educational or theological one'.[104] Newton discusses the identity of the 'weak' and the 'strong' arguing that each group represents a 'range of viewpoints'. He wishes to leave each category open but does, for example, comment on the 'strong', 'Some may have been strong in political, social or economic terms but weak in terms of Christian faith and love'.[105] Therefore Newton does not accept Theissen's rigid division into 'socio-economic groups'.[106]

Cheung too provides a critique of Theissen's work, which he finds unconvincing, because it is based on 'highly questionable, and probably mistaken, assumptions'.[107] Moreover, David Hall critiques 'fundamental

99. Gooch, *Dangerous Food*, pp. 99–108. Gooch comments on 1 Cor. 8, 'Paul's appeal concerning the weak is hypothetical' (p. 103).

100. Gooch, *Dangerous Food*, p. 108.

101. Horrell, 'Review of Peter D. Gooch', p. 281.

102. Derek Newton, *Deity and Diet: The Dilemma of Sacrificial Food at Corinth* (JSNTSup, 169; Sheffield: Sheffield Academic Press, 1998); Alex T. Cheung, *Idol Food in Corinth: Jewish Background and Pauline Legacy* (JSNTSup, 176; Sheffield: Sheffield Academic Press, 1999) and Hall, *Unity of the Corinthian Correspondence*.

103. Newton, *Deity and Diet*, p. 384.

104. Newton, *Deity and Diet*, p. 35.

105. Newton, *Deity and Diet*, pp. 310–12 (311).

106. Newton, *Deity and Diet*, p. 32.

107. Cheung, *Idol Food in Corinth*, pp. 311–14.

weaknesses' in Theissen's arguments.[108] He also interacts with Meggitt's criticism of Theissen.[109] He finds himself disagreeing with both Theissen and Meggitt because 'the evidence is not sufficient to justify their conclusions'.[110] Although Hall argues that Theissen's thesis of an elite group of strong believers is imposed on chapters 8–10 he still sees social-status divisions in Paul's letter.[111] His conclusion on 1 Cor. 1.26–29 is that most Christians were of low status before they were called but others were not. He recognises a 'small upper-class minority' together with very poor Christians but sees most believers as possessing a social status between these extremes.

In conclusion, this section has demonstrated the lively debate regarding social-status issues in 1 Cor. 8–10. Although Hall remains unconvinced by the evidence for either Theissen's or Meggitt's position he does, nevertheless, affirm the presence of a small number of elite believers. Thus his position coincides with my understanding of elite believers at Corinth.

d. *The Lord's Supper (1 Corinthians 11.17–34)*

Theissen provided a new interpretation of the abuse of the Lord's Supper (1 Cor. 11.17–34). He argued that the difficulties arose from a socially stratified community and not, as previously thought, from theological differences. He saw the conflict as one between rich and poor Christians. Thus Theissen comments:

> The core of the problem was that the wealthier Christians made it plain to all just how much the rest were dependent on them, dependent on the generosity of those who were better off. Differences in menu are a relatively timeless symbol of status and wealth, and those not so well off came face to face with their own social inferiority at a most basic level. It is made plain to them that they stand on the lower rungs of the social ladder. This in turns elicits a feeling of rejection which threatens the sense of community.... Paul rightly raises his voice in protest against the wealthy Christians: "You despise the church of God and humiliate those who have nothing" (1 Cor. 11:22).[112]

Theissen demonstrated that the conflict was neither purely material nor theological but primarily social. These were the problems of a socially

108. Hall, *Unity of the Corinthian Correspondence*, pp. 50–85. This is chapter 3, 'The Social Background to 1 Corinthians'. Hall rightly recognises that Theissen's articles although published many years ago are foundation documents and it is important to examine these for the presuppositions (p. 51). He addresses social backgrounds relevant to 1 Cor. 8–10 in pp. 59–64.

109. Hall, *Unity of the Corinthian Correspondence*, pp. 74–77.

110. Hall, *Unity of the Corinthian Correspondence*, p. 77.

111. Hall, *Unity of the Corinthian Correspondence*, pp. 64, 79.

112. Theissen, *Social Setting*, p. 160.

stratified community. There was a conflict rooted in 'a consistent theory of community' which collided with 'behaviour produced by social differences'. This existed not only in the Christian tradition but, as Theissen comments, in Greek traditions also. Yet his evidence only amounts to one sentence of references with no discussion.[113] Finally, the conflict is not seen from the perspective of the upper strata and is not mentioned in the congregational letter but appears to originate in an oral correspondence.[114] A weakness in Theissen's argument is his reliance on Latin authors (Pliny, Martial and Juvenal).[115] He attempts to mitigate this by demonstrating how strong the Roman influence was in Corinth, that the congregation 'in all likelihood included people of Latin origin', and by supposing that this practice was not widespread in the church. The hosts would only need to treat their guests differently depending on their social status for the situation to arise.[116] However, Justin Meggitt argued that Theissen's view on the consumption of meat is incorrect.[117] Nevertheless, his approach reveals a new way of interpreting the text. Malherbe notes Theissen's approach is 'not always convincing' but 'provides a welcome new perspective'.[118] The significance of Theissen is his change of focus.

Peter Lampe explains how a pagan Graeco-Roman dinner party of the first century AD was celebrated and compares this with the Corinthian Eucharistic 'Potluck' Dinner (*Eranos*).[119] He sees in this Graeco-Roman cultural setting an explanation of the Corinthians' behaviour. The dinner party had 'First Tables', at which several courses were served, a break and then 'Second Tables', with more food, often with guests who had newly

113. Theissen, *Social Setting*, p. 162.

114. Theissen, *Social Setting*, pp. 162–63. He remarks, 'It is instructive, then, that Paul does not derive his information from the congregational letter. It can be assumed that this letter was written by those from the upper strata. Some *topoi* of popular philosophy, which in all probability had their origin in that letter, so indicate. One would hardly expect that the authors divulged anything unfavorable about themselves. Others must have done that.' However, this is rather speculative. The non-elite in the church could use a scribe to write a letter.

115. Theissen, *Social Setting*, pp. 156–58.

116. Theissen, *Social Setting*, p. 158.

117. Justin J. Meggitt, 'Meat Consumption and Social Conflict in Corinth', *JTS* 45 (1994), pp. 137–41.

118. Abraham J. Malherbe, *Social Aspects of Early Christianity* (Philadelphia, PA: Fortress Press, 2nd edn. enl., 1983) p. 84.

119. Peter Lampe, 'The Eucharist: Identifying with Christ on the Cross', *Int* 48 (1994), pp. 36–49 (39). He explains that the *eranos* custom can be traced back to Homer and it still existed in the second century AD. He roughly translates *eranos* as 'potluck dinner' where the food brought by the participants is shared on a common table. But the term is broader: either participants ate their own food brought along in a basket or the provisions were put on a common table as at a potluck dinner.

arrived. After Second Tables a symposium may be held. Lampe comments that it is likely the richer Christians ate early and then Christians of 'lower social strata' arrived in the break. This appeared to be the usual custom in the 'pagan context' and so would not seem unusual here.[120] However, this inconsiderate behaviour of the richer Christians arising from their adherence to the Graeco-Roman meal custom produced problems in the church. Thus Lampe and Theissen see social-status issues at the Lord's Supper. Dunn, however, sees a flaw in Lampe's analysis because Paul mentions 'only one common meal (the Lord's Supper)'.[121] Paul does not rebuke the Corinthians for a preceding shared meal but for one in which some Christians eat while others are hungry (1 Cor. 11.21). So Dunn concludes that although details are obscure the problems were caused by social status rather than theological differences.[122]

Nevertheless, Meggitt and Hall have challenged Theissen's view.[123] In return Theissen has answered Meggitt's comments.[124] I find it unnecessary to repeat, and review, the ongoing debate here but I do wish to point out the lively debate surrounding social-status issues related to this passage. Let us examine one more topic before I outline further studies on social-status issues within Paul's letter.

e. *Society-as-Body Topos (1 Corinthians 12.12–27)*

Martin examines Paul's use of the 'society-as-body' topos[125] where the human body is an analogy for society. It was used to explain how unity could exist within diversity and occurs in political and philosophical discussions of concord. Thus Martin remarks, 'Paul's use of the body analogy in 1 Corinthians 12:12–27 stands squarely in the Greco-Roman rhetorical tradition'.[126] He notes that Paul uses a variety of status terms and shows how Paul relates the body hierarchy to high- and low-status believers but his rhetoric pushes for a reversal of the norm. In the body analogy Paul uses the same rhetorical strategy (of status reversal directed towards the strong), that he employs elsewhere in the letter: 'he identifies with the strong and calls

120. Lampe, 'The Eucharist', p. 40.

121. Dunn, *1 Corinthians*, p. 79.

122. Dunn, *1 Corinthians*, p. 79.

123. Meggitt, *Paul, Poverty and Survival* and Hall, *Unity of the Corinthian Correspondence*, pp. 64–74.

124. Gerd Theissen, 'Social Conflicts in the Corinthian Correspondence: Further Remarks on J.J. Meggitt, *Paul, Poverty and Survival*', *JSNT* (2003), pp. 371–91 (377–81).

125. Martin, *Corinthian Body*, pp. 92–96.

126. Martin, *Corinthian Body*, p. 94.

on them to consider the weak'.[127] This sensitive analysis again demonstrates the social issues involved throughout Paul's letter.

Jerome Neyrey considers Paul's body imagery from the perspective of Mary Douglas' anthropological model.[128] Her model sees the physical body as a symbol of the social body and her 'ideas on bodily control offer a cross-cultural model for appreciating Paul's strong sense of custom, structure and order in his churches, a model applicable not only to 1 Corinthians, but to all his letters'.[129] His analysis identifies Paul's viewpoint as according to the cosmology of a controlled body (strong 'group'/high 'grid'), but his opponents in 1 Corinthians fit the weak 'group'/low 'grid.' He sees these as the pneumatics with their ideology of individualism and freedom. The model proves 'to be an accurate and useful heuristic device for evaluating the contrasting attitudes to body in 1 Corinthians'.[130] Neyrey sees the model and approach as an aid to recovering the cultural *Sitz im Leben* of Paul and his churches. Timothy Carter uses the same model to read 1 Cor. 1–4 in the light of Douglas' matrix, but takes issue with Neyrey's inadequate application.[131] He concludes that the model supports the view of rival groups in the church who competed for more followers.[132]

Once again these approaches enable an analysis of 1 Corinthians that identifies social-status issues within congregational conflicts. Finally, I turn to outline some further studies.

7. *Further Studies on Social Status in 1 Corinthians*

The above examples identify a range of passages within 1 Corinthians in which scholars have observed, and disputed, the presence of social-status issues. The further studies below have also identified social-status issues in Paul's letter. However, to limit the length of my study I minimise my discussion.

Dale Martin has studied 1 Cor. 9.19-23 for Paul's use of slave imagery and sees 'the positive, soteriological use of slavery as a symbol for the Christian's relationship to God or Christ'.[133] His analysis of Paul's rhetorical strategy in 1 Cor. 9 considers various aspects of Graeco-Roman

127. Martin, *Corinthian Body*, p. 103.

128. Jerome H. Neyrey, 'Body Language in 1 Corinthians: The Use of Anthropological Models for Understanding Paul and His Opponents', *Semeia* 35 (1986), pp. 129–70. His discussion covers all of 1 Corinthians and is not restricted to 1 Cor. 12–14.

129. Neyrey, 'Body Language in 1 Corinthians', p. 129. Nevertheless, Neyrey recognises that 'Of all Paul's letters, 1 Corinthians is thoroughly and intensely concerned with BODY'.

130. Neyrey, 'Body Language in 1 Corinthians', p. 163.

131. Timothy L. Carter, '"Big Men" in Corinth', *JSNT* 66 (1997), pp. 45–71.

132. Carter, '"Big Men" in Corinth', p. 69.

133. Martin, *Slavery as Salvation*, p. xiv.

slavery but concentrates on middle-level, managerial slaves.[134] He uses inscriptions from the West and East of the Empire.[135] Martin argues, 'Paul himself exploits the antibanausic prejudice of the higher-status Christians, admitting the servility of his labor and then calling on the strong to imitate it. This is a radical challenge to patronal ideology because following Paul's example necessitates social self-lowering on the part of these high-status Christians.'[136] Nevertheless, S.R. Llewelyn has criticised Martin's methodology for relying on slave inscriptions.[137] However, Martin's view presents an interesting alternative way of examining Paul's imagery of slavery and social-status issues. The value of his approach is its ability to interact with the text in a further examination of social-status issues.

Martin also observes that no studies addressed the issue of glossolalia as a status indicator.[138] He poses four questions and suggests that in Graeco-Roman society if glossolalia had any status significance at all 'it would probably be construed as high status activity'.[139] It seems that glossolalia, as other issues, was dividing the church along social-status lines. In his analysis Martin shows that, '1 Corinthians, in spite of an initial appearance of eclecticism in its issues, is thematically unified by the issues of conflict between higher-status and lower-status points of view'.[140] Philip Esler likewise acknowledges status issues in the manifestation of the Holy Spirit through glossolalia, discussing ascribed and acquired honour.[141] Martin revisited his earlier work on glossolalia and again concluded that tongue

134. Martin, *Slavery as Salvation*, p. xxi, states, 'By middle-level slaves I mean these who ran a business or worked as an agent or manager, those who occupied positions somewhere between top imperial slave bureaucrats and the slaves involved in common, manual labor and services. This aspect of slavery is often ignored by biblical commentators'.

135. On inscriptions as valuable sources for understanding the New Testament see Stanley E. Porter, 'Inscriptions and Papyri: Greco-Roman', in Evans and Porter (eds.), *Dictionary of New Testament Background*, pp. 529–39 and D. Noy, 'Inscriptions and Papyri: Jewish', in Evans and Porter (eds.), *Dictionary of New Testament Background*, pp. 539–41.

136. Martin, *Slavery as Salvation*, p. 147.

137. S.R. Llewelyn, 'The Sale of a Slave-Girl: The New Testament's Attitude to Slavery', in Llewelyn and Kearsley, *New Documents Illustrating Early Christianity*, 6: *A Review of the Greek Inscriptions and Papyri Published in 1980–81* (NSW: Macquarie University, 1992 no. 6), pp. 48–55. He considers a papyrus document from Side in Pamphylia (AD 142) on the sale of a slave girl and comments that the description of a slave's lot may be considered too negative by some. He cites Martin, *Slavery as Salvation*, for a more positive assessment from funerary and other inscriptions dedicated to, or by, slaves. But Llewelyn warns that other factors need to be taken into account beside inscriptions, which have bias.

138. Dale B. Martin, 'Tongues of Angels and Other Status Indicators', *JAAR* 59 (1991), pp. 547–89 (547).

139. Martin, 'Tongues', p. 558.

140. Martin, 'Tongues', p. 579.

141. Philip F. Esler, 'Glossolalia and the Admission of gentiles into the Early Christian Community', *BTB* 22 (1992), pp. 136–42 (140).

speakers may have been high-status members of the church, although he admits his brief survey of ancient speech cannot be regarded as proof, 'But it does suggest that they *may* have been, given that people in Greco-Roman society regularly associated esoteric speech with other high-status indicators'.[142] Anders Eriksson follows Martin and comments, 'Contrary to some prejudice in the exegetical literature which regards tongue speaking as a phenomenon among the uninfluential and marginalized, tongue speaking in the Corinthian church very likely gave a high status in the group and was probably regarded as a qualification for spiritual leadership.'[143] Martin, Esler and Eriksson concur on the relationship between glossolalia and high social status in 1 Cor. 12–14. This is in contrast to modern exegetical studies that see the manifestation as associated with low status. Hall, though, does not want the sociological approach to ignore the Holy Spirit's revolutionary work within the Corinthian Christians.[144] This is a valid point.

David Gill's essay examines Roman portraiture in relation to Paul's discussion of head-coverings for men and women in 1 Cor. 11.2–16.[145] From his analysis he suggests that the reason why men drew the toga over their heads in worship was 'members of the social élite were wanting to establish a Roman element into their worship'.[146] In a later article Gill also examined the social elite in the Corinthian church.[147] Bruce Winter recently revisited the issue of veiling in 1 Cor. 11.2–16 drawing upon Gill's earlier essay.[148] He too sees activity of the social elite but identifies a difference from Gill, in his concluding comment, 'It would seem rather that there were some who wished to draw attention to their own status and themselves as they addressed God or spoke in his Name. The above evidence also points to the power struggle among the élite within the congregation'.[149]

Winter's study also identifies elitist ethics operating within the congregation in his analysis of the passages: 6.12–20, 10.23 and 15.29–

142. Martin, *Corinthian Body*, pp. 88–92 (91).

143. Anders Eriksson, '"Women Tongue Speakers, Be Silent": A Reconstruction Through Paul's Rhetoric', *BibInt* 6 (1998), pp. 80–104 (84). She cites Martin, 'Tongues', for evidence of her view. She regards female pneumatics as Paul's main concern in 1 Corinthians 12–14.

144. Hall, *Unity of the Corinthian Correspondence*, p. 77.

145. David W.J. Gill, 'The Importance of Roman Portraiture for Head-Coverings in 1 Corinthians 11:2–16', *TynBul* 41 (1990), pp. 245–60.

146. Gill, 'The Importance of Roman Portraiture', p. 260.

147. David W.J. Gill, 'In Search of the Social Élite in the Corinthian Church', *TynBul* 44 (1993), pp. 323–37.

148. Winter, *After Paul Left Corinth*, pp. 121–41. This is chapter 6 'Veiled Men and Wives and Christian Contentiousness (1 Corinthians 11:2–16)'.

149. Winter, *After Paul Left Corinth*, p. 141.

34.[150] He draws upon the literary works of the educated elite, with crucial evidence from Philo, and argues how the elite justified their lifestyles from philosophy. After developing his argument Winter asks, 'Were any Christians among the "elite" of Corinth?' and answers in the affirmative. In these passages, he maintains, elitist ethics are being shown by the elite in the ἐκκλησία.[151]

Thus the above studies show the importance of social-status issues in the situation at Corinth. There appear to be elite members in the congregation. My study will focus on the education of the elite. However, to complete this section it will be valuable to mention briefly hidden assumptions within my discussion so far. An unwritten assumption has been that 1 Corinthians is a single letter. I consider it is helpful to readers to make this assumption explicit. Some scholars believe that 1 Corinthians is a composite of other separate Pauline letters and so they argue for partition theories. However, there are solid grounds for reading 1 Corinthians as a single letter. Anthony Thiselton highlights the controversy over the integrity of the letter, identifying the proponents, and arguments, for various views and showing that 1 Corinthians is a single letter with a unifying theme.[152] For a recent robust defence of both the integrity of 1 and 2 Corinthians see Hall's book.[153]

Thus in my above discussion on the various texts I consider that these situations all occur coincidently and Paul writes our 1 Corinthians to address the conflict and questions. I hold that Paul's initial visit to Corinth and the writing of 1 Corinthians occurred in the period from early to mid fifties AD.[154] On the size of the whole congregation I accept a basic figure of about 40 persons but recognise that the number of members could have been larger.[155] Indeed, David Balch's recent article re-evaluates assump-

150. Winter, *After Paul Left Corinth*, pp. 76–109. This is chapter 5 'Elitist Ethics and Christian Permissiveness (1 Corinthians 6:12–20; 10:23; 15:29–34)'.

151. Winter, *After Paul Left Corinth*, pp. 106–9 (106). See also his appendix: 'Roman Homosexual Activity and the Elite (1 Corinthians 6:9)', pp. 110–120

152. Thiselton, *First Epistle*, pp. 36–41. Thiselton, and others, argue, 'the unifying theme of the epistle is a *reproclamation of the different value system of grace, gifts, the cross, and the resurrection as divine verdict, criterion, and status bestowal within the new framework of respect and love for the less esteemed "other". Glorifying in the Lord and receiving status derived from identification with the crucified Christ (1:30–31) lead to a new value system demonstrable in a wide array of life issues*' (p. 40). Emphasis in original.

153. Hall, *Unity of the Corinthian Correspondence*. Hall's thesis is that 1 and 2 Corinthians are two stages in one conflict where Paul meets the same opponents (p. 1). And he states, 'Attempts to divide 1 and 2 Corinthians into a number of separate letters fail to appreciate Paul's pastoral strategy, and employ arguments that are logically flawed' (p. 2).

154. See Thiselton, *First Epistle*, pp. 29–32 for his discussion on the dates.

155. See Jerome Murphy-O'Connor, *St. Paul's Corinth: Texts and Archaeology* (Good News Studies, 6; Wilmington, DE: Michael Glazier, Inc., 1983), pp. 155–8; Dunn, *1 Corinthians*, pp. 17–18 and Carolyn Osiek and David L. Balch, *Families in the New Testament World: Households and House Churches* (The Family, Religion, and Culture; Louisville, KY:

tions on the size of house churches based on domestic space.[156] He comments that Jerome Murphy-O'Connor's argument for house churches as being both necessarily small (with up to 30–40 people) and also private is mistaken on both accounts (Pompeiian *domus* show both conclusions are incorrect).[157] His interesting article discusses the houses of the wealthy, and from this focus, 'We learn that the conclusions in many books that early Pauline house churches were *necessarily* small and private are mistaken'.[158] He recognises that some, or many, house churches may have been small but this conclusion cannot be drawn from the archaeological work on house sizes in Pompeii. He concludes, 'Archaeological investigation of *domus* in Pompeii and Herculaneum does not sustain the current consensus that early Pauline churches were necessarily small or that they were private. The size of many Christian assemblies may indeed have been small, but Pompeiian *domus* could have accommodated numbers far greater than 40 persons'.[159]

This section has shown useful studies on social status but because of the range of secondary literature I have needed to be selective.[160] I now turn to an outline of the claims and challenges to the so-called 'new consensus'.

8. *The 'New Consensus': Claims and Challenges*

Justin Meggitt's *Paul, Poverty and Survival* challenged Theissen's claims that elite (upper-class) members dominated the Corinthian church. Meggitt argued that there were no elite but the Corinthian Christians were among the 99% of the inhabitants in the Roman Empire who suffered poverty.[161] He regards this view as the one generally accepted before the rise of the 'new consensus' championed by Theissen. Clearly this is a

Westminster John Knox Press, 1997), pp. 201–3. Osiek and Balch offer reasons, based on house sizes, why the number of members could be larger. For a recent discussion on the contributions of these scholars see David G. Horrell, 'Domestic Space and Christian Meetings at Corinth: Imaging New Contexts and the Buildings East of the Theatre', *NTS* 50 (2004), pp. 349–69.

156. David L. Balch, 'Rich Pompeiian Houses, Shops for Rent, and the Huge Apartment Building in Herculaneum as Typical Spaces for Pauline House Churches', *JSNT* 27 (2004), pp. 27–46.

157. Balch, 'Rich Pompeiian Houses', p. 28.

158. Balch, 'Rich Pompeiian Houses', p. 30.

159. Balch, 'Rich Pompeiian Houses', p. 41.

160. For another contribution on the social sciences see David G. Horrell, 'Social Sciences Studying Formative Christian Phenomena: A Creative Movement', in Blasi, Duhaime and Turcotte (eds.), *Handbook of Early Christianity: Social Science Approaches* (Walnut Creek, CA: Altamira Press, 2002), pp. 3–28.

161. Meggitt, *Paul, Poverty and Survival*, pp. 50, 52, 59. Meggitt's approach is social-historical.

radically different position to that propounded by Theissen. Where there no elite believers at Corinth?

Theissen responded to Meggitt's book with gratitude and respect but vigorously defended his own position in two articles.[162] Further scholars entered the fray. For particular contributions see: Jongkind, Hall, Friesen, Barclay, Oakes and Horrell.[163] I shall focus on Theissen's response because if Meggitt's view is correct then there were no elite and consequently no basis for studying the 'educated elite'. Theissen recognises Meggitt's argument for a 'socially homogenous lower class' before discussing the 'new consensus', which he notes is neither new nor a consensus.[164] He criticises Meggitt for not locating his study within the Roman-Hellenistic society. To aid his discussion of social status Theissen presents Figure 1, 'Stratification and rank in Roman-Hellenistic society according to Geza Alföldy', which is a pyramid divided by horizontal lines to show the various orders. At the top are the senators, then the equestrians followed by the decurions, and finally the ordinary people (free, freed and slaves) sub-divided (vertically) into city (*plebs urbana*) and country (*plebs rustica*).[165] Theissen recognises that most Christians belonged to the majority below the decurions (the 'politically powerful families'). But in his discussion on the status of individuals in the church he argues, from Jewish communities and also clubs, that some were elite. For Theissen, 'Early Christianity was located in the *plebs urbana*, but attracted also a small minority of people at the periphery of the local upper class'.[166] I find Theissen's arguments for the existence of elite believers in Corinth convincing. Even Hall, who does not accept Theissen or Meggitt's theses, still sees a 'small upper-class minority' in the Corinthian church

162. Gerd Theissen, 'The Social Structure of Pauline Communities: Some Critical Remarks on J.J. Meggitt *Paul, Poverty and Survival, JSNT* 84 (2001), pp. 65–84 and Gerd Theissen, 'Social Conflicts in the Corinthian Correspondence'.

163. Dirk Jongkind, 'Corinth in the First Century AD: The Search for Another Class', *TynBul* 52 (2001), pp. 139–48; Hall, *Unity of the Corinthian Correspondence*, pp. 52–53, 74–77; Steven J. Friesen, 'Poverty in Pauline Studies: Beyond the So-called New Consensus', *JSNT* 26 (2004), pp. 323–61; John M.G. Barclay, 'Poverty in Pauline Studies: A Response to Steven Friesen', *JSNT* 26 (2004), pp. 363–66; Peter Oakes, 'Constructing Poverty Scales for Graeco-Roman Society: A Response to Steven Friesen's "Poverty in Pauline Studies"', *JSNT* 26 (2004), pp. 367–71 and Horrell, 'Domestic Space and Christian Meetings at Corinth'.

164. Theissen, 'The Social Structure of Pauline Communities', pp. 65–67. 'There was neither an "old consensus" in the nineteenth century nor did there develop a "new consensus" in the twentieth century. The latter was rather a renewed socio-historical interest with different results' (p. 66).

165. Theissen, 'The Social Structure of Pauline Communities', p. 74. For a more developed figure for ancient society see James Malcolm Arlandson, *Women, Class and Society in Early Christianity: Models from Luke-Acts* (Peabody, MA: Hendrickson Publishers, 1997), p. 22 and his discussion.

166. Theissen, 'The Social Structure of Pauline Communities', p. 73.

although he is not willing to concede that these monopolized the church leadership.[167]

Finally, I accept that there were elite Corinthian Christians who, according to Theissen, were located among the decurions. Nevertheless, I wish also to agree with Malcolm Arlandson who notes on elites, 'Since the senate in Rome and the councils in cities throughout the empire seated only a few hundred men, other elites did not necessarily occupy political positions, though many may have served as decurions for a season'.[168] Thus I accept that there were elites without a political office. However, I need to clarify the use of this term 'elite' with that used in classical scholarship. Myles McDonnell, in a valuable article on writing, discusses the famous Pompeian portrait of a man and his wife with a papyrus roll, writing tablet and stylus. He mentions that they do not appear to be from the elite decurion class but from the sub-elites. McDonnell comments, 'Defining social categories in Roman history is a dicey business. By "elite" and "upper-class" I mean senators and equestrians. There were wide social and economic distinctions in this category'.[169] However, he notes 'sub-elites', as defined by Keith Hopkins for Roman Egypt, refers to 'people wealthy enough not to have to work with their hands – "local town-councillors, ... leading temple priests".'[170] Theissen's work places the 'elite' within the lower upper class, the decurions, not with senators and equestrians. In McDonnell's terms they would be called 'sub-elites', although McDonnell confusingly writes, in the body of his article, about the couple as not in 'the elite decurions class'. I shall continue to use the term 'elite' as used by New Testament scholars while recognising that classical scholars such as McDonnell may prefer to speak, at times, of 'sub-elites'. John Barclay helpfully notes, in response to Steven Friesen, that he knows of nobody within the 'new consensus' who proposes that there were 'super-wealthy elite' in Paul's churches.[171]

167. Hall, *Unity of the Corinthian Correspondence*, pp. 74–77, 79. Hall, in fact, sees the church as composed of 'the small upper-class minority', with most believers of low social status and then those who were very poor (p. 79). Jongkind, *Corinth in the First Century AD*, p. 148, concludes from his argument on the variety of Corinthian housing that the society 'cannot be simply divided into an élite and a very poor non-élite'. All the Christians are not very poor.

168. Arlandson, *Women, Class and Society in Early Christianity*, p. 26.

169. Myles McDonnell, 'Writing, Copying and Autograph Manuscripts in Ancient Rome', *ClQ* 46 (1996), pp. 469–91 (469 n. 1).

170. McDonnell, 'Writing, Copying and Autograph Manuscripts in Ancient Rome', p. 469 n. 1.

171. Barclay, 'Poverty in Pauline Studies', p. 365. He notes the possible exception of Erastus. See also Philip A. Harland, 'Connections with Elites in the World of the Early Christians', in Blasi, Duhaime and Turcotte (eds.), *Handbook of Early Christianity: Social Science Approaches*, pp. 385–408.

Before concluding this chapter I turn to address the debated nature of the city of Corinth.

9. *Greek and Roman Corinth*

To understand the relation between Paul and the Corinthians it is essential to see them within the social context of first-century Corinth. Fortunately, the social context of first-century, or Roman, Corinth has been addressed in a number of works including commentaries. It is unnecessary to summarize all that has been written. Horrell and Savage provide detailed descriptions.[172] Barrett, Conzelmann and Fee give overviews.[173] Recently, Thiselton has addressed Roman Corinth in Paul's time.[174] Nevertheless, caution is needed. Richard Oster rightly criticises scholars who typically present two Corinths, one Greek and one Roman.[175] Oster notes Barrett, who draws a sharp distinction when he says:

> In 146 B.C. a sharp line is drawn through the history of Corinth, when Rome brought the Achaean League to an end.... After 100 years of desolation Corinth was refounded by Julius Caesar as a Roman colony.
>
> New Corinth naturally possessed the topographical characteristics of the old city; otherwise it bore little relation to its predecessor.[176]

However, Oster comments that the archaeological evidence demands caution when dealing with ancient authors who wrote about Corinth. The material evidence does show activity at Corinth between 146–44 BC. He notes the ambiguity in the evidence and urges care in understanding the religious and cultural situation of Paul's Corinth. Therefore, 'it would be a grave error to suppose that the inhabitants of colonial Corinth lived in a

172. Horrell, *Social Ethos*, pp. 64–73; Timothy B. Savage, *Power Through Weakness: Paul's Understanding of the Christian Ministry in 2 Corinthians* (SNTSMS, 86; Cambridge: Cambridge University Press, 1996), pp. 19–53. Other descriptions include: Leon Morris, *The First Epistle of Paul to the Corinthians* (Grand Rapids, MI: Eerdmans; Leicester: InterVarsity Press, 2nd edn, 1985), pp. 17–19, Talbert, *Reading Corinthians*, pp. xvi–xviii, Ben Witherington III, *Conflict and Community in Corinth: A Socio-Rhetorical Commentary on 1 and 2 Corinthians* (Grand Rapids, MI: Eerdmans; Carlisle: Paternoster, 1995), pp. 5–19, while Chow, *Patronage and Power*, pp. 38–82, examines, in particular, patronage in Roman Corinth.

173. C.K. Barrett, *The First Epistle to the Corinthians* (London: A&C Black, 1971), pp. 1–3; Hans Conzelmann, *1 Corinthians* (trans. James W. Leitch; Hemeneia; Philadelphia, PA: Fortress Press, 1975), p. 11; Fee, *First Epistle*, pp. 1–3.

174. Thiselton, *First Epistle*, pp. 1–17.

175. Richard E. Oster, 'Use, Misuse and Neglect of Archaeological Evidence in Some Modern Works on 1 Corinthians', *ZNW* 83 (1992), pp. 52–73 (54).

176. Barrett, *First Epistle*, pp. 1–2.

setting which was mono-cultural and homogeneous at the time of nascent Christianity'.[177]

Indeed, Irene Romano provides evidence from Hellenistic deposits to show that life did continue at the site of Corinth during the period 146–44 BC.[178] Have we any further evidence on Corinth's interim activity? Elizabeth Gebhard and Matthew Dickie have more recently re-assessed the evidence for the interim period.[179] They recite the familiar story of the destruction of Corinth before asking three questions including 'Did the city remain devoid of population, its buildings and walls levelled?'[180] Then follows a thorough critique of the literary, physical and inscriptional evidence. They conclude that the literary evidence for the destruction of Corinth presents a set theme. It cannot be relied upon. For the physical evidence they review published reports covering a range of material items and conclude that people lived in the central part of the city in the interim period up to the founding of the colony.

Finally, Gebhard and Dickie consider inscriptional evidence in Latin. The first inscription regulated the activities of 'the Isthmian–Nemean Guild of the Artists of Dionysos' and appears to have been erected after 146 BC in, or near, the South Stoa. People must have been passing by who were interested in the dispute.[181] The second inscription commemorates the hauling of a fleet over the Isthmus under Marcus Antonius. They argue that the inscription dates from the end of the second century BC.[182] This Roman general wanted to impress people who could read Latin. They were not squatters. Who were they? Gebhard and Dickie argue that these people were Italians involved in trade and commerce. Finally, they observe

177. Oster, 'Use, Misuse and Neglect', pp. 54–55 (55). See Gill, 'In Search of the Social Élite', pp. 327–28, for examples of arguments used for the Roman nature of the city of Corinth. Gill states that, 'Some scholars have argued for a Greek presence in the colony and therefore Greek cultural interpretations of the epistles', and, 'The Romanness of the colony should not be underestimated' (p. 327). Gill's article, 'The Importance of Roman Portraiture', p. 245, argues for reading Corinth as a Roman, not a Greek, city. Here he takes issue with Alan Padgett, 'Paul on Women in the Church: The Contradictions of Coiffure in 1 Corinthians 11.2–16', *JSNT* 20 (1984), pp. 69–86, who considers Greek cultural norms. But Gill's arguments seem to be reductionist. He is ensuring that 'The Romanness of the colony should not be underestimated', but he appears to argue that it was almost totally Roman, and therefore a monolithic culture. Nevertheless, I agree with his conclusion that members of the social elite were in the Corinthian church.

178. Irene Bald Romano, 'A Hellenistic Deposit from Corinth: Evidence for Interim Period Activity (146 – 44 B.C.)', *Hesp* 63 (1994), pp. 57–104.

179. Elizabeth R. Gebhard and Matthew W. Dickie, 'The View from the Isthmus, ca. 200 to 44 B.C.', in Williams and Bookidis (eds.), *Corinth: Corinth, The Centenary 1896–1996* (ASCSA, 20; The American School of Classical Studies at Athens, 2003), pp. 262–78.

180. Gebhard and Dickie, 'The View from the Isthmus', p. 261.

181. Gebhard and Dickie, 'The View from the Isthmus', pp. 270–72 (270).

182. Gebhard and Dickie, 'The View from the Isthmus', pp. 272–77.

Spawforth's suggestion that 'Some of the very early duovirs ... were Italian *negotiatores* who had settled in Corinth immediately upon its foundation'. However, although this is possible they state 'it is also possible that some of them were already well established in Corinth or its immediate environs more than fifty years before the colony was officially founded'.[183] Thus Gebhard and Dickie show that while the literary evidence concerning Corinth is unreliable the physical and inscriptional evidence points to interim activity, not of squatters but of more important people.

A.H.M. Jones comments that the emperors made no attempt to romanize the Greek-speaking provinces, although planting Roman colonies in the Greek East may give this impression.[184] But Jones remarks, 'These settlements were clearly too few and far between seriously to modify the predominantly Greek culture of the regions in which they were planted, and in point of fact they for the most part gradually took the tone of their surroundings'.[185] Renée Forsell has investigated the presence of Roman citizens in the Argolid countryside (in the Peloponnese) during the first centuries AD. Pausanias (2.17.6) mentions that Roman emperors, e.g. Nero and Hadrian, visited the Argolid, and inscriptions confirm the interest of Roman citizens in the towns and sanctuaries.[186] However, Forsell considers evidence for acquisition of land and signs of an elite living in the countryside. Changes in landowning may indicate 'the presence of a new dominant élite landowning stratum living in the countryside' but these do not need to be Roman – they could be Greek.[187] In general, the countryside indicates a lack of Roman interest so that Forsell remarks, 'the poor tenant or farmer who lived in the country and worked the land, did not notice much of Roman culture and was just as Greek as he had always been'.[188]

On the origin of the colonists Jones observes:

> The origin of the Roman colonists in the East may in part explain the rapidity with which the majority of the colonies were hellenized. The settlers, though legally Roman citizens, must to a very considerable

183. Gebhard and Dickie, 'The View from the Isthmus', p. 277.

184. A.H.M. Jones, *The Greek City from Alexander to Justinian* (Oxford: Clarendon Press, 1940), pp. 60–61.

185. Jones, *Greek City*, p. 61.

186. Renée Forsell, 'The Argolid Countryside in the Roman Period', in Ostenfeld (ed.), *Greek Romans and Roman Greeks: Studies in Cultural Interaction* (ASMA, 111; Aarhus: Aarhus University Press, 2002), pp. 64–69.

187. Forsell, 'The Argolid Countryside in the Roman Period', p. 64.

188. Forsell, 'The Argolid Countryside in the Roman Period', p. 68. She notes this is in contrast to the Roman interest in the Peloponnese's western parts, e.g. Patras, which was a Roman colony. 'With Methana as an exception, the Argolid countryside retained the sleepy existence that started in the Late Hellenistic period.'

> extent have been of oriental origin. Caesar's colonists at Corinth were for the most part freedmen, and to the majority of them Greek was probably more familiar than Latin.[189]

Thus it seems that too much emphasis should not be placed on the Roman origin of the colonists at Corinth without giving due accord to their 'Greekness' as well.

In his search for religious cults behind 1 Cor. 8–10 and sacrificial food, Derek Newton has reviewed the state of archaeological investigation in Corinth.[190] He specifically addresses scholars' discussions on the issue of continuity and discontinuity in the city before concluding 'Scholarship thus lies in two camps'.[191] Consequently, his study recognises 'the continued uncertainty' and he explores both Roman and Greek practice.

Witherington's commentary argues for the Roman nature of Corinth, which is not just a 'Hellenistic city' but rather its best description is 'Greco-Roman'.[192] Anthony Thiselton's extensive commentary also discusses Roman Corinth.[193] In his analysis he concludes, '*the city community and city culture of Corinth were formed after a Roman model*, not a Greek one, even if many immigrants came from Achaea, Macedonia, and the East to constitute an equally cosmopolitan superstructure'.[194] Moreover, Bruce Winter forcibly argues for the Roman nature of Corinth, as a Roman colony, by using a range of evidence.[195] While he stresses the city's *Romanitas*, Winter does comment that an assumption that only Roman citizens populated the city would be wrong. He concludes, 'the cultural milieu which impacted life in the city of Corinth was *Romanitas*. This does not mean that there were no ethnic minorities, but it does mean that the dominant and transforming cultural influence was Roman'.[196] In an earlier article, Winter recognises the presence of important Greeks in Roman Corinth by the time of Claudius, citing Anthony Spawforth.[197] However, in

189. Jones, *Greek City*, p. 63.

190. Newton, *Deity and Diet*, pp. 72–114 (chapter 3).

191. Newton, *Deity and Diet*, pp. 81–85 (84). He notes that New Testament scholars caution against both underestimating and overestimating the Roman nature of Corinth. Moreover, he observes the caution of the two archaeologists, C.K. Williams II and Professor Bookidis, on the relation of Greek and Roman aspects in the city.

192. Witherington, *Conflict and Community in Corinth*, pp. 5–9 (7–8).

193. Thiselton, *First Epistle*, pp. 1–17.

194. Thiselton, *First Epistle*, pp. 3–4 (his italics).

195. Winter, *After Paul Left Corinth*, pp. 7–25. His evidence is: 'archaeological, numismatic, epigraphic, literary and, finally, a crucial, first-century official source' (p. 7).

196. Winter, *After Paul Left Corinth*, p. 22.

197. Bruce W. Winter, 'Gallio's Ruling on the Legal Status of Early Christianity', *TynBul* 50 (1999), pp. 213–24 (216). He cites, Antony J.S. Spawforth, 'Roman Corinth: the Formation of a Colonial Elite', in Rizakis (ed.), *Roman Onomastics in the Greek East*, *Meletemata*, 21 (1996), pp. 167–82 (175).

After Paul Left Corinth, Winter notes Spawforth's suggestion, 'the appearance of outside notables as office-holders from Claudius on marks a significant step in the integration of this enclave of *Romanitas* into the surrounding Greek world' but then questions his conclusion.[198] Winter sees not the colony but these Greeks as undergoing change. But is it quite this clear cut? Could it be that both are undergoing change? Certainly, Greeks could become Romans while still remaining Greek as G. Woolf shows.[199]

More recently, Mary Walbank states the current position of scholarship on Corinth, 'It is now accepted that it was founded as a Roman colony in accordance with traditional Roman practice, rather than being simply a refoundation of Greek Corinth'.[200] Walbank's article discusses centuriation at Corinth in a critique of D.G. Romano's arguments against the colony founded in 44 BC.[201] Winter, under his archaeological evidence, uses centuriation as evidence that Corinth was laid out as Roman city.[202] However, Romano argues that the Roman colony was failing by the 70s AD and so refounded under the Flavians as a new colony. Thus he sees two Roman colonies at Corinth: the original Julian colony and the new colony in the Flavian era. However, in a detailed discussion Walbank refutes his position and argues convincingly for the existence of only one Roman colony, the Julian one.[203] However, this debate does not substantially impact on my study.[204] Nevertheless, I wish to consider

198. Winter, *After Paul Left Corinth*, p. 22; citing Spawforth, 'Roman Corinth', p. 175.

199. G. Woolf, 'Becoming Roman, Staying Greek: Culture, Identity and the Civilising Process in the Roman East', *PCPS* 40 (1994), pp. 116–43.

200. Mary E. Hoskins Walbank, 'What's in a Name? Corinth under the Flavians', *ZPE* 139 (2002), pp. 251–64 (251). She refers here to her own article, based on her PhD thesis: M.E.H. Walbank, 'The Foundation and Planning of Early Roman Corinth', *JRA* 10 (1997), pp. 95–130.

201. D.G. Romano, 'A Tale of Two Cities: Roman Colonies at Corinth', in Fentress (ed.) *Romanization and the City: Creation, Transformation, and Failures* (JRA Supp., 38; Portsmouth: R.I.; *Journal of Roman Archaeology*, 2000), pp. 81–104.

202. Winter, *After Paul Left Corinth*, p. 8. Winter cites D.G. Romano, 'Post-146 B.C. Land Use in Corinth, and Planning of the Roman Colony of 44 B.C.', in Gregory (ed.), *The Corinthia in the Roman Period* (JRA Supp., 8 Ann Arbor, MI: Journal of Roman Archaeology, 1993), pp. 9–30. However, Walbank, 'What's in a Name? Corinth under the Flavians', p. 252, first recognised centuriation in Corinth. Centuriation is the Roman practice of using a grid for land division in town planning.

203. Walbank, 'What's in a Name? Corinth under the Flavians', p. 251 outlines his position before refuting it.

204. Romano divides Corinth into three distinct time periods: the interim period, 146–44 BC, the Caesarian colony and the Flavian colony. See his more recent article: D.G. Romano, 'City Planning, Centuriation, and Land Division in Roman Corinth: *Colonia Laus Iulia Corinthiensis & Colonia Iulia Flavia Augusta Corinthiensis*', in Williams and Bookidis (eds.), *Corinth: Corinth, The Centenary 1896–1996*, pp. 279–301.

some evidence for Corinth's relationship to its Greek past, for as a Roman colony it was not totally isolated from its own history.

In his numismatic evidence, Winter observes that all Corinth's minted coins were in Latin up to AD 67.[205] However, this comment needs supplementing as Katharine Edwards states:

> Notwithstanding their Latin legends, the coins preserve the old Greek tradition. They have for reverse types true Greek gods, Poseidon, Athena, Aphrodite, Asclepius, Dionysus, and others, with their usual attributes; the city-goddess is Tyche with turret-crown, not Roma; the local legendary heroes, Bellerophon with Pegasos and the Chimaera, Ino with Melicertes, Melicertes with his dolphin, and Isthmus are regularly represented, and Pegasos flies through the whole series.[206]

Moreover, there are small bronze anonymous coins without names of any duoviri or emperor. They have short legends and Greek subjects, e.g. Pegasos, Melicertes and Isthmus. One group has Poseidon's head (on the obverse) and athletes (on the reverse) including boxers, a runner and a discus-thrower. Edwards infers that these coin-types were popular during Augustus' reign and attributes these athletic types to his reign.[207] Images show Greek figures: two naked boxers, a naked athlete and a naked runner.[208] Edwards also discusses the Corinthian 'tesserae' which were found with early Roman coins. One type has a dolphin and another Pegasos. They are not coins but appear to be special issues, 'perhaps on the occasion of an athletic festival, to be used as admission tickets of honoured guests'.[209] Thus Edwards' work shows that Roman Corinth had clear links with its Greek past, which continued into the present with its athletic games.

205. Winter, *After Paul Left Corinth*, p. 11. He also notes (pp. 11–12) their Roman types, reflection of imperial changes and coin denominations. See also David W.J. Gill, 'In Search of the Social Élite in the Corinthian Church', pp. 327–28, who notes 'Its magistrates issued coinage with Latin texts'. For an introduction on coinage and the New Testament see L.J. Kreitzer, 'Coinage: Greco-Roman', in Evans and Porter (eds.), *Dictionary of New Testament Background*, pp. 220–22 and R.F. Stoops, 'Coinage: Jewish', in Evans and Porter (eds.), *Dictionary of New Testament Background*, pp. 222–25.

206. Katharine M. Edwards, *Corinth: Coins, 1896–1929* (ASCSA, 6; Cambridge, MA: Harvard University Press, 1933), p. 2. Her comments apply to the period when Corinth produced its own coins from 44 BC until the reign of Septimius Severus with his family. There was a short period from the end of Galba's reign to Domitian's reign when Corinth did not have the right to produce coins. Greek traditions appear on the duovirate coinage and not just on the later coinage. See Edwards *Corinth: Coins, 1896–1929*, pp. 16–24 and Plates I-II.

207. Edwards, *Corinth: Coins, 1896–1929*, p. 7. The short legends include COR, CORIN, SE or COL.

208. Edwards, *Corinth: Coins, 1896–1929*, nos. 83–85, pp. 25–26 and Plate III.

209. Edwards, *Corinth: Coins, 1896–1929*, p. 9. She dates them as probably belonging to the early Roman period. The 'tesserae' are 'coin-like bronzes' with diameters of 19.5 to 21 mm.

Recently, Mary Walbank has examined later Corinthian coinage.[210] She identifies the main characteristics of the earlier duovirate coinage as a focus on local types and the imperial family. However, she observes:

> There is no doubt as to the Roman character of Corinth during the 1st century. But the Roman colony also inherited the traditions of one of the most important cultural centers of Classical Greece, which included controlling the important sanctuary of Poseidon at Isthmia. It is also clear that, as time went on, Corinth was increasingly influenced by its Greek environment.[211]

Changes in coinage shows that the Corinthians placed less emphasis on their contact with Rome, they reintroduced Greek deities (or they make their first appearance), and the reign of Hadrian had more stress on 'myths and legends' to connect Corinth with its Greek past.[212] Walbank therefore sees the coinage as showing two things. The first-century coins show that 'Corinth was primarily a Roman colony' (as Winter argues) while later Corinth still retains this identity but focuses more on its Greek past.[213] However, the first-century duovirate coinage and the anonymous coins together with the Corinthian 'tesserae' do show Corinth's link to its Greek past, even if this becomes much more of a focus in the second century AD.

Under his epigraphic evidence, Winter discusses Latin and Greek inscriptions arguing that Latin in official inscriptions demonstrates Corinth's *Romanitas*.[214] He argues that since the Greek inscription to Iunia Theodora comes from Lycia, where Greek was spoken, her public benefaction (which was not from the Corinthians) should be in Greek.[215] However, he admits that there are also ostraca in Greek including one against athletes.[216] Nevertheless, Winter does not see these as overthrowing

210. Mary E. Hoskins Walbank, 'Aspects of Corinthian Coinage in the Late 1st and Early 2nd Centuries A.C.', in Williams and Bookidis (eds.), *Corinth: Corinth, The Centenary 1896–1996*, pp. 337–49. She recognises that the Corinthian coinage falls into two distinct periods. She covers the earlier period (44 BC to AD 68/9) but her focus is on the later period from Domitian's reign (AD 81–96) to AD 192 (end of the Antonine era).

211. Walbank, 'Aspects of Corinthian Coinage in the Late 1st and Early 2nd Centuries A.C.', p. 343.

212. Walbank, 'Aspects of Corinthian Coinage in the Late 1st and Early 2nd Centuries A.C.', pp. 343–45.

213. Walbank, 'Aspects of Corinthian Coinage in the Late 1st and Early 2nd Centuries A.C.', p. 348. She states that Roman Corinth never became a Greek city but managed to hold Greek culture with Roman government in the second-century.

214. Winter, *After Paul Left Corinth*, p. 12.

215. Winter, *After Paul Left Corinth*, pp. 12–13.

216. Winter, *After Paul Left Corinth*, p. 14. These are curse tablets on lead. He mentions that of those found in the temple of Demeter only one was in Latin the remaining ones are in

other evidence for Corinth's *Romanitas* and he is probably correct here. But there is other evidence for Greek inscriptions that Winter has not discussed. There are the victors' lists for the Isthmian Games. Even in Roman Corinth these inscriptions were in Greek not Latin. They are a clear link with Corinth's illustrious Greek past.[217] Moreover, C. Iulius Spartiaticus, of the famous Spartan Eurycles family, had Latin and Greek inscriptions in Corinth. The Latin inscription gives his *cursus honorum*. He was a Corinthian magistrate (including president of the games) and held imperial offices.[218] But the fragmentary Greek inscription, dated from the time of Claudius, also names him. The inscription seems to have belonged with a statue of Spartiaticus (no longer present).[219]

A further link with Corinth's Greek past is provided in Room 'C' of the South Stoa. Oscar Broneer identified Room 'C' as the *Agonotheteion*, 'probably constructed in the reigns of Augustus or Tiberius'.[220] The room's inner dimensions are about 9 m (north to south) and 7.6 m (east to west) and on the floor there is a mosaic, which Broneer describes as in a 'comparatively good state of preservation'.[221] The mosaic is constructed with a number of panels but the inner panel provides the chief design. It measures 1.295 m (east to west) by 1.27 m (north to south). Broneer describes the panel as follows:

Greek (including those found in other locations in Corinth). One curse tablet from Roman Corinth is 'an Isthmian curse against other competitors' (p. 168). It attempts to control four men running a race.

217. See Benjamin Dean Meritt, *Corinth: Greek Inscriptions, 1896–1927* (ASCSA, 8.1; Cambridge, MA: Harvard University Press, 1931), no. 14, pp. 14–18; no. 15, pp. 18–21; no. 16, pp. 21–25 and no. 17, pp. 25–27. No. 14 is a headless herm inscribed in Greek on three sides and found in a field near the Gymnasium. The inscription, dated as 33 years after Augustus' Actium victory, i.e. 3 AD, is a victor list for the Isthmian Caesarea. No. 15 is a pedestal inscribed in Greek on all thee sides and found near the Gymnasium. The inscription is dated in the latter part of the second century AD but is linked to the first century AD by mention of Augustus' adopted son Lucius Caesar (died 2 AD). No. 16 has two fragments in Greek dated 181 AD. No. 17 is four fragments that belong to inscription no. 16. Meritt comments on the Isthmian Games, 'the large number of cities represented in these lists indicates the cosmopolitan character of the festival, at least in the first and second centuries A.D.' (p. 24).

218. Allen Brown West (ed.), *Corinth: Latin Inscriptions, 1896–1926* (ASCSA, 8.2; Cambridge, MA: Harvard University Press, 1931), no. 68, pp. 50–53. His family (the Eurycles) was associated with Corinth. His father, C. Iulius Laco, was also a Corinthian magistrate. His grandfather C. Iulius Eurycles was active at the time of Augustus. Spartiaticus himself was Paul's contemporary. See chapter 3 for a further discussion on the Eurycles.

219. Meritt, *Corinth: Greek Inscriptions, 1896–1927*, no. 70, pp. 53–54.

220. Oscar Broneer, *Corinth: The South Stoa and Its Roman Successors* (ASCSA, 1.4; Princeton, NJ: The American School of Classical Studies at Athens, 1954), p. 110.

221. Broneer, *Corinth: The South Stoa and Its Roman Successors*, p. 107. The mosaic is shown in Plates 30–31 and Plan II. The inner panel is also shown as a coloured plate on p. 108. Plan XXI shows the location of Room 'C' with respect to the other rooms in the South Stoa.

> On a light ground is depicted in naturalistic colors a nude athlete in front view, holding a palm branch and standing before a seated female figure. He is represented in an attitude of triumphant victory, symbolized by the palm branch and the wreath and fillet on his head. Before him sits the goddess of Good Fortune, holding a shield on her knee, on which the name Ẹ[YTY]XIA appears in Greek letters.[222]

He observes that the goddess sits in a three-quarter view facing the athlete who is probably a runner. It appears that the runner arrives immediately from his victory. From both the style of the figures and the decorative patterns Broneer suggests the most likely date for the mosaic as second half of the first century AD.[223]

The athletic scene suggests a connection to the Isthmian Games. Thus Broneer considers that Room 'C' is probably the office for the *agonothetes*. He was the chief official of the games and this title was highly esteemed among honours given by the city.[224] Two other rooms appear to belong to the same complex so Broneer speculates that Room 'A' may have belonged to the ten *Hellenodikai* and Room 'B' to the *eisagogeus*.[225] The first-century athletic mosaic shows important continuity with Corinth's Greek past.

Finally, I consider the Julian Basilica where first-century Roman portraits also have links to local Greek traditions. Catherine Vanderpool has addressed Roman portraiture in Corinth including the early imperial statues found in the Julian Basilica.[226] She argues that statues of Augustus with his adopted sons Lucius Caesar and Gaius Caesar form a family group.[227] Unlike earlier scholars whose analyses focused on portrait heads she shows that studying body types also yields meaning for the individuals.

222. Broneer, *Corinth: The South Stoa and Its Roman Successors*, p. 108. He notes that the inscription originally consisted of two lines. However, the top line of four letters only has a corner of the *epsilon* preserved.

223. Broneer, *Corinth: The South Stoa and Its Roman Successors*, p. 108.

224. Broneer, *Corinth: The South Stoa and Its Roman Successors*, p. 110. For inscriptions where the elite record that they held this important office of president of the games, see John Harvey Kent, *Corinth: The Inscriptions, 1926–1950* (ASCSA, 8.3; Princeton, NJ: The American School of Classical Studies at Athens, 1966) and Allen Brown West (ed.), *Corinth: Latin Inscriptions, 1896–1926*.

225. Broneer, *Corinth: The South Stoa and Its Roman Successors*, pp. 110–11. The *Hellenodikai* are officials for the Isthmian Games. The *eisagogeus* appears to have held responsibilities related to contests associated with the emperor. See the discussion on this position in chapter 4.

226. Catherine de Grazia Vanderpool, 'Roman Portraiture: The Many Faces of Corinth', in Williams and Bookidis (eds.), *Corinth: Corinth, The Centenary 1896–1996*, pp. 369–84.

227. Vanderpool, 'Roman Portraiture: The Many Faces of Corinth', pp. 375–79. The adopted sons do look like Augustus because, as Vanderpool observes (p. 376), they were actually his grandsons from Livia (his daughter) and Agrippa (Livia's husband). An Augustan female portrait may possibly represent Livia and be part of the group but Vanderpool (pp. 379–80) regards her assessment of this association as 'very tentative'.

In particular, both statues of Gaius and Lucius Caesar are 'identical in outline and measurements to a group of statues in the theatre in Leptis Magna'.[228] This group includes the 'well-known Dioskouroi' (Divine Twins). Vanderpool therefore considers that Gaius and Lucius were meant to be seen as the Divine Twins (at least on one level). The statue type indicates a common ancestor for the four figures, which she associates with the famous Dioskouroi figures erected at Delphi (Greece) as a victory monument to commemorate the Spartan victory at Aigospotamoi (405/4 BC). However, this victory monument was not restricted to the Spartans but also celebrated the Peloponnesian contribution included the Corinthians.[229] From her analysis, Vanderpool identifies the significance for our understanding of Corinth of the nude Corinthian statues of Gaius and Lucius:

> While Corinth as Roman colony was proud of its ties to Rome itself, it was also Peloponnesian and Greek, and proud of that too. Is it just a coincidence that among Corinth's chief benefactors in the Early Empire was the Spartan Eurykles, who, with other Spartan nobles, traced his descent from Castor and Pollux? Could it have been Spartan patrons who selected Antiphanes' Dioskouroi to represent Gaius and Lucius? They would thus not only flatter the imperial family, but also pay tribute to local pride.[230]

Thus Vanderpool sees the Corinthian statue group as an expression of the Corinthian elite celebrating the Julian family. Although the nudity of the statutes has been used to date them after Gaius died, Vanderpool notes that nudity was acceptable in the Greek East, more so than in Rome. Therefore she dates the statues during Gaius' lifetime and suggests that the patrons initially had them erected in Corinth before they were moved to the completed Julian Basilica early in Tiberius' reign.[231] This statue group therefore shows Corinth's concern with its Greek past.

228. Vanderpool, 'Roman Portraiture: The Many Faces of Corinth', p. 376. Leptis Magna is in North Africa.

229. Vanderpool, 'Roman Portraiture: The Many Faces of Corinth', pp. 377. Aigospotamoi was in the Hellespont. The Peloponnesian fleet achieved victory over the Athenian fleet. The monument was by Antiphanes of Argos.

230. Vanderpool, 'Roman Portraiture: The Many Faces of Corinth', pp. 377. Castor and Pollux (the Dioskouroi or Divine Twins) are mentioned in Acts 28.11 when Paul boards a ship at Malta to go to Rome. This was 'an Alexandrian ship with the Twin Brothers (Διοσκοῦροι) as its figurehead' (NRSV). The NIV translates, 'with the figurehead of the twin gods Castor and Pollux'. The Spartan Eurykles was G. Julius Eurykles (died c. 2 BC).

231. Vanderpool, 'Roman Portraiture: The Many Faces of Corinth', pp. 379. Gaius died in AD 4 and Vanderpool notes that Lucius died in AD 2. The Julian Basilica was completed in reign of Tiberius (AD 14–37).

Paul's letter (1 Cor. 1.22–24) specifically mentions Jews, Ἰουδαῖοι, and Greeks, Ἕλληνες, whose respective interests are signs and wisdom, and they are called by God (1.22, 24). However, in 1.23 Paul mentions Jews and gentiles, ἔθνη. Fee notes the change from 'Greeks' to 'gentiles' and states that 'While under most of this discussion the two terms could be interchangeable, it was especially the "Greek" who sought after wisdom'.[232] In these passages Thiselton reads 'Greeks' as equivalent to 'gentiles'.[233] Further, Winter too argues that Ἕλληνες should be translated as 'gentiles' throughout as it is 'an all-embracing term' which tells us nothing about the 'ethnic origin' of those in the Corinthian church.[234] Yet Winter does not discuss in which sense gentiles seek wisdom. How does this seeking wisdom apply to all gentiles? Fee, though, recognises the pre-eminence of Greeks in seeking wisdom.

Indeed, Anthony Corbeill shows the Roman dependence upon Greeks for wisdom noting that in the Republican period, 'the Romans selectively fashioned Greek educational principles into a uniquely Roman form of citizenship'.[235] Joy Connolly further discusses this relationship of Greeks and Romans in 'The Problems of the past in Imperial Greek education'.[236] My point here is that a more nuanced interpretation of Paul's use of Jews, Greeks and gentiles may be possible if we consider the ancient context for wisdom and education. For further investigations of interaction between Greeks and Romans see Erik Nis Ostenfeld (ed.) *Greek Romans and Roman Greeks*.[237] Moreover, Christopher Stanley has argued that in Gal. 3.28 ('neither Jew nor Greek') and 1 Cor. 12.13 ('Jews or Greeks') that Paul means 'real "Jews" and real "Greeks"' not just 'gentiles'.[238] Charles

232. Fee, *First Epistle*, p. 76 n. 40.

233. Thiselton, *First Epistle*, pp. 169–72.

234. Winter, *After Paul Left Corinth*, pp. 23–25.

235. Anthony Corbeill, 'Education in the Roman Republic: Creating Traditions', in Too (ed.), *Education in Greek and Roman Antiquity* (Leiden: E. J. Brill, 2001), pp. 261–87 (261). The Roman education system drew from Greek education to suit its own needs. This resulted in the intentional reproduction of 'social hierarchies' through education. There was no intention of producing an egalitarian system. Corbeill aptly summarises the situation, 'The willingness of Roman education to assimilate Greek elements, elements difficult for the non-elite to access because of their inherent foreignness, serves to maintain the Roman status quo' (p. 284). Nevertheless, this addition of Greek culture was disguised (termed 'genesis amnesia').

236. Joy Connolly, 'The Problems of the Past in Imperial Greek Education', in Too (ed.), *Education in Greek and Roman Antiquity*, pp. 339–72.

237. Erik Nis Ostenfeld (ed.) with the assistance of Karin Blomqvist and Lisa Nevett, *Greek Romans and Roman Greeks: Studies in Cultural Interaction* (ASMA, III; Aarhus: Aarhus University Press, 2002).

238. Christopher D. Stanley, '"Neither Jew nor Greek": Ethnic Conflict in Graeco-Roman Society', *JSNT* 64 (1996), pp. 101–24.

McNelis provides a detailed discussion on the important relationship between Romans and Greek intellectuals.[239]

To sum up, I agree that Corinth is a Roman colony, not a Greek city, and agree with Winter that its dominant culture is Roman. Nevertheless, I have shown that Roman Corinth was not in total isolation from its Greek past. Moreover, Roman Corinth, in the Greek East, was not in total isolation from its surrounding Greek culture. My study does not focus on Corinth's dominant Roman culture but rather on Greek aspects. Nevertheless, certain Greek aspects, such as the Isthmian Games, were incorporated into Corinth's Roman culture.[240] For a nuanced discussion of Greek and Roman influences in Corinth and how they combined with each other see Jason König's informative discussion. He argues for 'a model whereby some members of the elite were able (although differently in different contexts) to combine elements of both Greek and Roman affiliation and self-presentation within versions of Corinthian identity'.[241]

10. *Summary*

This chapter has demonstrated the importance of social-status issues in 1 Corinthians. I have surveyed New Testament scholarship identifying developments, particularly those stemming from Theissen's sociological study, that have contributed to our understanding of the letter in its first-century AD context. Active areas of debate remain but the discipline of social-scientific criticism has made considerable advances in examining Paul's letter and showing the importance of social-status issues in various passages. The 'new consensus' view of recent scholarship that the Corinthian church was a socially stratified community in which social-status issues played a significant part in the community conflict has been challenged, particularly by Meggitt. Nevertheless, there are grounds for seeing elite and non-elite believers in the congregation. Scholars often describe the elite as the 'educated elite' or refer to the education of the elite. This description is built upon an understanding of the 'educational systems' in antiquity. I also examined the nature of first-century Corinth.

239. Charles McNelis, 'Greek Grammarians and Roman Society during the Early Empire: Statius' Father and his Contemporaries', *ClAnt* 21 (2002), pp. 67–94.

240. See Jason König, 'Favorinus' *Corinthian Oration* in its Corinthian Context', *PCPS* 47 (2001), pp. 141–71, who argues that the Isthmian festival and sanctuary did present 'a combination of Greek and Roman influences, traditional and untraditional much like the city of Corinth itself' (p. 150). I owe this reference to Elizabeth R. Gebhard who kindly pointed it out to me.

241. König, 'Favorinus' *Corinthian Oration* in its Corinthian Context', p. 146. Here he argues against Donald Engel's handling of the evidence, e.g. on Latin inscriptions.

My next chapter develops the focus on the educated elite in 1 Corinthians by investigating the descriptions that New Testament critics employ for the education of the elite and ancient education models. From this survey I indicate my particular study will focus on the Greek gymnasium. Thus chapters 1 and 2 progressively focus my study. Let us turn to education and the elite.

Chapter 2

FIRST CORINTHIANS AND ANCIENT EDUCATION MODELS

1. *Introduction*

In Chapter 1 I examined New Testament scholarship's understanding of social-status issues and the elite in 1 Corinthians. This chapter develops my study by focusing more closely on the educated elite. I describe, and evaluate, the ancient education models that New Testament scholars use for examining the elite in the church. By ancient education models I mean those models that critics use to reconstruct the education of these elite in antiquity.[1] I consider scholarship on the Corinthian correspondence that primarily addresses research in 1 Corinthians. Their models are evaluated against education models for the Graeco-Roman world described by biblical and classical scholarship. Finally, I address the understanding gained through recent works by historians of education. This chapter highlights the omission of the Greek gymnasium from education models employed for interpreting Paul's letter.

First, I consider primary and secondary education in the Roman Empire by looking at the contributions of Alan Booth and Robert Kaster. They examine, and critique, the traditional three-stage education model used in histories of ancient education. Kaster argues for a two-stage model, and diversity, rather than the single traditional three-stage education model. Second, I examine studies by the New Testament scholars: Fitzgerald, Pogoloff, Litfin, Bullmore, Glad, Martin, Clarke, Winter, and Braxton.[2] Fitzgerald investigates Paul's lists of hardships in the light of the Graeco-

1. See my discussion in the Introduction.

2. John T. Fitzgerald, *Cracks in an Earthen Vessel: An Examination of the Catalogues of Hardships in the Corinthian Correspondence* (SBLDS, 99; Atlanta, GA: Scholars Press, 1988); Pogoloff, *Logos and Sophia*; Litfin, *St. Paul's Theology of Proclamation*; Bullmore, *St. Paul's Theology of Rhetorical Style*; Clarence E. Glad, *Paul and Philodemus: Adaptability in Epicurean and Early Christian Psychagogy* (NovTSup, 81; Leiden: E.J. Brill, 1995); Martin, *The Corinthian Body*; Clarke, *Secular and Christian Leadership in Corinth*; Bruce W. Winter, *Philo and Paul Among the Sophists* (SNTSMS, 96; Cambridge: Cambridge University Press, 1997), now available in a second edition as *Philo and Paul among the Sophists: Alexandrian*

Roman concept of the sage. The next three studies consider the important role that Graeco-Roman rhetoric played in the problems Paul met in Corinth. Glad explores Epicurean communities and their educational practices in relation to Paul's methods. Martin addresses the ancient construction of the body in interpreting 1 Corinthians, and Clarke examines the elite and leadership. Winter examines the impact of the sophistic movement on the Corinthian church. Finally, as Brad Braxton assumes the presence of a gymnasium in Corinth I briefly address his contribution. Their models are evaluated against contemporary New Testament scholarship and ancient education models for the Graeco-Roman world. Third, I introduce recent histories of ancient education that have become available since the above works were written. These should be used to inform future work on the New Testament. I draw upon these in my study. My identification of the omission of the Greek gymnasium from studies of 1 Corinthians then leads on to chapter 3 where I discuss the Greek gymnasium and the Corinthian Christians.

2. *Ancient Education: Universality, Uniformity and Diversity*

There is a danger of reducing education in the Graeco-Roman world to one uniform system in the first-century AD. For example, Marrou comments in his history of education:

> The three chapters that follow are in a sense unnecessary, for the general principles, the syllabus and the methods used in Roman schools were simply copied from their Hellenistic prototypes: the change-over to a Latin-speaking society caused no important modifications in teaching. The reader will certainly be surprised when he discovers how mechanically the change-over was made. It was not even a case of imitating; it was on the whole a pure and simple transfer.[3]

According to Marrou, over time Roman education became virtually identical to Greek education. He describes the three successive stages in education operating in Greek-speaking countries and Rome. But these comments, emphasising universality and uniformity, when taken alone are misleading. The emphasis on sameness neglects differences. For example, the Greek emphasis on physical education and the gymnasium is lost.

John Townsend makes similar comments on universality when he remarks that in the New Testament world:

and Corinthian Responses to a Julio-Claudian Movement (Grand Rapids, MI and Cambridge, UK: Eerdmans, 2nd edn, 2002). Finally, Brad Ronnell Braxton, *The Tyranny of Resolution. I Corinthians 7:17–24* (SBLDS, 181; Atlanta, GA: Society of Biblical Literature, 2000).

3. H.-I. Marrou, *A History of Education in Antiquity* (trans. George Lamb; London and New York: Sheed and Ward, 1956; Second Impression 1977), p. 265.

> Educational theory and practice were essentially Hellenistic. The Greco-Roman world had settled into a single, universal educational system that was to dominate the ancient scene.... One should not see this system as a corruption of education in classical Athens but rather as the culmination of its development. Nor should education in the Latin West be viewed as developing out of Roman educational practice in early republican times. Rather, late republican and imperial Roman educators simply adopted the main tenets of the Hellenistic system with Latin added to the curriculum and with less emphasis on physical training.[4]

Thus Townsend, like Marrou, emphasises the 'single, universal educational system,' but he does indicate that there was less emphasis on physical training in the Roman education system. He discusses the contribution of the gymnasium to education and states, 'The decline in the importance of physical education should not be exaggerated. In NT times, it still played a significant role in all levels of education, particularly in the East.'[5] This is a valid point. However, the structure of the article tends to blurs the distinctive difference of the gymnasium for Greek rather than Roman education. A better approach is that in *The Oxford Classical Dictionary* with separate entries for Greek and Roman education.[6]

The *Dictionary of New Testament Background* has separate entries for 'Education: Jewish and Greco-Roman' and 'Gymnasia and Baths'.[7] Here Watson notes that Greek education was established before Rome's conquest of Greece and he recognises the role of the Greek gymnasium (as a public institution) in the Hellenistic period for primary education. Pearson provides a fuller description of gymnasia as educational centres in both the Hellenistic and Roman eras and discusses changes that occurred with time.

Unfortunately, New Testament scholarship often sees Greek and Roman education as identical and tends to treat them together as 'Graeco-Roman' education. This model fails to recognise and examine distinctive features of the Greek system, particularly the importance of physical education. Graeco-Roman education was not monolithic, as New

4. John T. Townsend, 'Education (Greco-Roman Period)', in Freedman (ed.), *The Anchor Bible Dictionary*, Vol. 2, pp. 312–17 (312). He also notes Hellenic influence on Jewish education.

5. Townsend, 'Education (Greco-Roman Period)', p. 313.

6. Frederick A.G. Beck and Rosalind Thomas, 'Education, Greek', in Hornblower and Spawforth (eds.), *The Oxford Classical Dictionary* (Oxford: Oxford University Press, 3rd edn., 1996), pp. 506–9; J.V. Muir, 'Education, Roman', in Hornblower and Spawforth (eds.), *The Oxford Classical Dictionary*, pp. 509–10.

7. D.F. Watson, 'Education: Jewish and Greco-Roman', in Evans and Porter (eds.), *Dictionary of New Testament Background*, pp. 308–13; B.W.R. Pearson, 'Gymnasia and Baths', in Evans and Porter (eds.), *Dictionary of New Testament Background*, pp. 435–36.

Testament scholars often portray it, and cannot be confined within a universal three-stage model as traditionally taught in modern histories of education and used by New Testament scholars.

Scholarship may incorrectly assume that what is a suitable education model for ancient Rome is also suitable for ancient Corinth in the Greek East. Using this transferred model, scholars 'understand' 1 Corinthians. This chapter, then, assesses the contributions of Pauline scholars to examining the educated elite in 1 Corinthians and the education models the critics apply. I recognise valuable contributions, and identify a major omission in scholarship because of the neglect of the Greek gymnasium. Claims that ancient education was universal and uniform although correct in some aspects are also misleading. Booth and Kaster, to whom I now turn, investigate diversity within ancient education.

3. *Primary and Secondary Education in the Empire*

New Testament scholars rely upon standard histories of ancient education and articles such as those by Alan Booth and Robert Kaster for their understanding of ancient education.[8] Therefore, before considering the Pauline scholars' understanding of education and its relationship to the exegesis of 1 Corinthians, it is important to review these works.

First, Alan Booth challenges the traditional prevalent pattern confidently accepted by modern scholars, which sees a progression from primary to secondary education.[9] He argues that the sources frequently ignore the existence of the primary stage for a liberal education and present the secondary teacher as the first instructor. Booth comments, 'Quintilian's silence indicates, then, that he and his public readily assumed that the elements would be taught by one of those mentioned in the child's entourage. The most likely candidate is the *paedagogus*, whom the ancients did not regard as a teacher.'[10] Again, Booth remarks that for receiving a liberal education the *grammatistes* was often avoided and instruction could be given at home perhaps by the *paedagogus* 'or be subsumed into the instruction of the *grammaticus*'.[11] Moreover, Booth concludes that in first-century Rome the *ludi magister* 'ran a lowly type of technical school which

8. Alan D. Booth, 'Elementary and Secondary Education in the Roman Empire', *Florilegium* 1 (1979), pp. 1–14, and Robert A. Kaster, 'Notes on "Primary" and "Secondary" Schools in Late Antiquity', *TAPA* 113 (1983), pp. 323–46.

9. Booth, 'Elementary and Secondary Education', p. 1. The pattern depicts the child attending the school of the *grammatistes* (from age six or seven) for learning the 3 R's. After this elementary education the child progresses to the school of the *grammaticus* (at age 11 or 12) for more advanced linguistic and literary studies. This is the secondary education.

10. Booth, 'Elementary and Secondary Education', p. 3.

11. Booth, 'Elementary and Secondary Education', p. 10.

peddled craft literacy to children, slave and free, to enhance their employability, but that the elements were usually acquired elsewhere by children embarking on a liberal education'.[12]

Robert Kaster successfully develops Booth's work and notes, 'The standard histories of ancient education teach us that a student pursuing a full course of literary instruction typically passed through three stages of schooling and attribute to each stage its own teacher and discrete curriculum'.[13] Kaster then identifies the primary school, secondary school, and the school of rhetoric. The standard histories say that the scheme originated in Hellenistic Greece and after adoption by the Romans (in the first century BC) continued during the history of the Empire. Kaster recognises that Booth's analysis shows 'separate parts of a socially segmented system composed of two tracks' one of which catered for the lower orders while the other provided a liberal education for upper-class children.[14] Children received elementary instruction either at home or in the grammarian's school. Nevertheless, apart from this last observation on some elementary instruction with the grammarian's school, Kaster notes that:

> Booth's view is rather a modification of than a break with the received opinion, since even those historians who favor the sequential or three-stage model commonly modify their position by noting that many students of the *ludus* would not have gone on to the grammarian's school, while many upper-class students of the *grammaticus* would have received private tuition in the elements.[15]

However, Kaster observes that the controversy raises important questions on the social organisation of ancient education. He limits his discussion to the later Roman Empire and remarks, 'while the available evidence does much to support the criticisms made by Booth, we are not dealing with a set of facts which resolve themselves into a clear picture simply faithful to one model or another'.[16] He draws together material that confirms or contradicts the three-stage sequence and then offers observations 'on the

12. Alan D. Booth, 'The Schooling of Slaves in First-Century Rome', *TAPA* 109 (1979), pp. 11–19 (19).

13. Kaster, 'Notes on "Primary" and "Secondary" Schools', p. 323. He cites as the most complete recent accounts, H.-I Marrou, *Histoire de l'éducation dans l'antiquité* (Paris, 1965); S.F. Bonner, *Education in Ancient Rome: From the Elder Cato to the Younger Pliny* (London: Methuen & Co Ltd., 1977), and M.L. Clarke, *Higher Education in the Ancient World* (London: Routledge & Kegan Paul, 1971).

14. Kaster, 'Notes on "Primary" and "Secondary" Schools', p. 324.

15. Kaster, 'Notes on "Primary" and "Secondary" Schools', p. 324 n. 5.

16. Kaster, 'Notes on "Primary" and "Secondary" Schools', p. 325.

different models of scholastic organization that have been proposed and on the neglected question of local variation'.[17]

After examining the evidence Kaster produces two different models of the regular institutional arrangement of schools.[18] His figure A shows the sequence customarily described with three schools formally distinct but allowing a regular progression. Allowance is made for attrition on the sequence and for lateral entry into the sequence for those receiving private elementary tuition. His figure B is the system described by Booth for first-century Rome.[19] It is socially segmented along two essentially separate tracks. The most important distinction is the division in the two tracks with the *ludus litterarius* providing common literacy for those of relatively humble origin and the *scholae liberales* catering for the more privileged. He assumes attrition and lateral entry for those upper class students instructed at home. An uneven trickle indicates those crossing the educational divide.

Kaster's evidence, he admits, discourages him from accepting figure A as 'typical' but he is also unwilling to accept figure B as 'typical or generalized', although he finds the idea of a socially segmented system attractive. He believes that figure B existed in *some* circumstances. Thus Kaster remarks, 'the schools of "vulgar" and "liberal" letters were surely segregated socially, in the sense that only the latter were regularly frequented by the upper classes' because these students met the grammarian as their first teacher in the formal school setting.[20] Yet, first, there is insufficient evidence to demonstrate that this was 'typical'. Second, the strongest hints of a two-track system come from the greatest centres of administration and education'. So Kaster notes, 'The social and economic life of such cities could demand and support a differentiated system of schools: but there would be few cities indeed in which we could expect to find replicated the pattern of schooling that might be found in the great metropolitan centers'.[21]

In summary, Kaster notes that the evidence:

> Tends to support recent arguments that (1) the organization of schools under the Empire did not regularly conform to the three-stage sequence presented in modern histories of ancient education, and, more specifically, that (2) the assumption of a normal differentiation between schools described as 'primary' and 'secondary' is seriously flawed: for in the education of the upper classes, the distinction between the 'primary' teacher (γραμματιστής/*litterator*) and 'secondary' teacher (γραμματικός/

17. Kaster, 'Notes on "Primary" and "Secondary" Schools', p. 325.
18. Kaster, 'Notes on "Primary" and "Secondary" Schools', p. 337.
19. Kaster, 'Notes on "Primary" and "Secondary" Schools', p. 337.
20. Kaster, 'Notes on "Primary" and "Secondary" Schools', p. 338.
21. Kaster, 'Notes on "Primary" and "Secondary" Schools', p. 341. Kaster includes as evidence Quintilian of Rome (first century AD).

> *grammaticus*) would frequently have been effaced, with the latter performing the function of both.[22]

He recognizes that in some circumstances the two-track or socially segmented pattern existed. The 'school of letters' served the lower classes with basic literacy while the 'liberal schools' provided the more privileged clientele with more refined skills. Nevertheless, Kaster does not reject the three-stage model to replace it with a two-track model, for this new model, where it can be seen, appears only in sources from great cities. Kaster concludes that *all* the evidence constantly supports only one view, i.e. that throughout the Empire there were 'schools of all shapes and kinds, depending on local needs, expectations and resources. And in a world without centralized direction of education of any sort, that is only what we should expect.'[23]

The analyses of Booth, and particularly, Kaster offer valuable insights not present in the standard histories of education. Kaster's model identifies diversity. Their models will be used in examining New Testament scholars' studies in 1 Corinthians. Are New Testament scholars aware of this diversity?

4. *Studies in the Corinthian Correspondence*

a. *John T. Fitzgerald*

John Fitzgerald studies the '*peristasis*' catalogues in the Corinthian correspondence from the conviction that they provide a vital role in the apostle's self-presentation (*Selbstdarstellung*).[24] These are 'catalogues of circumstances' ('good', 'bad' or both) but in the Corinthian correspondence they are 'catalogues of hardships' – what he sees as a subset of the basic type. Although various kinds of catalogues exist, Fitzgerald focuses on the wise man's hardships.[25]

He notes that in Graeco-Roman philosophy the sage was 'an immensely popular figure' who embodied reason and virtue and 'played a central role in both the propaganda and the pedagogy of philosophy'.[26] After documenting the intimate connection between virtue and adversity in the hardships of the sage, Fitzgerald observes:

> Since *peristaseis* constitute a test of human character, they have both a revelatory and a demonstrative function. The man with little or no

22. Kaster, 'Notes on "Primary" and "Secondary" Schools', p. 346.
23. Kaster, 'Notes on "Primary" and "Secondary" Schools', p. 346.
24. Fitzgerald, *Cracks in an Earthen Vessel*, pp. 2–4. He examines three of Paul's five catalogues: 1 Cor. 4.9–13; 2 Cor. 4.8–9, and 2 Cor. 6.4–10.
25. Fitzgerald, *Cracks in an Earthen Vessel*, pp. 47–49.
26. Fitzgerald, *Cracks in an Earthen Vessel*, p. 203.

> integrity collapses under the weight of his burdens. His *peristaseis* reveal and prove his deficiencies as a person. The *proficiens*, by contrast, shows greater strength of character in dealing with his hardships, so that his *peristaseis* reveal his progress, what he is *becoming*. Since they help to form his character, they play a crucial role in his *paideia*. For the *sapiens*, however, *peristaseis* no longer have this educative character. They provide instead the proof that he is educated. Consequently, they exhibit who he *is*, what he *has become*. His serene endurance of the greatest possible calamities is the definitive proof of his virtue and serves to distinguish him from every charlatan who merely claims to be 'wise'.[27]

Thus Fitzgerald ably demonstrates the relationship of philosophy, sufferings and education (*paideia*) for the sage.

Moreover, Fitzgerald shows that in 1 and 2 Corinthians Paul frequently depicts himself as the ideal philosopher and his use of *peristasis* catalogues is an integral part of this *Selbstdarstellung*. Hellenistic moralists used the suffering sage figure to admonish their students and to show a proper model for their conduct. In 1 Cor. 4 Paul admonishes the young converts and through the catalogue presents himself as a model.[28] Thus Fitzgerald helpfully concludes that Paul is familiar with the Greek concept of the sage:

> Paul's use of *sophos*-imagery and *peristasis* catalogues clearly shows that he is familiar with the traditions about the sage and the means used to depict him. In his Corinthian correspondence he adopts and adapts these traditions for his own purposes and uses them in the ways that have been indicated. Such adoption and adaption are not unique to Paul... But Paul's own use of these traditions and the catalogues associated with them is highly creative. It is informed by OT traditions about the afflicted righteous man and suffering prophet, and it is transformed by his fixation on the cross of Christ. His *peristasis* catalogues thus represent the convergence of several traditions and reflect his own personal experiences of suffering and divine power.[29]

An important contribution to understanding the problematic text in 1 Cor. 4.6 is Fitzgerald's argument, from Plato (*Prt*. 326D, the speech of Protagoras) and Seneca (*Ep*. 94.51), that the text refers to elementary education and learning to write.[30] Children learnt to write by copying a model and this occurs in the context of moral guidance. Paul gives the

27. Fitzgerald, *Cracks in an Earthen Vessel*, pp. 114–15. Fitzgerald says that the *proficiens* was one making moral progress but had not achieved the ideal (pp. 56–57).

28. Fitzgerald, *Cracks in an Earthen Vessel*, p. 204.

29. Fitzgerald, *Cracks in an Earthen Vessel*, p. 207.

30. Fitzgerald, *Cracks in an Earthen Vessel*, pp. 122–27. 1 Cor. 4.6 reads, 'Do not go beyond what is written' (NIV).

Corinthians a slogan that treats them as children. Fitzgerald's conclusion fits within an education model for reading 1 Corinthians and it is addressed in chapter 6. His work thus assists modern readers in understand-ing the ancient world and how Paul used sage traditions in his Corinthian correspondence. Philosophy, suffering and education are linked.

b. *Stephen M. Pogoloff*

Stephen Pogoloff examines the rhetorical situation of 1 Corinthians. After helpfully discussing the contribution of Plato, Socrates, Aristotle and Isocrates to the form and content of classical rhetoric, he comments:

> Isocrates brought together and developed the various strands of Hellenic rhetoric ... in his educational system. Successors to Isocrates' school flourished and became the basis of most education of the Hellenistic world and eventually of Rome as well. This widespread dominance of rhetoric in Hellenistic *paideia* (in both senses of education and culture) means that we can reconstruct that culture with a certain degree of confidence.[31]

Isocrates' educational system was enduring. Pogoloff remarks, 'this educational model was so universal that four centuries later in Rome, the Elder Seneca still testifies, that "you can easily pass from this art [eloquence] to all others; it equips even those whom it does not train for its own ends.... The practice of declamation will help you in those pursuits to which you are wholly-heartedly devoted".'[32]

The aim of Isocrates was to cultivate the ability 'to think and speak well'.[33] Pogoloff sees Isocrates' education model as universal but this assumption could give the mistaken impression that this is the single education model of antiquity. However, Pogoloff does recognise the availability of philosophy for study. For example, he comments:

> Although philosophy competed for students on the tertiary educational level, on the whole it was a minority counter-culture 'for an intellectual

31. Pogoloff, *Logos and Sophia*, pp. 41–42. By 'culture' Pogoloff, p. 42 n. 19, means 'the dominant integrated pattern of values, social forms, and linguistic and literary norms of Greco-Roman society'. He comments, this *paideia* varied even among the upper classes, and that its relevance decreased as we move down the social scale. Yet its strength was such that all lived within its world-defining power, even if with weaker articulation among οἱ πολλοί. However, we must also be sensitive to differences where we can detect them'. I note that Beck and Thomas, 'Education, Greek', p. 507, comment on Isocrates' methods, 'It was this primarily rhetorical basis of further education that became the dominant characteristic of ancient education'. See also Niall Livingstone, 'The Voice of Isocrates and the Dissemination of Cultural Power', in Too and Livingstone (eds.), *Pedagogy and Power*, pp. 263–81.

32. Pogoloff, *Logos and Sophia*, p. 43; Seneca, *Contra*. 2. pr. 3–4.

33. Pogoloff, *Logos and Sophia*, p. 43; Isocrates, *Antidosis* 244.

> elite prepared to make the necessary effort. It meant breaking with the usual culture, whose general tone was literary, rhetorical and aesthetic'. Even under the Principate, when opportunities for public speech declined, parents who paid for their children's education did not 'have much time for philosophy. Rhetoric was what everybody wanted'.[34]

Nevertheless, the studies by Fitzgerald and Glad (see below) show how philosophical models are used by Paul in 1 Corinthians.

Pogoloff's discussion of the rise of rhetorical education omits specific references to the Greek gymnasium (γυμνάσιον). Here Clarence Forbes comments that in the late fifth century BC sophists were the first to use rooms in the γυμνάσιον as lecture rooms.[35] While the sophists were itinerant, Socrates was permanent in Athens 'and one of the best known habitués of the city's gymnasia'.[36] Thus Forbes remarks, 'The casual and desultory frequenting of the gymnasia by such educators as the Sophists and Socrates gave an idea to the Athenian philosophers. Plato acquired the gymnasium called the Academy as an established headquarters for his philosophical school'.[37] Aristotle took over the grounds of another gymnasium, the Lyceum, for his school. In the third Athenian gymnasium, the Cynosarges, Antisthenes founded the Cynic school. Thus Forbes observes that all three Athenian gymnasia in the fourth century BC were used as schools of philosophy.[38]

Pogoloff makes a passing reference to the γυμνάσιον. He discusses the Corinthians, money and status, and remarks, 'even if money alone could not buy the "old boy" connections of the most acceptable *gymnasia*, it could buy teachers to lend a pretense of culture or even to actually educate oneself or one's children. It could also buy books (like Tramalchio's [*sic*] two libraries of Greek and Latin works)'.[39] But although Pogoloff notes the importance of the Greek gymnasium he does not develop his gymnasia reference.

Yet, he helpfully links the spread of Greek rhetoric to Romans and the situation in Corinth:

> [Roman] writings reveal a fairly consistent picture of the same ideals of [Greek] *paideia*, changed only by the peculiar values of Roman public

34. Pogoloff, *Logos and Sophia*, p. 50. He first cites Marrou, *A History of Education in Antiquity*, p. 206 and then M. Winterbottom, 'Introduction', in *The Elder Seneca: Declamations* (trans. M. Winterbottom, LCL; Cambridge: Harvard University Press, 1974), p. ix.

35. Clarence Allen Forbes, 'Expanded Uses of the Greek Gymnasium', *CPhil* 40 (1945), pp. 32–42 (33).

36. Forbes, 'Expanded Uses', p. 33.

37. Forbes, 'Expanded Uses', p. 34.

38. Forbes, 'Expanded Uses', p. 34. See also my comments in chapter 3.

39. Pogoloff, *Logos and Sophia*, pp. 125–26. On Trimalchio see: Raymond J. Starr, 'Trimalchio's Libraries', *Hermes* 115 (1987), pp. 252–53.

> and political life: the production of the educated, cultured, civicly minded individual who could speak persuasively by dint of his wisdom – i.e., his character, knowledge, understanding, education, and practical ability to use the language. Since Corinth lay on the cusp of Greek and Roman culture, we can assume both the traditional strength of Greek rhetorical teaching and the direct influence of its Roman heirs.[40]

He shows the importance of both form and content in classical rhetoric and develops this to support his assumption on Corinth. Pogoloff cites the Roman orator Cicero as carrying forth the ideals of Isocrates and opposing the separation of form and content.[41] He also cites the educator Quintilian who 'greatly admired Cicero as one who fulfilled the ideals of liberal rhetorical education'.[42] Quintilian also asserted that content and form were fundamentally united. Thus Pogoloff concludes:

> The leading theorists of rhetoric treated their subject as concerned with far more than the ornaments of style. However, their statements are apologetic and polemical, confronting those (especially philosophers) who would accuse rhetoric of concern with mere appearances. For this reason, we might be tempted to dismiss their apologies as irrelevant to the reality of Paul's Corinth. However, the unity of form and content they espoused was, in large measure, lived out in the wider rhetorical culture.[43]

From here Pogoloff examines rhetoric and culture and the importance of παιδεία (education and culture).

He remarks, 'Since most Hellenistic peoples could be Greek only through language and culture, they particularly valued the *paideia* acquired in the rhetorical schools. Thus, through rhetorical education and the general use of speech, the culture itself became rhetorical,' and so he notes that, rhetorical education is central to a true picture of Hellenistic civilization.[44] And, Hellenism, he rightly states is a 'civilization of paideia.'[45] He recognises that rhetoric, not philosophy, dominated in

40. Pogoloff, *Logos and Sophia*, p. 44.

41. Pogoloff, *Logos and Sophia*, p. 46.

42. Pogoloff, *Logos and Sophia*, p. 47. But Simon Swain, 'Plutarch's Lives of Cicero, Cato and Brutus', *Hermes* 118 (1990), pp. 192–203, shows that Plutarch regarded Cicero as lacking *paideia*.

43. Pogoloff, *Logos and Sophia*, p. 48.

44. Pogoloff, *Logos and Sophia*, pp. 48, 49, citing Marrou, *A History of Education in Antiquity*, p. 97.

45. Pogoloff, *Logos and Sophia*, p. 49, citing Martin Hengel, *Judaism and Hellenism: Studies in Their Encounter in Palestine During the Early Hellenistic Period*, Vol. I (trans. John Bowden; Philadelphia, PA: Fortress Press; London: SCM Press, 1974), p. 65.

Graeco-Roman schools. Rhetoric prepared free men for life.[46] However, Pogoloff notes that rhetoric's influence reached past the upper class:

> Except for specialized 'trade schools' for slaves and lower class free in large urban centers, virtually all education, including the learning of 'letters' (roughly, age 7 to 12) and 'grammar' (13–17), as well as 'rhetoric' (up to age 20 or even higher) was viewed as a continuum which aimed to produce the complete eloquent individual. Even if one's economic status limited a student to only part of this progression, that part would communicate a certain amount of rhetorical and literary theory and practice.[47]

Yet in his explanation of this system Pogoloff relies upon Bonner and Quintilian who is a Roman educator.[48] Bonner is concerned with Rome not Corinth, primarily Romans not Greeks. In discussing declamation in the imperial age he cites Clarke, but this is still Rome not Corinth, and although he cites Greek declamations from Russell his comment is restricted to the second century AD.[49] Pogoloff demonstrates the importance of *paideia*, but does not mention the importance of the γυμνάσιον in its transmission.

Pogoloff's analysis of ancient education does refer to Robert Kaster's article, and Alan Booth's works in the bibliography.[50] However, he appears to over condense, and consequently, oversimplify both Kaster's and Booth's analyses. For teaching 'letters' Pogoloff identifies two routes: the primary schools or home-based instruction for upper class children.[51] He mentions the progression to grammar and rhetoric schools, but he recognises that not all would complete the system because one's economic status may limit progress. He could have added that it also depended on one's sex with far more boys than girls completing this education. In her study of literate education Teresa Morgan make this important note on gender. There were educated women and women

46. Pogoloff, *Logos and Sophia*, p. 49, citing Donald Lemen Clarke, *Rhetoric in Greco-Roman Education* (New York: Columbia University Press, 1957), p. 65. He also cites James L. Kinneavy, *Greek Rhetorical Origins of Christian Faith: An Inquiry* (Oxford: Oxford University Press, 1987), p. 20, 'The concept of rhetoric ... dominated the schooling of the time in Greek and Roman education, and it was conspicuous in Jewish schools also. It was an honorific concept, much more complex than just a combination of intellectual and emotional appeals'.

47. Pogoloff, *Logos and Sophia*, p. 50.

48. Bonner, *Education in Ancient Rome*.

49. M. L. Clarke, *Rhetoric at Rome: A Historical Survey* (London: Cohen & West, 1953), pp. 85–86, 97; Russell, *Greek Declamations*, p. 76.

50. Pogoloff, *Logos and Sophia*, p. 50, citing Kaster, 'Notes on "Primary" and "Secondary" Schools' and in his bibliography Booth, 'Elementary and Secondary Education', and 'The Schooling of Slaves'.

51. Pogoloff, *Logos and Sophia*, p. 51.

teachers but she effectively argues that 'literate education's self image is that of an essentially masculine process, one which leads to power and authority, social and political, of a kind which was inaccessible to women'.[52]

Thus Pogoloff's summary seems to oversimplify Kaster's analysis and does not specifically mention that he describes a two-stage model against the traditional three-stage model. Pogoloff gives the impression that the two-stage system was 'typical or generalized', which is what Kaster denies. Pogoloff states that changes occurred as Rome adapted *paideia* for its own needs.[53] However, he does not sufficiently consider differences, thereby omitting a discussion of the Greek gymnasium, although one reference shows his awareness of the importance of this institution. Nevertheless, his work is a valuable contribution to understanding rhetoric's origin and importance in both education and society in a way that helps us to read 1 Corinthians as considerate readers. He observes that comparisons of character included references to noble birth, education (*paideia*), children, public offices and reputation.[54] Thus education (*paideia*) was so important.

c. *Duane Litfin*

Litfin's study investigates the relationship between Paul's preaching and the apostle's theological assumptions.[55] He examines the passage in Paul's epistles that addresses this issue (1 Cor. 1–4) and shows the rhetorical background of the problems by beginning in fifth century BC Athens. From here Litfin traces rhetoric through the sophists, Plato, Isocrates, Aristotle to Cicero, Quintilian and other Greek and Latin first-century writers. He shows rhetoric's nature and importance in first-century Corinth. Litfin uses this historical material to investigate the problems Paul faced in Corinth and his responses in 1 Cor. 1–4. A contrast exists between Paul's stated *modus operandi* as a preacher and that of the first-century rhetor.

Litfin's comprehensive examination of ancient authors clearly shows the development and importance of rhetoric in written and oral form and its place in education and culture. He explains that the sophists taught rhetoric at the oral level. He mentions the importance of Plato, the disciple of Socrates, who founded the Academy in 387 BC. Then he investigates the contribution of the sophist Isocrates who ennobled rhetoric. Litfin also

52. Morgan, *Literate Education*, p. 48.

53. Pogoloff, *Logos and Sophia*, p. 44.

54. Pogoloff, *Logos and Sophia*, p. 232. He is addressing the issue of self-praise in 2 Corinthians.

55. Litfin, *St. Paul's Theology of Proclamation*.

discusses Aristotle who opened the Lyceum (Peripatetic School) where he taught until he died (322 BC). Yet he does not explain about the location of their schools in the γυμνάσιον. He does not mention that in the fourth century Athens' three gymnasia were used as schools.[56] Bruce Winter evaluates Litfin's study and while recognising its considerable merits he comments:

> His view is that 1 Corinthians 1.17–25 is Paul's *apologia* against the Corinthians' criticism that his preaching failed to measure up to Graeco-Roman eloquence. While Litfin's work is a very important contribution to the discussion of 1 Corinthians 1.17–31, it does not probe the influence of the sophistic movement on the thinking of the Christian community which is the wider issue at stake in the Corinthian letters.[57]

Further, Litfin's study while clearly establishing the importance of rhetoric in antiquity does not discuss models of ancient education. His contribution considers the study of rhetoric, the importance of educators such as the sophists, Isocrates and Quintilian, but there is no wider discussion on Greek, Roman or Jewish education in the first century. Nevertheless, his contribution to understanding the culture of Corinth is very helpful. He recognises that the Roman influence in Corinth remained an important one, yet he usefully stresses its Greek identity:

> Because the city was situated crucially in the center of Greece and continued to uphold many long established Greek traditions – for example, the Isthmian Games and various other festivals were held here – Corinth quickly reclaimed much of its Greek identity, becoming once more, as Favorinus put it, 'thoroughly Hellenized'. With its deeply rooted Greek heritage, its close proximity to other distinctly Greek cities such as Athens, and its unavoidable location for north-south travel in Greece, it is hardly surprising that Hellenism firmly reasserted itself in Corinth.[58]

Litfin believes that although dominated by Greeks and Romans, Corinth represented a cross section of the Empire. Thus he remarks, 'More Greek than Rome, more Roman than Athens, if any city of the first century deserved the hyphenated designation "Greco-Roman" it was Corinth'.[59] He sees it as a significant Graeco-Roman city. This recognition of its

56. For philosophy and the gymnasia in classical Athens see R.E. Wycherley, 'Peripatos: The Athenian Philosophical Scene – I', *GR* 8 (1961), pp. 152–63, and 'Peripatos: The Athenian Philosophical Scene – II', *GR* 9 (1962), pp. 2–21.

57. Winter, *Philo and Paul*, p. 12.

58. Litfin, *St. Paul's Theology of Proclamation*, p. 141.

59. Litfin, *St. Paul's Theology of Proclamation*, p. 142.

'Greekness' is the basis for my later discussion on a Greek education model.

d. *Michael A. Bullmore*

Michael Bullmore's study also considers rhetoric. He describes the specific rhetorical practice with which Paul compares his preaching and comments:

> There was in first century Corinth A.D. a strong predilection for rhetoric which honored the aesthetics of presentation above all else and made of stylistic virtuosity the ground of persuasion. It is against the backdrop of this specific rhetorical tradition that 1 Corinthians 2.1–5 is best understood. Over against this rhetorical tradition Paul purposefully had chosen to adopt a plain and unadorned style in his preaching ministry so as not to distract from his message and to ensure that the faith of his hearers was rightly grounded.[60]

Bullmore provides a reconstruction of first century rhetorical culture and determines the level of Paul's rhetorical awareness before offering an exegesis of 1 Cor. 2.1–5. His study, with Pogoloff's and Litfin's, constitute three largely independent studies. As Litfin remarks they basically argue the same position, 'that Greco-Roman rhetoric lay at the core of the Corinthian *sophia logou* (1:17) that Paul was at pains to disavow'.[61] Their theses are similar, he admits, but do reflect differences. Nonetheless, Litfin rightly observes that three similar studies in the nineties arguing for the same background, 'surely indicates the power of this historic understanding of 1 Corinthians 1–4'.[62]

In his discussion on the historical background to hellenization after Alexander, Bullmore notes the importance of the Greek city, 'In its political structure and operation, its business administration and currency, its education centered in the gymnasium, its civic engineering and architecture, and its domestic and social organization, the city of the Near East was Greek'.[63] He refers to A.H.M. Jones for the role of the gymnasium in Greek communal life.[64] Although this is a promising start he does not develop his thoughts on the gymnasium.

His approach is to examine both Roman and Greek sources to reconstruct the situation in Corinth, but his primary approach is to

60. Bullmore, *St. Paul's Theology of Rhetorical Style*, preface.

61. Litfin, 'Review of Michael A. Bullmore', p. 568.

62. Litfin, 'Review of Michael A. Bullmore, p. 570.

63. Bullmore, *St. Paul's Theology of Rhetorical Style*, p. 26.

64. Bullmore, *St. Paul's Theology of Rhetorical Style*, p. 26 n. 8; citing A.H.M. Jones, *The Greek City*, pp. 220ff.

reconstruct the situation from Roman sources.[65] This leads him to describe 'The Hellenization of Rome' including the impact of Greek language, literature and learning.[66] He describes 'The Roman Reaction' illustrating this from Cato the Elder's views on education.[67] Nevertheless, Bullmore observes that 'by the beginning of the first century B.C. instruction in Greek rhetoric had an absolutely established place in Roman education'.[68]

Bullmore discusses the 'Political and Educational Developments Affecting First Century Rhetoric' and the loss of political oratory and the shift to the schools.[69] He considers the role of rhetoric in Greco-Roman education.[70] Earlier he mentioned the importance of the gymnasium but this is omitted here. He unfortunately gives the impression that all Greek children went to public schools. He fails to mention that education was private, and fee-paying, thus restricting access to the elite (apart from early ephebic training). He appears unaware of recent discussions on the restriction of literacy even in democratic Athens.[71]

65. For example, Bullmore states, 'In the attempt to determine the nature of first century Greek rhetorical culture the temptation is strong to rely on Roman sources for they are abundant and it is easy to assume they are descriptive of the whole empire. Such an assumption is suspect however, particularly as it applies to Greece, for it was Greece that, culturally speaking, took Rome "captive"' (p. 43). Yet he argues and concludes, 'The result of Rome's contribution was that even in Greece the culture was Greco-Roman.... By the end of the first-century B.C. a coherent Greco-Roman culture was firmly in place in Greece' (p. 50). Moreover, Bullmore, pp. 65–66, argues for the necessity of understanding first-century Greek rhetorical culture through Roman sources because, first, virtually all the important Greek sources of the last three centuries BC are not extant and have to be accessed through extant Roman sources which quote them. Second, and more significant, he notes that Rome became 'the cultural center of the world and as such came to largely control the direction and momentum of the rhetorical culture of the empire' (p. 66).

66. Bullmore, *St. Paul's Theology of Rhetorical Style*, pp. 30–36. He concludes, 'It is due to these factors then – the assimilation of Greek literature, the influx of Greek artifacts, the use of the Greek language and the presence of numerous learned Greeks – that a cultural fusion took place and Roman culture became Greco-Roman culture' (p. 36).

67. Bullmore, *St. Paul's Theology of Rhetorical Style*, pp. 36–43 and pp. 37–38 for Cato.

68. Bullmore, *St. Paul's Theology of Rhetorical Style*, p. 52. In Roman education he examines the life, education and influence of Cicero (pp. 82–90).

69. Bullmore, *St. Paul's Theology of Rhetorical Style*, pp. 150–71, for the section 'Political and Educational Developments Affecting First Century Rhetoric'; 'The Loss of Political Oratory and the Shift to the Schools', pp. 151–54.

70. Bullmore, *St. Paul's Theology of Rhetorical Style*, pp. 155–57, on 'Rhetoric in Greco-Roman Education'.

71. See, for example, William V. Harris, *Ancient Literacy* (Cambridge, MA and London: Harvard University Press, 1989); Marc Kleijwegt, *Ancient Youth: The Ambiguity of Youth and the Absence of Adolescence in Greco-Roman Society* (Dutch Monographs on Ancient History and Archaeology, 8; Amsterdam: J.C. Gieben, Publisher, 1991) (I owe this reference to Onno M. van Nijf who kindly pointed it out to me). I discuss these works in chapter 4.

Bullmore concludes that by the end of the first century BC Roman and Greek education were almost the same:

> The only significant difference being the inclusion of Latin in the Roman curriculum. As a result there existed, throughout Rome and the Greek-speaking countries of its empire, a homogeneous, firmly entrenched and widespread educational program of which rhetoric was the focus. With the political changes which accompanied the transition from the Republic to the Empire and the subsequent shifting of the weight of rhetoric to the schools rhetoric came to monopolize secondary education even more.[72]

But this general picture, although it has merits, needs to distinguish between the types of education available to the elite and non-elite. Furthermore, when Rome adopted Greek education, it did not embrace Greek physical education in the gymnasium. Bullmore emphasises the 'homogeneous' education programme with similarities but he overlooks the differences.[73]

Nonetheless, his aim of interpreting 1 Cor. 2.1–5 through ancient rhetoric is valuable, for it demonstrates, with Pogoloff and Litfin, that reconstructing ancient education and a culture of rhetoric aids us in understanding the problems Paul faced in the Corinthian church.

e. *Clarence E. Glad*

The contribution of Clarence Glad to Pauline studies, and especially 1 Corinthians, is notable.[74] Harold Attridge's favourable review notes, 'Glad offers his treatment of Philodemus within a broad context of ancient educational theory'.[75] Glad's thesis is that 1 Cor. 9.22b ('I have become everything in turn to men of every sort' NEB) 'is part of a tradition in Greco-Roman society which underscores, in the light of human diversity, the importance of adaptability in conduct and speech in the unreserved association with all and in the psychagogic adaptation to different human dispositions'.[76] He argues that the pericope 1 Cor. 9.19–23 'reflects Paul's concern with adaptation in light of human diversity both in the unreserved association with all in recruitment and in the practice of psychagogy or

72. Bullmore, *St. Paul's Theology of Rhetorical Style*, pp. 156–57.

73. See the above discussion on Booth's and Kaster's articles.

74. Glad, *Paul and Philodemus*. Glad, p. 5 n. 8, notes that Philodemus was born in Syria c. 110 BC and died *c.* 40/35 BC. He probably had Greek parents and received a Greek education. He was the leader, and probably a founder, of an Epicurean school based in Herculaneum.

75. Harold W. Attridge, 'Review of Clarence E. Glad, *Paul and Philodemus: Adaptability in Epicurean and Early Christian Psychagogy*', *JBL* 116 (1997), pp. 376–77 (376).

76. Glad, *Paul and Philodemus*, p. 1.

"care of the young"'.[77] Here Paul's leadership model gives the wise an example of how to treat the weak and to implement a proper form of psychagogic guidance.[78]

Glad develops a model complementary to that of Abraham J. Malherbe (who argues that Paul's teaching and self-understanding were in the form of the gentle Cynics) but Glad argues for redressing the balance, and that Epicurean practice is the closest comparison with Paul's psychagogy and nurture in his communities. Thus Glad's thesis is the tradition of psychagogy, 'in the practices of the Epicureans in Athens, Naples, and Herculaneum less than a century before Paul that we find the closest comparison to Paul's psychagogic nurture of the proto-Christian communities'.[79] His purpose is to show a widespread communal practice shared by Epicureans and the early Christians. However, he does not aim to demonstrate influence or borrowing.[80] He observes that the social practice of *mutual* edification and exhortation with *mutual* correction occurs among both Epicureans and Christians. Glad comments, 'My thesis agrees with E.A. Judge's recognition that Paul is a participant in adult education, but is at variance with his claim that Paul is promoting a "new kind of community education for adults"'.[81]

His analysis of Epicurean psychagogy is applied to Pauline communities in Rom. 14.1–15.14 and 1 Cor. 8.1–11.1. Glad identifies Paul's leadership style as belonging to the psychagogic traditions of harsh and gentle guidance. Paul's advice to the Corinthians is modelled both on the advice

77. Glad, *Paul and Philodemus*, p. 2. He remarks, 'I use the term "psychagogy" or the "guidance of the soul" to describe a mature person's leading of neophytes in an attempt to bring about moral reformation by shaping the neophyte's view of himself and of the world. Such a reshaping demands in many cases a radical reorientation through social, intellectual and moral transformation. Psychagogic discourse attempts to effect such a transformation. Such a discourse is then a form of paraenesis or moral exhortation having a twofold focus: on dissuasion and on persuasion'. Glad focuses 'on the psychagogue's method of exhortation, as well as on his perception of the status of his clients'.

78. Glad, *Paul and Philodemus*, p. 3.

79. Glad, *Paul and Philodemus*, p. 4. He sees these practices witnessed primarily in Philodemus' *On Frank Criticism*.

80. Glad, *Paul and Philodemus*, p. 9.

81. Glad, *Paul and Philodemus*, p. 12 n. 24; Edwin A. Judge, 'The Reaction Against Classical Education in the New Testament', *JCE 77* (1983), pp. 7–14 (12). Judge argues that, 'In 1 Cor 1:20 Paul challenges the three main types of tertiary scholar of his world: the rationalistic philosopher ("the wise"), the Jewish legal expert ("the scribe") and the rhetorician ("the debater")' (p. 11). Moreover, Judge sees in Paul's vocabulary 'persuasiveness of speech' (2.4), and 'philosophy' (2.8) that both great divisions (rhetoric and philosophy) of Greek higher education are 'explicitly discounted' (p. 12). Paul occupies the territory that belongs to higher education and promotes a new kind of community education. Therefore Judge concludes, 'This involved him in a confrontation with his own churches because they wanted him to adopt the status in life that was appropriate to a tertiary teacher' (p. 12).

of a frank friend and the guidance of a loving but stern father.[82] Paul, like Philodemus, portrays 'a variation of two different types of students, namely, the strong or recalcitrant ones, and the weak or tender ones. Paul is gentle towards the weak but more forceful and overbearing in his guidance of the recalcitrant and stubborn students'.[83] Paul's discourse 'supposes education and growth,' and the reference to the 'weak' and 'strong' is Paul's attempt at character portrayal.[84] Attridge notes that some suggestions challenge much contemporary scholarship, and aptly summarises, 'He [Glad] rejects the notion that the wise and strong were contemptuous of the weak; their activity aimed at the moral education of their fellow Christians. Finally, he rejects a social reading of the category 'weak'; the designation is a psychological or dispositional term, common in the psychagogic literature'.[85]

Glad's work is commendable in its analysis of the two communities and the construction of his education model. He demonstrates that Paul's adaptable behaviour is part of a recognised strategy for building new communities. However, as Attridge rightly remarks, 'Not all the analysis is equally convincing. The construction of mutual psychagogy in Pauline communities is strained and the attempt to downplay the conflict between Paul and the 'superlative apostles' overlooks too much in 2 Corinthians'.[86]

Glad includes some useful discussion on social-status issues but admits his study is not concerned with social status.[87] Consequently, his engagement with contemporary scholarly discussion on social-status issues at Corinth is minimal.[88] Although he discusses Epicurean and Christian social communities he appears reticent in developing his thoughts along the line of social status although he is willing to identify the 'wise' with patronage in 1 Cor. 9.3–12 and concludes:

> The rejection of an exclusive allegiance to a few patrons is explained in light of the need to associate with the many in order to recruit or benefit them. Here different views have emerged relating to the question of with whom one should associate. Paul seems to treat the wealthy patrons and the 'wise' who probably belonged to the entourage of these patrons as community leaders with whom he debates issues of leadership. In the

82. Glad, *Paul and Philodemus*, pp. 326–27.
83. Glad, *Paul and Philodemus*, p. 328.
84. Glad, *Paul and Philodemus*, p. 329.
85. Attridge, 'Review of Clarence E. Glad', p. 377.
86. Attridge, 'Review of Clarence E. Glad', p. 377.
87. Glad, *Paul and Philodemus*, p. 209–10.
88. For his above citation he notes that 'Gerd Theissen has demonstrated that issues of social status exacerbated the tensions among the Corinthians' (p. 209 n. 81); Theissen, *The Social Setting of Pauline Christianity*. He (p. 210 n. 82) cites Theissen, pp. 94–95, and Meeks, *The First Urban Christians*, pp. 55–63.

> context of 1 Cor. 8–9 this debate concerns not only questions of versatility and the association of different character types but also matters of psychagogic guidance.[89]

Here Glad has the 'wise' among the social group of the wealthy patrons. Later, in discussing the ironic list of hardships in 1 Cor. 4.10, Glad sees the 'wise' Corinthians as 'the honored, strong and wise of this world'.[90]

Glad's education model has merits and shows the diversity evident in the first-century AD. His overall unwillingness to engage in depth with the social-status issues identified in 1 Corinthians, by contemporary scholarship, weakens his conclusions. Graham Tomlin's article on Epicureans in 1 Corinthians takes a different tack when he says, 'The argument complements rather than contradicts the sociological and rhetorical approaches mentioned above, by suggesting a plausible philosophical source for arguments used to back up the behaviour of a group of fairly well-off Corinthian Christians, with whom Paul is far from happy'.[91] A valuable recent article on basic education in Epicureanism may further assist scholars investigating Epicureanism in Corinth.[92]

f. *Dale B. Martin*

In his important book, *The Corinthian Body*, Dale Martin suggests two ways of reading his work. It can be read as *either* an interpretation of 1 Corinthians (primarily) that then focuses on the 'ancient construction of the body' for analysis *or* as an investigation of 'ancient ideologies of the body' (primarily) that then takes 1 Corinthians as an entrance into the Graeco-Roman world for understanding the body.[93] Either approach benefits the exegete of 1 Corinthians. Martin explains his methodology of using various sources (Greek, Roman, and Jewish) to 'construct Graeco-Roman ideologies' and his study spans eastern Mediterranean urban

89. Glad, *Paul and Philodemus*, p. 272.

90. Glad, *Paul and Philodemus*, p. 307.

91. Graham Tomlin, 'Christians and Epicureans in 1 Corinthians', *JSNT* 68 (1997), pp. 51–72 (53).

92. Elizabeth Asmis, 'Basic Education in Epicureanism', in Too (ed.) *Education in Greek and Roman Antiquity*, pp. 209–39. This chapter is outlined below.

93. Martin, *Corinthian Body*, p. xi. He explains that his book is not a full commentary or a comprehensive study on how the ancients saw the body. Martin, p. xii, writes for New Testament scholars (to encourage them in a fuller contextualisation of early Christian texts) and classical historians (to convince them, if needed, of the value of early Christian literature in examining ancient culture from a non-elite standpoint).

culture from about 300 BC to AD 300.[94] He reconstructs Graeco-Roman culture using Jewish sources on the basis that Judaism in the cities (Greek and Roman) was a Graeco-Roman religion that had been deeply affected by Hellenism and Rome. For Martin, Judaism is an ethnic subculture and 'Any firm distinction between "Greco-Roman" and "Jewish" in this period is therefore historically misleading, even if, for some people, it is theologically important'.[95]

His main thesis is 'that theological differences reflected in 1 Corinthians all resulted from conflicts between various groups in the local church rooted in different ideological constructions of the body'.[96] This is an important point for Martin's book. He notes:

> Whereas Paul and (probably) the majority of the Corinthian Christians saw the body as a dangerously permeable entity threatened by polluting agents, a minority in the Corinthian church (...'the Strong') stressed the hierarchical arrangement of the body and the proper balance of its constituents, without ever evincing much concern over body boundaries or pollution. The different stances taken by Paul and this minority group on various subjects ... spring from their different assumptions regarding both the individual human body and the social body – in this case, the church as the body of Christ. Furthermore, these positions correlate with socioeconomic status, the Strong being the higher-status group, who enjoy a relatively secure economic position and high level of education, and Paul, like many members of the Corinthian church, being among the less educated, less well-off inhabitants of the Roman Empire.[97]

However he does not see Paul as *coming from* a lower-class background.

Education occupies a key position in Martin's theses. Martin calls Paul's opponents 'upper-class' and the 'educated elite' but he does not imply that

94. Martin, *Corinthian Body*, p. xv, states, 'By calling a statement *ideology*, I indicate the *way* I want to look at it, without implying that I intend to replace some false statement with an objectively true alternative; I mean only that I will examine it *as it relates to the (usually) asymmetrical social relations of power and domination*... I am willing to conceive of liberating "counterideologies" employed by subordinated groups to oppose the oppressive ideologies of the dominant class or powerful social groups. But in my usage *ideology* usually refers to the system of symbols that supports and enforces the power structures of the dominant class and ruling groups; it therefore retains a generally negative tone with good reason, without implying that it can be overcome by recourse to some objective truth'. Emphasis in original.

95. Martin, *Corinthian Body*, p. xiv. For my discussion on Judaism and Hellenism see chapter 3.

96. Martin, *Corinthian Body*, p. xv.

97. Martin, *Corinthian Body*, p. xv.

they were members of the true elite.[98] There is no doubt that Martin successfully identifies status issues in the conflict at Corinth. Indeed, David Horrell finds Martin's reconstruction of the Corinthian situation persuasive: believers are divided by social status issues so Paul responds to challenge 'the dominant ideology' urging the Strong believers to change their behaviour towards the Weak.[99] Nevertheless, Horrell raises questions about vulnerable aspects of Martin's case. I have a few concerns on his treatment of education.

In 'The Status of Rhetoric' Martin engages with Paul's disparagement of rhetoric in 1 Cor. 1–4. Relying on Pogoloff's work, Martin comments, 'in both his disparagement of rhetoric and his claim to be only a layman [in 2 Cor 11:6], Paul stands in a great tradition of rhetorical disavowals of rhetorical activity'.[100] He correctly observes that in Paul's day it would be impossible for an urban person to avoid exposure to rhetoric. After indicating that rhetoric was ubiquitous Martin comments, 'anyone who received any Greek education whatsoever would thereby receive at least a modicum of rhetorical education'.[101]

Martin shows that some rhetorical training occurred during elementary education. However, he recognises that proper rhetorical education came later and those who could pay, especially the upper classes, gave their sons a rhetorical education (possibly private but usually with a teacher of rhetoric).[102] He notes that some educated people would be exposed to philosophy but that 'Greco-Roman education *was* rhetorical education'. Consequently, Martin rightly observes that rhetorical education served as an essential statues indicator in the Graeco-Roman world.[103]

Nevertheless, Martin's consideration of ancient education does not follow Pogoloff's work but relies upon Gwynn, Bonner, Marrou and Quintilian, while showing no knowledge of Booth's or Kaster's articles.[104] This leads him to rely on dated modern histories for his model of

98. Martin, *Corinthian Body*, p. xvii. 'It is doubtful that any of them was of the equestrian or decurion order, much less the senatorial. My guess is that the more affluent members of Paul's churches were in that middle area between the true elite and the poor'. He comments 'the Strong being the higher-status group, who enjoy a relatively secure economic position and high level of education' (p. xv). Thus Martin's understanding of 'elite' appears to equate with Hopkins' 'sub-elite' (see chapter 1).

99. David Horrell, 'Review of Dale B. Martin, *The Corinthian Body*', *JTS* 47 (1996), pp. 624–29 (628).

100. Martin, *Corinthian Body*, p. 49. He relies on Pogoloff, *Logos and Sophia*, pp. 108–27 and pp. 158–72.

101. Martin, *Corinthian Body*, p. 49.

102. Martin, *Corinthian Body*, p. 49–50.

103. Martin, *Corinthian Body*, p. 50.

104. Pogoloff, *Logos and Sophia*, pp. 50–52; Aubrey Gwynn, *Roman Education from Cicero to Quintilian* (Oxford: Clarendon, 1926); Bonner, *Education in Ancient Rome*; Marrou, *A History of Education in Antiquity*, and Quintilian, *Inst*. 2.1.1–6.

education. Although he refers to 'Greek education' he focuses on a Roman model. Beck and Townsend demonstrate development and differences between Greek and Roman education, but Martin does not use these.[105]

Martin's summary of ancient education uses the traditional three-stage model. He does not use Booth's, and Kaster's, insights (see my earlier discussion) and appears unaware of the two-stage model and Kaster's desire not to replace the three-stage system by a two-stage system, but to recognise diversity. Insights from these scholars would provide a more accurate understanding of ancient education. Moreover Martin does not consider distinctive features of Greek education, such as the gymnasium, and Jewish education in the Greek gymnasium.[106] Including a discussion of the Greek gymnasium would enhance Martin's work on the body.

Nonetheless, he notes the developing consensus that Paul would have received some rhetorical education and argues that Paul came from a social level that would have valued a rhetorical education.[107] Paul's letters demonstrate knowledge of Graeco-Roman rhetoric and could not have been written by someone uneducated in rhetoric. Indeed, Martin sees evidence for Paul's rhetorical education everywhere. His education, for Martin, is evidence that his family had 'relatively high status'.[108]

Apart from the three-stage model Martin briefly describes philosophical education and the elite in the Corinthian church. He argues that some believers' knowledge of philosophy indicates either they had a philosophical education or were exposed to it in the households of the upper class. Whatever alternative occurred, Martin understands that their knowledge of moral philosophy 'implies a higher-class position', although Martin does not consider them as Cynics or Stoics.[109] Rather, their knowledge of philosophy indicated their elevated social environment.[110].

105. Beck, *OCD*^{2}, pp. 369–73, and Townsend, 'Education (Greco-Roman Period)', pp. 312–17. Townsend's discussion while examining Greek, Roman and Jewish education tends to focus on the unity of Greek and Roman education without sufficient emphasis on the differences. He discusses the gymnasium but fails to emphasise that this was part of Greek physical education not Roman. More recently, differences are discussed in Beck and Thomas 'Education, Greek', pp. 506–9, and in Muir 'Education, Roman', pp. 509–10.

106. See my chapter 3 for a discussion on the use of the Greek gymnasium by Jews.

107. Martin, *Corinthian Body*, p. 51.

108. Martin, *Corinthian Body*, p. 52. For a discussion on Paul's education see Jerome Murphy-O'Connor, *Paul: A Critical Life* (Oxford: Clarendon Press, 1996).

109. On Cynics and the Pauline churches see Downing, *Cynics, Paul and the Pauline Churches*, and 'Paul's Drive for Deviants'. Downing's article notes that Grant sees the Corinthian radicals as 'Cynic in outlook' (p. 371 n. 42). See Grant, *Paul in the Roman World.*

110. Martin, *Corinthian Body*, p. 73.

Martin's arguments for the elite and understanding of body in 1 Corinthians are very useful. However, despite arguing for the conflict in the church over social status divisions and the essential difference between the educated Strong and the less educated Weak, Martin devotes relatively little space to discussing education. Where he does he uses the three-stage model from the histories of education, which have now been critiqued by Kaster.

g. *Andrew D. Clarke*

Andrew Clarke's study does not specifically consider ancient education models but it is a valuable study of secular and Christian leadership in Corinth that addresses the elite. Clarke's thesis is that some people from the 'élite Corinthian society also belonged to the Pauline community and that, both in practices adopted and perceptions of leadership in the church, some of these were strongly influenced by a secular model'.[111] His methodology highlights the imbalance in studying church leadership. He notes that studies either narrowly focus on theological ideals or they rely on modern social theory. However, he chooses the method of social history.[112]

His study focuses on 1 Corinthians 1–6 where he uses socio-historical and exegetical approaches to reconstruct an understanding of leadership in the Corinthian church. First, using a range of sources, he describes the structures and dynamics of elite secular leadership in Roman Corinth.[113] Second, he uses 1 Corinthians to show that Paul addresses some church members who were among the elite in secular society. This includes a discussion of Erastus (Rom. 16.23) and the Corinthian inscription dedicated by an Erastus in Roman Corinth to see if there is a common identity.[114] He concludes that, irrespective of whether these Erasti were the

111. Clarke, *Secular and Christian Leadership*, p. 1.

112. Clarke, *Secular and Christian Leadership*, pp. 1–7. He notes that the consensus view of institutionalisation in the Pauline churches focused on theological studies. Some scholars termed this the 'idealistic fallacy' because the method ignored historical and social aspects and determined the situation only on the theological content of Paul's letters. See B. Holmberg, *Paul and Power: The Structure of Authority in the Primitive Church as Reflected in the Pauline Epistles* (Lund: Gleerup, 1978), p. 205.

113. Clarke's sources include: epigraphic, numismatic, literary and secondary sources. For example, his chapter 1 'Evidence of Secular Leaders in Corinth' looks at the literary and non-literary evidence (using inscriptions discovered during the excavations of Corinth). His Appendix A is a useful compilation of prosopographical information on leading figures in Roman Corinth (with 160 entries).

114. Clarke, *Secular and Christian Leadership*, p. 47 notes that the inscription is from two paving slabs near the Roman theatre that read, 'Erastus in return for his aedileship laid (the pavement) at his own expense'. See also, Andrew D. Clarke, 'Another Corinthian Erastus Inscription', *TynBul* 42 (1991), pp. 146–51.

same person, Erastus belonged to the powerful mentioned in 1 Cor. 1.26. Clarke also includes Crispus, Gaius and Stephanus among the influential in 1 Cor. 1.26. Next, Clarke examines secular practices and perceptions of leadership in 1 Cor. 1–6 and shows that these demonstrate some Christians were among the Corinthian elite.[115] Finally, Clarke argues that Paul's principles for Christian leadership stand against models of secular leadership. Paul directly accuses Corinthian Christians of secular leadership in 1 Cor. 3.3–4 but then redefines the true nature of Christian leadership.

Clarke's study effectively demonstrates his thesis that some members of the Corinthian church were also from the elite in Corinthian society. Thus his study helpfully underpins my work, which focuses on the education of the elite. His more recent study is also helpful.[116]

h. *Bruce W. Winter*

Bruce Winter's work examines the sophistic movement in Alexandria and Corinth.[117] For Alexandria, he examines a student among the Alexandrian sophists using *P.Oxy*. 2190, which is a private letter from a student to his father dated at the end of the first century AD. He also considers the contributions of Dio and Philo to establishing a picture of the sophists. For Corinth, Winter gathers evidence from non-Biblical sources (Epictetus and the Corinthian student of the sophists, Dio and Plutarch) and Paul's letters to the Corinthians. From his analysis Winter cogently argues for the presence of a first century sophistic movement in these two cities and demonstrates that Paul contends with these sophists in both 1 and 2 Corinthians. Winter's contribution identifies the importance of education in antiquity.

In *P.Oxy*. 2190 Neilus (a student of rhetoric) writes to his father, Theon, in Oxyrhynchus regarding the educational arrangements that he made because he was unable to enrol in a reputable sophist's school. He mentions important educators in the sophistic tradition: sophist, tutor and declaimer. Winter notes that it 'confirms the picture that has recently emerged of first-century *paideia* over against the traditional view of a more structured three-tier education system,' and he acknowledges the challenges of Booth and Kaster to the standard three-tier education system.[118] While Kaster does not discuss *P.Oxy*. 2190 Winter rightly

115. Clarke, *Secular and Christian Leadership*, examines 'going to court' (1 Cor. 6.1–8) and 'incest'.

116. Andrew D. Clarke, *Serve the Community of the Church: Christians as Leaders and Ministers* (First-Century Christians in the Graeco-Roman World; Grand Rapids, MI and Cambridge, UK: Eerdmans, 2000).

117. Winter, *Philo and Paul.*

118. Winter, *Philo and Paul*, p. 20. See my earlier discussion on the contributions of Booth and Kaster.

remarks this is a first-century example of variation in the content of *paideia* thus supporting the general thesis of Kaster.[119] So Winter demonstrates the diversity of education systems in the ancient world. The Alexandrian schools of the sophists were full so Neilus intended to continue his education outside the sophist's classroom by listening to public displays of declamation and employing a tutor.[120] Thus Winter remarks:

> Neilus believes that if he listens to orators or sophists declaiming publicly, especially Poseidonius, and makes use of Didymus as an *ad hoc* tutor to help him in his own declamations, then he will succeed. It is significant that such an alternative existed for an advanced student of rhetoric. It demonstrates both the central role declamations played in *paideia* in first-century Alexandria, and the prominence that teachers of rhetoric and sophists had secured for themselves through them.[121]

He considers Neilus 'a credible witness' and sees the text to be indicating sophists were important within Alexandria's education market.[122] They were in great demand and a teacher shortage shows demand outstripping supply.

In his detailed discussion on the Hellenised Jew Philo of Alexandria, and Philo's critique of the Alexandrian sophistic tradition, Winter recognises that Philo did not resist Greek '*paideia per se*' for he had enjoyed its advantages in his own education.[123] But Philo opposed its misuse. Winter incidentally cites Harris' work on Philo as a source of athletic terms and as a previous pupil in the gymnasium.[124] This is an important point because although Philo was a Jew he received his education in the Greek gymnasium. Other Jews also received training in the gymnasia. Winter comments, 'Some Jews pursued *paideia* not for virtue but "with no higher motive than parading their superiority, or from desire of office under our rulers", *LA* III.167. That such civic ministrations were open to Jews

119. Winter, *Philo and Paul*, p. 20, n. 3.

120. For a recent discussion on declamation, with its lurid subject matter and its intention in training the elite, see Robert A. Kaster, 'Controlling Reason: Declamation in Rhetorical Education at Rome' in Too (ed.), *Education in Greek and Roman Antiquity*, pp. 317–37. Kaster refers to the criminal themes, and associated punishments, as a 'social mess' and concludes, 'How to clean up such a mess – and, no less, how one should learn to fear it – were two valuable lessons that such themes were eminently well suited to teach' (p. 335).

121. Winter, *Philo and Paul*, p. 34.

122. Winter, *Philo and Paul*, p. 39.

123. Winter, *Philo and Paul*, p. 84.

124. Winter, *Philo and Paul*, p. 60–61, n. 2; H.A. Harris, *Trivium, Greek Athletics and the Jews* (Cardiff: University of Wales Press, 1976), pp. 13, 51–91. For an introduction to Greek athletics see J.R.C. Couslan, 'Athletics', in Evans and Porter (eds.), *Dictionary of New Testament Background*, pp. 140–42. Couslan notes that because of the popularity of ancient athletics its terms were used metaphorically by philosophers (p. 142).

possessing Greek *paideia* even before the letter of Claudius to the Alexandrians is no longer contested'.[125] In a detailed note he gives the evidence for Jews among the list of ephebes.[126] Moreover, in his discussion on Paul's opponents in 2 Cor. 10–12, Winter argues that they were trained in Greek rhetoric and answers that the fact they were Jews is no objection because Philo, and other Jews, were 'trained in Greek *paideia*'.[127] Therefore, Winter confirms Jewish participation in the Greek education system.

Winter gives incidental references to the gymnasium in his discussion of Epictetus and the Corinthian sophist. Epictetus states that a citizen trained in rhetoric could become the 'the superintendent of the *ephebi* (ἐφήβαρχος),' and Winter notes, 'The ἐφήβαρχος was responsible for the *ephebeia* whom they trained in the gymnasium'.[128] Favorinus, a sophist and a Roman of the equestrian order, made three visits to Corinth and delivered his Corinthian oration (*Or*. 37) on his last visit. Thus Winter remarks:

> While the 'best of the Greeks' had been inclining to Rome, Favorinus favoured the rich heritage and glories of Greece at enormous political and economic cost to himself. In fact, to his mind it had cost him everything, for he did not want merely to appear a Greek, but actually to be one. He had devoted himself to oratory in Athens and athletics in Sparta. Because he had pursued the study of wisdom in all the cities he visited, he had been instrumental in encouraging many Greeks to follow this pursuit. Indeed, he persuaded many barbarians to do the same.[129]

This demonstrates the willingness of some Romans to pursue a Greek education. Favorinus' reference to athletics at Sparta (φιλογυμναστεῖ) implies he trained in the gymnasium.

Winter's work demonstrates the availability of different education routes than the traditional three-stage model. He shows how a student could receive a rhetorical education in first-century Alexandria even when all the reputable sophist schools were full. Further, he shows that Jews could be educated in Greek παιδεία. For Philo and others this included training in the gymnasium. The Roman sophist Favorinus reveals an

125. Winter, *Philo and Paul*, p. 96. He, p. 96 n. 73, notes that this includes Jews because Philo writes 'our race' in his *LA* III.167.

126. Winter, *Philo and Paul*, p. 96 and n. 74.

127. Winter, *Philo and Paul*, p. 221.

128. Winter, *Philo and Paul*, pp. 119–20. Winter uses *Diss*. 3.1. The reference to the ἐφήβαρχος occurs in *Diss*. 3.1.34.

129. Winter, *Philo and Paul*, pp. 133–34. Winter, p. 132, dates Favorinus of Arles *c*. AD 80–150, and he notes that the Corinthians erected a statue of Favorinus in the most prominent place in the library to inspire the young (p. 133). His *Or*. 37 occurs in *Dio Chrysostom*, Vol. IV (trans. H. Lamar Crosby; LCL; London: William Heinemann Ltd; Cambridge, MA: Harvard University Press, 1946).

education in παιδεία that included travel to Athens for oratory and to Sparta for athletics (and implied training in the γυμνάσιον). Winter cogently argues that sophists, those educated in Greek παιδεία, were Paul's opponents in 1 and 2 Corinthians.[130]

In his second edition of *Philo and Paul* Winter continues to show his familiarity with writers on ancient education by drawing on Teresa Morgan's book on literate education.[131] His work recognises diversity, rather than uniformity, in ancient education. My study on the Greek gymnasium is a contribution to this diversity.

i. *Brad Ronnell Braxton*

Finally, I include, briefly, the study by Brad Braxton. His work provides an exegesis of 1 Cor. 7.17–24 with a particular interest in ambiguity in the text. He addresses two levels of ambiguity: that in the text and that in the social and cultural worlds of 1 Corinthians. He sees these as related issues with the latter giving rise to the former. He focuses primarily on ethnicity and social status in 7.17–24 and suggests that 'circumcision and uncircumcision' arise in the social context of the Corinthian congregation and concern both Paul and the believers. Thus Braxton comments, 'In particular, I will maintain the plausibility that Paul may be in "competition" with two important and alluring institutions, the gymnasium and the synagogue'.[132] Although Braxton does not discuss ancient education models he is aware of the importance of the Greek gymnasium and convincingly argues his case for this important institution being behind Paul's comments on circumcision. He does not discuss the gymnasium in great detail but indicates some important features related to the text he is considering. Thus his work is closely related to my study, which will develop the gymnasium as an ancient education model relevant to first-century Corinth. In chapter 6 I apply my model and interact with Braxton's valuable study.

This completes my review of New Testament scholars in relation to ancient education, the elite and 1 Corinthians. Doubtless there are other books that I could have considered. Nevertheless, this selection gives some indication of the ancient education models that scholars have used. There is now a move away from recognising an ancient education system that is universalistic and uniform. New Testament scholars need to recognise diversity and see how this impacts on our understanding of the educated elite in 1 Corinthians. New contributions to the history of ancient

130. For a review of Winter's book see David Runia, 'Review of *Philo and Paul Among the Sophists* by Bruce Winter', *EvQ* 72 (2000), pp. 89–91.

131. Winter, *Philo and Paul Among the Sophists: Alexandrian and Corinthian Responses*, p. x, citing Morgan, *Literate Education in the Hellenistic and Roman Worlds*.

132. Braxton, *The Tyranny of Resolution*, p. 3.

education can assist us in our quest here. I now turn to some new important contributions. These are used to inform my study and my questions.

5. *Histories of Ancient Greek and Roman Education*

a. *Education in Greek and Roman Antiquity:* Yun Lee Too (ed.)

New Testament scholars have rightly used histories of ancient education to help understand the cultural and social situation in Corinth when Paul established the church there. Included here is one work of particular distinction, i.e. Henri Irenée Marrou's comprehensive history.[133] Yun Lee Too regards this as '*the* authoritative history of ancient education'.[134] Although Too praises aspects of Marrou's history and summarises its main arguments she also effectively analyses its own history and shortcomings. *Education in Greek and Roman Antiquity* is a new history of Greek and Roman education. She admits that it is not the discoveries of new material that require a new history but the different questions we now ask. When we ask new questions about teaching and learning in antiquity she notes that the material now speaks in other ways to us. Marrou saw ancient education as confined to children and young men (occasionally women) in the home and/or school classroom but separate from adulthood, politics and power.[135] However, Too notes that in antiquity 'education' is concerned with *paideia*, which was a political issue. Thus she observes:

> In antiquity, education was not disinterested. It was a process of socialization, one that seeks above all to create the productive and loyal citizen with the aim of maintaining the community in a state of equilibrium. It was implicated in the structures of power, and specifically in training rulers to rule and the ruled to be ruled. It was largely an exclusive process, and birth and class, rather than ability ... were the operative criteria for determining who would be given training and 'knowledge'.[136]

Too's introduction helpfully locates the history of education in current scholarship, including our modern understanding of education and pedagogy. This new history of ancient education recognises the social and political components. In future, New Testament scholars will need to use this new history if they are to accurately address ancient education. My

133. Marrou, *A History of Education in Antiquity*.

134. Yun Lee Too, 'Introduction: Writing the History of Ancient Education', in Too (ed.), *Education in Greek and Roman Antiquity* (Leiden: E. J. Brill, 2001), pp. 1–21 (1).

135. Too, 'Introduction: Writing the History of Ancient Education', p. 10.

136. Too, 'Introduction: Writing the History of Ancient Education', p. 13.

study uses appropriate chapters although there is no single contribution on the Greek gymnasium.

Too's volume contains entries on Greek classical education that prepare the ground for Hellenistic and Roman education.[137] Elizabeth Asmis helpfully discusses education in Epicureanism. This consists of two education stages: basic (memorization of main doctrines with personal guidance) and advanced (developing the details of the doctrines).[138] Her focus on the basic stage shows diversity in ancient education. Epicurean philosophy's admission policy was to permit access to all (men and woman, slaves and masters, both the educated and uneducated, plus the poor and rich).[139] The education available is non-elitist but, nevertheless, only available to individuals and not the masses.[140] Epicureanism spread even into high society so that while Cicero spoke against it, other late Republican politicians were adherents. They could study the philosophy in Greece, learn from Greek philosophers living in Italy or obtain their own 'house philosophers'.[141] However, Epicureanism did not require any preparatory traditional education (this may badly affect the mind). Rather, 'Just as Epicurean education was intended for all, so it was intended to take the place of all other education. It was conceived as an alternative education, replacing both the traditional education and any other attempt at reform ... The Epicureans claimed that their education was the only real education'.[142] Again this demonstrates diversity in ancient education.

Raffaella Cribiore discusses the selection of Euripides' tragedy *Phoenissae* by grammarians in Hellenistic and Roman education.[143] She makes the important point that in antiquity the same texts were used at different levels of instruction starting at the elementary stage and finishing with learning rhetoric.[144] *Phoenissae* was popular as both a school text and with 'the cultivated public'.[145] She notes that Greeks could identify with its themes, e.g. exile, fatherland and power. They were, to some extent, exiles

137. For these entries see my chapter 3.

138. Asmis, 'Basic Education in Epicureanism', pp. 209–39.

139. Asmis, 'Basic Education in Epicureanism', p. 209. Only one distinction exists: those who want to learn philosophy and all others.

140. Asmis, 'Basic Education in Epicureanism', p. 210.

141. Asmis, 'Basic Education in Epicureanism', pp. 212–13.

142. Asmis, 'Basic Education in Epicureanism', pp. 214–15.

143. Raffaella Cribiore, 'The Grammarian's Choice: The Popularity of Euripides' *Phoenissae* in Hellenistic and Roman Education', in Too (ed.), *Education in Greek and Roman Antiquity*, pp. 241–59.

144. Cribiore, 'The Grammarian's Choice', p. 241.

145. Cribiore, 'The Grammarian's Choice', pp. 241–42. She goes on to explain the many reasons for its popularity in school and among readers after their school years were over. It addresses 'the royal house of Thebes'.

from their homeland, Greece. Education gave them a connection and a Greek identity.[146] They could associate with Polyneices' desire for his fatherland. Cribiore notes Polyneices' words, as he weeps, and sees 'the halls, the altars of the gods, the gymnasia where I was nurtured, and the streams of Dirke'.[147] Finally, Cribiore observes that the first part of *Phoenissae* used maxims (*gnômai*) for its development. As maxims were fundamental in ancient education, the tragedy provided a rich store for the grammarian to use with his mainly male pupils. Their ethical content was copied, memorized and developed during the pupils' education.[148] Paul uses maxims in 1 Corinthians. The important point about Cribiore's study is that the educated elite in 1 Corinthians will probably have been familiar with this literary text from their schooldays. Students would read and master the text in school and revisit it when the school years were completed, not because of nostalgia but because the training shaped tastes. Cribiore concludes, 'The popularity of the *Phoenissae* in and out of school is a further demonstration of the powerful ties that existed between *paideia* and ancient culture'.[149]

Three final articles should be briefly mentioned. First, Ruth Webb discusses the *progymnasmata*, which were preliminary exercises prior to studying rhetoric. This series of exercises bridged the gap between the study of grammar and texts, and writing and speaking.[150] Second, Robert Kaster discusses declamation in rhetorical education.[151] Third, Joy Connolly examines imperial Greek education and its selected use of the past.[152] She recognises that the learned man (*pepaideumenos*) has a consistency that depends upon the almost uniform teaching methods across the 'Greek-speaking empire'.[153] Although Too's history does not

146. Cribiore, 'The Grammarian's Choice', p. 246. She notes, 'Education provided people with a Greek identity to be used as a badge of belonging to a world of culture and privilege. While these Greeks in the Eastern world could not claim to be born in Greece and had very distant connections with it, nevertheless, they could speak a common tongue, read and write in an artificial Greek of the past, and follow the same aesthetic and ethical ideals promoted by the schools of grammar and rhetoric'.

147. Cribiore, 'The Grammarian's Choice', p. 247.

148. Cribiore, 'The Grammarian's Choice', pp. 248–49.

149. Cribiore, 'The Grammarian's Choice', p. 248.

150. Ruth Webb, 'The *Progymnasmata* as Practice', in Too (ed.), *Education in Greek and Roman Antiquity*, pp. 289–316 (289). The exercise range may go from recounting a mythological episode, addressing an anecdote, and a developed argument for or against something like 'one should marry'. Webb notes the *progymnasmata* were 'crucial in laying the foundations for elite discourse' (p. 290) and 'a first step towards ... the competitive culture of declamation' (p. 291).

151. Kaster, 'Controlling Reason, pp. 317–37.

152. Connolly, 'The Problems of the Past in Imperial Greek Education'.

153. Connolly, 'The Problems of the Past in Imperial Greek Education', p. 348. This is the teaching of the liberal arts, termed the *egkyklios paideia*.

have a chapter on the Greek gymnasium the various contributions serve to make the reader sensitive to issues in the history of education and inform my study.

b. *Literate Education in the Hellenistic and Roman Worlds*: Teresa Morgan

Another recent important history of education is Teresa Morgan's *Literate Education in the Hellenistic and Roman Worlds*. Her study of education focuses on literary texts and papyri from Graeco-Roman Egypt.[154] She notes that literary and numerate education were considered a separate category within educational practice. They were addressed separately to physical education. However, she justifies her selection of only literary education for her work. Hence, she focuses on literature, grammar and rhetoric. Importantly she compares literary texts and the papyri to see where they coincide or diverge depending on social groups.[155] She argues for a new model distinct from the 'curricular model' as portrayed by Bonner and Marrou. This is the 'core' and 'periphery' model.[156] Everyone could not learn the entire 'curriculum' but would cover what was in the 'core'. 'It includes what most people learned, what they learned first and, in the case of reading, what they went on practising longest'.[157] The 'periphery' includes all things not in the 'core' but this is not homogenous. However, even with the 'periphery' some areas are more central then others. She notes the function of this education, '"Core and periphery" education performed two social tasks very efficiently. It constituted a mechanism for the admission of cultured non-Greeks or non-Romans into Greek or Roman cultural groups, while simultaneously controlling the numbers admitted'.[158] Morgan shows us that ancient education has a purpose but we must not assume that its aims were the same as in the modern Western world. Its aims were different. I shall use insights from Morgan's perceptive work in my study.

c. *Gymnastics of the Mind: Greek Education in Hellenistic and Roman Egypt*: R. Cribiore

Cribiore examines Greek education over a long time period in Egypt, but throws light on educational practices elsewhere in the Mediterranean. She also investigates literary education from primary level up to rhetorical study (from about aged seven to eighteen) noting, 'In antiquity, education served well the interests of the elite and the preservation of the hierarchical

154. Morgan, *Literate Education*, pp. 4–6.
155. Morgan, *Literate Education*, p. 6.
156. Morgan, *Literate Education*, pp. 67–73.
157. Morgan, *Literate Education*, p. 71.
158. Morgan, *Literate Education*, p. 74.

status quo'.[159] Again, this recent study will be used to enrich my focus on the Greek gymnasium and its relevance to the conflict and social status issues in 1 Corinthians.

6. *Summary*

This chapter examined different ancient education models used by New Testament scholars for the exegesis of 1 Corinthians. In my analysis some diversity in the identity and application of models was seen. One area of weakness was the acceptance by some scholars of 'Graeco-Roman' models which assume that Greek and Roman education were identical in the first century AD. Earlier modern histories of education, and related works, explain that Rome took over Greek education and a universal system of education existed across the Empire. While there is some truth in this universality, it remains the case that diversity is also evident in our period.

The traditional three-tier, or three-stage, model of education expounded by Marrou, and other scholars, has been criticised by Booth and Kaster. Indeed, Kaster maintains that the organisation of schools in the Empire did not regularly conform to this sequence. Moreover, 'the assumption of a normal differentiation between schools described as "primary" and "secondary" is seriously flawed'.[160] The existence of a socially segmented two-tier, or two-track, model was demonstrated by Kaster who comments that the 'school of letters' provided the lower classes with a basic literacy, while 'liberal schools' provided more cultured children with more advanced skills. Nevertheless, Kaster does not wish to exchange one overly-generalised scheme for another. He believes that both systems operated, and diversity is the most typical feature of ancient education.[161]

However, some New Testament scholars continue to use the three-stage system as a universal situation in their Corinthian studies without any awareness of the diversity in the Empire. Winter refers to the work of Kaster and notes that his own method is part of the diversity he identified. Winter demonstrates that for investigating the situation in 1 Corinthians valuable ancient education models can be identified and applied. He traces Paul's opponents in 1 and 2 Corinthians to the sophistic movement in the first century AD and people educated in Greek *paideia*. Brad Braxton, although he does not discuss ancient education models as

159. Raffaella Cribiore, *Gymnastics of the Mind: Greek Education in Hellenistic and Roman Egypt* (Princeton and Oxford: Princeton University Press, 2001), p. 9. She has published a number of works on ancient education.

160. Kaster, 'Notes on "Primary" and "Secondary" Schools', p. 346.

161. Kaster, 'Notes on "Primary" and "Secondary" Schools', p. 346.

such, assumes the relevance of the gymnasium in Corinth for exegesis of 1 Corinthians.

Finally, I discussed new histories of education and how these recent works can assist us in understanding ancient education more sensitively than just seeing it as a universalistic and uniform system. I shall draw upon the insights they provide in my study.

However, New Testament studies highlight the importance of the Greek education system and its relationship to Roman education in understanding Graeco-Roman society. Nevertheless, the emphasis on 'Graeco-Roman' education and sameness has been costly, for it has robbed New Testament scholars of a more sensitive analysis of education, and its diversity, in the Empire that should be applied to the exegesis of 1 Corinthians. My contribution to this diversity is the Greek gymnasium education, which was available in the first century AD. I investigate this in my next chapter.

Part II

The Greek Gymnasium, Education and the Ancient World

Chapter 3

THE GREEK GYMNASIUM AND THE CORINTHIAN CHRISTIANS

1. *Introduction*

In Part I (Chapters 1 and 2) I surveyed how New Testament scholarship had identified social-status issues and the educated elite in 1 Corinthians. I also reviewed ancient education models and identified the omission of the Greek gymnasium from these models. This chapter rectifies this deficiency by considering how the elite believers in the Corinthian church could have received a gymnasium education. The focus is on aspects that are relevant to a sensitive interpretation of Paul's letter, and its educational language, but largely ignored by the scholarship.[1] The Greek gymnasium must not be confused with the modern western gymnasium, for although there are similarities, in the provision of sports facilities, there are substantial differences.

This chapter begins by examining the development of the gymnasium to locate it historically in the New Testament world. A section considers gymnasiarchs, ephebes, and the *neoi*. After this general introduction I consider three routes by which residents at Corinth, and hence church members, may have received education in the gymnasium. I consider Corinth's gymnasia and then mobility within the Graeco-Roman world. People educated outside Corinth may become residents or Corinthian residents could send their sons away for a gymnasium education. Finally, my chapter uses the analytical tools developed by John Barclay to investigate the Greek gymnasium, education and the Diaspora Jews.[2] Although the Corinthian church contained gentiles, its Jewish component

1. I use the word 'largely' because in chapter 2 I showed that Bruce W. Winter discusses Epictetus, the visit of the Corinthian student of rhetoric and the gymnasium. There I referred to his *Philo and Paul Among the Sophists*. He again refers to this incident in his *After Paul Left Corinth*, pp. 33–34. In his earlier work, *Seek the Welfare of the City*, pp. 145–52, Winter also discusses circumcision, the gymnasium and social mobility. The relationship of circumcision and the gymnasium has also been analysed by Braxton, *The Tyranny of Resolution*. These issues are considered in chapter 6.

2. As given in Barclay, *Jews in the Mediterranean Diaspora*.

must not be ignored. This section examines the evidence for Jewish involvement in Greek education and forms an integral part of the chapter. Its location is determined by the prior need to consider the Greek gymnasium historically, and its relevance to the Corinthian church, before investigating Jewish responses to the institution. I demonstrate that the gymnasium is an important educational institution primarily for the male social elite, whether Greeks, Romans or Jews. Although gymnasium education is an aspect largely neglected by New Testament critics, this chapter demonstrates the relevance of the Greek gymnasium model for understanding 1 Corinthians, and therefore fills this lacuna within the scholarship. Chapter 4 builds on my model of the Greek gymnasium by considering education in relation to family and society.

It is essential to consider these aspects if scholars are not to distort the ancient world by claiming that Corinth was a 'Roman' city. Corinth, in the Greek East, did not stand in total isolation from Greek culture, or its own historic past. Therefore claims that it was 'Roman', implying, if not explicitly stating, that it did not have significant relationships with Greek culture are surely too restrictive. Now Corinth was a Roman colony, yet arguments advanced for the 'Roman' city are not proof that Greek institutions have no relevance to Corinth, and especially to the Corinthian church. By emphasising the Roman aspects of Corinth, scholars mistakenly marginalize its Greek inheritance and, unfortunately, exclude this aspect from an exegesis of Paul's letter.[3]

2. *Development of the Gymnasium*

a. *The Archaic and Classical Periods*

The aim of this section is to introduce the beginning of the Greek gymnasium. It is not to discuss ancient Greek education in detail – that would be too long a task and deviate from describing my model. Scholars frequently use Marrou's monumental work because he examines Greek education from Homeric times to the Hellenistic age but my introduction

3. Tomlin, 'Christians and Epicureans in 1 Corinthians', while arguing for the arrival of Epicureanism with the original colonists, acknowledges the shift in identity when he states, 'Donald Engel's study of Roman Corinth points to the shift in ethnic and cultural identity from Roman (Latin) to Greek which took place in Corinth through the middle of the first century. He shows how the original social élite of the city, arriving in the new colony from Rome, tried to resist this process of Hellenization' (p. 54). He cites Donald Engels, *Roman Corinth: An Alternative Model for the Classical City* (Chicago and London: The University of Chicago, 1990), p. 73. However, see Jason König, 'Favorinus' *Corinthian Oration*', p. 146, for his concerns over Engel's reconstruction. See my earlier comments on Greek and Roman Corinth in chapter 1.

does not require a full historical examination.[4] Marrou's work has recently been updated so that Yun Lee Too (ed.) *Education in Greek and Roman Antiquity* provides substantial contributions on early Greek education and Teresa Morgan also addresses classical education. Interested readers should consult these works.[5] I do not wish to give the impression that the gymnasium was the totality of Greek education, as the contributions in Too show there was change, variety, restrictions and debate. Nevertheless, I focus on the beginnings of the gymnasium to put my study in its socio-historical context.

In examining the gymnasium it is important to recognise that the ancient terms 'gymnasium' and 'palaestra' are not identical. There is some fluidity in the terminology in both ancient and modern usage. My Appendix clarifies these issues. The institution of the gymnasium was founded in the early sixth century BC although the only gymnasia of this period that scholars know about are in Athens: the Academy, the Lyceum and the Kynosarges.[6] In the fourth century BC the Academy reached its height, after Plato founded his school here. Olga Tzachou-Alexandri notes, 'The fame of the Academy continued, as one may conclude from an honorary decree of 122/1 BC (*IG* II^2, 1006, 1.20) in which the ephebes of the preceding year are praised for their contribution for instruction in philosophy. The Academy is mentioned for the last time by Cicero.'[7] In the fourth century BC Aristotle founded his school at the Lyceum and Antisthenes founded the Cynic philosophical school at the Cynosarges.

4. H.-I. Marrou, *A History of Education in Antiquity*, pp. 3–15.

5. Yun Lee Too (ed.), *Education in Greek and Roman Antiquity* (Leiden: E.J. Brill, 2001). On early Greek education see the contributions: Mark Griffith, '"Public" and "Private" in Early Greek Institutions of Education', pp. 23–84; Andrew Ford, 'Sophists Without Rhetoric: The Arts of Speech in Fifth-Century Athens', pp. 85–109; Yun Lee Too, 'Legal Instructions in Classical Athens', pp. 111–32; Andrea Wilson Nightingale, 'Liberal Education in Plato's *Republic* and Aristotle's *Politics*', pp. 133–73; Josiah Ober, 'The Debate Over Civic Education in Classical Athens', pp. 175–207. Morgan, *Literate Education in the Hellenistic and Roman Worlds*, pp. 9–21 and Teresa Morgan, 'Literate Education in Classical Athens', *ClQ* 49 (1999), pp. 46–61.

6. Olga Tzachou-Alexandri, 'The Gymnasium. An Institution for Athletics and Education', in Tzachou-Alexandri (ed.), *Mind and Body: Athletic Contests in Ancient Greece* (trans. Judith Binder, Timothy Cullen, *et al.*; Athens: Ministry of Culture – the National Hellenic Committee I.C.O.M., 1989), pp. 31–40 (32).

7. Tzachou-Alexandri, 'The Gymnasium', p. 32. She does not expand on precisely what was 'their contribution for instruction in philosophy.' For a translation of *IG* II^2.1006 see Stephen G. Miller, *Arete: Greek Sports from Ancient Sources* (Berkeley, Los Angeles, Oxford: University of California Press, 2nd ed., 1991), no. 128, pp. 140–45. This inscription is in three main parts (a) a decree honouring the *epheboi* for 123/2 BC with mention of most of the teachers, (b) a decree honouring the *kosmetes* for that year, and (c) a list of *epheboi* who have become Athenian citizens. Miller notes that the total number of *epheboi* was 58 and they had at least 32 instructors: 'kosmetes, didaskaloi, *swordsmen, archer, etc*'. (p. 145).

Thus all three gymnasia in Athens were used in the fourth century BC as schools of philosophy. As chapter 2 demonstrates, New Testament scholars who trace the threads of rhetoric from Athens to first-century Corinth miss this connection with the gymnasia. However, as Mark Griffith observes, in the context of the spread of schools, boys could receive physical training in a gymnasium or palaistra but 'by no means every community boasted a separate *gymnasion or palaistra* before the 4th or 3rd C'.[8] The Greek city (*polis*), from the fourth century onwards, often appointed officials with responsibilities for overseeing ephebes and young athletes on their 'training and moral well-being'.[9]

Athens provided ephebic training for young men who were potential citizens. Aristotle describes the selection, supervision, training and responsibilities of these young men.[10] The emphasis is on the military needs of the state and the ephebes are required to provide guard duty for two years. After this period they become full citizens. Nevertheless, changes occurred over time, as Josiah Ober notes, the *ephêbeia* was reformed in 335/4 BC. Prior to the 330s young citizens acted as border-guards but from 335/4, the *ephêbeia* included more education. The city provided two years 'military education and moral training' for Athenian males aged eighteen.[11] How many ephebes were there in each class? John Dillery, in discussing the location for drilling of ephebes in Athens, notes that Habicht estimates 500 young men per ephebic class.[12] But this is when service was compulsory. After 307 BC attendance was not compulsory and so the numbers decreased 'and the Ephebeia developed into the aristocratic institution so familiar and widespread in the Hellenistic period'.[13] So let us consider the gymnasium in the Hellenistic and Roman periods.

8. Griffith, '"Public" and "Private" in Early Greek Institutions of Education', pp. 66–67.

9. Griffith, '"Public" and "Private" in Early Greek Institutions of Education', p. 66. He identifies the officials as *didaskaloi* = 'teachers', *sôphronistês* = 'supervisor' and *kosmetês* = 'keeper-of-order' (p. 55).

10. Miller, *Arete*, no. 127, pp. 139–40. Aristotle's *Constitution of the Athenians* 42, dated *c.* 325 BC. For Aristotle's view on education see Miller, *Arete*, no. 130, pp. 147–50, on Aristotle, *Politics* 1337a–1339a, *c.* 325 BC. See also Nightingale, 'Liberal Education in Plato's *Republic* and Aristotle's *Politics*', pp. 133–73.

11. Ober, 'The Debate Over Civic Education in Classical Athens', pp. 202–4.

12. John Dillery, 'Ephebes in the Stadium (not the Theatre): *Ath. Pol.* 42.4 and *IG* II^2.351', *ClQ* 52 (2002), pp. 462–70. He cites Christian Habicht, *Athens from Alexander to Antony* (trans. Deborah Lucas Schneider; Cambridge, MA and London: Harvard University Press, 1997), p. 24.

13. Dillery, 'Ephebes in the Stadium (not the Theatre)', p. 463 n. 10. See also Griffith, '"Public" and "Private" in Early Greek Institutions of Education', p. 55, who states on the Athenian *ephêbeia*, 'By the 3rd and 2nd C., it became little more than a prep-school for the wealthy (even including some non-Athenians), with gym and school-rooms'. He cites Marrou, *A History of Education in Antiquity*, pp. 105–12.

b. *The Hellenistic and Roman Periods*

If gymnasia existed in the classical period what was the situation in the Hellenistic age? Richard Billows observes that the Hellenistic era was an important period for Greek cities.[14] Geographically there was an enormous expansion with several hundred new cities stretching from western Asia eastwards to modern Afghanistan and Pakistan. The size of the Greek cities increased from the classical period. Moreover, Billows notes that the Hellenistic cities modelled themselves on classical Athens regarding language, culture, physical infrastructure and their institutions. Citing Dio Chrysostom (*Or*. 48.9) and Pausanias (10.4.1), Billows lists the requirements for a city (*polis*): surrounding walls, a monumentally defined *agora*, a theatre, at least one *gymnasion*, stoas, fountain houses, a council house and/or *prytaneion* (town hall). Various administrative offices were held including that of the *gymnasiarchos* (head of gymnasium).[15] Royal letters illustrate how a Hellenistic king, King Eumenes II, granted recognition of a *polis*. The inhabitants of the Toriaians requested the right to become a *polis*. The king agrees to their request 'that a *polis* constitution be granted to you, and your own laws, and a gymnasium, and as many things as consistent with these'.[16]

Billows discusses three cities: Priene (a moderate size town), Ephesus (a large important city) and Pergamon (a royal city).[17] Ancient Priene was an Ionian city that moved to a new site at the end of the classical period and the beginning of the Hellenistic. This very early Hellenistic city lost importance in the early Roman period, was abandoned in antiquity and left undisturbed. It has little Roman building upon it and the excavated site is 'an almost perfectly undisturbed Hellenistic city'. Priene had two gymnasia. Billows' figures show a reconstruction of Priene with the large gymnasium located at the south wall.[18] The large outside running track has spectators' seats on one side. Ephesus had four Roman gymnasia but Billows states that several continue the Hellenistic gymnasia. At Pergamon, he notes the 'gymnasium complex', commenting:

14. Richard Billows, 'Cities', in Erskine (ed.), *A Companion to the Hellenistic World* (Oxford: Blackwell Publishing, 2003), pp. 196–215.

15. Billows, 'Cities', p. 197.

16. Roger Bagnall and Peter Derow (eds.), *The Hellenistic Period: Historical Sources in Translation* (Oxford: Blackwell Publishing, 2nd edn, 2004), pp. 80–81. Tyriaion was in rural Phrygia (Asia Minor) and the letters were written after 188 BC. Eumenes II was an Attalid ruler (in Pergamon) from 197–157 BC (p. 291). He ruled by authority of the Romans, as his letter indicates. (Note that Scholars Press published the first edition of this book in 1981 as *Greek Historical Documents: The Hellenistic Period.*)

17. All three cities are in modern Turkey.

18. Billows, 'Cities', pp. 200–3. Priene has a gymnasium at the city centre and the large second gymnasium by the city wall. His Figures 12.1 (a plan) and 12.2 (a reconstruction) show the large gymnasium/stadium.

> The three-part gymnasium is one of the most remarkable structures of Pergamon. The upper gymnasium, the largest and most elaborate of the three, was for general use by the 'young men' of Pergamon, while separate gymnasia were provided for youths (the middle gymnasium), and boys (lower gymnasium), which probably doubled as schools for the youngsters of the citizen class.[19]

Much of the upper gymnasium's architecture is Roman. Billows concludes by emphasizing the idea of the Greek city in the Hellenistic Era. This idea was striven for as a reality. His final piece of evidence relates this to the gymnasium, 'It has long been pointed out that in the Hellenistic period the gymnasium became the most characteristic institution of social and cultural life in the cities, that frequenting the gymnasium was the hallmark – the *sine qua non* almost – of the Greek citizen'.[20] In the early second century BC the town Beroia (in Macedonia) established a law to regulate the gymnasium. Why did they do this? They became aware that other Greek cities had such laws and they needed one so that their city could conform to the ideal.[21]

F.W. Walbank also discusses the expansion of Greek cities and the importance of the gymnasium. On Ptolemaic Egypt he remarks:

> The usual Greek aloofness was reinforced by addiction to the gymnasium... which was not only the centre of their education, where as adolescents they studied Greek literature, rhetoric and mathematics, as well as physical training, but also the focus of their social life and culture. Gymnasia existed in Alexandria and also in the nome capitals and even in the countryside.[22]

Walbank mentions the excavated gymnasium in Ai Khanum (Afghanistan) while Robin Lane Fox includes a photograph of the large exedra.[23] This recess has benches against its walls. Here philosophers and other teachers

19. Billows, 'Cities', p. 208. His Figure 12.5 (a plan) shows the location of the gymnasium (p. 207). For a slightly more detailed plan of Pergamon showing the upper, middle and lower gymnasium see Peter Levi, *Atlas of the Greek World* (Oxford: Phaidon, 1984), pp. 188–89 (188). Pergamon is well-worth visiting, especially to see the remains of the gymnasia. The tourist guide Fatih Cimok, *Pergamum* (Istanbul: A Turizm Yayinlari, 1999), with its coloured photographs, shows the grandeur of the gymnasia.

20. Billows, 'Cities', p. 213.

21. As Billows observes this inscription is preserved. I discuss it further below.

22. F.W. Walbank, *The Hellenistic World* (Fontana History of the Ancient World; London: Fontana Press, 3rd impression, 1992), p. 117.

23. Walbank, *The Hellenistic World*, p. 61 and Robin Lane Fox, 'Hellenistic Culture and Literature' in Boardman, Griffin and Murray (eds.), *The Oxford History of the Classical World* (Oxford and New York: Oxford University Press, 1986), pp. 338–64 (340). The gymnasium is late second century BC.

instructed the young men. Lane Fox notes that the *gymnasion* shows Greek culture spread to remote parts of the Hellenistic world.

François Chamoux also identifies the gymnasium as essential to Hellenistic city life and its importance 'cannot be overestimated'. He helpfully describes its arrangement:

> It housed first and foremost a palaestra, a specialized building that grouped around a large quadrangular court changing rooms, training rooms, sanitary installations, as wells as exedras, open courtyards providing benches for relaxation and conversation, even lecture halls. Close to the palaestra was an open-air running track, twinned with a covered one for use in bad weather: both were one *stadion* (about 190 meters) long. Depending on circumstances, a stadium for competitions was provided near the gymnasium. Finally, it happened occasionally that, as at Delphi, an open-air swimming pool was added to these facilities; but scarcity of water did not allow such a facility to be offered in many locations, in Greece proper at least. On the other hand, bathrooms were found as a rule in every gymnasium, often provided with troughs for washing one's feet.[24]

Chamoux provides an overview of the gymnasia in Athens. By the Hellenistic era Athens had five gymnasia. To the three ancient gymnasia (the Lyceum, the Academy and the Cynosarges) were added the Gymnasium of Ptolemy and the Gymnasium of Diogenes. He notes that the Gymnasium of Diogenes focused on 'literary and scientific studies'. This gymnasium continued beyond New Testament times into the third century AD. Interestingly, Chamoux observes that at the start of the second century AD Plutarch saw Ammonius 'subjecting ephebes who studied there to tests in literature, geometry, rhetoric and music'.[25] Thus Chamoux summaries, 'The gymnasium was thus a teaching institution, a place for relaxation and human contact, and a group of buildings and facilities intended for the practice of physical exercise'.[26]

What impact did such Hellenization have on Jewish culture in Palestine? In his discussion Erich S. Gruen argues that in the second century BC the Greek gymnasium was introduced in Jerusalem not as a compromise but on the initiative of the Jewish High Priest. Moreover, 'other Jewish priests soon found themselves in the palaestra, engaging in physical exercise and exploiting the institution to their advantage (2 Macc. 4.9). They evidently

24. François Chamoux, *Hellenistic Civilization* (trans. Michel Roussel in cooperation with Margaret Roussel; Oxford: Blackwell Publishing, 2003), pp. 293–95.

25. Chamoux, *Hellenistic Civilization*, p. 297. He cites Plutarch, *Mor*. 736d. Chamoux observes that the five gymnasia were not limited to athletics but the three ancient gymnasia were 'each the birthplace of a great philosophical tradition.' Sulla's army destroyed the Academy during his siege in 87/6 BC.

26. Chamoux, *Hellenistic Civilization*, pp. 297–98.

did not regard this activity as undermining their priestly duties for the Temple. The notion of an irreconcilable cultural conflict needs to be abandoned.'[27] He sees no confrontation between Hellenism and Hebraism. Jason the High Priest, introduced the gymnasium and ephebate and these continued with Judas Maccabaeus, his brothers and successors.[28] Gruen notes that Herod the Great built at least three gymnasia in Palestine (Jos. *Ant.* 15.268–271, 15.341, 17.194).[29] He also discusses Jewish involvement in the gymnasium in the Diaspora, which I address later.

Gruen aptly comments, 'The gymnasium marked the capstone of higher education in Greek cities all around the Mediterranean and beyond. That institution, with its attendant corps of ephebes, the select youth of upper echelon families, signalled the cultural and intellectual elite of the Hellenistic world.'[30] However, we should not think of Greek cities and gymnasia in isolation. Athletes who trained in the gymnasia participated in local contests and travelled to international contests where they competed for prizes and glory as Walbank illustrates with an inscription that shows the different categories of events.[31]

By the Hellenistic period the gymnasium had developed into the main education centre where philosophy was taught. Clarence Forbes observes:

> In the Hellenistic age the gymnasium flourished to an extraordinary degree in Egypt and Asia Minor as well as in Greece proper, and for the most part it was utilized for both intellectual and gymnastic purposes. The saying of Salvianus was applicable in this period and later: 'Colitur et honoratur Minerva in gymnasiis.' Vitruvius includes spacious exedrae, with seats for the accommodation of professors and students, as a regular part of the floor plan of the typical, fully elaborated Greek gymnasium.[32]

James Bowen comments that in the Hellenistic East racial penetration, initiated by Alexander the Great, proved attractive to many indigenes, including the Jews. The term 'Greek' now became cultural and this shared

27. Erich S. Gruen, 'Jews and Greeks', in Erskine (ed.), *A Companion to the Hellenistic World*, pp. 264–79 (264–65). He is speaking of cultural conflict between Jews and Greeks.

28. Gruen, 'Jews and Greeks', p. 269. He qualifies his comment on continuity with 'so far as the evidence goes'. However, for a view on conflict see Christopher D. Stanley, ' "Neither Jew nor Greek" '.

29. Gruen, 'Jews and Greeks', p. 275.

30. Gruen, 'Jews and Greeks', p. 274.

31. Walbank, *The Hellenistic World*, pp. 71–2. I discuss athletes below and in chapter 5.

32. Forbes, 'Expanded Uses', p. 34. Miller, *Arete*, no. 121, pp. 121–22, explains that Vitruvius was an architect whose treatise *On Architecture* 5.11 (dated ca. 28 BC) describes the gymnasium. Miller notes that Vitruvius' description is very similar to the palaestra-gymnasium at Olympia (third century BC). The translation explains the layout, functions and the use of the Greek terms.

culture depended on Greek education. The *ephebeia* became the way to citizenship. He remarks:

> The gymnasion was a prominent and important building and we have either documentary evidence or the remains of twenty-nine gymnasia that were constructed in the Hellenistic Orient before the birth of Christ. Higher education and the ephebeia were centred in the gymnasion, which was in effect the only architectural institution the Greeks ever devised for the purpose of education. In its architecture the gymnasion was unchanged from that of earlier centuries: the open-air palaistra was the centre around which was constructed a roofed, colonnaded walk, forming a square or rectangle, and within which were the various rooms used for storing equipment, for oiling and massaging. The exhedrae – spacious recesses – were set aside for philosophers and rhetors. Only one further development seems to have occurred: in some cases the baths were heated.[33]

Bowen thus indicates the importance of the gymnasium. However, the architecture did change over the centuries. Donald Kyle notes that the earliest 'gymnasia' were simply sites used by athletes and these predate the architectural development noted by Delorme and the earliest known architectural remains.[34] He distinguishes between the 'rudimentary' or 'pre-architectural gymnasium' with space for a δρόμις and παλαίστρα for open air exercising but no fixed constructions and the 'architectural gymnasium', which refers to sites enclosed by walls and subdivided by fixed constructions into specialised areas.[35] However, by New Testament times architectural gymnasia had been established for centuries.[36]

The Younger Pliny is a witness to the rebuilding of an architectural gymnasium in the early second century AD. In his letter (*Ep.* 10.39.) to the Emperor Trajan he comments:

> The citizens of Nicaea have also begun to rebuild their gymnasium (which was destroyed by fire before my arrival) on a much larger and more extensive scale than before. They have already spent a large sum, which may be to little purpose, for the buildings are badly planned and too scattered. Moreover, an architect – admittedly a rival of the one who

33. James Bowen, *A History of Western Education*. Vol. 1. *The Ancient World: Orient and Mediterranean 2000 B.C. – A.D. 1054* (London: Methuen & Co Ltd, 1972), p. 159.

34. Donald G. Kyle, *Athletics in Ancient Athens* (Leiden: E.J. Brill, 1987), p. 66.

35. Kyle, *Athletics in Ancient Athens*, p. 66.

36. Onno M. van Nijf observes that pre-Hellenistic gymnasia did not need much in the way of buildings, in the Roman period gymnasia tended to be built up, but not always. Personal communication. Reproduced with kind permission. See Jean Delorme, *Gymnasion. Étude sur les monuments consacrés à l'éducation en Grèce (des origines à l'Empire romain)* (BEFAR, 196; Paris: E. De Boccard, 1960), Plates I-XLI (Figures 1–68) for helpful examples of the locations and styles of gymnasia. Figure 6 shows the location of the gymnasium in Corinth during the Roman period. It is north of the theatre near the Asklepieion.

> drew up the designs – has given the opinion that the walls cannot support the superstructure in spite of being twenty-two feet thick, as the rubble core has no facing of brick.[37]

Trajan's brief reply (*Ep.* 10.40) shows Greek devotion to the gymnasium, 'These poor Greeks all love a gymnasium; so it may be that they were too ambitious in their plans at Nicaea. They will have to be content with one which suits their real needs'.[38] Thus the Greek gymnasium was important in the Hellenistic and Roman periods. What were its typical features?

c. *The Greek Gymnasium: Typical Features*

Tzachou-Alexandri describes typical features of the gymnasium and an outline of them is appropriate to avoid anachronistic misinterpretations based on modern conceptions of a gymnasium.[39] She notes that the earliest preserved example with 'all the features of a fully developed gymnasium' is the one at Delphi (dated the last third of the fourth century BC).[40] The palaestra (παλαίστρα) is a central courtyard enclosed by porticoes (i.e. a peristyle court) and at the back are the main, and auxiliary, rooms. There is a covered running track called the *xystos* (χυστός) and the open air running track called the *paradromis* (παραδρομίς or δρόμις). These are parallel to each other. The bath is a large circular reservoir in the open air. Training in the palaestra covered the 'heavy' sports: wrestling, boxing and the *pankration* (a combination of boxing and wrestling). The so-called 'light' sports (track events) used the gymnasium.[41]

In the palaestra the most important room was the *konisterion* (κονιστήριον), which was used mainly for wrestling but also for *pankration*. The floor had a thick layer of fine sand to avoid injuries. The athletes

37. Translation by Betty Radice, *The Letters of the Younger Pliny* (London: Penguin Books, reprinted 1969), p. 273. Pliny represented Trajan in Bithynia and Pontus, a province by the Black Sea. Nicaea was one of the cities. He opens his letter explaining that the theatre at Nicaea was being built but there were structural and cost problems.

38. Radice, *The Letters of the Younger Pliny*, p. 274.

39. The following description uses Tzachou-Alexandri's article with her transliterated Greek terms. I add the Greek in brackets after the first use of the transliterated word. Her description covers the period from the pre-Classical to the Roman era. She uses literary sources, inscriptions, representations from art and data from excavated gymnasia. A more detailed description of the gymnasium is provided by Delorme, *Gymnasion*, pp. 324–36, in the important chapter XI, 'Le Gymnase, Institution Intellectuelle'. Tzachou-Alexandri cites Delorme in her bibliography.

40. Tzachou-Alexandri, 'The Gymnasium', p. 34. See her photograph of the model of the Gymnasium at Delphi (by the French Archaeological School at Athens) in the Roman era (p. 38). For a plan of the location of the Gymnasium at Delphi and a photograph of the excavated remains see Olivier Picard, 'Delphi and The Pythian Games', in Tzachou-Alexandri (ed.), *Mind and Body*, pp. 69–81 (70–71).

41. Tzachou-Alexandri, 'The Gymnasium', p. 35.

maintained this area to ensure it was suitable for their matches. It seems that pankratiasts and boxers used separate rooms. These were called the *korykeion* (κωρυκεῖον) and the *sphairisterion* (σφαιριστήριον) respectively. Before wrestling the athletes rubbed their body with oil for hygienic reasons. However, Michael Carter notes that Dickie has shown that besides the gymnasium and palaestra being used for heavy sports (boxing, the pancratium or wrestling) they did include events for inculcating 'beauty of form and graceful, elegant movement in the youth'.[42] In earlier gymnasia, a room called the *apodyterion* was used. This has been identified in Delphi and it is reported in the accounts. Originally the room was an assembly place for those who provided religious ceremonies. Many activities occurred here but by Hellenistic times it lost connection with intellectual activities and became a cloakroom.[43]

Tzachou-Alexandri discusses the term *elaiothesion* (only mentioned by Vitruvius), which appears to be a room for distributing oil. Originally athletes provided their own oil but eventually gymnasiarchs supplied the oil. The *aleipterion* (ἀλειπτήριον) was a heated room for applying oil. However, the word was linked to the citizens who used the gymnasium, as C.P. Jones discusses in relation to an Ephesian Greek inscription by the citizens in honour of Atticus.[44] Jones observes that the inscription, which begins:

> 'The citizens who anoint themselves in the *aleipterion*' must be similar to the *aleiphomenoi* found in many gymnasial inscriptions, that is, those who used the athletic facilities of the gymnasium in question as opposed to the educational ones. *Aleipteria* are often mentioned as rooms or divisions of gymnasia dedicated to the distribution of olive-oil, that cherished commodity of Greek life which was inseparable from athletics and civilized living in general; in the course of time, the word *aleipterion* comes to be used of the whole gymnasium, as may already be true here.[45]

42. Michael Carter, 'A *Doctor Secutorum* and the *Retiarius* Draukos from Corinth', *ZPE* 126 (1999), pp. 262–68 (267). He uses M. Dickie, 'Παλαιστρίτης / "palaestrita": Callisthenics in the Greek and Roman Gymnasium', *Nikephoros* 6 (1993), pp. 118–20.

43. Tzachou-Alexandri, 'The Gymnasium', p. 36.

44. C.P. Jones, 'Atticus in Ephesus', *ZPE* 124 (1999), pp. 89–94 (89). Jones notes the inscription, from a marble statue-base, was published by Mustafa Büyükklolancı and Helmut Engelmann, 'Inschriften aus Ephesos', *ZPE* 86 (1991), pp. 137–44 (142 no. 8 with Plate 10). It is *SEG* 41.964. The citizens from the gymnasium honour a certain Atticus for his benefactions. Jones argues that this Atticus is the friend of Cicero (106–43 BC). The inscription recognises Atticus (a Roman citizen) as a prefect 'of the deified Caesar and his heir' (i.e. Julius Caesar and Octavian). Jones (pp. 92–93) also observes that Atticus collected objects to furnish Cicero's gymnasium in his villa and was a friend of Mark Antony (a gymnasiarch – see below), thus showing his association with gymnasia.

45. Jones, 'Atticus in Ephesus', p. 89, who notes that Atticus' benefactions could be provision of oil (or a subsidy for it) or something for the building/ornamentation of the *aleipterion*. He references for the *aleipterion*, C. Foss, ''Ἀλειπτήριον', *GRBS* 16 (1975), pp. 217–26.

From the start baths were provided and swimming pools may be available. Hellenistic gymnasia have inscriptions referring to a *pyriaterion*, which Tzachou-Alexandri identifies as a type of steam bath.[46]

The *akroaterion* (ἀκροατήριον) was a hall designed for lectures (*akroaseis*, ἀκροάσεις), although in most gymnasia it was called the *exedra* (ἐχέδρα). These first appear in the third century BC and many inscriptions refer to them, as does Vitruvius. Tzachou-Alexandri remarks, 'Philosophers and rhetoricians taught there. Names of young men who attended courses of instruction were written in the palaestra at Priene. The *exedra* is a hall of considerable size with a facade of columns and it is equipped with benches. It is located in the palaestra building behind the porticoes'.[47] The *ephebeion* (ἐφηβαῖον), a developed form of the *exedra*, is the largest room and had benches.[48]

The *paidagogeion* (παιδαγωγεῖον) is located in the palaestra on Delos and elsewhere. This is usually considered to be the place where the *paidagogoi* (παιδαγωγοί) waited for the boys they escorted to and from home. Tzachou-Alexandri notes that it is difficult to identify the area because it has no distinguishing features.[49] In 1 Cor. 4.15 Paul contrasts his position in the church, as 'father,' with those who are παιδαγωγοί. Both the construction of gymnasia and Paul's letter maintain a social distinction. Libraries are attested at later gymnasia. They became indispensable components and in imperial Roman times their numbers increased. 'Groves, brooks and springs' surrounded gymnasia.[50]

46. Tzachou-Alexandri, 'The Gymnasium', p. 37.

47. Tzachou-Alexandri, 'The Gymnasium', p. 38. There were two gymnasia at Priene: the upper gymnasium (in the north) and the lower gymnasium (in the south). The lower gymnasium is in a much better state of preservation than the upper gymnasium. Tzachou-Alexandri's comments apply to the lower gymnasium. Guidebooks include photographs showing the gymnasia at Priene. During a visit to Priene (modern Turkey), I purchased the guidebook by Ahmet Sinanoğlu, *Didyma, Miletus, Priene* (trans. Bülent Özgöz; Şti: Hakan Ofset Ltd., 1997). The section on Priene, pp. 66–90, provides a general view of the city with the lower gymnasium located in the south of Priene adjacent to the city walls (p. 66). The guidebook photographs show the *ephebeion* (classroom), examples of students' mural inscriptions and a reconstruction of a class being held (pp. 86–87). The lower gymnasium running track still has the spectators' seating in position.

48. Tzachou-Alexandri, 'The Gymnasium', pp. 38–39.

49. Tzachou-Alexandri, 'The Gymnasium', p. 39. She notes that later the term denoted a school. See Clarence A. Forbes, 'The Education and Training of Slaves in Antiquity', *TAPA* 86 (1955), pp. 321–60 (334–37). He states, 'The Roman *paedagogium* was antiquity's most systematic and durable plan for educating slave children' (p. 334).

50. Tzachou-Alexandri, 'The Gymnasium', p. 39. She notes the 2nd century BC inscription for the library at Rhodes where the gymnasiarch managers the donations made. These donations were mainly orators' speeches. The library from the Ptolemaion Gymnasium (Athens) is mentioned in 116/5 BC. Forbes, 'Expanded Uses', pp. 36–37, provides evidence of libraries from the second century BC to the second century AD. The Ptolemaeum in Athens,

Teachers ('professors') taught in the gymnasium. Inscriptions identify *skolai* (σχολαί) and *akroaseis* (ἀκροάσεις). Tzachou-Alexandri argues that *skolai* were courses taught through the year (with permanent teachers) and *akroaseis* were lectures (taught by visiting teachers).[51] Moreover, Forbes notes that often the Hellenistic architects and their successors had an auditorium in their plans for a gymnasium. Excavations at Ephesus and Pergamon have shown that these rooms were filled with tiers of permanent seats, as in present-day classrooms. These lectures were attended by organised groups (e.g. the ἔφηβοι at Athens, Eretria, Haliartus) or by the general public.[52]

Forbes observes that the peripatetic lecturers in the gymnasia were received and cared for by gymnasiarchs.[53] Inscriptions show that the lecturers were varied with philosophers perhaps the most numerous. An Athenian Homeric scholar, Dionysius, lectured in the Eretrian gymnasium to the παῖδες, ἔφηβοι, and others interested in culture.[54] A physician, Asclepiades of Perge (Pamphylia), lectured on health to his fellow-citizens and to the people in Seleucia-on-the-Calycadnus. A musician taught in the gymnasium at Delos.

A literary scholar was provided for instructing the ἔφηβοι and νέοι of the gymnasium in Priene by the gymnasiarch Zosimus. Menander, a professor of literature, lectured at Delphi. This was a centre for pilgrims, travellers and tourists, and therefore there were many opportunities to provide hospitality for itinerant lecturers. Not all lecturers were old for an inscription shows a poet from Scepsis was still a boy when he read his epic poem in Delphi's gymnasium.[55] Moreover, Teresa Morgan notes that in the first century BC in addition to philosophers and rhetors we see grammarians (*grammatikoi*) appear as teachers of ephebes.[56] They received a liberal education.

built 275 BC, benefited from a late second century BC civic decree that required each year's graduating ephebes to provide a hundred volumes to the school library. This regulation continued in effect for at least seventy-five years.

51. Tzachou-Alexandri, 'The Gymnasium', p. 37.

52. Forbes, 'Expanded Uses', p. 34.

53. Forbes, 'Expanded Uses', p. 35.

54. Forbes, 'Expanded Uses', p. 35. *IG*, XII, 9, 235 (1st century BC). A companion inscription (234) mentions an unnamed rhetor in another year that lectured in the same gymnasium to a similar audience.

55. Forbes, 'Expanded Uses', p. 35. *Fouilles de Delphes*, III, 1, 273 (*c.* 132 BC). However, Onno M. van Nijf considers that this delivery may have been in a poetry contest rather than a lecture. Personal communication. Reproduced with kind permission.

56. Morgan, *Literate Education*, p. 156. She includes, '*IG* II 2. 1039.17f, 1042b.19f, 1042c.7f (41/0 BCE), 1043.20 (38/7 BCE).

Exhibitions or speeches (ἐπιδείξεις) and examinations (ἀποδείξεις) of the students occurred in the large halls of the gymnasium.[57] Forbes cites how students in the gymnasia rushed out of a philosopher's lecture when they hear the gong sound for the oil rub.[58] Paul uses the word ἀπόδειξις in his important argument on the rejection of rhetoric and his demonstration or proof of the Spirit's power (1 Cor. 2.4–5).[59]

Like other ancient public events, and festivals, the Greek gymnasia were religious centres. Hermes and Herakles were known as 'the gods of the palaestra' or 'the gods established in the gymnasium' and statues of Achilles (the ideal athlete) were popular.[60] Tzachou-Alexandri notes the link, right from the beginning, of religion and athletics in the gymnasia and in Hellenistic times cults arose in the gymnasium associated with 'donors, benefactors and rulers'.[61] Moreover, Diskin Clay discusses the inscriptions of gymnasium inventories at Delos and Athens and comments that the fragments for Hellenistic Athens offer 'the most extensive evidence which has come to light for the furnishing of a Greek gymnasium.'[62] Statues of gods and demigods, with the names of their sculptors, included: Centaur(s), the Kouretes, Komoidia, Asklepios, Hermes, Hygieia, Artemis, the Muses, Hermaphroditos. They stood in 'the exedrae which were the center of the intellectual life of a Greek gymnasium'.[63] Statues, and herms, of Herakles were common in gymnasia.[64] A double herm with the heads of Hermes and Apollos from the second-century AD Panathenaic stadium in Athens demonstrates the

57. Forbes, 'Expanded Uses', p. 35.

58. Forbes, 'Expanded Uses', p. 36. He cites a passage in Cicero, who studied philosophy in Athens in 79 BC. Crassus declares to Catulus in the *De oratore* (II.5.21): 'Gymnasia were invented many centuries before philosophers began to babble in them; and even in our day, although philosophers occupy all the gymnasia, yet their auditors are more eager to hear the gong than the sage. As soon as the gong sounds, though the philosopher be in the midst of a discourse descanting on matters of the greatest weight and import, they all abandon him to go and take an oil-rub'. Forbes notes that *discus* (gong) here refers to the cymbal-like gong used to indicate the time of anointing in the gymnasium, and not the discus of athletes.

59. 1 Cor. 2.4–5 (NIV) reads, 'My message and my preaching were not with wise and persuasive words, but with a demonstration (ἀποδείξει) of the Spirit's power, so that your faith might not rest on men's wisdom, but on God's power.' For a discussion of ἀπόδειξις see Duane Litfin, *Paul's Theology of Proclamation*, pp. 17, 80, 207, 214 n. 4, 244 and 249 n. 18.

60. Tzachou-Alexandri, 'The Gymnasium', pp. 39–40.

61. Tzachou-Alexandri, 'The Gymnasium', p. 39.

62. Diskin Clay, 'A Gymnasium Inventory from the Athenian Agora', *Hesp* 46 (1977), pp. 259–67 (266).

63. Clay, 'A Gymnasium Inventory', pp. 262–63.

64. Tzachou-Alexandri (ed.), *Mind and Body*, no. 39, pp. 150–51, shows a marble statue of a naked youthful Herakles (Athens, 350–325 BC).

type of herms that may be located in a gymnasium.[65] Statues of deserving citizens, rulers and victorious athletes were erected and parts of the gymnasium had pictures.[66] Miller draws attention to the gymnasium inventories on the island of Delos. These inventories identify movable items, by their locations, as these were transferred from outgoing annual officials to the new ones. Statues included humans and gods. Many statues with inscriptions were dedicated by gymnasiarchs and vice-gymnasiarchs. There were trophies from victors obtained in local events.[67] Jean-Charles Moretti also provides evidence of the religious aspects of the gymnasium.[68]

Tzachou-Alexandri sums up the gymnasium's central importance:

> The gymnasium, the product of centuries of historical and spiritual development, was the centre of lofty intellectual enquiry. It was the decisive factor in forming the character of the youth. The young men who took part in the victorious wars against the barbarian received their training in the gymnasia. It was there that faith in the gods and the ideal of free men competing in contests was instilled. The gymnasium was the main agent in maintaining the cultural identity of the Greek colonists, the connecting link with their homeland. The development of the characteristic Greek achievements, oratory and philosophy, and the spread of Greek culture in the East and West is due to the institution of the gymnasium. The ancient Greek gymnasium is the symbol of Greek culture.[69]

She asserts the fundamental and enduring position of this institution.[70] However, her article may give the impression that education in the γυμνάσιον and access to the ἐφηβεία was open to all except slaves who had to wait in the παιδαγωγεῖον. This is unfortunate. From the time when the ephebate was no longer compulsory it developed into an elite organisation.

65. Tzachou-Alexandri (ed.), *Mind and Body*, no. 40, pp. 152–53. This is huge herm (partly preserved). It may have been placed in the stadium by Herodes Atticus when it was rebuilt (140–144 AD). She remarks that it is more common to find a combination of Hermes and Herakles but this particular uncommon herm may have indicated a connection between athletics and music in contests.

66. Tzachou-Alexandri, 'The Gymnasium', p. 40.

67. Miller, *Arete*, no. 122, pp. 123–24. See the translation of the inventory *ID* 1417AI.118–154, dated 155 BC.

68. Jean-Charles Moretti, 'Le gymnase de Délos', *BCH* 120 (1996), pp. 617–38.

69. Tzachou-Alexandri, 'The Gymnasium', p. 40.

70. For the continuing military aspects of the gymnasium in New Testament times see Clarence Allen Forbes, *Greek Physical Education* (New York and London: The Century Company, 1929. Reprint, New York: AMS Press, 1971), pp. 177–78, (page citation refers to the reprint edition), who notes that in Athens in the third century AD there are still gymnastic and military exercises. He refers to the inscription *IG* III. 1202 which includes the teachers and functionaries.

She states, 'One of the purposes of the gymnasium was to raise the level of education amongst all of the people. Thus it functioned as a university.'[71] But, even with officials and benefactors contributing financially 'towards instructing the boys and educating the youth' it seems that the gymnasium did not provide a universal free education. The emphasis is on male athletics and education. Moreover, wealth at least was required for entry into the later ephebate. The comparison with the modern university is problematic. What education do universities provide – is it elite education or mass education? For example, higher education in the United Kingdom has changed within recent decades. Leslie Wagner gives a thirty-year perspective on UK higher education (from the sixties to the nineties) and comments, 'The external changes have produced a mass higher education system whilst the lack of internal change has resulted in the retention of values of an élitist system'.[72] The National Committee of Inquiry into Higher Education examined the changing face of the university in the UK and made many recommendations for further changes.[73] I therefore prefer not to compare the Greek gymnasium with the modern university.[74]

In conclusion, the gymnasium as an important education centre considerably pre- and post-dates Paul's Corinthian correspondence. Gymnasia continued well beyond New Testament times before disappearing.[75] The continuity or survival of the γυμνάσιον is not in doubt but its relevance to the exegesis of 1 Corinthians has not been appreciated. The above description focuses on important aspects that contribute to our

71. Tzachou-Alexandri, 'The Gymnasium', p. 37.

72. Leslie Wagner, 'A Thirty-Year Perspective: From the Sixties to the Nineties', in Schuller (ed.), *The Changing University?* (Buckingham: SRHE and Open University Press, 1995), pp. 15–24. Further chapters in this volume also discuss changes. See also Frank Coffield and Bill Williamson (eds.), *Repositioning Higher Education* (Buckingham: SRHE and Open University Press, 1997).

73. National Committee of Inquiry into Higher Education, *Higher Education in the Learning Society* (London: HMSO, 1997). Also called the Dearing Report from Ron Dearing, the chairman.

74. However, for a discussion on ephebes and U.S. education see Charles W. Hedrick Jr., 'The American Ephebe: The Ephebic Oath, U.S. Education, and Nationalism', *CW* 97 (2004), pp. 384–407.

75. Charlotte Roueché, *Performers and Partisans at Aphrodisias in the Roman and Late Roman Periods* (JRS Monograph, 6; London: Society for the Promotion of Roman Studies, 1993), p. 137, discusses their disappearance. She notes that they were expensive to run (the office of *gymnasiarch* was very burdensome) but remarks, 'There was apparently no longer the will to maintain them in their previous condition. As was said above, the function of the gymnasia had been to educate the ruling classes of the cities in a manner appropriate to citizens; but from the third century, the purpose of education was increasingly to produce, not the ruling élite of the cities, but the governing class of the empire. For that, the expensive installations of the gymnasium, intended to provide physical as well as intellectual education, were not necessary.'

understanding of its relevance to New Testament studies and which should not be overlooked. Now it is necessary to consider personnel and pupils associated with the ancient gymnasium.

3. *Personnel and Pupils*

a. *Gymnasiarchs*

In the Hellenistic and Roman city the γυμνασίαρχος was the general supervisor of the civic gymnasium (or gymnasia). He (or she) did not teach. Antony Spawforth states that, assisted by other people, s/he was responsible for practical aspects of the civic gymnasium and the moral supervision of its youths (the ἔφηβοι).[76] Moreover, the gymnasiarch 'was a fearsome authority-figure (e.g., Plut. *Amat.* 755a) empowered to fine and flog.'[77] The gymnasium's centrality in civic life meant that gymnasiarchs were prominent people. The 'Athenian gymnasiarchy', comments Spawforth, 'was prestigious enough for Mark Antony ... to don its insignia with relish (Plut. *Ant.* 33.10)'.[78] The ἔφηβοι were looked after by experts called the παιδοτρίβης (Athens) and the κοσμήτης (Egypt). They often had a subordinate officer who took direct charge of the young ephebes called 'the master of the ephebes' or ἐφήβαρχος, who could be an ephebe himself.[79]

The substantial costs of physical exercise, mainly stemming from the provision of free oil for athletics and fuel for the hot baths, meant that the office was 'a target for the euergetism of rich citizens.'[80] They were expected to spend their money and demonstrate their generosity. Spawforth observes that many inscriptions honour generous gymnasiarchs. Norman Gardiner reproduces a drawing of the funeral stele of Diodorus, gymnasiarch of Prusa in the Imperial period, with the oil tank and ladles prominently displayed because he 'had probably celebrated his term of office by providing oil.'[81]

Forbes discusses the provision of public feasts in the gymnasium (a large

76. A.J.S. Spawforth, 'Gymnasiarch', in Hornblower and Spawforth (eds.), *The Oxford Classical Dictionary*, p. 659.

77. Spawforth, 'Gymnasiarch', p. 659.

78. Spawforth, 'Gymnasiarch', p. 659.

79. Marrou, *A History of Education in Antiquity*, pp. 110–12, discusses the ephebic magistrates. However, there was not complete uniformity in the use of the terms. For example, he notes that even when the actual word γυμνασίαρχος was not used the office still existed (p. 110). In Athens the title κοσμήτης was used instead.

80. Spawforth, 'Gymnasiarch', p. 659. For 'euergetism' see Stephan J. Joubert, 'One Form of Exchange or Two? "Euergetism," Patronage, and Testament Studies', *BTB* 31 (2001), pp. 17–25.

81. E. Norman Gardiner, *Athletics of the Ancient World* (Oxford: Clarendon Press, 1930), pp. 78–79.

structure for containing many people) and Tzachou-Alexandri notes that some gymnasia had special rooms for symposia.[82] Two first-century AD inscriptions record that gymnasiarchs provided feasts. Epaminondas of Acraephia gave breakfast in the gymnasium for everyone: citizens, strangers who happened to be in the city, free-born boys, and even slaves.[83] A gymnasiarch of Aegina spread a feast in the gymnasium for the Club of Anointers (οἱ ἀλειφόμενοι).[84] Even a private meal for a large group might be arranged in the gymnasium. Thus, a late Oxyrhynchus papyrus reads, 'Eudaemon invites you to dine at the gymnasium on the 1st at the 8th hour.'[85] Bruce Winter, in his discussion on civic rights in 1 Cor. 8–11.1, cites an inscription about a feast in a gymnasium.[86] Thus the γυμνάσιον provides a social situation in which Paul's discussion on eating idol food in 1 Cor. 8–10 would be applicable.

Derek Newton's study *Deity and Diet: The Dilemma of Sacrificial Food at Corinth* examines 1 Cor. 8–10 and also identifies locations for eating sacrificial food. His discussion of images in the Roman Imperial Cult identifies gymnasia as locations for sacrifices and banquets.[87] Moreover, he cites an inscription from Pergamon (Asia Minor) where in the Middle Gymnasium the *exedra* has a dedication not only to the traditional gods of the gymnasium Hermes and Herakles but also to 'the "new gods" Augustus and Livia'.[88] Newton examines the use of dining rooms in mid-first century Corinth and concludes, from doubts about their use, 'we must give serious thought to the possibility that the meals were being eaten in some other "place of idols", such as a gymnasium, hall or athletic games location'.[89] Again, on the problem of statues, Newton mentions an

82. Forbes, 'Expanded Uses', p. 39; Tzachou-Alexandri, 'The Gymnasium', p. 40.

83. Forbes, 'Expanded Uses', p. 39. However, this list appears to include males but not females. The inscription is *IG* VII, 2712 (*c*. 40 AD).

84. Forbes, 'Expanded Uses', p. 39. Forbes notes that οἱ ἀλειφόμενοι 'probably included all who frequented the building for gymnastic purposes.' This inscription is *IG* IV, 4 (early first century AD).

85. Forbes, 'Expanded Uses', p. 39. *P.Oxy* XVII, 2147 (early 3rd century AD).

86. Winter, *Seek the Welfare of the City*, p. 169. This is a second century BC inscription (*IG* XII, 7515) from Aigiale on the island of Amorgos (in the Aegean Sea). Kritolaos provides the finances for an annual feast in the gymnasium that includes resident citizens of Aigiale, 'and the alien residents and the foreigners and those of the Romans and their wives who are present'.

87. Derek Newton, *Deity and Diet*, p. 141. He refers to the inscription *SEG* 15.330.13–14 from Acraephia in Boeotia and dated about 42 AD.

88. Newton, *Deity and Diet*, p. 141. The inscription is *IGR* 4.318.1–2. Augustus was emperor 27 BC – 14 AD, Livia was his wife.

89. Newton, *Deity and Diet*, p. 142. His conclusion follows from Professor Bookidis' assessment of the cults of Demeter and Kore and also Asklepios. Dining in their sanctuaries around 50 AD is uncertain (Newton, *Deity and Diet*, pp. 91–99).

inscription from Lapethos (Cyprus) in which Adrastos, a priest and a gymnasiarch, erects a statue in the gymnasium to the divine emperor. He did this for the Cult of Tiberius and the statue stood with those of the traditional gods.[90] Finally, Newton also highlights an inscription where the gymnasiarch Menas sacrifices in the gymnasium to the gods Hermes and Heracles and shares the sacrifice with those people who are active in the gymnasium and foreigners.[91] Thus Newton helpfully shows that Imperial Cult worship was propagated by gymnasiarchs in gymnasia even if we do not have direct evidence of their worship procedures for Corinth.[92]

Men and women could occupy the office of gymnasiarch. R.A. Kearsley discusses an Ephesian inscription (93 AD/4–104) on the woman Vedia Marcia, who is described as: *prytanis*, priestess and high-priestess of Asia, and she comments, 'Epigraphic evidence for women carrying civic burdens other than as *prytanis*, for example as gymnasiarch, agonothete and, much more rarely, *grammateus* or secretary, is also to be found'.[93] Kearsley discusses inscriptions honouring Claudia Metrodora from the island of Chios near Ephesus.[94] She was a Greek woman who was a Roman citizen and a citizen of Chios where she holds magistracies. Included in her many offices are *agonothete* and gymnasiarch (held four times). Later, as a married woman, she appears on a building inscription in Ephesus. This bilingual inscription includes the Emperor Nero's name and locates her during his reign (54 AD–68). James Arlandson, in *Women, Class and Society*, discusses women in the context of the governing classes and urban elite. Among the many offices they held 48 women can be identified as gymnasiarchs in 23 cities during the first to third centuries AD.[95]

90. Newton, *Deity and Diet*, p. 170. The inscription is *OGIS* 2.583.1, 9–11.

91. Newton, *Deity and Diet*, p. 199. The inscription, *OGIS* 339 (130–100 BC), is from Sestos (Dardanelles).

92. Newton, *Deity and Diet*, p. 303. Diverse locations included: 'temples, gymnasia, halls and athletic locations'. For a helpful detailed discussion of the Imperial Cult in Corinth, see Winter, *After Paul Left Corinth*, pp. 269–86. This is chapter 12, 'The Imperial Cult, the Games, and Dining in a Temple (1 Corinthians 8–10:21)'.

93. R.A. Kearsley, 'Women in Public Life', in Llewelyn and Kearsley, *New Documents Illustrating Early Christianity*, 6, no. 3, pp. 24–27 (25–26). The *prytanis* was one of the chief magistracies of the city. For a survey of female gymnasiarchs Kearsley refers to L. Casarico, 'Donne ginnasiraco', *ZPE* 48 (1982), pp. 117–23. See also Harold Arthur Harris, *Greek Athletes and Athletics* (London: Hutchinson & Co Ltd, 1964), pp. 183–84, for his references to women as gymnasiarchs in imperial times.

94. R.A. Kearsley, 'Women in Public Life in the Roman East: Iunia Theodora, Claudia Metrodora and Phoebe, Benefactress of Paul', *TynBul* 50 (1999), pp. 189–211 (198–201, 208–09).

95. Arlandson, *Women, Class and Society in Early Christianity*, p. 33. His source is P.R. Trebilco, *Jewish Communities in Asia Minor* (Cambridge: Cambridge University Press, 1991), pp. 116–17.

Greek inscriptions from Ephesus, mention T. Flavius Pythio, who was asiarch in 104/05 and *archiereus* of the city's imperial cult in 115/16: 'By that year Pythio and his wife had also performed the exceptional service of undertaking not once only, but on six occasions, the expenses for one of the city's gymnasia which would otherwise have fallen to the treasury of Artemis (*I.Eph.* V.1500)'.[96] Thus his wife shared with him his term as gymnasiarch.

Ti. Claudius Aristio was *archiereus* of Asia in 88/89 AD. From 92/93 AD he was active in the administration of the city. One inscription was found on a statue base in the Harbour Gymnasium. He also contributed to the cost of its construction. An inscription records that he served as a gymnasiarch (*I.Eph.* III.638), probably of the Harbour Gymnasium following its completion.[97]

Earlier, during the Second Triumvirate, Antony held the office of gymnasiarch in Athens (39/38 BC), Alexandria (33 BC) and Tarsus (but indirectly via his friend Boethos). We do not have a record of him being gymnasiarch in Ephesus but C.P. Jones considers this likely as he stayed there in 41 and 33/32 BC.[98] Moreover, Lewis considers official letters discovered in the Ephesus excavations on the privileges for the city's gerousia.[99] The original three letters are dated from about 29 BC to 31/32 AD. Envoys to the provincial governor consisted of the gymnasiarchs Ti. Julius Heras and L. Cusinius and 'Alexander son of Alexander, gymnasiarch-designate of all the gymnasia for the coming year'.[100]

Thus we have evidence from Ephesus covering Paul's period in Corinth for gymnasiarchs in the city where Paul worked and wrote 1 Corinthians (1 Cor. 16.8).

A large marble stele from second-century BC Beroia in Macedonia provides one of the few surviving 'gymnasiarchal laws' detailing conduct in

96. R.A. Kearsley, 'Some Asiarchs of Ephesos', in Horsley, *New Documents Illustrating Early Christianity*, 4, no. 14, pp. 46–55 (51).

97. Kearsley, 'Some Asiarchs of Ephesos', pp. 49–50.

98. Jones, 'Atticus in Ephesus', p. 93. Jones notes (p. 93) that Antony claimed his descent from Heracles, who was 'the reputed founder of Greek athletics', moreover his winter in Ephesus 33/32 BC occurred before his break with Octavian and the Triumvirate, after expiring, was not renewed. For his gymnasiarchy in Athens, Jones cites Plut., *Ant.* 33.7.

99. Naphtali Lewis, 'The New Evidence on the Privileges of the Gerousiasts of Ephesos', *ZPE* 131 (2000), pp. 99–100. Lewis identifies the inscriptions as late first/early second century but points out these are copies of the earlier letters. She notes that 'in each case the envoy chosen by the gerousia to wait upon the governor was a local notable', i.e. the gymnasiarchs which are named in the separate inscriptions.

100. Lewis, 'The New Evidence', p. 100.

the gymnasium.[101] Interestingly, Side A of the stele states that as other cities with gymnasia had gymnasiarchal laws their city should have them. The city adopted the law proposed by the gymnasiarch Zopyros (and two other men) and inscribed it on a stele in the gymnasium with a record in the public archives. When the gymnasiarch was elected he was obliged to swear an oath of office, '[I swear] by Zeus, Ge, Helios, Apollo, Herakles (and) Hermes that I shall discharge the office of gymnasiarch in accordance with the law on the gymnasiarchy.'[102] He also promised not to steal or allow others to steal. The gymnasiarch is empowered to flog and fine the disobedient. For example, 'The gymnasiarch shall have the power to flog the boys and the physical trainers who show indiscipline, if they are not free and to fine those who are free.'[103] Moreover, at the *Hermaia*, 'the gymnasiarch shall have the power to flog and fine those who cheat and do not complete fairly in the contests, and similarly if anyone hands the victory to another'.[104]

H.A. Harris notes that the Apostolic Father Clement in his second Epistle to the Corinthians (7.4) 'writes that if an athlete is detected cheating ... he is flogged and expelled from the stadium'.[105] Second Clement, 7.1-6, uses imagery from the Isthmian Games as exhortation for Christians to strive in the contest of life. Here athletic officials use corporal punishment like the gymnasiarch does. This insight is useful when 1 Cor. 4.21 is examined in chapter 6 for Paul's use of the rod.

Miller notes that conduct in the gymnasium '*seems to have been a*

101. David W.J. Gill, 'Macedonia', in Gill and Gempf (eds.), *The Book of Acts in Its Graeco-Roman Setting*, Vol. 2 (Grand Rapids, MI: Eerdmans; Carlisle: Paternoster, 1994), pp. 397–417 (416 n. 131), notes the law from Styberra (74/5 AD) as another known in the Roman period from other cities in the province.

102. Bagnall and Derow (eds.), *Hellenistic Period*, pp. 133–138 (134). Bagnall and Derow, p. xxi, use square brackets to show places where the damaged original is restored and parenthesis for editorial insertions for clarity or the probable sense of a passage not restored. A translation is given also in Miller, *Arete*, no. 126, pp. 133–38 (134). The inscription is *SEG* 27.261. Bagnall and Derow use the spelling Beroia and Miller uses Verroia. On the date of the inscription Bagnall and Derow have 200/170 BC and Miller before 167 BC.

103. Bagnall and Derow (eds.), *Hellenistic Period*, pp. 133–138 (135).

104. Bagnall and Derow (eds.), *Hellenistic Period*, pp. 133–38 (136). Miller, *Arete*, no. 126, pp. 133–38 (137) notes that the *Hermaia* was an athletic festival dedicated to Hermes (p. 214).

105. H.A. Harris, *Trivium, Greek Athletics and the Jews*, p. 87. For the community to which it was sent, and its date, see Kirsopp Lake's discussion in *The Apostolic Fathers*, Vol. I (trans. Kirsopp Lake; LCL; London: William Heinemann; New York: The Macmillan Co., 1912), pp. 125–27. The biblical scholars Harnack and Lightfoot associate it with the Corinthian church. It is dated about the mid-second century AD.

frequent and widespread concern in antiquity.'[106] Yun Lee Too also discusses Aeschines' oration *Against Timarchus* which indicates this concern in classical Athens.[107] Aeschines refers to Solon's supposed legislation regulating teachers and those entering the gymnasium. Concerning those who are not to enter the gymnasium the stele orders, 'no one may (enter) the gymnasium and take of his clothes (who is) a slave, a freedman, or a son of these, if he has not been through the palaistra, if he has been a prostitute or has practised a *banausic* trade, or is drunk, or mad.'[108] The gymnasiarch was required to enforce this on threat of a fine.[109] Anyone insulting, or striking, the gymnasiarch in the gymnasium was to be fined. This law also includes provision for appointment of three male assistants to the gymnasiarch and physical trainers (*paidotribai*).

Inscriptions show how gymnasiarchs were honoured.[110] In Greek cities we see the social hierarchy through the processions. Here festivals are a political tool not just entertainment as the following text, which refers to a festival in Oenoanda, demonstrates:

> The following will process through the theatre and will sacrifice together during the days of the festival, according to the way the agonothete gives written instructions for each communal sacrifice:
> The agonothete himself, one bull; the civic priest of the emperors and the priestess of the emperors, one bull; the priest of Zeus, one bull; the three panegyriarchs, one bull; the secretary of the council and (70) the five prytaneis, two bulls; the two market supervisors of the city, one bull; the two gymnasiarchs, one bull; the four treasurers (*tamiai*), one bull; the two *paraphylakes* [rural police-officers], one bull; the ephebarch, one

106. Miller, *Arete*, p. 131. Emphasis in the original. The three sources he uses are: Aischines, *Against Timarchos* 9–12 (Athens, 345 BC), *SIG*^{3} 578 (Teos, third century BC), and *SEG* 27.261 (Verroia/Macedonia, before 167 BC).

107. Yun Lee Too, *The Pedagogical Contract: The Economies of Teaching and Learning in the Ancient World* (Ann Arbor: The University of Michigan Press, 2000), p. 28. See Miller, *Arete*, no. 124, pp. 131–32, for the extract *Against Timarchos* 9–12 on governing conduct in the gymnasium.

108. Bagnall and Derow (eds.), *Hellenistic Period*, pp. 133–138 (135).

109. Forbes, 'The Education and Training of Slaves in Antiquity', pp. 354–58 discusses the physical education of slaves and demonstrates that gymnasiarchs may distribute anointing oil and sacrificial meat to slaves, but they were usually excluded from the gymnasium.

110. For example, see Forbes, *Greek Physical Education*, pp. 197–98, for a first century BC inscription in which the gymnasiarch is honoured for discharging the duties of his office. At his own expense he furnished an instructor in rhetoric and one in heavy armed fighting. Holland Hendrix, 'Benefactor/Patron Networks in the Urban Environment: Evidence from Thessalonica', *Semeia* 56 (1991), pp. 39–58 (43–45), provides an example from 95 BC (Thessalonica) in which οἱ νέοι honour their gymnasiarch, including placing their honorific decree engraved on a stone stele in a conspicuous place in the gymnasium.

> bull; the paidonomos, one bull; the supervisor of the public buildings, one bull; of the villages....[111]

The whole city parades to the theatre. The ritual made the social order visible and enduring and the gymnasiarchs are evident. This is the fullest surviving record of the foundation and other arrangements for holding a quadrennial, or a penteteric, agonistic festival.[112] The ἐφήβαρχος is also evident. Gymnasiarchs fit into the group of those who Paul considers to be wise, influential and of noble birth (1 Cor. 1.26).[113] In the various festivals at first-century AD Corinth, such as the Isthmian Games (see Paul's imagery in 1 Cor. 9.24–27), the social elite would display their importance. Their important positions (e.g. *agonothete*) were made enduring as shown by the excavated inscriptions from Corinth.

In addition to the gymnasiarch, other personnel were active in the gymnasium. I have already indicated that there were teachers, itinerant lecturers, grammarians, philosophers and instructors for physical activities. Miller's translation of *IG* II^2.1006 (122 BC) gives an indication of personnel. He notes that although the total number of ephebes was only 58 the total number of instructors (excluding philosophers) was at least 32![114] *Kosmetes* were honoured by herms. For example, the marble herm (inscribed in Greek) of the *kosmetes* Heliodorus was erected, and paid for, by instructors (e.g. *paidotribes* and *grammateus*) and ephebes in Athens.[115] He is shown as a bearded mature man. A similar herm was erected for the *kosmetes* Sosistratos.[116]

111. *SEG* 38.1462. Translation in Stephen Mitchell, 'Festivals, Games, and Civic Life in Roman Asia Minor', *JRS* 80 (1990), pp. 183–93 (185–86). Oenoanda was a Lycian city. The inscription is dated 125 AD. The festival occurred every four years.

112. Mitchell, 'Festivals, Games, and Civic Life', p. 183. On processions see Onno M. van Nijf, *The Civic World of Professional Associations in the Roman East* (Dutch Monographs on Ancient History and Archaeology, 17; Amsterdam: J.C. Gieben, Publisher, 1997), pp. 191–206. This is chapter 5 'Professions on Parade'.

113. Marrou, *A History of Education in Antiquity*, notes that the gymnasiarch was always a very important person chosen 'from amongst the most influential and above all the most affluent of the citizens' (p. 110).

114. Miller, *Arete*, no. 128, pp. 140–45. The inscription is Athenian. See also Miller *Arete*, no. 126, pp. 133–38.

115. Tzachou-Alexandri (ed.), *Mind and Body*, no. 85, pp. 192–94. Its provenance is Athens (dated early second century AD) and probably from the Gymnasium of Diogenes. 'In the Roman period...the *kosmetai* were primarily instructors in the gymnasia. The office of *kosmetes* (which was honorific as well as functional) was generally held by men of about forty who came from distinguished Athenian families' (p. 194).

116. Tzachou-Alexandri (ed.), *Mind and Body*, no. 86, pp. 193–94. The Greek inscription on the front shows it was dedicated by the ephebes to their own *kosmetes*. Its provenance is Athens (dated 141/2 AD) and probably from the same gymnasium as no. 85. He is shown as a bearded mature man with plenty of hair. 'The office of *kosmetes* was one of the highest distinctions in Athenian society' (p. 194).

b. *Ephebes and the* Ephebeia

The ephebes were young men with their own institution, the *ephebeia* (ἐφηβεία).[117] Tzachou-Alexandri aptly summarises the relationship between the institutions of the gymnasium and the development of the ἐφηβεία in the Hellenistic period. She notes that it had a military character from the beginning to the end, however, after the fourth century BC:

> It emphasized instruction in intellectual subjects for the ephebes in the gymnasium. The ephebes, organized in groups, took part in contests, attended courses in the company of their *kosmetes*, their director who was responsible for maintaining good order.... In the ephebic lists ...the ephebes are praised together with the *kosmetes* for successfully attending courses and lectures in various Athenian gymnasia: the Ptolemaion, the Lyceum and the Academy.[118]

John Townsend notes that after secondary school young Greeks of good family commonly finished their education in the ἐφηβεία.[119] In higher education there were other study-options: rhetoric, philosophy, law and medicine. However, after mentioning options for law and medical training, he observes that more importance was attached to the Hellenistic *ephebeia* (and the *collegia juvenum* – Rome's equivalent):

> By Hellenistic times the *ephebeia* had become an exclusive municipal male finishing school housed in the gymnasium where future aristocrats (*epheboi*) leisurely pursued their studies with an emphasis on physical education. Apart from athletics, learning was not rigorous. Even though various grammarians, rhetoricians, and philosophers offered courses on a variety of subjects and even though the students usually had a library available, the time for study was relatively short. Students on the island of Chios were serving three years in the *ephebeia*... but one or two years was more the norm, with much of that time spent at the palaestra and the stadium. The importance of the *ephebeia* lay, however, not in its curriculum, but in its social significance. Study in the *ephebeia* certified that one was truly civilized (i.e., Hellenized) and was essential for full social and political acceptance.[120]

117. For an ephebe statuette from Aï Khanum (Afghanistan) see Chamoux, *Hellenistic Civilization*, p. 321, Plate10. Chamoux comments on the quality of this unfinished Hellenistic sculpture.

118. Tzachou-Alexandri, 'The Gymnasium', p. 37. She comments that very many ephebic lists are preserved.

119. Townsend, 'Education (Greco-Roman Period)', p. 314.

120. Townsend, 'Education (Greco-Roman Period)', p. 315. He notes that Jason, the high priest, showed his Hellenism by introducing to Jerusalem 'a gymnasium and *ephebeion*' (2 Macc. 4.9, 12).

This shows the importance of the ἐφηβεία in Greek education from Hellenistic times into the New Testament period. Continuity and change occurred with the gradual transformation of the ἐφηβεία from a military to a more educational institution. Townsend rightly remarks that it was 'an exclusive municipal male finishing school' and future aristocrats studied here. Indeed, its importance lay in its social significance because study there certified a man was civilized, or Hellenized, and it was essential to obtain full social (and political) acceptance. Yet for all these insights, coupled with Townsend's description of the importance of the gymnasium in education and for the ἔφηβοι, it is surprising that New Testament scholarship has not applied these insights sufficiently to the Corinthian church.

The important social-status issues discovered by scholarship in 1 Corinthians and the identification of the educated elite at Corinth have, as I described in chapter 2, produced an interest in ancient education models. Nevertheless, the importance of the ἐφηβεία for research has been overlooked in Pauline studies even though 1 Corinthians contains many points of contact with Townsend's description of the ἐφηβεία. It is regrettable that his *Anchor Bible Dictionary* article has been overlooked, together with his earlier article, which also addressed this area.[121] Moreover, Martin Hengel's outstanding studies in Judaism and Hellenism have demonstrated the central position of Greek education and the gymnasium.[122] E.A. Judge notes, 'from adolescence boys were admitted to the privileged ephebic education in the gymnasium, originally intended for military training. It became a kind of public school system in the elite sense, conferring social status'.[123] However, biblical scholars have not developed these comments on classical education to examine the educated elite in 1 Corinthians. More recently, Pearson's article outlines the importance of the gymnasium.[124]

In the Classics literature Hornblower and Spawforth note the importance of the *ephebeia*:

121. John T. Townsend, 'Ancient Education in the Time of the Early Roman Empire', in Stephen Benko and John J. O'Rourke (eds.), *The Catacombs and the Colosseum* (Valley Forge, PA: Judson Press, 1971), pp. 139–63, and in Stephen Benko and John J. O'Rourke (eds.), *Early Christianity: The Roman Empire as the Setting of Primitive Christianity* (London: Oliphants, 1972), pp. 139–63.

122. See Martin Hengel, *Judaism and Hellenism: Studies in Their Encounter in Palestine During the Early Hellenistic Period*, 2 Vols. (trans. John Bowden; Philadelphia, PA: Fortress Press; London: SCM Press Ltd, 1974), pp. 165–83; *Jews, Greeks and Barbarians: Aspects of the Hellenization of Judaism in the Pre-Christian Period* (trans. John Bowden; London: SCM Press Ltd, 1980); *The 'Hellenization' of Judaea in the First Century After Christ* (London: SCM Press and Philadelphia, PA: Trinity Press International, 1989), pp. 19–29.

123. Judge, 'The Reaction against Classical Education in the New Testament' p. 7.

124. Pearson, 'Gymnasia and Baths', pp. 435–36.

> From the 3rd cent. BC the *ephebeia*, based on the gymnasium, was a universal feature of the *polis*; the usual assumption, that Athens is the model, is probably exaggerated. The institution flourished for as long as the *polis*: in Paphlagonia it was still being introduced under Commodus (*IGRom*. 3.1446). Attested at Oxyrhynchus as late as 323 AD (*POxy*. 42), its final disappearance in the 4th cent. reflects the depleted finances of the late Roman city and the eventual devaluation of physical education.[125]

They comment that in 305 BC it ceased to be compulsory at Athens and from 282 BC service was reduced from the original two-year period to one year, 'thereafter, there and elsewhere, it increasingly resembled an association for young 'gentlemen', with a (superficial) intellectual training (notably classes in philosophy, letters, rhetoric, and music are attested) coming to supplement athletics and arms-drill'.[126]

They therefore confirm Townsend's view. The institution of the ἐφηβεία, based on the gymnasium, was a feature of the city for young 'gentlemen'. It spanned New Testament times and provided physical exercise and intellectual education. However, Hornblower and Spawforth's necessarily brief remarks may leave the impression that ephebic education covered one year from the age 18 to 19 years.

Frederick Beck and Rosalind Thomas, who note that the *ephebate* 'spread over the Greek world with enormous vitality, and became a kind of cultural-athletic institution for the leisured classes', divide pupils into educational age groups, although they admit these seem to vary with location: παῖδες, aged 12–17, ἔφηβοι, aged 18–20 in Athens (younger elsewhere) and νέοι (ex-ephebes, in their twenties).[127] Similarly, Marc Kleijwegt roughly divides education into three types: primary, secondary and higher. Primary is from 7–14 years (the child is a παῖς or *puer*) but he assumes that children only followed lessons for one or two years at the most.[128] However, he finds evidence that some subjects were taught to both παῖδες and ἔφηβοι. Unlike Townsend, who puts ἔφηβοι under higher education, Kleijwegt puts them in secondary. Whereas in classical Athens the age of entry to the ἐφηβεία was eighteen years Kleijwegt notes that during the Hellenistic-Roman period in Egypt and some parts of Asia Minor the regular age for entrance seems to have been fourteen. He shows that ἔφηβοι were regularly registered before eighteen and concludes that the ephebe was a teenager. The post-classical ἐφηβεία was one year in Athens

125. Simon Hornblower and Antony J.S. Spawforth, 'Epheboi', in Hornblower and Spawforth (eds.), *The Oxford Classical Dictionary*, pp. 527–28 (527). Commodus was emperor 180–192 AD.

126. Hornblower and Spawforth, 'Epheboi', p. 527.

127. Beck and Thomas, 'Education, Greek', p. 508.

128. Kleijwegt, *Ancient Youth*, p. 89.

and elsewhere, although there were, of course, regional variations, one year was normal.

A fundamental change occurred in third-century BC Athens when state payment to the ἔφηβοι ceased and the young men had to pay. Kleijwegt comments that the institution then became 'an aristocratic club' for the children of the elite.[129] They elected their own officials (e.g. treasurer) and the supervisor of the ἔφηβοι (κοσμήτης) ceased as a state-office and functioned as a liturgy.[130] In the Hellenistic-Roman period ἔφηβοι even performed as gymnasiarch or *agonothete*. Kleijwegt notes a second/first century BC inscription from Apollonis (Lydia) when a father was gymnasiarch and his son an ἐφήβαρχος (he had left the ἐφηβεία that year).[131] However, there were regional variations so that the ἐφήβαρχος could be a member of the ἐφηβεία or not (he may be older or younger).

Kleijwegt notes that ἔφηβοι had a central part to play in religious feasts.[132] At Athens they were involved in the mysteries of Eleusis but they also celebrated their own feasts. After an extensive study Kleijwegt concludes that the ἐφηβεία in the Hellenistic and Roman period was an aristocratic institution by which the ephebes were introduced into the adult world. Their internal organisation intentionally imitated the civic institutions.[133]

An essential element in Kleijwegt's argument is the distinction between modern adolescents and ἔφηβοι, who in contrast, were expected to act as adults. Although there was an overlap in their ages he forcefully argues that members of the *ephebeia* were not similar to modern adolescents. This has implications for the education model used in 1 Corinthians because of Paul's metaphorical language. He refers to the Corinthians as νηπίοις (1 Cor. 3.1) and as those who are mere men and still worldly (1 Cor. 3.1–4). He is their father and they are his children, who have pedagogues (1 Cor. 4.14–15).[134] His language is in contrast to the social expectations for the elite enrolled in ephebic education, who were to behave as social adults.

129. Kleijwegt, *Ancient Youth*, p. 97.

130. A.H.M. Jones, and P.J. Rhodes, 'Liturgy, *Greek*', in Hornblower and Spawforth (eds.), *The Oxford Classical Dictionary*, p. 875, comment that the liturgy is an institution, 'by which rich men were required to undertake work for the state at their own expense. It channelled the expenditure and competitiveness of rich individuals into public-spirited directions, and was perhaps felt to be less confiscatory than an equivalent level of taxation'.

131. Kleijwegt, *Ancient Youth*, p. 99.

132. Kleijwegt, *Ancient Youth*, p. 100.

133. Kleijwegt, *Ancient Youth*, p. 101.

134. This language occurs in 1 Cor. 13.11 on behaviour as a child compared with that of a adult. In 1 Cor. 14.20, Paul charges them, 'Brothers, stop thinking like children. In regard to evil be infants, but in your thinking be adults' (NIV).

It is worth briefly examining the relevant information on gymnasium education in Sparta, as this data is contemporary with Paul's work in Corinth.[135] Nigel Kennell's investigation of education and culture in ancient Sparta shows that in the Hellenistic phase the age grades of ἔφηβοι spanned the ages 14 to 20 years and in the Roman phase from 16 to 20 years.[136] He comments, from his reconstruction, 'we can now state with some confidence that Spartans during the Roman period were enrolled in the *agōgē* from sixteen through twenty years old.'[137] Each grade of the ἔφηβοι was divided into several smaller groups called *bouai* with a leader called the *bouagos* (cattle leader). However, the earliest epigraphic evidence is from the late first century AD, and thus an earlier date for the two terms is unlikely.[138] The ἔφηβοι were divided into tribes that spanned more than one age grade. Thus all boys belonged to one of five age grades and one of five tribes. Ex-ephebes were called *sphaireis*. From the second half of the first century AD a connection that some ephebes entered into was '*kasen*-ship' as a process which 'enabled poorer Spartans to pass through the *agōgē* by establishing a form of foster tie with wealthier contemporaries'.[139] Kennell notes that relationships developed among ἔφηβοι had a semi-official character that lasted a lifetime, he says:

> We find a large number of adult Spartan notables identifying themselves as fellow ephebes (*sunephēboi*) of particular men who had been *bouagoi*. The title *sunephebos* appears in catalogs of magistrates as well as individual careers from the Flavian period onwards and is perhaps to be associated with the first epigraphical attestation of the *bouagos* at this

135. Moreover, Spartans could be resident in Corinth during this period and there would be no racial barrier to them becoming members of the church. See my discussion below under 'Mobility in the Empire' for the important Eurycles family and its residence in both Sparta and Corinth at the end of the first century BC and the beginning of the first century AD. The same section addresses the Corinthian benefactor Herodes Atticus, and other family members, who were enrolled in the ἔφηβοι in Sparta.

136. Nigel M. Kennell, *The Gymnasium of Virtue: Education and Culture in Ancient Sparta* (Chapel Hill, NC and London: The University of North Carolina Press, 1995), pp. 28–39. He uses ephebic contest inscriptions from the sanctuary of Artemis Orthia comprising *stelai* with iron sickles attached to them. They range in date from the fourth century BC to the third century AD, with most from the first two centuries AD. The victor's name is expressed as an age grade. He comments that this is like 'the terms "freshman," "sophomore," "junior," and "senior" are given to undergraduate students at American universities' (p. 29). His work also uses a wide range of ancient literary sources, including Plutarch and Pausanias.

137. Kennell, *Gymnasium of Virtue*, p. 38.

138. Kennell, *Gymnasium of Virtue*, p. 38. *Bouai* is derived from the same semantic route as *bous*/*boes* (bull/cattle). See Paul Cartledge and Antony Spawforth, *Hellenistic and Roman Sparta: A Tale of Two Cities* (London and New York: Routledge, 1989), pp. 203–4, for the evidence.

139. Kennell, *Gymnasium of Virtue*, p. 43.

> time. The relationship appears to have had overtones of patronage and dependency.[140]

This demonstrates the ongoing importance attached to being an ephebe and how notables had been educated as ephebes.

The social position of ἔφηβοι can be seen in their public roles. G.H.R. Horsley cites a Greek posthumous honorific decree from Kyzikos in Mysia (Asia) in which the *demos* and the Romans engaged in business in the city honour Apollonis the daughter of Prokles:

> As a result, indeed, the *demos* has resolved: the totality of all men and women who live in the *polis* are to be in mourning. The temples, sacred areas and all the shrines are to be closed... until her burial. The presidents and the eponymous magistrates are to follow the cortege, as also are the boys, ephebes, citizens, and all free males in the city; likewise, unmarried girls, female citizens, and the remaining free women who live in the city.[141]

Horsley notes that she is given a state funeral with 'public and general mourning by all free people, adult and child, citizen and non-citizen of Kyzikos'.[142] However, he does not comment on the ἔφηβοι as a group distinct from the male citizens. Nevertheless, Charlotte Roueché indicates their importance:

> At Aphrodisias, as in many other cities, the ephebes, and their elders, the *neoi*, had special seating in the Stadium. Between them, these groups will have included all the young men of the city, that is those aged between about seventeen and twenty-two, and particularly those who belonged to the curial class, the future members of the Council. These were the young men whose life centred on the gymnasium, or probably more than one gymnasium in a city as prosperous as Aphrodisias. They will have had their own contests, and from their ranks will have come the victors whose successes at various contests were recorded in inscriptions.[143]

A late Hellenistic inscription from Athens demonstrates official recognition of ephebes and their teachers. The three-part inscription comprises (a) a decree honouring the ephebes and most teachers, (b) a decree honouring

140. Kennell, *Gymnasium of Virtue*, p. 43. The Flavian dynasty was initiated by Vespasian (emperor 69–79 AD).

141. G.H.R. Horsley, '" ... in memory of her,"' in Horsley, *New Documents Illustrating Early Christianity*, 4, no. 2, pp. 10–17 (12). Dated to the second quarter of the first century AD. The inscription is *SEG* 28 (1978) 953.

142. Horsley, '" ... in memory of her"', p. 14.

143. Roueché, *Performers and Partisans at Aphrodisias*, p. 135. See also Nijf, *The Civic World of Professional Associations in the Roman East*, pp. 209–40. This is chapter 6 'Seats and Civic Memory'.

the *kosmetes*, and (c) a list of ephebes who became Athenian citizens.[144] Again, their importance is recognised. In the Imperial Roman period a stele with an ephebic list shows five ephebes in a boat.[145] It includes the names of festivals and athletic events ephebes participated in. The list includes Athenians and non-Athenians. An Athenian marble commemorative stele recalls the friendship of two ephebes. It shows three competition prizes and mentions the *kosmetes*.[146]

Our discussion so far addresses males but what was the situation for girls? Although they were not ἔφηβοι, girls in Sparta trained and competed in contests similar to their brothers and cousins. On this aspect Kennell helpfully remarks that contests for girls indicated:

> Girls were considered to be just as much members of the *agōgē* as the ephebes. Regrettably, apart from this and what has justly been called 'a scatter of evidence' for the physical training of girls in the Roman period, nothing survives that might enable us to venture any guesses whatsoever about the organizational framework of the female version of the *agōgē*. Despite this ignorance, we can assume that Spartan girls had training that mirrored to some extent that of the ephebes during every phase of the *agōgē*'s history.[147]

Cartledge and Spawforth consider other evidence for girls' contests and conclude that if Roman Sparta encouraged athletics for girls these were no longer uncommon in the Graeco-Roman world.[148] While Thomas Scanlon provides a detailed study of the evidence, Kennell states he 'goes far beyond what the evidence can support.'[149] Unfortunately, Kennel only

144. Miller, *Arete*, no. 128, pp. 140–45. The inscription is *IG* II^2.1006, dated 122 BC. The ephebes are for 123/2 BC and the *kosmetes* are for the same year.

145. Tzachou-Alexandri (ed.), *Mind and Body*, no. 87, pp. 194–96. The inscription is *IG* II^2, 2087 (dated 163/4 AD). The provenance is Athens, the Gymnasium of Diogenes. 'It is known that foreigners often enrolled in the *ephebeia*; in this way they were able to enjoy the cultural benefits offered by the greatest educational centre the world has every known, and at the same time they hoped to acquire political rights' (p. 196).

146. Tzachou-Alexandri (ed.), *Mind and Body*, no. 102, pp. 210–11. The provenance is Athens, the Gymnasium of Diogenes. The epigram is *IG* II^2, 3734 (dated 126/7 AD). Diogenes paid for the stele to commemorate his friend Marcianus. Herodes Atticus was the *eponymous archon* (in Athens) at this time. Marcianus probably won all three prizes for the games, which were possibly held in the gymnasium, although the amphora and wreath may be from the Panathenaic Games.

147. Kennell, *Gymnasium of Virtue*, p. 46.

148. Cartledge and Spawforth, *Hellenistic and Roman Sparta*, pp. 205–6.

149. Thomas F. Scanlon, '*Virgineum Gymnasium*: Spartan Females and Early Greek Athletics', in Raschke (ed.), *The Archaeology of the Olympics: The Olympics and Other Festivals in Antiquity* (Madison, WI and London: The University of Wisconsin Press, 1988), pp. 185–216; Kennell, *Gymnasium of Virtue*, p. 186 n. 114.

provides this remark and does not engage with Scanlon to rebut his handling of the evidence.

More recently, Raffaella Cribiore addresses Greek education in Hellenistic and Roman Egypt.[150] In her discussion of the importance of the gymnasium she observes, 'Membership in the "metropolitan class" was granted to individuals who could show Greek ancestry on both maternal and paternal sides, and parents belonging to this class registered their children with the gymnasium officials as soon as they reached fourteen years of age.' Cribiore notes that although most applications were for boys there are two from families to register girls to obtain privileges. However, she does not know if registration did secure them automatic participation in gymnasium activities.[151]

Kennell sums up the situation for the Greek gymnasium:

> Greek urban culture had been dominated by the gymnasium for centuries. As the centers of physical and literary training, the gymnasia assumed an importance visible even today in the immensity of their ruins. Sparta did not stand apart from this trend: the city was studded with gymnasia, which had to be maintained and staffed. Ephebes would have made up only a portion of their clientele; the rest were professional athletes and local enthusiasts who could not bear to forsake the camaraderie of ephebic life. Elsewhere in Greece, such people formed organizations of young men (*neoi*) who met together and kept up with the old exercises. At Sparta those past ephebic age belonged to an association of *neaniskoi*, headed by a *neaniskarchēs*. The *sphaireis*, as ex-ephebes, would have formed a contingent within the *neaniskoi*, since *neoi* were usually young men older than twenty, but younger than thirty years old, the age at which they would normally assume the responsibilities and privileges of full citizenship.[152]

Their curriculum was heavily weighted towards physical education but music was important in Sparta, as it continued central to Greek education.[153] In conclusion, ἔφηβοι, although very important were only part of a larger picture. We now turn to another aspect of this picture – *neoi*.

150. Cribiore, *Gymnastics of the Mind*.

151. Cribiore, *Gymnastics of the Mind*, pp. 35–36. Registration for boys did secure automatic participation in gymnasium activities. See also her chapter 3 'Women and Education', pp. 74–101.

152. Kennell, *Gymnasium of Virtue*, p. 47. Moreover, Kennell notes, 'At any time from the first to the third century of our era, visitors to the city of Sparta saw a prosperous provincial city of the Roman Empire, decked out with all the facilities thought necessary for civilized life – gymnasia, baths, shopping arcades, theatres, and a good range of public sculpture' (p. 5). Thus this situation is contemporary with Paul.

153. Kennell, *Gymnasium of Virtue*, p. 110.

c. *Neoi*

The ἔφηβοι were organised in many cities in the Greek world during the Hellenistic and Roman periods. At the same time organisations of νέοι flourished. They were youths older than ἔφηβοι ranging from the age of nineteen or twenty upwards. They were ephebic alumni based in the gymnasium. Here, Forbes remarks, 'Although the *neoi* were no longer an integral part of the educational system, they were still held together by the close bonds of friendship formed during the ephebic years; and they modelled their organization on that with which they had grown familiar in the period of ephebic training'.[154]

From his geographical survey of the νέοι Forbes concludes that the institution, a Hellenistic development, functioned from the late fourth century BC to the third century AD, i.e., for seven centuries. His earliest evidence is the Peloponnesian city of Troezen yet these associations stretched from Delphi to Babylon.[155] Forbes notes that in Cyzicus (Mysia) the νέοι were established by 277–276 BC and still existed in the middle of the second century AD – a period of over five hundred years. In the great gymnasium of the νέοι excavated at Pergamum nearly forty inscriptions show evidence for the association over three hundred years.[156] Thus the institution was well established in the Greek East during New Testament times.

Inscriptions demonstrate that a gymnasiarch directed the youths. This leadership shows their close association 'with the gymnasium and their prime interest in gymnastic activities.'[157] The gymnasiarch may just supply free oil, but often performed other roles, such as acting as a real supervisor (maintaining order and good behaviour), exhibited or directed games of the νέοι (as *agonothete*), provided benefactions for the gymnasium (e.g. reconditioning or rebuilding it), and adorned the building with statues or other artistic works. Inscriptions honour gymnasiarchs for their good services and conduct.[158] The gymnasiarch of the νέοι may control another group as well, so frequently there was a combination of ἔφηβοι and νέοι (groups of similar ages/tastes) and occasionally he controlled παῖδες, ἔφηβοι and νέοι.[159] Other leaders and officials were needful and there were variations in different cities and times. However, a treasurer and a

154. Clarence Allen Forbes, *Neoi: A Contribution to the Study of Greek Associations* (Philological Monographs, 2; Middletown, CT: The American Philological Association, 1933), pp. 2–3.

155. Forbes, *Neoi*, pp. 16–17.

156. Forbes, *Neoi*, pp. 18–19.

157. Forbes, *Neoi*, p. 21. This discussion expands the earlier examination of the gymnasiarch.

158. Forbes, *Neoi*, p. 24.

159. Forbes, *Neoi*, p. 30.

secretary were usually required.[160] With the leadership of the gymnasiarch, secretary and treasurer the νέοι were a corporate group.[161] They may have elite benefactors. For example, as Harland notes, C. Antius Aulus Julius Quadratus was an important Pergamene and a senator who was a benefactor for local associations 'including the synod of young men (*neoi*)'.[162]

Unfortunately, Forbes mentions that no evidence exists for how many νέοι there were in any city. Even on individual νέοι there is scant evidence.[163] Nevertheless, Forbes comments, 'That resident foreigners of the proper age might be welcomed to some sort of membership among the *neoi* is possible.' During the Roman empire the νέοι, like other associations, may proclaim their loyalty to the emperor.[164]

Forbes notes, 'The most important activity of the *neoi* everywhere was gymnastics. During their ephebic years and earlier, they became habituated to physical education, to the sports of the gymnasium and athletic field.'[165] He remarks that the vast quantity of oil used by them speaks of their devotion to exercise. The only building they used was the gymnasium. Often, perhaps regularly, the ἔφηβοι and νέοι exercised together so that they shared the gymnasium with the ἔφηβοι or other gymnastic groups (including the γερουσία).[166] Yet, Forbes observes that ten cities had a separate gymnasium used exclusively by the *neoi*.[167] Strabo (14.1.43–14.5.12) noted the gymnasium of the νέοι at Nysa and Tarsus.[168] However, Forbes cautions that in general the purpose of their gymnasia was committed to physical exercise, 'whereas the gymnasia of ephebi and boys were educational institutions'.[169] Yet he does cite a gymnasiarch (of Pergamum) for the ἔφηβοι and νέοι who gave educational prizes and made

160. Forbes, *Neoi*, p. 35.

161. Forbes, *Neoi*, p. 38.

162. Philip A. Harland, 'Connections with Elites in the World of the Early Christians', in Blasi, Duhaime and Turcotte (eds.), *Handbook of Early Christianity: Social Science Approaches*, pp. 385–408 (402–3). Harland notes that he held the consulate in 94 and 105 AD and also held many provincial offices throughout the Greek East. In 109–10 AD he was proconsul of Asia.

163. Forbes, *Neoi*, p. 39.

164. Forbes, *Neoi*, p. 39.

165. Forbes, *Neoi*, p. 45.

166. Forbes, *Neoi*, p. 31. The γερουσία were older men, called in inscriptions: 'fathers,' 'senators,' 'gerusia,' 'elders,' or 'old men.' Forbes, *Neoi* comments, 'These so-called elders were men of a ripe age, no doubt, but hardly what we should deem old. Their age was not so advanced as to prevent their sharing with the *neoi* in gymnastic exercises and in other interests of active life' (p. 31). Forbes notes they had a gymnasiarch (who could be a woman).

167. Forbes, *Neoi*, p. 47.

168. Forbes, *Neoi*, p. 48.

169. Forbes, *Neoi*, p. 48.

arrangements for them to practice in all branches of study. Moreover, Kleijwegt refers to Sestos (Thrace) for a second-century AD inscription mentioning *paides*, *epheboi* and *neoi* who honoured the same geometry teacher.[170] So clearly the νέοι did, at least on some occasions, receive some instruction besides being involved in physical exercises.

Holland Hendrix has recently examined two inscriptions of benefactions at Thessalonica related to νέοι, which demonstrate their presence in 95 BC and the early first century AD.[171] Case I 'The Youths and a Gymnasiarch' (95 BC) is an honorific decree issued by the νέοι (the youth organization) commending their gymnasiarch Paramonos. He was honoured with a crown, bronze likeness (life-size and painted) and the decree, on a stone stele, was to be erected in a conspicuous location in their gymnasium.[172] Hendrix notes that Thessalonian gymnasiarchs in this period contributed honours on behalf of the νέοι to 'the gods and Roman benefactors,' and 'He [Paramonos] was the mediator in satisfying the organizations honorific responsibility to its divine patrons.'[173]

In conclusion, οἱ ἔφηβοι and οἱ νέοι were teenagers and youth groups centred on the γυμνάσιον in New Testament times. They were among the social elite. In addition, the γερουσία used the gymnasium. It is clear from the work of these scholars that the gymnasium was a central part of Greek civic culture and an educational institution for the ἔφηβοι. Moreover, adults relaxed there showing their status as 'Greek men of leisure.'[174] This general discussion provides a foundation for examining the situation with the educated elite and the community conflict that Paul addresses in 1 Corinthians. Further, Corinth itself merits study to examine the evidence for its gymnasia.

4. *Gymnasia and Corinth*

a. *Greek Corinth*

In assessing the evidence and relevance of gymnasium education, for the educated elite in 1 Corinthians, it is essential to examine the historical situation in Corinth. An appreciation of the evidence for Greek Corinth provides a fuller picture for understanding the period of Paul. This is best achieved by considering first Greek, and then Roman,

170. Forbes, *Neoi*, p. 24. Kleijwegt. *Ancient Youth*, p. 90. The inscription is *I.Sestos* 5.

171. Hendrix, 'Benefactor/Patron Networks in the Urban Environment', pp. 39–58. Acts 17.1–11 records Paul's missionary work in Thessalonica. He also wrote to the church there, e.g. 1 Thessalonians.

172. Hendrix, 'Benefactor/Patron Networks in the Urban Environment', p. 45.

173. Hendrix, 'Benefactor/Patron Networks in the Urban Environment', pp. 45, 49.

174. I owe this insight to Onno M. van Nijf. Personal communication. Reproduced with kind permission.

Corinth.[175] There was continuity and change following the destruction and colonisation of Corinth, but there were not two Corinths, one Roman and one Greek.[176] James Wiseman notes, 'The destruction of Corinth was far less extensive than scholars have preferred to believe. Few of the buildings excavated, in fact, can be shown to have been subjected to the great violence that has customarily been associated with the plundering of Corinth in 146 B.C.'[177] Excavations at Corinth have not yet found a Hellenistic or Classical gymnasium. However, from the literary evidence Clarence Forbes notes that 'during a massacre of the peace-loving oligarchs at Corinth in 393/2, the Craneum was a place of refuge for the younger men.'[178] This appears to be the gymnasium. Kent no. 30 is a fragmentary third century BC reference to a gymnasiarch (with the line above, it seems, as part of a name).[179] Kent no. 33 is a third century BC list of thirty-eight men 'but there is nothing to show whether the names are part of an ephebic list, a casualty list, or some other kind of record'.[180] Sterling Dow convincingly argues that this is not an ephebic list.[181] Kent no. 49 is a fragmentary inscription prior to 44 BC and he notes that, 'Line 3 indicates that the fragment is associated in some way with the Corinth gymnasium, which lay about 200 m. north of the spot where the stone was found (cf. Pausanias, 2.4.5)'.[182] Thus the sparse literary and epigraphic evidence suggests a gymnasium and gymnasiarch, but unfortunately, no direct evidence exists for the ephebate.

Nevertheless, the Corinthian archaeologist Richard Scranton argues for the institution from the results of the excavation of the Stoa north of the Archaic Temple.[183] About thirty stone catapult balls, dated in the second century BC, were found in the ruins of the fourth century Stoa. He rejects

175. I use 'Greek Corinth' for the period before 44 BC and the term 'Roman Corinth' for the period after the founding of the colony.

176. See the discussion in chapter 1.

177. James Wiseman, 'Corinth and Rome I: 228 B.C. – A.D. 267', *ANRW* II 7.1 (1979), pp. 438–548 (494). His section 'The Interlude: 146–44 B.C.', pp. 491–96, evaluates the evidence for occupation of Corinth in this period. He shows that the city had inhabitants, construction occurred, and cults show continuity from Hellenistic to Roman imperial times.

178. Forbes, 'Expanded Uses', p. 38.

179. Kent, *Corinth: The Inscriptions, 1926–1950*, no. 30, p. 9. The inscription (shown in Plate 3) is on white marble and was engraved in a vertical channel of an original column drum. The second line reads: [– – – –]γυμνασιά̣[ρχης– – – –].

180. Kent, *Corinth: The Inscriptions, 1926–1950*, no. 33, pp. 9–11 (11).

181. Sterling Dow, 'Corinthiaca', *HSCP* 53 (1942), pp. 89–119 (90–106, 96).

182. Kent, *Corinth: The Inscriptions, 1926–1950*, no. 49, p. 16. The inscription (Plate 5) is on a fragment of gray limestone slab discovered in the Theatre. It reads: ἐπι γυμν̣α̣[– – – –].

183. Robert L. Scranton, *Corinth: Monuments in the Lower Agora and North of the Archaic Temple* (ASCSA, 1.3; Princeton, NJ: The American School of Classical Studies at Athens, 1951).

the idea that these balls were hurled by the besieging Romans during the final siege of Corinth and argues that the North Stoa was an arsenal.[184] A building complex included the Stoa, the Area in front of it, and the bath in the Painted Building. Scranton comments:

> As a complex, it has a generalized parallel in the gymnasium at Delphi which also consisted of a stoa, an open area for running, and a bath (of a different type). But the concept of gymnasium combined with military associations is a normal element in Greek life, and means simply the ephebate. Although there is no specific record of this institution at Corinth we may confidently assume that it existed in some form, and suppose that the complex as a whole was devoted to the use, training, and equipment of the young Corinthian men undergoing training at arms. The Area would serve as a ground for exercise, the bath for its own purpose, the Stoa for storage and shelter for any permanent or semi-permanent guard. It is true that the Area is not long enough for a full stadium course, by a good deal, but it is large enough for gymnastic practise in general, as in an ordinary palaestra.[185]

After further arguing for this location as plausible for an arsenal, he concludes, 'The defect is the scantiness of the evidence; the other side of the picture is that the evidence which is available points in this direction.'[186] Nevertheless, Wiseman observes the restricted exercise space and that it has no resemblance to other palaestras.[187] He notes that Jean Delorme rejects the Painted Building as a bath and the complex as a gymnasium or palaestra.[188] Thus Scranton's deductions on the complex are challenged, however, his confidence in the existence of the ephebate remains intact, although its location is doubtful. Let us now examine the situation in Roman Corinth.

b. *Roman Corinth*

Pausanias (2.4.5) records the location of Corinth's gymnasium as follows:

> Above the theatre is a sanctuary of Zeus surnamed in the Latin tongue Capitolinus, which might be rendered into Greek *Coryphaeos*. Not far from this theatre is the ancient gymnasium (γυμνάσιον τὸ ἀρχαῖον), and a spring called Lerna. Pillars stand around it, and seats have been made to refresh in summer time those who have entered it. By this gymnasium are temples of Zeus and Asclepius.[189]

184. Scranton, *Corinth: Monuments*, pp. 176–77.
185. Scranton, *Corinth: Monuments*, p. 179.
186. Scranton, *Corinth: Monuments*, p. 179.
187. Wiseman, 'Corinth and Rome I', pp. 485–86.
188. Wiseman, 'Corinth and Rome I', p. 486.
189. Pausanias, *Description of Greece*, Vol. I (trans. W.H.S. Jones; LCL; London: William Heinemann Ltd; New York: G.P. Putnam's Sons, 1918). He visited Corinth mid-second-

The excavator of the Corinthian gymnasium James Wiseman comments, 'Pausanias records that the "old" gymnasium and a spring called "Lerna" were located not far from the theatre and that a temple of Zeus and a temple of Asklepios were near the gymnasium.'[190] Delorme too notes that at the time of Pausanias the Craneion gymnasium at Corinth was in a cypress wood.[191] Pausanias refers to the Old Gymnasium at Corinth and Forbes infers from this that there was also a new gymnasium at Corinth in the second century AD.[192] Furthermore, in the second century AD, Aelius Aristides describes Corinth and notes, 'the gymnasiums and schools are in themselves instructions and stories.'[193]

What evidence exists for a first-century gymnasium at the time of Paul? Wiseman remarks:

> A large Gymnasium occupied a prominent position near the edge of the first plateau above the coastal plain of Corinth during the early Roman Empire. The Gymnasium which lies almost due north of the theatre ... was probably preceded by a Hellenistic and perhaps Classical Gymnasium, but no architectural remains of an earlier building have yet been identified with certainty.[194]

From the excavated foundations and remains of the stoa (including many drums and fragments of Doric and Ionic columns and capitals) Wiseman dates the gymnasium's stoa from the late first century or early second century AD. This is near Paul's time at Corinth and just coincides with dates attributed to the writing of 1 Corinthians.[195] However, the

century AD. For the location of the gymnasium in Corinth see Charles K. Williams II, and Nancy Bookidis (eds.), *Corinth: Corinth, The Centenary 1896–1996* (ASCSA, 20; The American School of Classical Studies at Athens, 2003), p. xxviii, Plan V. Site Overview. It is north of the theatre by the Asklepieion at the north wall. Also see Wiseman, 'Corinth and Rome I', Figure 2, p. 442.

190. James Wiseman, 'Excavations at Corinth, the Gymnasium Area, 1965', *Hesp* 36 (1967), pp. 13–41 (13).

191. Delorme, *Gymnasion*, p. 333.

192. Forbes, *Greek Physical Education*, p. 187.

193. *Or.* 46.28. See the translation and discussion in Murphy-O'Connor, *St. Paul's Corinth*, pp. 114–19.

194. James Wiseman, 'The Gymnasium Area at Corinth, 1969–1970', *Hesp* 41 (1972), pp. 1–42 (1).

195. Wiseman, 'Excavations at Corinth, the Gymnasium Area, 1965', p. 21, remarked that the foundations of a large stoa were found and this seems to have been built in the late first or early second century after Christ. Again, James Wiseman, 'Excavations in Corinth, The Gymnasium Area, 1967–68', p. 67 notes, 'The thick stucco and the profiles of the capitals also suggest that the capitals should date to about the time of building the Gymnasium in the late 1st century after Christ.' In 'The Gymnasium Area at Corinth, 1969–1970', pp. 4–5, he dates ceramic material associated with the walls as late 1st or early 2nd century after Christ and an Attic base to the middle of the first century after Christ. F.W. Grosheide, *The First Epistle to*

gymnasium was probably in use before Paul's time. Wiseman observes, 'Evidence for the date of the Gymnasium Stoa is still mid to second half of the first century A.D., but they could make do without the stoa, using the flat area on the plateau as an exercise ground.'[196] He also comments that elaborate architecture is not needed to serve the needs of a gymnasium.[197] The exercise ground on the plateau would be sufficient.

On the availability of rooms for teaching, Wiseman remarks, 'There is a very large exedra in the courtyard, but it was built as part of the renovations by Hadrian. There may well have been rooms there, however, replaced by the exedra. Besides, the courtyard would have been a pleasant place and had benches.'[198] Thus evidence is lacking for rooms at the time of Paul but, as Wiseman states, the courtyard at least was available and suitable for use.

Next to the gymnasium is a bath and fountain complex and here the Greek bath, dated before the fall of Corinth, was in use in the early first century AD. Wiseman again comments, 'The bathing complex was repaired and adorned sumptuously, inside and out, during the early life of the Roman colony of Corinth.'[199] He describes the complex:

> The bath and fountain in the hollow to the west of the Asclepieium was ... remodelled during the early life of the colony. At least by the time of Tiberius the complex consisted of a large open courtyard in the center of which was a swimming pool nearly 2 m. deep. Walls of poros blocks were on three sides of the court and on the south there were passages into three underground chambers .... The westernmost chamber was a bath with six water basins on stands preserved from the pre-Mummian period; the south wall of the vaulted chamber was rusticated to give the appearance of a natural grotto .... The middle chamber was a fountain where water was obtained from a small pool below a masonry arch and a semi-domical construction of large rocks, again giving the effect of a

the Corinthians (NICNT; Grand Rapids, MI: Eerdmans, 1953), p. 13, dates 1 Corinthians to the spring of 53 or 54 AD; C.K. Barrett, *The First Epistle to the Corinthians*, pp. 4–5, dates 1 Corinthians at the end of 53, or more probably early in 54 AD; Ralph P. Martin, *2 Corinthians* (WBC, 40; Waco, TX: Word Books, 1986), p. xlvi, dates the letter to 54 AD; Fee, *First Epistle*, pp. 4–5, dates Paul as leaving Corinth in 51–52 AD, and 1 Corinthians as written approximately three years later. Thiselton, *First Epistle*, pp. 29–32 reviews the dates and accepts spring 54 or 55 for the date of 1 Corinthians.

196. Wiseman. Personal communication. Reproduced with kind permission.

197. Wiseman. Personal communication. Reproduced with kind permission. Onno M. van Nijf also makes a general comment that even in the Roman period when gymnasia were built up this was not always the case. Personal communication. Reproduced with kind permission.

198. Wiseman. Personal communication, reproduced with kind permission. Hadrian was emperor 117–138 AD.

199. Wiseman, 'The Gymnasium Area at Corinth, 1969–1970', p. 16. The complex was in use during the first three centuries AD.

> natural grotto from which water issued. The easternmost chamber was a large reservoir from which water could also be drawn.[200]

Wiseman remarks that the bath and swimming pool served the athletes who practised in the gymnasium. The bathing complex is contemporary with Paul.

Finds in this complex include Roman terracotta lamps.[201] The most interesting inscription 'is a list of athletic officials and victors carved on a herm (I-70–39). One of the *xystarchs* named is Gnaeus Babbius Italicus who was probably the son of the well-known Cn. Babbius Philinus and was active in Corinth in the mid-1st century after Christ.'[202] In 1972 this inscribed herm was unpublished and, unfortunately, remains unpublished. However, James Wiseman provides details in a personal communication.[203] I-70–39 (in Greek) identifies the agonothete T. Claudius Dinippus who presided over the Neronea, Isthmia and Caesarea Games. West produced fairly strong evidence that his agonothesia was probably 55 AD.[204] He also held it again when Nero visited Corinth. Wiseman remarks, 'The same inscription includes a list of "Gymnasium Victories," and two of the contests mentioned are a "youth's race" and "men's race". It is reasonable to conclude that the Gymnasium Victors named belong to the gymnasium of which the courtyard, bath, and pool are components'.[205] The second inscribed herm I-71–15 (in Latin) honours T. Manilius Iuvencus.[206] He was

200. Wiseman, 'Corinth and Rome I', p. 511. See Wiseman, 'The Gymnasium Area at Corinth, 1969–1970', for a more detailed discussion on the complex and the associated finds.

201. Wiseman, 'The Gymnasium Area at Corinth, 1969–1970', pp. 19–20. These were manufactured in the first century AD. No. 8 shows the scene of a gladiatorial combat, no. 9 shows a draped animated female, who may be dancing. No. 11 shows a nude Herakles, with his lion's skin over one shoulder, gently resting his weight on the club in his right hand. A draped female figure, Athena or Nike, stands nearby. These were deposited in the first Roman construction period earlier than when the bath was opened (before the middle of the first century, perhaps as early as the reign of Tiberius). They were found at the junction of water channels for the bath and above a lower channel where Hellenistic pottery was found.

202. Wiseman, 'The Gymnasium Area at Corinth, 1969–1970', p. 20. Cn. Babbius Philinus was a duovir in the Augustan period. The herm was found in the swimming pool.

203. Wiseman. Personal communication. Reproduced with kind permission. Publication of the herm is forthcoming.

204. West (ed.), *Corinth: Latin Inscriptions, 1896–1926*, no. 86, pp. 71–74. West nos. 87–90, pp. 74–79 and no. 203(?), p. 126 also mention him. See also Kent, *Corinth: The Inscriptions, 1926–1950*, nos. 158–163, pp. 74–75. Kent notes that at least ten inscriptions from the Corinthian excavations honour Tiberius Claudius Dinippus. Clarke, *Secular and Christian Leadership in Corinth*, pp. 18–19, 144, discusses his offices and from the ten inscriptions makes a reconstruction. Clarke dates his office of *quinquennial duovir*, with Tiberius Claudius Anaxilaus, to 57/58 AD (p. 144). He dates him as agonothete of the Neronea Caesarea and the Isthmian and Caesarean games (67 AD).

205. Wiseman. Personal communication. Reproduced with kind permission.

206. Wiseman. Personal communication. Reproduced with kind permission.

the first man to hold the Caesarean Games before the Isthmian.[207] He seems to have been agonothete in the reign of Tiberius. Wiseman notes that athletic officials in Corinth included gymnasiarchs, but does not date these.[208]

An exceptionally well-carved head of a marble portrait statue was found in the pool. It is a young man and Wiseman suggests a member of the Julio-Claudian family.[209] Two marble statue heads found in the pool represent athletes. One is a young boy. A fillet in his hair suggests he was a victor in a boy's contest.[210] The other head 'probably also represents a youthful victorious athlete who was commemorated at the bath he frequented.'[211] Wiseman remarks, 'Statues of athletes or dignitaries doubtless stood in the courtyard and in rooms and niches along its perimeter.'[212] Catherine de Grazia Vanderpool in her recent review of Corinthian Roman portraiture confirms this situation. She observes that in Roman Corinth the preferred public locations for portraiture of private citizens were the South Stoa, Central Shops, Bema, the Lechaeum Road, Gymnasium and Theatre.[213] Vanderpool notes the diversity of sculpture styles in Corinth. In contrast to Roman Athens and Aphrodisias, 'the material from Corinth appears to have a style that is only distinctive because it is a composite, a mix of trends – suitable for a city that, established by Rome as a commercial and administrative centre, soon attracted a diverse populace from around the eastern Mediterranean'. The sculpture retrieved from the gymnasium excavations in the 1970s (and portraits in the Julian Basilica) come from the early years of the Roman colony and shows Western influences. However, 'Both groups show that

207. Kent, *Corinth: The Inscriptions, 1926–1950*, no. 154, p. 73. West, *Corinth: Latin Inscriptions, 1896–1926*, no. 81, pp. 64–66. Clarke, *Secular and Christian Leadership*, p. 150, records Titus Manlius Juvencus as aedile at the time of Augustus, *praefecus iure dicundo* in 32/33 AD (?) possibly when Tiberius was emperor and also as *agonothete* in 15 AD (?) of both the Isthmian and Caesarean games. Clarke also notes that he was first in scheduling the Caesarean games before the Isthmian games.

208. Wiseman, 'Corinth and Rome I', p. 500. His statement refers to Corinth within the period 44 BC to 267 AD but is not more specific. No references are provided.

209. Wiseman, 'The Gymnasium Area at Corinth, 1969–1970', pp. 19–20. Dated before mid-first century AD.

210. Wiseman, 'The Gymnasium Area at Corinth, 1969–1970', no. 14, p. 21.

211. Wiseman, 'The Gymnasium Area at Corinth, 1969–1970', no. 15, p. 21. This head was found near the preceding one. However, Brunilde Sismondo Ridgeway, 'Sculpture from Corinth', *Hesp* 50 (1981), pp. 422–48 (434) notes that the athletic monuments 'Rather than depicting specific victors, they may simply represent ideal types, some of them quite young, perhaps for boys' competitions'.

212. Wiseman, 'The Gymnasium Area at Corinth, 1969–1970', p. 21.

213. Vanderpool, 'Roman Portraiture: The Many Faces of Corinth', p. 372. She notes, 'Of central importance to understanding the use and role of portraiture in the social fabric of the city is its context and setting' (p. 372).

amalgam of Roman iconography and classicizing forms – Roman patronage and probably Attic hands – which characterize many works of Augustan and Early Imperial art.'[214]

A fragmentary Latin dedicatory plaque may indicate a library, and Wiseman notes, 'A library would have been an altogether appropriate element in a gymnasium-bath complex. The library at Corinth was evidently a much frequented place in the 2nd century after Christ.'[215] However, a library and/or archives existed in first century AD, but Saul Weinberg's work demonstrates that this was not near the gymnasium.[216] Nevertheless, members of the gymnasium might have had access to it.

Wiseman believes that in a large prosperous city like Corinth there would have been other gymnasia.[217] Richard Oster cannot personally conceive of Roman Corinth not having a gymnasium prior to 55 AD, even if it is yet undiscovered.[218] Onno M. van Nijf considers that Corinth would be remarkably untypical if it did not have a gymnasium in the New Testament period.[219] Indeed, the building of a gymnasium stoa in the second half of the first century demonstrates an interest in, and financial commitment to, having this distinctly Greek institution at Corinth. The Corinthian excavator Wiseman comments on the gymnasium complex:

> The whole complex is certainly the one Pausanias mentions in ii.4.5; perhaps it was the one that was re-founded first after the colony was

214. Vanderpool, 'Roman Portraiture: The Many Faces of Corinth', p. 374. She records the portraits as follows (p. 374 n. 29), 'S-70–13, portrait of boy from swimming pool in the Gymnasium: Wiseman 1972, p. 21, pl. 8, Ridgeway 1981, p. 434 (probably Augustan in date); S-71–25, portrait of boy from Gymnasium pool, Augustan (?); S-71–15, portrait of boy from Gymnasium pool, Augustan (?); S-69–22 and S-70–20 (neck fragment), portrait of man from Gymnasium pool: Wiseman 1972, pp. 19–20, Augustan or Early Tiberian'.

215. Wiseman, 'The Gymnasium Area at Corinth, 1969–1970', pp. 38–39. Wiseman suggests that the inscription may be as early as Hadrian (p. 39).

216. Wiseman. Personal communication. Reproduced with kind permission. Saul S. Weinberg, *Corinth: The Southeast Building, The Twin Basilicas, The Mosaic House* (ASCSA, 1.5; Princeton, NJ: The American School of Classical Studies at Athens, 1960), pp. 11–12 (28). The library and/or archives were in the Southeast Building. Weinberg notes a second century library in Corinth (drawing upon Dio Chrysostom's 37th discourse).

217. Wiseman. Personal communication. Reproduced with kind permission. Many cities had more than one gymnasium. See Edwin M. Yamauchi, *The Archaeology of New Testament Cities in Western Asia Minor* (London and Glasgow: Pickering & Inglis, 1980), pp. 38–41. Kleijwegt, *Ancient Youth* remarks, 'Every community which prided itself on being a Greek city possessed at least one gymnasium. Bigger cities possessed more gymnasia, possibly one for every age group: paides, ephebes, young men and old men' (p. 250).

218. Oster. Personal communication. Reproduced with kind permission. For his interest in Corinth see his 'Use, Misuse and Neglect'. Excavations at Corinth have been mainly in the forum area so future discoveries are possible.

219. Nijf. Personal communication. Reproduced with kind permission.

> created — the bath area certainly had a Hellenistic phase, and so was 'old'. The covered running track on the plateau above the courtyard, pool, and bath seems to have been built in the second half of the first century A.D., but the bath-courtyard complex ... was in operation probably during the reign of Augustus, and no later than Tiberius; there is a fair amount of archaeological evidence for the dating, not just the inscriptions.[220]

This gymnasium was a civic gymnasium in which both youths and men exercised.[221]

Moretti's discussion on the identification of the gymnasium on Delos, at the location GD 76, has yielded relevant results for Corinth.[222] He argues that GD 76 is not the gymnasium mentioned in the Delian accounts, or Athenian inventories, and that the latter is GD 67.[223] His thesis is that by its plan, and the collection of its contents, the Palaestra of the Lake (GD 67) can be identified as a gymnastic establishment.[224] He concludes that a transfer occurred between 95 and 88 BC from GD 67 to the new gymnasium with its covered race track.[225] The Palaestra of the Lake did not have such a facility yet inscriptions show that it provided ephebic training.[226] Clearly, as Wiseman states for the gymnasium at Corinth, a covered race track was not essential. Moreover, at Delos the ephebes were trained in the Palaestra. Thus the absence of a covered race track in Corinth at the start of the first century AD need not prevent ephebic training.

Although there is no direct evidence for this training, the circumstantial evidence suggests that this was available at the time Paul was active in Corinth. The inscribed herm (I-70–39) discussed by Wiseman shows that the gymnasium was in use. A list of 'Gymnasium victories' is recorded and two of the contests mentioned are a 'youth's race' and a 'men's race.'[227]

Antony Spawforth also makes the useful suggestion that as the colony was running Greek-style agonistic contests as early as Augustus and Corinthian citizens are competing in them in athletic events as 'boys' or 'beardless youths' then the circumstantial case for a civic gymnasium running some kind of ephebic training is quite strong.[228] Onno van Nijf

220. Wiseman. Personal communication. Reproduced with kind permission.
221. Wiseman. Personal communication. Reproduced with kind permission.
222. Moretti, 'Le gymnase de Délos.'
223. Moretti, 'Le gymnase de Délos', p. 632.
224. Moretti, 'Le gymnase de Délos', p. 631.
225. Moretti, 'Le gymnase de Délos', p. 633.
226. Moretti, 'Le gymnase de Délos', p. 635. See *ID* 1923, *ID* 1950, *ID* 2594, *ID* 2598, *ID* 2600 and *ID* 2633.
227. Wiseman. Personal communication. Reproduced with kind permission.
228. Spawforth. Personal communication. Reproduced with kind permission.

confirms this view noting that Corinthian athletes and rhetors must have trained somewhere.[229]

We have further evidence for Corinth in Epictetus's *Discourses* as reported by Arrian. Arrian writes to the Corinthian aristocrat Lucius Gellius Menander (Book 1.1). These shorthand notes were made *c.* 108 AD.[230] Bruce Winter uses this work to discuss the visit of the young Corinthian student of rhetoric to Epictetus at Nicopolis (III.1.1 and III.1.34).[231] Oldfather translates that passage, 'Shall we make a man like you a citizen of Corinth, and perchance a warden of the city (ἀστυνόμον), or superintendent of ephebi (ἐφήβαρχον), or general (στρατηγὸν), or superintendent of the games (ἀγωνοθέτην)?'[232] The significant point here is that Epictetus speaks to the Corinthian student as a citizen in Corinth being elected to positions in the city.[233] Winter notes, and discusses the status positions in the list and the hierarchy.[234] He comments, 'The ἐφήβαρχος was responsible for the *ephebeia* whom they trained in the gymnasium'.[235] This then is evidence for the position of ἐφήβαρχος in Corinth, from Arrian's notes made *c.* 108 AD, for the aristocratic Corinthian L. Gellius Menander.[236] Helpfully, Winter observes that Epictetus referred to the students ' "paltry" body, hardly a compliment to a youth who, as part of his education, worked out regularly in the gymnasium in order to shape his body'.[237] This literary evidence demonstrates ephebic training in Corinth at the very beginning of the second century and is consistent with the date of the excavated Corinthian gymnasium. Pausanias (2.10.7) observes, when he came to the gymnasium at Sicyon, 'This gymnasium (γυμνάσιον) was built for the Sicyonians by Cleinias, and they still train the youths (ἐφήβους) here'. It is hard to image that Corinth, which regained control of the

229. Nijf. Personal communication. Reproduced with kind permission.

230. Winter, *Philo and Paul*, p. 116.

231. Winter, *Philo and Paul*, pp. 116–21.

232. Epictetus, *Diss.* 3.1.34.

233. Winter, *Philo and Paul*, p. 119 n. 13, notes that the procedure here is one 'by which citizenship is recognised and does not mean the conferring of citizenship upon a foreigner.' Winter comments that Oldfather, 'rightly concludes that the interlocutor must have been a citizen'.

234. Winter, *Philo and Paul*, pp. 119–21. The list gives an ascending status hierarchy.

235. Winter, *Philo and Paul*, p. 120.

236. For a discussion on Arrian and the Gellii see James H. Oliver, 'Arrian in Two Roles', in *The Civic Tradition and Roman Athens* (Baltimore and London: The John Hopkins University Press, 1983), pp. 66–75. He, p. 66, observes that Kent, *Corinth: The Inscriptions, 1926–1950*, no. 124, pp. 55–56, is an inscription erected at Corinth to Arrian by the Gellii family (L. Gellius Menander and his son L. Gellius Justus). See also Oliver, 'Arrian and the Gellii of Corinth', *GRBS* 11 (1970), pp. 335–37, who sees the dedication as made to L. Gellius Iustus.

237. Winter, *After Paul Left Corinth*, p. 34.

Isthmian Games from Sicyon early in the life of the Roman colony, did not have its own civic gymnasium and ephebes if Sicyon had such a well-established institution.

Finally, in *1 Clement*, written to the Corinthian church perhaps within fifty years of Paul writing 1 Corinthians, Clement deals with the disruption caused by the young men (οἱ νέοι) in the church.[238] Horrell's discussion on the social ethos of *1 Clement* concludes it is most likely 'that the deposed elders were among the socially prominent members of the community, heads of households. It is probable that the rebels were those of lower social position.'[239] He agrees that this is hard to substantiate but sees this as seeming, 'the most plausible assessment.'[240] However, a tentative suggestion is whether the use of οἱ νέοι conveys more than just young men and refers to those who were members of οἱ νέοι in the gymnasium at Corinth. As young men they may be of lower status than the elders but could be among the educated elite.

5. *Mobility in the Empire*

Gymnasia in Corinth represent one educational route for the elite Corinthians and Corinthian Christians.[241] However, gymnasia existed in many cities and persons freely moved during the Empire for various needs, including their educational requirements. The New Testament provides evidence of mobility, for example, teachers could travel to the Corinthian church.[242] People educated in gymnasia outside Corinth might become residents (not necessarily permanent). Conversely, Corinthian residents

238. *1 Clement* is in *The Apostolic Fathers*, Vol. I (trans. Kirsopp Lake; LCL; London: William Heinemann; New York: The Macmillan Co., 1912). *1 Clem.* 3.1-3 mentions that in the troubles at Corinth there rose up the 'young against the old.'

239. Horrell, *Social Ethos*, p. 250. See chapter 6 'The social ethos of 1 Clement.'

240. Horrell, *Social Ethos*, p. 250.

241. In discussing the Corinthian Christians I do not wish to unnecessarily restrict my study. For example, I accept that there could be patrons of the Corinthian congregation who may not be believers. I am particularly thinking of the possibility that Erastus could be an interested person, or a patron, but not yet a believer as discussed in Theissen, 'The Social Structure of Pauline Communities', pp. 79–80. Clarke, *Serve the Community of the Church*, pp. 175–76, accepts 'The possibility remains... that a prominent figure from Corinthian civic life was also closely associated with the Christian community in Corinth' (p. 176). He agrees that Rom. 16.23 does not require Erastus to be a Christian but other texts may indicate he was one.

242. In the New Testament Paul's residences include Jerusalem, Antioch, Corinth, Ephesus and Rome. Aquila and Priscilla are resident in Rome, Corinth, Ephesus and Rome again (Acts 18.1; 1 Cor. 16.8, 19; Rom. 16.3). Apollos, a native of Alexandria, is resident in Ephesus, Corinth and Ephesus again (Acts 18.24; Acts 19.1; 1 Cor. 16.8–12). Chloe's people, at least, travelled (1 Cor. 1.11).

may send their sons away for a gymnasium education. I examine these routes in this section.

However, a comment on the original colonists is appropriate. Antony Spawforth, in his analysis of the colonists, considers the arrival of Roman *negotiatores*.[243] His primary material is the names of the 42 individual duovirs who 'signed' the colony's 24 emissions of coinage over the century or so from Corinth's refoundation in 44 BC. He identifies in the magistrates a significant number (19%) who can be 'classified as probably or certainly of freedman stock'.[244] Only 6% of magistrates were of veteran stock.[245] Yet 29% are attributed to Roman residents in the East, *negotiatores*, who moved to the new colony at Corinth.[246] In some cases these were already partly hellenized.[247] Recently, Elizabeth Gebhard and Matthew Dickie have noted Spawforth's suggestion that after Corinth's foundation Italian *negotiatores* settled there and some became very early duovirs.[248] They note that this is possible but some of these could have already been established in the city, or nearby, over fifty years before the official foundation of the colony.[249]

In chapter 2 I considered Winter's work which examined mobility with the example of the student among the Alexandrian sophists in *P.Oxy.* 2190.[250] Neilus, accompanied by his slave was studying rhetoric in first-century AD Alexandria and wrote to his father Theon, who lived in Oxyrhynchus. His letter informs Theon about educational difficulties he has experienced.[251] Moreover, S.R. Llewelyn discusses a first-century AD epitaph of a student of rhetoric who died away from home.[252] The Greek inscription, from Claudiopolis, is one of two surviving consolation decrees for the deceased student Theodoros, son of Attalos. Theodoros left home and came to Claudiopolis to study rhetoric. Llewelyn comments that it was

243. Spawforth, 'Roman Corinth: the Formation of a Colonial Elite'.

244. Spawforth, 'Roman Corinth: the Formation of a Colonial Elite', p. 169.

245. Spawforth, 'Roman Corinth: the Formation of a Colonial Elite', pp. 170–71.

246. Spawforth, 'Roman Corinth: the Formation of a Colonial Elite', pp. 171–73.

247. Spawforth, 'Roman Corinth: the Formation of a Colonial Elite', p. 174.

248. See Clarke, *Serve the Community of the Church*, pp. 41–49 on political leadership in the Roman colony. Duovirs were the two chief magistrates who were elected annually (p. 42).

249. Gebhard and Dickie, 'The View from the Isthmus', pp. 262–78 (277).

250. Winter, *Philo and Paul*, pp. 19–20.

251. Winter, *Philo and Paul*, p. 27, also shows that students studied away from home in the first century BC. Cicero sent his son Marcus (aged twenty-one) to study oratory and philosophy in Athens (*c.* 44 BC).

252. S.R. Llewelyn, 'The Epitaph of a Student Who Died Away from Home', in Llewelyn, *New Documents Illustrating Early Christianity*, 8, no. 8, pp. 117–21. The inscription is *SEG* XXXIV 1259.

not uncommon for members of the elite to travel for educational reasons.[253] Cartledge and Spawforth also consider the evidence for the habit of wealthy Spartan families sending their children abroad for their education, which was probably formed in the Hellenistic period.[254] However, in the first century AD at Sparta this educational opportunity, at least for the sons of prominent families, competed with their native gymnasium education as ephebes.[255] On the practice of elite boys studying away from home in Hellenistic and Roman Egypt see Raffaella Cribiore.[256] In her interesting chapter she discusses communication between teachers, parents and boys studying away. Finally, Epictetus speaks of students not crying for their nurse and mammy and asks them: 'In what respect are you superior to the man who weeps for a maid, if you grieve for a trivial gymnasium (γυμνασίδιον), a paltry colonnade, a group of youngsters, and that way of spending your time?'[257] This appears as a clear reference to their former experiences in the gymnasium before they took up philosophy. He talks to the poor man who longs for Athens and the Acropolis and asks if he will sit and cry as little children cry.[258] Thus students from a gymnasium background were now studying away from home.

Another funerary inscription (second/third century AD) concerns an athlete who died and was buried far from home but his friends erected a stele for him in his native Termessos.[259] His father's pain as well as the athlete's youthfulness and athletic success are recorded. This particular

253. Llewelyn, 'The Epitaph of a Student', p. 120. The inscription uses the two *topoi* of death at a young age and death in a foreign land. On these Llewelyn remarks, 'Death as a young person … was a chief cause of lament for three reasons: (a) the deceased had no time to enjoy life; (b) the parent or older person outlived the child; and (c) premature death threatened the continuity of the family' (p. 119).

254. Cartledge and Spawforth, *Hellenistic and Roman Sparta*, p. 177.

255. Cartledge and Spawforth, *Hellenistic and Roman Sparta*, p. 204.

256. Cribiore, *Gymnastics of the Mind*, pp. 102–23. This is chapter 4 'Parents and Students'. Her chapter addresses elite boys because although elite girls may receive grammatical education they stayed at home (p. 104).

257. Epict., *Diss*. 2.16.29. Ronald F. Hock, 'The Workshop as a Social Setting for Paul's Missionary Preaching', *CBQ* 41 (1979), pp. 438–50 (448 n. 50) observes, 'On the importance of the gymnasium as a social setting for intellectual discourse in the early empire, see Epictetus, *Diss*. 3.16.14; 4.1.113'.

258. Epict., *Diss*. 2.16.32–33.

259. Llewelyn, 'The Epitaph of a Student', p. 119. The fate of the deceased results in the advice, 'to rejoice, eat and drink and enjoy the gifts of Aphrodite' (p. 119). This 'carpe diem' motif is another important funeral topos. In 1 Cor. 15.32 Paul opposes this viewpoint as he argues for the resurrection of the dead. Another funeral topos was life as a race in the stadium (cf. 1 Cor. 9.24-27). Termessos is in modern Turkey near Antalya. The excavated site is well-worth visiting. The ancient gymnasium still retains its walls and structure. At the entrance a Greek inscription refers to the gymnasium.

inscription illustrates movement in the Empire for competitive athletes who may reside in other cities. Corinth as an important city with responsibility for the Isthmian Games may have provided an attractive temporary, or permanent, residence for foreign athletes. Thus people educated elsewhere in the gymnasium may subsequently live in Corinth.

Moreover, Michael Poliakoff describes combat athletes of later antiquity and comments on Aelius Aurelius Menander of Aphrodisias who was from 'eminent and well-reputed lineage.'[260] In his *pankration* career (mid-second century AD) he won as a boy, youth and man in three consecutive years and was crowned at Delphi, Nemea, Isthmia, Naples, Rome and other festivals. He travelled widely, served as *xystarch* 'and received, as successful athletes often did, citizenship and the office of senator in several different cities.'[261] Marcus Aurelius Demetrios, a wrestler and *periodonikes* in *pankration*, was a citizen of Alexandria and Hermopolis but his son, Marcus Aurelius Asclepiades, also a victor, served on the senates of six important cities while holding citizenship and civic office in others.[262] Emiel Eyben also refers to this 'super-athlete' who over six years travelled and competed in Italy, Greece and Asia.[263] Kent no. 370 is a partial Latin inscription on a marble block listing cities, which may indicate an itinerant athlete or artist.[264] However, the incomplete inscription makes this uncertain. Communication occurred between Corinth and other cities. For example, Alexandrians of all ages (boys, youths and men) attended the games at Corinth on a regular basis and are recorded in victor lists.[265] Girls also traveled and attended the Isthmian

260. Michael B. Poliakoff, *Combat Sports in the Ancient World: Competition, Violence and Culture* (New Haven and London: Yale University Press, 1987), p. 125.

261. Poliakoff, *Combat Sports*, p. 125. A *xystarch* is the head of an athletic synod.

262. Poliakoff, *Combat Sports*, pp. 125–26. A *periodonikes* was a man who won at the four festivals in the four-year circuit (*periodos*). The games were in: Olympia, Delphi (the Pythian festival), Corinth (the Isthmian festival) and Nemea. Thus he was a victor in the Isthmian Games. Marcus Aurelius Asclepiades won victories in many cities and was also a *periodonikes*. Thus he travelled to Corinth for the Isthmian Games.

263. Emiel Eyben, *Restless Youth in Ancient Rome* (trans. Patrick Daly; London: Routledge, 2nd rev. edn, 1993), pp. 86–87. His citizenship included Alexandria, Hermopolis, Puteoli and Naples. The inscription reveals that he was a senator of named cities plus 'citizen and senator of many other cities'.

264. Kent, *Corinth: The Inscriptions, 1926–1950*, no. 370, p. 143. The inscription was cut by two engravers and mentions: Ephesus, Laodikeia, Sardis, Settai (in Lydia), Antioch (Daphne), Patros, Chalkis and Sikyon. He argues there appears to be no direct connection between the locations so an itinerant athlete or artist seems likely. But he admits his approach lacks foundation. The inscription is late second/early third century AD.

265. Meritt, *Corinth: Greek Inscriptions, 1896–1927*, no. 16, pp. 21–25. Meritt comments on the Isthmian Games, 'the large number of cities represented in these [victor] lists indicates the cosmopolitan character of the festival, at least in the first and second centuries A.D. In 3 A.D. all three of the boxing contests (boys, youths, and men) were won by Alexandrians, a

(and other) Games as an inscription on a statue base from Delphi demonstrates. The statue was for three sisters. The inscription begins, 'Hermesianax son of Dionysios, citizen of Kaisarea Tralles as well as of Athens and Delphi, dedicates this to Pythian Apollo on behalf of his daughters, who hold the same citizenships'.[266] He identifies their victories in various festivals.

Spawforth demonstrates that in his sample of Corinthian magistrates 6–8% are provincial Greek notables.[267] He observes, 'The fact that under Claudius and Nero, no fewer than five Greeks from neighbouring cities can be identified as holders of the highest colonial offices is striking.'[268] Spawforth concludes:

> Finally, the lapse of the best part of a century before Achaia's provincial 'aristocracy' took a detectable interest in the colony suggests the strength of the provincial Greek prejudice against Corinth's servile origins; the appearance of outside notables as office-holders from Claudius on marks a significant step in the integration of this enclave of *Romanitas* into the surrounding Greek world.[269]

Two women indicate the extent of travel in the first century. First, Iunia Theodora, a Roman Lycian woman, lived in Corinth during the mid-first century AD and is a contemporary of Paul. Five Greek inscriptions on the same stone honour her. Kearsley notes that three are from Lycian cities (Myra, Patara and Telmessos) and two are from the Federal Assembly of the Lycians.[270] Among the reasons for honouring her are: the will she has drawn up, the numerous benefits she bestowed on many citizens and acting as host in the provision of domestic hospitality for visiting Lycians, whether private individuals or ambassadors. This domestic patronage, as Kearsley comments, appears parallel to instances where Paul and his friends are given hospitality or protection by women. Phoebe

fact which indicates that even the younger groups were rather well represented from various points in the Roman world. It is but natural, perhaps, that Corinthians predominate in the victor lists, especially in the more expensive competitions with horses' (p. 24).

266. Miller, *Arete*, no. 106, pp. 103–4 (103). See the discussion on this inscription (*SIG*^{3} 802, dated 47 AD) in chapter 5.

267. Spawforth, 'Roman Corinth: the Formation of a Colonial Elite', pp. 173–74.

268. Spawforth, 'Roman Corinth: the Formation of a Colonial Elite', p. 174.

269. Spawforth, 'Roman Corinth: the Formation of a Colonial Elite', p. 175.

270. Kearsley, 'Women in Public Life', pp. 24–27 (24). On Lycia, which was made a Roman province in 43 AD, see Stephen Mitchell, 'Ethnicity, Acculturation and Empire in Roman and Late Roman Asia Minor', in Mitchell and Greatrex (eds.), *Ethnicity and Culture in Late Antiquity* (London: Duckworth; Swansea: The Classical Press of Wales, 2000), pp. 117–150 (122–24). Paul landed at Myra in Lycia on his way to Rome (Acts 27.5). He had also stopped at Patara on his way to Jerusalem (Acts 21.1).

'is described in similar terms to Iunia Theodora since she is called the προστάτις of the church at Kenchreai.'[271] Iunia Theodora's activities also included exerting influence on members of the Roman provincial government, although apparently not based on formal authority.[272] She was a wealthy and powerful foreign woman, but it is extremely unlikely that she was an exception. Indeed, Kearsley's more recent article helpfully discusses both Iunia Theodora and Claudia Metrodora (mentioned above). Our second woman, Claudia Metrodora also lived in the mid-first century AD, was Greek, a benefactor, and held Roman citizenship. She held high public office and travelled widely, as did her brother Claudius Phesinus. Thus Kearsley concludes, 'The apparent ease with which Metrodora, and her brother moved between the cities of Chios, Teos and Ephesus is typical of other leading families in the Greek East during this period. Multi-citizenship made it possible, and it was not uncommon for the wealthy to own estates within the territories of in [*sic*] several different cities'.[273] Intermarriage and adoption cemented relationships between members of the elite. Cities welcomed such people.[274] Kearsley briefly addresses the similarity between Paul's benefactor Phoebe and Metrodora. Phoebe lived in Kenchreai (Corinth's Aegean port) and travelled to Rome (Rom. 16.1).[275]

Other foreign residents (men and women) would belong to the social elite, and it is safe to conclude that these would include those with a gymnasium education.[276] Indeed, Claudia Metrodora was a gymnasiarch four times and *agonothete* three times for imperial games in Chios.[277] Moreover, Iunia Theodora performed an important role at Corinth for this was on the trade route from Rome to the east, including Lycia.[278]

Further, John Chow cites a monument of mid-first century AD Corinth inscribed to honour Julius Spartiaticus, a patron of the Corinthian tribe of Culpurnia and a powerful man under the emperor, who was a contemporary of Paul.[279] Spartiaticus was a member of the Eurycles

271. Kearsley, 'Women in Public Life', p. 25.

272. Kearsley, 'Women in Public Life', p. 25.

273. Kearsley, 'Women in Public Life in the Roman East', p. 201.

274. Kearsley, 'Women in Public Life in the Roman East', p. 201.

275. Kearsley, 'Women in Public Life in the Roman East', pp. 201–02.

276. For example, men who were educated as ἔφηβοι. Elite women from Sparta could receive a gymnasium education, as we saw earlier.

277. Kearsley, 'Women in Public Life in the Roman East', p. 199.

278. Kearsley, 'Women in Public Life in the Roman East', p. 195. Kearsley identifies the products and people. He notes that all three cities, which honoured her with inscriptions, were coastal cities. See also Winter, *After Paul Left Corinth*, pp. 12–13, 199–203, on Iunia Theodora.

279. Chow, *Patronage and Power*, p. 38. The text is in West, *Corinth: Latin Inscriptions 1896–1926*, no. 68, pp. 50–53.

family in Sparta whose rise and fall are considered by Chow, Chrimes, and Cartledge and Spawforth.[280] Clarke also mentions him.[281] Chow notes that in Corinth, a certain Laco, a procurator of Claudius was honoured with an inscription.[282] Many scholars believe that he was the son of the Eurycles who was granted Roman citizenship and the control of Sparta in *ca.* 30 BC.[283] Both were exiled from Sparta around 31 AD, nevertheless, both held offices and resided in Corinth.[284] Laco was the father of Spartiaticus. Over three generations this wealthy and influential Spartan family resided in Corinth, and Sparta, and had distinguished municipal careers. Spartiaticus also held Corinthian citizenship and he was awarded equestrian rank.[285]

These contemporary texts demonstrate that wealthy and powerful people took up residence in Corinth at the time of Paul. Moreover, it shows travellers (individuals and ambassadors) in Corinth. Its importance as a commercial centre, its situation on trade routes and the Jewish travellers' route to Jerusalem for festivals, as well as host for the important Isthmian Games, meant an influx of people.[286] Therefore it is reasonable to expect people trained in the gymnasia of other cities to be present in Corinth.

Winter describes the three visits of the sophist Favorinus of Arles, a Roman equestrian and a pupil of Dio Chrysostom, to Corinth.[287] On his first visit he began a good relationship with them and during his second visit 'the Corinthians did everything in their power to encourage him to stay, but to no avail. However, they did erect a statue of him in the most prominent place in their library in order to inspire the youth of their city to

280. Chow, *Patronage and Power*, pp. 48–51; K.M.T. Chrimes, *Ancient Sparta: A Re-examination of the Evidence* (Manchester: The University Press, 1949), Chapter V; Cartledge and Spawforth, *Hellenistic and Roman Sparta*, pp. 97–104.

281. Clarke, *Secular and Christian Leadership*, p. 19 and Appendix A, no. 101, p. 149. Clarke notes that he was a non-Corinthian who was prominent in both Corinth and Athens. Among his offices he was *quinquennial duovir* twice. Clarke dates these offices in 47/48 (?) and AD 52/53 (?). He was *agonothete* of the Isthmian and Caesarean games (47 AD).

282. Chow, *Patronage and Power*, p. 49. West, *Corinth: Latin Inscriptions, 1896–1926*, no. 67, pp. 46–49. See also Kent, *Corinth: The Inscriptions, 1926–1950*, pp. 19 n. 6, 25, 31.

283. Chow, *Patronage and Power*, pp. 48–50.

284. Chrimes, *Ancient Sparta*, p. 187.

285. Cartledge and Spawforth, *Hellenistic and Roman Sparta*, p. 104, state that, 'It was presumably as a citizen of Corinth, rather than Sparta, that Spartiaticus was chosen to be the first high-priest of the Achaean League's Imperial Cult.' Chow, *Patronage and Power*, p. 50.

286. For Corinth as a commercial centre see Charles K. Williams II, 'Roman Corinth as a Commercial Center', in Gregory (ed.), *The Corinthia in the Roman Period*, pp. 31–46. Also see Thiselton, *First Epistle*, pp. 6–12.

287. Winter, *Philo and Paul*, pp. 132–37. Favorinus of Arles lived *c.* 80–150 AD.

persevere in the pursuits which won such fame for Favorinus.[288] Favorinus studied oratory in Athens and athletics in Sparta. He is encouraged to take up residence but refuses. Nevertheless, he encourages Greeks and barbarians to imitate his ways 'so that no one even of the barbarians may despair of attaining the culture of Greece (τῆς Ἑλληνικῆς παιδείας) when he looks upon this man.'[289] If he speaks thus to the Corinthians then the youths must have access within Corinth to such Greek education.[290] Rhetoric and athletics were learnt in the gymnasium. More recently, in examining Greek and Roman identity, Jason König has critically assessed Favorinus' Corinthian speech, Aelius Aristides' speech to honour Poseidon (156 AD) and Pausanias' account of Corinth.[291] König insists that Favorinus' speech must be interpreted in its Corinthian context.

Again, Winter comments on one of Favorinus' pupils Herodes Atticus, the sophist and benefactor of Corinth who spent time there.[292] He cites the second-century inscription, found in Corinth, and erected by the *boule* in honour of his wife Regilla. Her husband erected the statue that honoured her during her life. Nevertheless, the inscription praises him as 'pre-eminent above others, who had attained the peak of every kind of virtue' and 'famous among the Hellenes'.[293] Winter concludes:

> Herodes Atticus epitomises all that a virtuoso rhetorician should be, and was deemed worthy of the longest treatment in Philostratus' *Lives*. Of his success as a declaimer there is no doubt. Furthermore he was well born and had vast financial resources which he used to erect fine buildings in a city not his own, namely Corinth. The accolades bestowed upon him were meant to secure further benefactions for this city. E. L. Bowie's discussion of the status of sophists surely finds its focus in this man who may rightly be called wise, powerful, and well-born.[294]

For Winter, Herodes Atticus shows the tremendous importance of a sophist at Corinth and supports his argument that Paul's opponents in 1 and 2 Corinthians were sophists. But his family also demonstrates how sons could be sent away to be educated.

288. Winter, *Philo and Paul*, p. 133. However, the statue was thrown down later.

289. *Or*. 37.27.

290. I owe this insight to Onno M. van Nijf. Personal communication. Reproduced with kind permission.

291. König, 'Favorinus' *Corinthian Oration*'. König notes that Aristides' speech seems to be for the Isthmian festival (p. 153).

292. Winter, *Philo and Paul*, pp. 137–41. Herodes Atticus lived *c*. 101–77 AD.

293. Winter, *Philo and Paul*, p. 138.

294. Winter, *Philo and Paul*, p. 141.

Antony Spawforth sets out the evidence that ties the family of Herodes Atticus, the Athenian consul, to Sparta.[295] Tib. Claudius Atticus Herodes, the sophist's father, served a term in Sparta's ephebate.[296] Herodes Atticus, and his son Regillus Atticus, were Spartan ephebes.[297] Thus Herodes Atticus' family enjoyed close ties with Sparta during which three members attended an ephebate away from their native city (Athens). The family exemplifies Paul's words concerning those who were wise, influential and of noble birth (1 Cor. 1.26–31). Access to the gymnasium was available to them in Sparta, a city that did not usually accept foreigners.

Likewise, Corinthians may enrol their sons in ephebic training outside Corinth, possibly at Athens. Forbes and Marrou list the inscriptional evidence for the number of Athenian and foreign ephebes at Athens and demonstrate that in New Testament times the number of foreigners exceeded Athenian ephebes.[298] Christian Habicht also notes that foreigners (not just Romans) were admitted to the Athenian ephebate from around 125 BC.[299] However, Antony Spawforth comments that Herodes' family is odd and so is the Athenian ἐφηβεία regarding foreigners.[300] Spawforth notes that students leaving home for 'tertiary' education (e.g., to study rhetoric) is well documented but this is not so for 'secondary' education. In the Roman *polis* passage through the ἐφηβεία was a *de facto* qualification for

295. A.J.S. Spawforth, 'Sparta and the Family of Herodes Atticus: A Reconsideration of the Evidence', *ABSA* 75 (1980), pp. 203–20.

296. Spawforth, 'Sparta and the Family of Herodes Atticus', p. 203. He had one-year in Sparta's ephebate (during *c*. 86–93 AD) when he was probably between 16–18 years old.

297. See Cartledge and Spawforth, *Hellenistic and Roman Sparta*, p. 113, for Herodes as an ephebe. His son is discussed in Spawforth, 'Sparta and the Family of Herodes Atticus'.

298. Forbes, *Greek Physical Education*, pp. 172–76, and Marrou, *A History of Education in Antiquity*, pp. 383–84. Marrou says it is seems quite certain 'that the great majority of these foreign ephebes were not the sons of foreigners who had settled in Attica or its dependencies but students who came to Athens for the particular purpose of completing their education; most of them came from Asia Minor – the majority of them were Milesians in the years 80–90 to 115 AD, but there were also quiet a few from Syria-Palestine; those who came from the West came chiefly from Sicily, Tarento, and above all Roman Italy' (p. 384). In the period 39/8 BC Marrou gives 53 Athenian and 66 foreign ephebes, in 84/5 – 92/3 AD he gives 80 Athenian ephebes and 151 foreigners and for 111/2 AD, 21 and 79 respectively. Athens not only accepted foreigners but also had a prestigious educative institution at this time. Nevertheless, Marrou does not cite any Corinthians in the lists. Forbes' inscriptions, p. 173, in 13/2 BC, 44/5 AD, and 41–54 AD give no indication whether the ephebes were partly foreigners. Forbes argues that 'Milesians' is a general term for foreigners (pp. 172–73).

299. Christian Habicht, 'Roman Citizens in Athens (228–31 B.C.)', in Hoff and Rotroff (eds.), *The Romanization of Athens* (Oxbow Monograph, 94; Oxford: Oxbow Books, 1997), pp. 9–17 (11).

300. Spawforth. Personal communication. Reproduced with kind permission.

active citizenship.[301] It seems that this route for education would be exceptional, not normal.

In conclusion, residents in Corinth, and hence Corinthian Christians, could receive a gymnasium education in Corinth. Mobility within the Empire meant that Corinthian residents (not necessarily permanent residents) would include those who had received a gymnasium education in other cities before moving to Corinth. Exceptionally, parents could send their sons away to receive ephebic training but this was not normal. Finally, in *After Paul Left Corinth* Winter argues that the Corinthian church was affected by 'secular educational mores in Corinth' and 'the secular élitist educational model which was promoted by the sophists', certainly my findings are consistent with his conclusion.[302]

6. *Jews in the Diaspora*

a. *Jews and Hellenization*

In 1 Corinthians we see a racially mixed church (cf. Acts. 18.8) and it is important to evaluate how this education model is applicable to both gentiles and Jews in the church, and to Paul, the Diaspora Jew.[303] Hengel has examined the Hellenization of Jews in first century Judaea.[304] He shows how widespread this process was and that the usual distinction between 'Palestinian' Judaism and 'Hellenistic' Judaism is not valid. This section investigates Diaspora Jews to see if any received a Greek education. On ancient terms for Jewish identity see the discussion by Naomi Janowitz.[305] I follow Barclay (below) who uses the term 'Jew'.

The Mediterranean Diaspora is a complex and diverse area and John Barclay states that the reluctance to generalise, 'reflects an important characteristic of current scholarship on post-biblical Judaism.'[306] There are

301. Spawforth. Personal communication. Reproduced with kind permission. Spawforth observes that this is discussed by M.-F. Baslez, 'Citoyens et non-citoyens dans l'Athènes imperiale au Ier et au IIe siècles de notre ère', in Walker and Cameron (eds.), *The Greek Renaissance in the Roman Empire: Papers from the Tenth British Museum Classical Colloquium* (Bulletin Supplement, 55; London: Institute of Classical Studies, University of London, 1989), pp. 17–36. In Roman Egypt passage through the gymnasium was also the route to citizenship.

302. Winter, *After Paul Left Corinth*, p. 43. This is his conclusion in Chapter 2 'Secular Discipleship and Christian Competitiveness (1 Corinthians 1–4)'. He compares the situation to secular disciples and teachers.

303. Horrell, *Social Ethos*, pp. 91–92 argues from 1 Corinthians, Romans and Acts that the believers included both Jews and gentiles by the time Paul wrote 1 Corinthians. Most would be gentiles I agree.

304. Hengel, *The 'Hellenization' of Judaea in the First Century After Christ*. See chapter 3, pp. 19–29, for his examination of 'Greek Education and Literature in Jewish Palestine.'

305. Naomi Janowitz, 'Rethinking Jewish Identity in Late Antiquity', in Mitchell and Greatrex (eds.), *Ethnicity and Culture in Late Antiquity*, pp. 205–19.

306. Barclay, *Jews in the Mediterranean Diaspora*, p. 4.

in fact 'Judaisms'. Barclay's recent study offers a comprehensive survey of Jews in the Mediterranean Diaspora. His time span (323 BC – 117 AD) includes the New Testament period and he covers the history of the Jewish communities and an analysis of the main Diaspora literature.[307] The sensitivity of the analytical tools defined and utilised in his work, together with his interest in the gymnasium, make his study particularly appropriate and forms the basis for my analysis. Moreover, Erich S. Gruen's recent study *Diaspora: Jews Amidst Greeks and Romans* also offers helpful perspectives. He follows Barclay in showing that although 'the testimony is slim' Jews could enter the Greek gymnasium.[308]

Barclay considers the categories that earlier scholars used to discuss Judaism (e.g. 'normative', 'classical' or 'native'), implying that 'native' was the 'purist' and dominant in Palestine.[309] 'Purist' was synonymous with 'Pharisaic' or 'rabbinic' Judaism. However, the old consensus has failed. 'Normative' Judaism cannot be applied to the Hellenized Diaspora. Even Palestine Jews were Hellenized. Although Feldman uses the category of 'deviation' plus the terms 'apostate' and 'apostasy', Barclay finds these inadequate.[310] Moreover, he criticises Feldman for his treatment of Hellenization and for using 'syncretistic' to describe diverse items.[311] This, Barclay rightly claims, does not seem of much analytical value, rather, he attempts 'to *weigh the significance* of such phenomena – an assessment which involves observing their social contexts and the perceptions of those who practised or witnessed such activities.'[312]

In Hellenization he sees seven principal components: political, social, linguistic, educational, ideological, religious, and material. Nevertheless, he admits this list is not exhaustive and the categories overlap.[313] But the advantage of Barclay's division is his recognition that Jews could engage with Hellenism in each sphere to 'differing degrees.'[314] Thus he helpfully

307. Barclay, *Jews in the Mediterranean Diaspora*, p. 9.

308. Gruen, *Diaspora*, pp. 123–26.

309. Barclay, *Jews in the Mediterranean Diaspora*, p. 82.

310. Barclay, *Jews in the Mediterranean Diaspora*, pp. 84–6. L.H. Feldman, *Jew and Gentile in the Ancient World* (Princeton: Princeton University Press, 1993). For a review of Feldman see: Fergus Millar, 'Review of L.H. Feldman, *Jew and Gentile in the Ancient World. Attitudes and Interactions from Alexander to Justinian*', *CR* 45 (1995), pp. 117–19.

311. Barclay, *Jews in the Mediterranean Diaspora*, p. 87.

312. Barclay, *Jews in the Mediterranean Diaspora*, p. 87.

313. Barclay, *Jews in the Mediterranean Diaspora*, pp. 88–90. He notes that Hellenization is the cultural engagement with 'Hellenism', which is 'the common urban culture in the eastern Mediterranean, founded on the Greek language . . . typically expressed in certain political and educational institutions and largely maintained by the social élite' (p. 88). Under 'Educational', he states that this is 'the acquisition of Greek *paideia* (training/education)' (p. 89).

314. Barclay, *Jews in the Mediterranean Diaspora*, p. 90.

distinguishes different kinds, and different degrees, of Hellenization while avoiding simple categories that are inadequate for addressing the evidence. To facilitate his analysis he constructs three scales for different kinds and degrees of Hellenization: assimilation, acculturation and accommodation.[315] Under assimilation the scale includes most of the political, social, and material aspects together with religious practice. It assesses the degree to which Diaspora Jews were integrated, or not, into their social environment. Both the frequency and quality of their contacts with gentiles need to be known to measure the assimilation. See Figure 1.[316]

The top of the scale shows social integration involving abandonment of Jewish social distinctiveness, while at the bottom of the scale, the social life is confined to the Jewish community and these people are the least assimilated.[317] Barclay's scale clearly highlights my focus on gymnasium education while including the related aspect of attending Greek athletics. In this process of assimilation a Diaspora Jew may receive a gymnasium education, which did not necessarily require abandoning key Jewish customs.

Under acculturation, Barclay includes education and remarks, 'In acquiring Greek *paideia* (to whatever level), Jews gained access not only to certain literary resources but also to a system of values which constituted, in Greek eyes, the very essence of civilization. Inasmuch as they acquired this common discourse of cultural ideals and recognized virtues, Diaspora Jews may be said to have become acculturated'.[318] His scale shows representative points. See Figure 2.[319]

At the top of the scale are 'those expert in the critical traditions of Hellenistic scholarship, the acme of scholarly attainment.'[320] He admits

315. Barclay, *Jews in the Mediterranean Diaspora*, p. 92. 'Assimilation' refers to '*social integration* (becoming "similar" to one's neighbours): it concerns social contacts, social interaction and social practices. By contrast, "acculturation" is here used to refer to the *linguistic, educational and ideological* aspects of a given cultural matrix.' Assimilation can be a means or result of acculturation but they can be distinguished. For example, Barclay notes that in Greek households Jewish slaves might be highly assimilated even if they received very little acculturation. But, 'Jews might acquire considerable expertise in Hellenistic *paideia*' while showing considerable care during social contacts with any non-Jews. For a summary of his three scales see P.R. Trebilco and C.A. Evans, 'Diaspora Judaism', in Evans and Porter (eds.), *Dictionary of New Testament Background*, pp. 281–96 (288–91).

316. Reproduced with permission.

317. Barclay, *Jews in the Mediterranean Diaspora*, p. 94. Barclay notes that although there were variations, taboos impeding Jewish assimilation included: refusing to worship other gods, Jewish dietary restrictions, Sabbath observance, and adherence to circumcision.

318. Barclay, *Jews in the Mediterranean Diaspora*, p. 95.

319. Reproduced with permission.

320. Barclay, *Jews in the Mediterranean Diaspora*, p. 95.

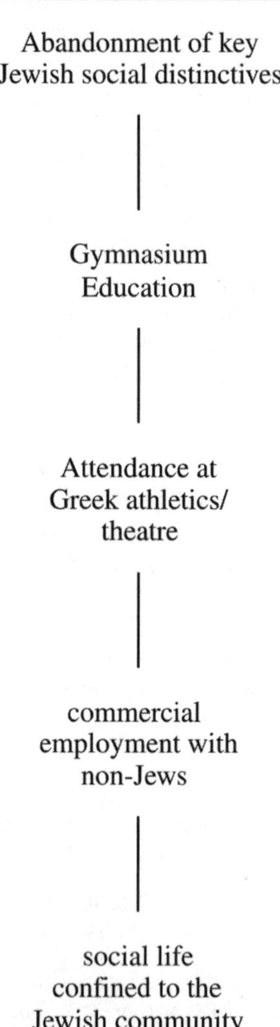
Assimilation
(Social Integration)
Abandonment of key
Jewish social distinctives
Gymnasium
Education
Attendance at
Greek athletics/
theatre
commercial
employment with
non-Jews
social life
confined to the
Jewish community

Figure 1

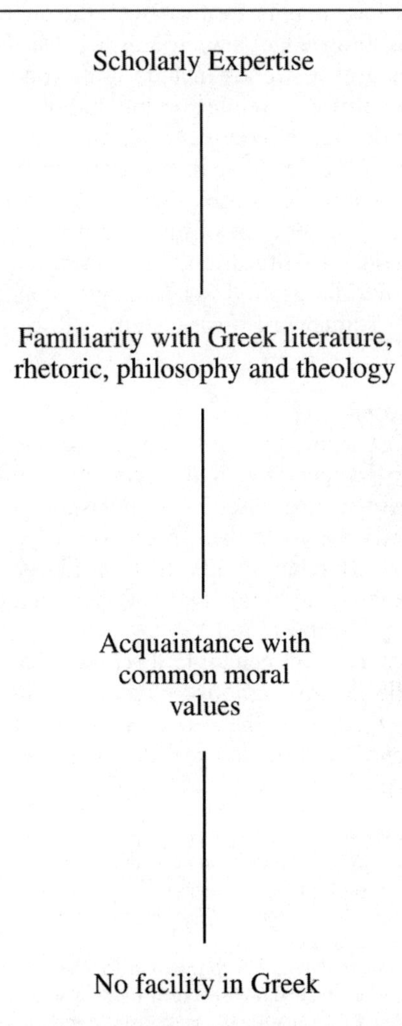

Figure 2

that his scale is vague in the centre but defends it because its heuristic value lies in showing that 'acculturation' is different from 'assimilation'. This is a valid point and the vagueness is acceptable in my study.

His final step distinguishes between acculturation and accommodation.[321] This is another useful distinction because it considers the degree to which Jewish and Hellenistic cultural traditions were merged or indeed polarized. Diaspora Jews may be familiar with the Greek heritage but how did they employ this knowledge? Two trends are distinguished: integrative or oppositional. Integrative trends include imitation, internalization and employment of the culture in reinterpreting Judaism, while oppositional trends comprise a defensive/resistive position and possibly employing Hellenistic weapons in a polemic against Hellenism.[322] See Figure 3.[323]

This scale indicates how Jews used their acculturation (not how much they were acculturated). The bottom of his scale is not a 'zero' point but an extreme reaction against acculturation.[324] Again, although the scale is not well-defined in the middle ground, as Barclay recognises, it nonetheless provided a sufficient framework for my study.

b. *Barclay's Analysis of the Evidence*

The Mediterranean Diaspora covered a large area but in practice, Barclay notes, there are only five locations in his period with sufficient literary and/or archaeological evidence to describe the Diaspora in any depth. These locations are: Egypt, Cyrenaica, the provinces of Syria and Asia and Rome. Yet even then, Barclay admits, there are large gaps in knowledge and just Egypt 'gives us anything like sufficient material to describe a Diaspora community "in the round"'.[325]

His three scales are commendable because they offer an orderly framework to handle the vast amount of material involved in discussing Hellenization.[326] He recognises the necessity of simplifications (to handle the amount of evidence) and the danger (they may cause misconstruing or

321. Barclay, *Jews in the Mediterranean Diaspora*, p. 96. Accommodation, as employed by Barclay, 'concerns the *use to which acculturation is put*, in particular the degree to which Jewish and Hellenistic cultural traditions are merged, or alternatively, polarized'.

322. Barclay, *Jews in the Mediterranean Diaspora*, pp. 96–97.

323. Reproduced with permission.

324. Barclay, Jews *in the Mediterranean Diaspora*, p. 97. Barclay explains the scale: 'At the top would be those whose accommodation entailed the loss of Jewish cultural uniqueness, those, that is, who merged Judaism with the Hellenistic tradition so far as to submerge it altogether. In the middle we may place those who propounded some Hellenistic interpretation of Judaism but preserved its difference or uniqueness in certain respects. At the other end of the spectrum are those whose employment of acculturation is purely oppositional, giving vent to perhaps well-educated but nonetheless virulent antagonism to Graeco-Roman culture... this scale depicts one of the many paradoxes of our topic: that acculturation could be used to construct either bridges or fences between Jews and their surrounding cultures' (p. 98).

325. Barclay, *Jews in the Mediterranean Diaspora*, p. 10.

326. Barclay, *Jews in the Mediterranean Diaspora*, p. 98.

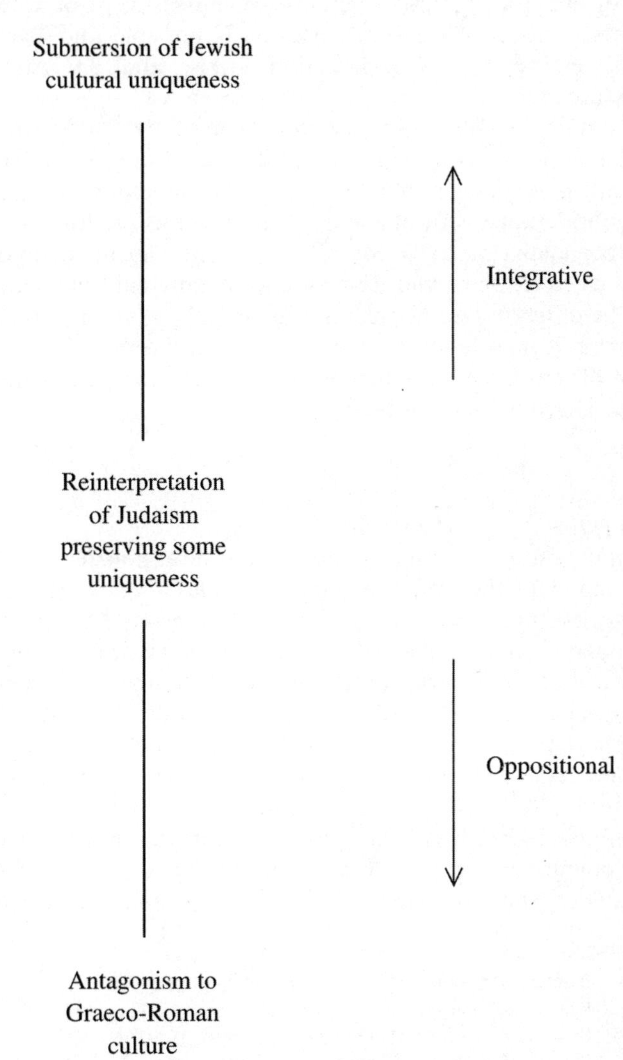
Accommodation
(Use of Acculturation)
Submersion of Jewish cultural uniqueness
Integrative
Reinterpretation of Judaism preserving some uniqueness
Oppositional
Antagonism to Graeco-Roman culture

Figure 3

distorting of the evidence). Nevertheless, inadequate evidence means that all Diaspora Jews cannot be plotted on his three scales. Papyri and inscriptional evidence indicate the degrees and kinds of assimilation, but offer little help in assessing acculturation and accommodation. However, Jewish Diaspora literature permits some assessment of acculturation and accommodation. Thus some analysis is possible and Barclay uses two kinds: assessment of assimilation levels, and analysis of Diaspora literature.[327]

My study examines gymnasium education and the Diaspora Jews, thus Barclay's study, with his wider remit, is used selectively. The material he presents is available in other studies and is therefore not unique. However, the considerable merit of Barclay's approach is the three scales he uses as sensitive analytical tools. My research follows his methodology because in contrast to scholars who have an undifferentiated treatment of Hellenization he differentiates between forms of Hellenization (different kinds and different degrees) and uses these as analytical tools. His approach has the merit of sensitively dealing with the evidence and permits an examination of the Diaspora Jews in their social context.

c. *Egyptian Jews and Assimilation*

Assimilation is the 'social integration into non-Jewish society'.[328] To accommodate the evidence Barclay divides his material into four wide categories: 'high', 'medium', 'low' and 'unknown'.[329]

Under 'high assimilation' Barclay uses a number of sub-categories to represent different forms of assimilation although my study does not need to consider each sub-category.[330] For Jews fully integrated into affairs of state, he cites the most famous example, Tiberius Julius Alexander, Philo's nephew, who held high office in the Roman administration, including procurator of Judea (Josephus, *Ant.* 20.100–3) and governor of Egypt (Josephus, *War* 2.309).[331] Barclay comments that inscriptions demonstrate his commitment to polytheism, and Josephus (*Ant.* 20.100) states that Alexander 'did not remain faithful to his ancestral customs.' Barclay

327. Barclay, *Jews in the Mediterranean Diaspora*, pp. 98–99.

328. Barclay, *Jews in the Mediterranean Diaspora*, p. 103.

329. Barclay, *Jews in the Mediterranean Diaspora*, p. 103.

330. Barclay, *Jews in the Mediterranean Diaspora*, pp. 104–12. His six sub-categories are: Jews fully integrated into the political/religious affairs of state, Social Climbers, Jews who married gentiles and failed to raise their children as Jews, Jewish Critics and Opponents of Judaism, Allegorists who abandoned key Jewish practices, and Isolated Jews.

331. Barclay, Jews *in the Mediterranean Diaspora*, pp. 105–6. Tiberius Julius Alexander (born *c.* 15 AD) was Roman procurator of Judea in 46–48 AD and governor of Egypt in 66–69 AD.

concludes, 'It appears that his assimilation required him to discard most if not all of the practices by which Jewish identity was distinguished.'[332]

For 'Social Climbers' Barclay notes that as the social/ political pressure intensified against Egyptian Jews in the early Roman period:

> Those whose Jewish identity counted against their admission into gymnasia must have been sorely tempted to abandon their Jewish loyalties for the sake of their social advancement. The violence of the middle years of the first century CE and the imposition of the Jewish tax after 70 CE may have increased this tendency, at least for those who were already somewhat on the edge of the Jewish community.[333]

Although Jews in Egypt were privileged, access to the gymnasia was of concern to them:

> In their reorganization of the social and economic structures of Egypt, the Romans attempted to make clear distinctions between native Egyptians and those of genuinely 'Greek' descent. A key aspect of this distinction was the right to enter children for the *ephebeia*, that gymnasium training in which young men were groomed for citizenship and future political participation. This attempt to define the social map involved a complex and controversial investigation of lineage, and this task was given particular urgency by its link with the taxation system.[334]

Following the troubles in Egypt, Claudius' edict (dated 41 AD) to the Alexandrian Jews fixed the fortunes of generations of Jews. The Jews were forbidden to participate in contests arranged by gymnasium officials, *gymnasiarchoi* and *kosmetae*. On the edict, Barclay comments it, 'appears to ban Jews from future gymnasium education and so from all the opportunities and privileges ... which the gymnasia provided. And this impression is confirmed by the following phrase, which urges the Jews to be content with the good things they enjoy *in a city not their own*.'[335] Claudius' comments on ephebes suggests that those already registered as ephebes were not to be removed (except those born of servile mothers) but no more could be added. The Jews, though given religious freedom, were now prevented from providing their children with the educational and

332. Barclay, Jews *in the Mediterranean Diaspora*, p. 106. See pp. 48–81 for Barclay's lucid explanation of the situation of the Jews in Roman Egypt (30 BC – 117 AD).

333. Barclay, Jews *in the Mediterranean Diaspora*, p. 107.

334. Barclay, Jews *in the Mediterranean Diaspora*, p. 49.

335. Barclay, *Jews in the Mediterranean Diaspora*, pp. 58–59 (59). For the edict Barclay, pp. 57–58, cites Josephus (*Ant*. 19.280–85) and the papyrus copy of Claudius' letter (*PLond* 1912 = *CPJ*153) but because of doubts on the authenticity of clauses in Josephus he discusses the papyrus letter as the best evidence. C.K. Barrett, *The New Testament Background: Selected Documents* (London: SPCK, 1956), pp. 44–47, provides a translation of *PLond* 1912.

social opportunities they desired for them. Barclay observes that this was a catastrophe for Philo and others in his social class.[336]

However, Erich Gruen, while agreeing that Jews could receive a gymnasium education in Alexandria, disagrees with scholars' analysis of the evidence in Claudius' edict.[337] Against the 'prevailing notion' Gruen argues that the two passages in the edict (one related to the games and the other on slave parentage/the ephebate) are not related.[338] He notes that nothing connects Claudius' comments on Jews and the ephebate, adding, 'Neither gymnasiarchal education nor access to citizenship is even hinted at here'.[339] Rather, Claudius is only directing Jews not 'to pour' into their games. The emperor was interested in maintaining order and so gymnasia and theatres, where demonstrations and disruption could occur among large crowds, were declared prohibited venues. Claudius, Gruen shows, was interested in being fair and restoring order, not in banning Jews from the gymnasium and its education.

If we follow Barclay's view, Jewish access to the gymnasium ceased after Claudius' edict. However, Gruen argues that this is a misreading of the evidence and Claudius did not prohibit Jewish access to gymnasium education. Either way, this means that during Paul's ministry to the Corinthian Christians, Diaspora Jews from Egypt, educated in Greek παιδεία lived in the Graeco-Roman world.

On Barclay's scale, 'medium assimilation' includes Jews with considerable social ties to the non-Jewish world but who carefully preserved their Jewish identity. Again, Barclay uses sub-categories to represent different forms of assimilation although my study does not consider each sub-category.[340] Among the well-educated Jews of Alexandria were the two brothers, Alexander the Alabarch (father of Tiberius Julius Alexander, mentioned above) and Philo. Philo's

336. Barclay, *Jews in the Mediterranean Diaspora*, p. 60. For an earlier discussion on this incident see A. Kasher, 'The Jewish Attitude to the Alexandrian Gymnasium in the First Century A.D.', *AJAH* 1 (1976), pp. 148–61. Also see John J. Collins, *Jewish Wisdom in the Hellenistic Age* (The Old Testament Library; Louisville, KY: Westminster John Knox Press, 1997), pp. 142–53 who shows that Jews may receive a gymnasium education.

337. Gruen, *Diaspora*, pp. 54–83. This is chapter 2 'The Jews in Alexandria'. For his discussion on Jews and the gymnasium as an institution in the Diaspora see pp. 123–26, where he briefly examines the evidence. He agrees with Barclay; concluding, 'The gymnasium emblematized the Hellenic commitment to the training of body and mind that would constitute the fashioning of the *kalos k'agathos*, the elite Greek gentleman. For Jews who had the wherewithal and the social status to share that ideal, the path, so far as we can tell, stood open' (p. 126).

338. Gruen, *Diaspora*, pp. 79–83.

339. Gruen, *Diaspora*, p. 81.

340. Barclay, *Jews in the Mediterranean Diaspora*, pp. 112–17, give the four sub-categories.

education can be located in the gymnasium. Barclay comments, 'As is typical in the Graeco-Roman world, the privileges of wealth were reflected in the quality of education. Philo talks repeatedly of the training of the gymnasium and of the school education (the 'encyclical education') given to the children of wealthy families.'[341] His works indicate that he was well trained in the core curriculum: literature, mathematics, astronomy, rhetoric and music.

However, Barclay's recognition that Philo received a Greek education is not new. He acknowledges the contribution of Mendelson and Harris.[342] Winter also cites Harris as evidence that Philo was a pupil in the gymnasium.[343] However, Philo was a devout Jew, brought up in a Jewish family, with a knowledge of Scripture and oral tradition that indicates a Jewish education besides his education in Greek culture.[344] He was probably an Alexandrian citizen who experienced ephebic training like other Greek youths of his social class. As an adult he spectated at sporting events and attended the theatre. Thus Barclay locates Philo on the 'medium assimilation' scale. He operates freely in his social environment and Barclay sees no tension evident between different values and no struggle between Jew and Greek in his life.[345]

Philo's life indicates that the 'Greek' and 'Jewish' worlds of late antiquity are perhaps too neatly divided by modern scholars.[346] This is an observation I made earlier when considering ancient education models. It may be convenient to sub-divide education into Greek, Roman and Jewish but this division is oversimplistic and fundamentally misleading if the reader then views these as impenetrable barriers erected and sustained by whether one is Roman, Greek or a Jew. The devout Jew Philo received, valued, and recommended Greek education.

341. Barclay, *Jews in the Mediterranean Diaspora*, p. 160. Barclay notes Philo's references here, e.g., *Spec. Leg.* 2.230, *Prov.* 2.44–46 and *Congr.* 74–76. Philo (*Vit. Mos.* 2.32) regards it praiseworthy that the LXX translators received a 'Greek education'. Elsewhere Barclay, p. 68 n. 45, comments that 'Philo praises those who give their children gymnasium education' (*Spec. Leg.* 2.229–230; cf. *Prov.* 2.44–46) and talks of Moses' Greek teachers (*Vit. Mos.* 1.21). See also Gruen, *Diaspora*, pp. 124–25 who includes Philo's positive comments on both culture and athletics associated with the gymnasium.

342. Barclay, *Jews in the Mediterranean Diaspora*, p. 160 n. 79. Alan Mendelson, *Secular Education in Philo of Alexandria*, pp. 28–33, and H.A. Harris, *Greek Athletics and the Jews*, pp. 72, 91, against H.A. Wolfson, *Philo. Foundations of Religious Philosophy in Judaism, Christianity and Islam* (2 vols.; Cambridge, MA: Harvard University Press, 1948), 1.78–91.

343. Winter, *Philo and Paul*, p. 60 n. 2. Moreover, Winter cites references for Jews among the ephebes, although he does not examine this further (p. 96 n. 74).

344. Barclay, *Jews in the Mediterranean Diaspora*, p. 161.

345. Barclay, *Jews in the Mediterranean Diaspora*, p. 161.

346. Barclay, *Jews in the Mediterranean Diaspora*, p. 161.

Although Barclay examines 'low' and 'unknown' assimilation these Jews did not receive Greek education and are not considered here. Nevertheless, it is now clear that in the first century AD some Egyptian Jews, of a particular social class, did receive a Greek education. Philo was among the educated elite.

d. *Acculturation and Accommodation*

With his other two scales Barclay examines some literature produced by Egyptian Jews. From the second century BC, Jewish writings suggest mastery at 'the highest social and educational levels', indicating a wide cultural awareness while presupposing a Jewish audience able to appreciate their works.[347] Such authors include Aristobulus, the author of *The Letter of Aristeas*, Ezekiel, and the author of *The Wisdom of Solomon*. Undoubtedly, as Barclay admits, these authors represent a tiny number, but he rightly notes, 'Nonetheless, their cultural sophistication indicates that at least some Jews could pass through the gymnasia of Alexandria – those prized organs of Greek culture whose training was the prerequisite for social success in the life of the city'.[348]

Barclay divides his authors into two categories according to the dominant ethos of their work. Cultural convergence as the dominant mood corresponds to the 'integrative' half of the Accommodation scale (see Figure 3 above) and cultural antagonism to the 'oppositional' half of the scale. Barclay's analysis of cultural convergence demonstrates the role of Greek education among devout Jews. It was not simply a matter of choosing either to remain a Jew, or to receive a Greek education, but that Egyptian Jewish authors could be both Jews and Greeks with regard to education. For example, Ezekiel presented the narrative of the Exodus (from the LXX) as a Greek tragedy where his mastery of the fifth-century Greek tragedians is evident. His work leads Barclay to deduce that Ezekiel received a gymnasium education with enthusiasm.[349] Thus he can be located in Barclay's cultural convergence.

Barclay's discussion need not be repeated since this chapter is already rather long. Interested readers should refer to his work. I merely identify conclusions relevant to my study. Philo is not typical of Alexandrian Jews or Mediterranean Jews, nevertheless, he drew on an established tradition in Alexandrian Judaism. Therefore Barclay properly states, 'we may take Philo to represent the intellectual and social stance of his own social

347. Barclay, *Jews in the Mediterranean Diaspora*, p. 42.
348. Barclay, *Jews in the Mediterranean Diaspora*, p. 42.
349. Barclay, *Jews in the Mediterranean Diaspora*, p. 134.

class.'[350] Within his class he received a Greek education as other Jewish authors did. Philo was certainly not the first loyal Jew to receive a gymnasium education, but he followed in a tradition which held together Jewish faith and practice with Greek παιδεία. However, this does not mean that Philo accepted all the associations of a Greek education for this was debased with mythology and immoral tales.[351] Nevertheless, he, like other authors, praised and recommended such an education.[352]

In conclusion, this section demonstrates the values attached to Greek education (παιδεία) by loyal Jews in Egypt. On the Assimilation scale they may receive a gymnasium education without rejecting key features of Jewish social distinctiveness, while on the Acculturation scale some reached the top in scholarly expertise. On the Accommodation scale (i.e., Use of Acculturation) highly educated Jews could use their training in two basic ways: integrative or oppositional. They may defend or attack Judaism. They may imitate Hellenistic culture to reinterpret their own Jewish tradition, and risk submerging their own cultural uniqueness, or they could use, at the other extreme, Hellenistic weapons against Graeco-Roman culture. The important point is that some Egyptian Jews received, respected, and recommended a Greek education while remaining loyal Jews.

e. *The Mediterranean Diaspora Outside Egypt*

While Egypt proves a fruitful ground for examining Greek education among the Diaspora Jews this section advances my discussion by showing the presence of Jewish ephebes in other Jewish communities.

Archaeology demonstrates Jewish communities in Cyrenaica (North Africa), which had five main cities (Cyrene, Apollonia, Ptolemais, Teucheira and Berenice). The inscriptional evidence provides two lists of ephebes in the city of Cyrene (one late first century BC and the other first century [3/4 AD]). Barclay notes that they include Jewish names, e.g., Jesus son of Antiphilos and Eleazar the son of Eleazar. This is proof that Jews could enter:

> The citizen body of Cyrene, though it is impossible to say what attitude they took to the religious aspects of their training (each list of names is dedicated to the Gods of the gymnasium, Hermes and Heracles). A

350. Barclay, *Jews in the Mediterranean Diaspora*, p. 159.

351. Barclay, *Jews in the Mediterranean Diaspora*, p. 176.

352. It is worth pointing out that Jews did not have their own separate gymnasia that were comparable with Greek gymnasia, as Gruen, *Diaspora*, p. 124 n. 132 observes (against Wolfson who maintained they were separate).

> similar phenomenon is probably discernible in Teucheira, where among the names scratched on the walls of the gymnasium are some which are almost certainly Jewish.[353]

Thus, as in Egypt, some Jews received their education in the gymnasium.

In Berenice one inscription (*SEG* 16.931), dated late first century BC/ early first century AD, records the thanks of the Jewish *politeuma* to Decimus Valerius Dionysius who paid for the stucco flooring, as well as the plastering and painting of the amphitheatre, as a contribution to the *politeuma*. Barclay discusses the problematic 'amphitheatre' because many find it difficult to imagine that the Jews mounted inscriptions in the civic amphitheatre and paid for its upkeep.[354] While he recognises the possibility that the community shared in the major civic amenities, and while he notes a century later Jews had their own block of theatre seats in Miletus in Asia (*CIJ* 748) he concludes, 'it is marginally more likely that the amphitheatre" was a specifically Jewish building. It is doubtful whether there was a permanent civic amphitheatre in Berenice at this time.'[355] But Barclay regards his argument here as 'marginal'. In a more thorough discussion on this inscription, and the relationship of Jews to their Graeco-Roman environment, R. Tracey remarks:

> Approached without the presupposition of a rigid, 'normative' Judaism, this inscription can go some way towards helping us to determine what the Jewish norm was at this time and in this particular place. Even on the most conservative interpretation it indicates a strong degree of assimilation, and amicable interaction with the community of Berenike at large.[356]

Even Barclay, while rejecting the standard interpretation of the amphitheatre, recognises the measure of assimilation. Thus two of the cities in Cyrenaica demonstrate Jewish assimilation and the ephebe lists indicate Jews may receive a Greek education in the gymnasium.

In Syria, Herod built the Greek city of Caesarea with amphitheatre, gymnasia, statues and temples. Moreover, Leonard Rutgers, noting how subtle Jewish sensitivities could be when confronted by Greek culture, remarks:

> After granting citizenship to the Jews in Asia, Lower Syria, and Antioch, Seleucus Nicator (ruled 312–281 B.C.) 'gave orders that those

353. Barclay, *Jews in the Mediterranean Diaspora*, pp. 234–35.

354. Barclay, *Jews in the Mediterranean Diaspora*, pp. 236–38.

355. Barclay, *Jews in the Mediterranean Diaspora*, p. 237.

356. R. Tracey, 'Jewish Renovation of an Amphitheatre', in Horsley, *New Documents Illustrating Early Christianity*, 4, no. 111, pp. 202–9 (209). See also the brief comments in Gruen, *Diaspora*, p. 126.

> Jews who were unwilling to use foreign oil should receive a fixed sum of money from the gymnasiarchs to pay for their own kind of oil.' In other words, some of the Jews one encounters here were willing to enjoy the pleasures of an essentially Greek athletic and educational institution, the gymnasium, but nonetheless insisted on using only oil provided by their own co-religionists.[357]

Barclay cites the same passage and also rightly judges that the oil supply was for those Jews training in the gymnasia on their way to Antiochene citizenship, rather than a general supply of oil to the city.[358] The oil distributed by the gymnasiarchs was 'impure' so the Jews had a special concession. Rutgers dates the incident by following Josephus and puts it a few centuries before Paul but Barclay thinks Josephus 'obscures the issue by generalizing it, and implausibly dates the origin of the privilege to the time of Seleucus I'.[359] Gruen too notes this incident and although he doubts its early date from Josephus' account he links the incident to the Jews and the gymnasium.[360] Barclay's reconstruction dates the incident to the Mucianus mentioned by Josephus who was governor of Syria in 67–69 AD which puts the incident shortly after 1 Corinthians was written. However, the incident, whichever date is accepted, again demonstrates the enrolment of Jews in the Greek gymnasium.

In Asia, an inscription from Iasus (early imperial period) mentions Ioudas as a Jewish ephebe and there were probably several other Jewish ephebes.[361] From the second century AD onwards there is more evidence. For example, in Miletus the Jews have prominent seats in the theatre. In the late second century Barclay mentions an inscription from Hypaepa on 'the *Jewish neoteroi*' (*CIJ* 755), suggesting 'an association of Jewish young men who have completed ephebe training.'[362] The Sardis synagogue within the gymnasium shows social integration in at least one location.[363] But the Jews acquired this after the 270s AD – much later than the New Testament period.[364]

357. Leonard Victor Rutgers, 'Archaeological Evidence for the Interaction of Jews and Non-Jews in Late Antiquity', *AJA* 96 (1992), pp. 101–18 (102–03). He quotes Josephus (*Ant.* 12.20).

358. Barclay, *Jews in the Mediterranean Diaspora*, pp. 256–57 n. 63.

359. Barclay, *Jews in the Mediterranean Diaspora*, pp. 256–57 n. 63.

360. Gruen, *Diaspora*, p. 126.

361. Barclay, *Jews in the Mediterranean Diaspora*, p. 271.

362. Barclay, *Jews in the Mediterranean Diaspora*, p. 280 n. 53.

363. Barclay, *Jews in the Mediterranean Diaspora*, p. 280.

364. Barclay, *Jews in the Mediterranean Diaspora*, p. 280 n. 55. Marianne P. Bonz, 'The Jewish Community of Ancient Sardis: A Reassessment of Its Rise to Prominence', *HSCP* 93 (1990), pp. 343–59, provides a discussion on the Jews and their acquisition of the synagogue.

In examining Rome, Barclay does not provide any evidence of Jewish integration into the gymnasium or Greek *paideia*. Nevertheless, Horsley discusses a third/fourth-century AD Greek epitaph from Rome. Kallistos, a child of Syrian parentage, was brought up at Rome but died aged nearly twelve, concerned himself 'with a good education and attending the gymnasium.'[365] Horsley thinks that this is of particular interest, for the child was 'given the opportunity of a thorough-going Greek education: not only *paideia* but also access to the gymnasium.'[366] However, this is well beyond our period.

In assessing the levels of assimilation among Diaspora Jews outside Egypt, Barclay helpfully summarises under 'medium assimilation' examples of Jewish ephebes and citizens:

> From Cyrenaica and Asia, we have already noted the probable presence of Jews among ephebes in Cyrene and Teucheira ... and in Iasus ... It is possible that some of these had begun to renounce their Jewish customs, but it does not seem necessary to assume so. Certainly at a date just beyond our limits an inscription from Hypaepa (Asia) indicates the existence of an association of Jewish youths (*CIJ* 755), apparently ephebes who have graduated from the gymnasium but retained their Jewish identity.[367]

Barclay considers the Diaspora Jew Paul with a brief discussion of his education and his relationship to *paideia*.[368] He concludes that Paul's literary and rhetorical training does not indicate he received a gymnasium education. Moreover, Paul does not appear to prize Greek *paideia*.[369] Instead Paul refers to his progress in Judaism. Barclay follows Hengel in arguing that his education must have taken place in Jerusalem in a school of Torah-interpretation and Paul was 'probably not an ephebe'.[370] What, though, about Paul's co-worker Apollos?

The Alexandrian Jew Apollos is described as learned or eloquent (ἀνὴρ λόγιος, Acts. 18:24). Winter translates this as a 'man of education' and notes that Luke describes him as 'an able speaker and debater (Acts 18.24, 28)'.[371] Donald Ker provides a useful discussion on Apollos and his

365. G.H.R. Horsley, 'Dearer than my mother...', in Horsley, *New Documents Illustrating Early Christianity*, 4, no. 9, pp. 33–35 (34). The inscription is *IG* XIV (1890) 1728.

366. Horsley, 'Dearer than my mother...', p. 34.

367. Barclay, *Jews in the Mediterranean Diaspora*, p. 327.

368. On the 'categorization' of Paul see Barclay's earlier article, 'Paul among Diaspora Jews: Anomaly or Apostate?' *JSNT* 60 (1995), pp. 89–120 and also James D.G. Dunn, 'Who did Paul think he was? A study of Jewish-Christian identity', *NTS* 45 (1999), pp. 174–93.

369. Barclay, *Jews in the Mediterranean Diaspora*, p. 383.

370. Barclay, *Jews in the Mediterranean Diaspora*, pp. 383–85 (385).

371. Winter, *After Paul Left Corinth*, p. 41.

education in relation to Acts and 1 Corinthians.[372] He considers Fee's tentative suggestion that Apollos may have had connections with Philo but dismisses this because the large size of the Jewish community in first-century Alexandria prevents a proof.[373] However, I wish to make the tentative suggestion that Apollos, like Philo, may have received an education in the Greek gymnasium. Nonetheless, I am not suggesting that he knew Philo but just that he too received a Greek education in the gymnasium. This connection may have made him preferable to Paul for some members of the Corinthian congregation (especially those who had also received their education in the Greek gymnasium and those with on-going connections to it).

Paul Barnett discusses Apollos and Paul noting that they were different regarding both their names and education.[374] He observes that while Saul of Tarsus was named after Saul (the first king of Israel) Apollos was named after a Greek god (Apollo). He makes a distinction between their educations. Paul received his education 'in the strict pharisaic academies in Jerusalem whereas Apollos of Alexandria, who was an *anēr logios* (Acts 18:24), would have been nurtured in an educational culture that we sense was different, despite not knowing how it was different'.[375] In a footnote, he concludes on Apollo's education:

> Ker, 'Paul and Apollos' (78) follows Litfin in making a connection between 'eloquence' and (rhetorical) 'education'. True as this was for Greeks and Romans it was not true for Jews. Apollos was an educated *Jew*. The assumptions regarding educated/eloquent gentiles do not obtain for Jews. The education of Apollos the Jew and his 'eloquence' could not have been more distinct from the educated and eloquent Gentile.[376]

But this view is mistaken as the evidence presented above demonstrates. Apollos, like the Jew Philo of Alexandria, could have been educated in the Greek gymnasium.

Thus this section has demonstrated that Jews could be educated in the Greek gymnasium. Barnett draws a distinction between Jews and gentiles. Perhaps it is worth pointing out that there were different views between some Romans and Greeks on education. It is true that Romans became ephebes as Christian Habicht notes that foreigners (not just Romans) were

372. Donald P. Ker, 'Paul and Apollos – Colleagues or Rivals?' *JSNT* 77 (2000), pp. 75–97 (76–79).

373. Ker, 'Paul and Apollos', p. 77; citing Fee, *First Epistle*, p. 57.

374. Paul Barnett, 'Paul, Apologist to the Corinthians', in Burke and Elliott (eds.), *Paul and the Corinthians*, pp. 313–326 (319).

375. Barnett, 'Paul, Apologist to the Corinthians', p. 319.

376. Barnett, 'Paul, Apologist to the Corinthians', p. 319 n. 19.

admitted to the Athenian ephebate from about 125 BC.[377] However, some moral Romans looked with suspicion on the Greek gymnasium as Michael Carter mentions.[378] Eyben also notes these concerns but observes that some Romans still went along![379]

Finally, I turn to one particular use of the term 'gymnasia' before concluding my chapter.

7. *Gymnasia as Gifts in Latin Inscriptions*

Before closing this long chapter I shall briefly address how the terms *gymnasium* and *gymnasia* were used in Latin inscriptions in a quite distinct way from the Greek gymnasium. Garrett Fagan's article captures this very clearly when he states:

> There are a number of inscriptions from the western provinces, especially North Africa, that commemorate gifts to a community by local officials of what the texts term *gymnasium* or *gymnasia*. At first glance, the interpretation of these inscriptions might appear unproblematic, since *gymnasia* are well-known as centers for exercise and education in the Greco-Roman world. A closer look at the inscriptions, however, reveals that the *gymnasia* recorded here cannot be buildings; in any case the term *gymnasium*, while routinely applied to structures in the Greek East, was never used in such a sense in inscriptions from the Latin West. Instead, the Latin inscriptions mentioning *gymnasia* clearly record the conferral of some sort of liberality for the benefit of the local population.[380]

Fagan examines forty-eight Latin inscriptions, including forty-five from North Africa and three from Germany and Spain, which refer to the *gymnasium*. The earliest inscription (no. 34) is from Spain and dated to the reign of Trajan while the latest inscription (no. 15) is African in the reign of Probus. Most datable inscriptions are attributed to the Severan

377. Habicht, 'Roman Citizens in Athens (228–31 B.C.)', pp. 9–17 (11).

378. Carter, 'A *Doctor Secutorum* and the *Retiarius* Draukos from Corinth', p. 267. He cites Plutarch's *Mor.* 274D, 'The Romans were exceedingly suspicious of rubbing down with oil, and believe that nothing has been so much the cause of the enslavement and effeminacy of the Greeks as their gymnasia and palaestra (τὰ γυμνάσια και τὰς παλαίστρας)'. However, as we saw earlier, Antony was a gymnasiarch.

379. Eyben, *Restless Youth in Ancient Rome*, pp. 84–86. He comments, 'Many (wealthy) youths did not lose any sleep over such objections from Romans of the old guard and were regular visitors to palaestras and gymnasia' (p. 85).

380. Garrett G. Fagan, 'Gifts of *gymnasia*: A Test Case for Reading Quasi-technical Jargon in Latin Inscriptions', *ZPE* 124 (1999), pp. 263–75 (263). However, he notes from the Latin literature 'dozens of examples of *gymnasium* used to denote buildings', e.g. Vitr. *De arch.* 1.7.1; Pliny *HN* 28.52; Quint. *Inst.* 12.2.8 and Pliny *Ep.* 10.39–40 (p. 263 n. 1).

era.[381] He concludes that we have a word with a regional use that was imported into Africa where it became popular. Thus *gymnasium* is used in a rather limited sense in his article. However, what did it mean and does this impact on my study?

Scholars have argued for two possible uses of the term *gymnasium* as either 'gymnastic displays or competitions' or as 'distributions of oil' (often by gymnasiarchs in the Greek East or with baths/bathing in the Latin West). Nevertheless, as both interpretations do not fit all the inscriptions Fagan offers a third possibility arguing against the way that the question is framed as either/or. He argues against the assumption that it must be one or the other and that it is too much to expect epigraphic language to be consistent. The term is 'quasi-technical' and it does not require a single meaning in all contexts. Consequently, '*gymnasium* in certain places and on certain occasions could have denoted distributions of oil and/or other supplies for exercise in the bathhouse ... while in other contexts ... it may have commemorated the staging of a gymnastic display or competition'.[382]

Thus Fagan helpfully indicates how the terms *gymnasium* and *gymnasia* where used in Latin inscriptions over a narrow time span, in the second and third centuries AD, and in a restricted geographical area. He demonstrates different usages but his article supports the use of *gymnasium*/*gymnasia* in the Greek East as buildings for exercise and education.

8. *Summary*

I began this chapter by examining the development of the Greek gymnasium. Besides describing the architecture and adornment of the gymnasium, I showed how it was a cultural and educational centre in antiquity both before, and after, the New Testament period. I described the important role of the gymnasiarch and considered the ephebes and *neoi*. This demonstrates that the gymnasium became an institution of particular importance for the social elite, an area relevant for the interpretation of 1 Corinthians.

381. Trajan was emperor 98–117 AD. Inscription no. 34 is dated AD 109. The Severan dynasty went from Septimius Severus (AD 193–211) to Severus Alexander (222–235 AD) but the Emperor Macrinus (217–218 AD) is excluded. The latest inscription (no. 15), in the reign of Probus, is dated 276–282 AD. Some inscriptions date from the Antonine period – the Emperors Nerva (96–98 AD) to Commodus (180–192 AD).

382. Fagan, 'Gifts of *gymnasia*', p. 271. He notes that 'oil distributions' appears as the most likely readings for North Africa inscriptions. However, he argues that uncertainty in the meaning of *gymnasium* is more related to our modern perspective than the ancient context where the local people would understand the jargon used.

After this general introduction I considered three routes by which residents at Corinth, and hence members of the church, might receive a gymnasium education. One route was through the gymnasia at Corinth. The two other routes investigated were based on the mobility of people in the Empire. People who had received a gymnasium education outside Corinth may become residents in the city. Moreover, Corinthians could send their sons away for ephebic education. However, this would be exceptional rather than normal. It is entirely feasible that Spartan women from the social elite residing in Corinth may have been educated in Sparta's gymnasia, in the *agoge*. Although not ephebes, they will have also experienced gymnasium education. Thus the model, while focusing on the reality of male education in the gymnasium, includes provision for the few females who received a gymnasium education.

My investigation of Diaspora Jews is important because the Corinthian church included Jews. Using the analytical tools developed by Barclay, I show that certain Jews from the social elite received a Greek gymnasium education in New Testament times while remaining loyal Jews. This practice was not restricted to Egypt but occurs in other areas of the Diaspora. Hengel demonstrates the 'Hellenization' of Judaea in the first century AD, so Jews there also had access to, and received, a Greek education.[383] Therefore, the education model recognises that Jews, both loyal and those abandoning their heritage, did mix with gentiles if they received a Greek gymnasium education. A final point is the fiction of kinship between the Jews and the Spartans.[384] Hengel notes that, 'Sparta was particularly attractive to the Jewish Hellenists, so that at an early stage they constructed a primal relationship between Jews and Spartans.'[385] Thus bonds existed between Jews and Spartans.

In chapter 2 I identified the oversight of New Testament scholarship in omission of the Greek gymnasium when considering the educated elite in 1 Corinthians. This chapter has rectified that oversight. Even Pauline scholars conducting social-science studies, which have discovered the role

383. More recently this has been demonstrated for Galilee by Santiago Guijarro, 'The Family in First-Century Galilee', in Moxnes (ed.), *Constructing Early Christian Families*, pp. 42–65. Guijarro, for example, concludes that, 'the omnipresence in the literary texts of families of the highest class, together with the widely attested evidence of big mansions of Hellenistic-Roman origin indicate that Galilee was deeply Hellenised, and that the families of this social class – who lived in cities – were not substantially different from those who lived in cities in other parts of the empire' (p. 62).

384. See Cartledge and Spawforth, *Hellenistic and Roman Sparta*, pp. 37, 85, 100, 114. Also Hengel, *Judaism and Hellenism*, II.329, under 'Spartans (and Jews).'

385. Hengel, *Judaism and Hellenism*, I.26. Hengel, p. 72, also notes that this legend of the affinity between the Jews and Spartans goes back to pre-Maccabean times. He explains the similarities between their beliefs and notes, 'It is certainly no coincidence that Jason, author of the Hellenistic reform in Jerusalem, ended his life in Sparta'.

of the educated elite in the community conflict between Paul and the Corinthians, have missed this crucial area for research. For example, Dale Martin's analysis of the body in 1 Corinthians overlooks gymnasium education for the elite.[386] Jerome Neyrey recognises the importance of athletic imagery to body language and the social body in 1 Corinthians but makes no connection with Greek education.[387]

Studies that characterise Corinth as a Roman city risk mistakenly marginalizing its Greek culture and heritage. Moreover, there has been a failure to investigate Corinth sufficiently within the Greek East as if the Corinthians lived in an impenetrable walled city with only connections to Rome. Its own gymnasium and the movement of people within the Graeco-Roman world clearly demonstrate the shortcomings of this too narrow approach. The Greek gymnasium as an ancient education model demands a voice in the social-scientific investigation of 1 Corinthians and fills a significant gap in New Testament scholarship. It is not that Pauline scholars are unaware of the survival of the gymnasium, but they fail to recognise its relevance to a sensitive exegesis of Paul's letter.

My next task, in the following chapter, is to investigate education, family and society in the Graeco-Roman world. This will provide a more rounded picture for understanding elite education.

386. Martin, *The Corinthian Body*.

387. Neyrey, 'Body Language in 1 Corinthians' Models for Understanding Paul and His Opponents'.

Chapter 4

Education, Family, and Society in the Graeco-Roman World

1. *Introduction*

In chapter 3 I described the development and relevance of the Greek gymnasium as an ancient education model for understanding the educated elite in 1 Corinthians. However, the Greek gymnasium, and its education, were not individualistic, isolated from society and family. In antiquity, education, family, and society were more closely aligned than in the modern western world, where the state provides, legislates, inspects, and controls education. Therefore an ancient education model for interpreting 1 Corinthians must examine the relationship between the individual, the family, and society in the Graeco-Roman world. This chapter, therefore, rectifies this omission in education models used by New Testament scholarship to understand 1 Corinthians. Consequently, this chapter locates the Greek gymnasium and education within the first-century family and society.

While Paul relativizes the social-status issues of wisdom, influence and noble birth in 1 Cor. 1.26–31 he uses family language in his letter, particularly in 1 Cor. 3–4, and presents himself as the father to his Corinthian children (1 Cor. 4.15). Moreover, he deals with issues related to families, e.g., 1 Cor. 7 concerns marriage. The commentator C.K. Barrett notes, 'The father-child relationship is unique, and corresponding to it is the relationship between the convert and the preacher responsible, under God, for his conversion'.[1] Similarly, Gordon Fee observes, 'His unique relationship to them was that of "father," and that gave him a special authority over and responsibility toward them. With this language, therefore, he is both reasserting his authority and appealing to their

1. Barrett, *First Epistle*, p. 115.

loyalty, which had obviously been eroded in this church'.[2] Clearly, Paul is not the natural father of the believers but their fictive father. David Bossman has helpfully discussed this fictive language.[3] Yet this concern with families is not unique to Paul. Plutarch wrote on brotherhood.[4] Philo, as we shall see, discussed families. And, as John Collins comments, about one half of Ben Sira's book addresses 'practical wisdom concerning relations with family members, women, rulers, servants, and friends and other aspects of social behaviour'.[5] He is the first Jewish writer to offer a detailed discussion on the honour of parents.[6] John Elliott demonstrates the significance of the role and function of the household theme in 1 Peter.[7] Moreover, Eva Marie Lassen observes, 'Metaphors of the family held a strong position among metaphors in Roman society and can be found in the religious as well as the social and political spheres'.[8]

Nevertheless, the study of families in antiquity is fairly recent. Halvor Moxnes comments, 'Strangely enough, although "family" is such an important topic in Christianity, there have been few comprehensive studies of family in early Christianity'.[9] He admits that there has been much interest in some aspects (e.g., ethics regarding marriage and 'household' codes) but much less interest 'in the social behaviour and forms of family'. This lack of interest also prevailed in Graeco-Roman studies until fairly recently.[10] Now discussion has focused on the family as a central topic in antiquity. Biblical scholars too have begun to address this area.[11] For

2. Fee, *First Epistle*, p. 185.

3. David M. Bossman, 'Paul's Fictive Kinship Movement', *BTB* 26 (1996), pp. 163–71.

4. Reidar Aasgaard, 'Brotherhood in Plutarch and Paul: Its Role and Character,' in Moxnes (ed.), *Constructing Early Christian Families*, pp. 166–82, discusses the similarities between Plutarch's view on carnal brotherhood and Paul's on spiritual brotherhood.

5. Collins, *Jewish Wisdom in the Hellenistic Age*, p. 62.

6. Collins, *Jewish Wisdom in the Hellenistic Age*, p. 63.

7. John H. Elliott, *A Home for the Homeless: A Sociological Exegesis of 1 Peter, Its Situation and Strategy* (London: SCM Press, 1982).

8. Eva Marie Lassen, 'The Roman Family: Ideal and Metaphor,' in Moxnes (ed.), *Constructing Early Christian* Families, pp. 103–20 (110).

9. Halvor Moxnes, 'Introduction', in Moxnes (ed.), *Constructing Early Christian Families*, pp. 1–9 (1).

10. Moxnes, 'Introduction', p. 1. He cites Keith R. Bradley, *Discovering the Roman Family: Studies in Roman Social History* (New York and Oxford: Oxford University Press, 1991), p. 5, who considers of family history as 'virtually a new field of Roman historical scholarship'.

11. Works here include Carolyn Osiek, 'The Family in Early Christianity: "Family Values" Revisited', *CBQ* 58 (1996), pp. 1–24 (Moxnes includes this article among two exceptions to his general statement, cited above, on lack of interest); Barton, (ed.), *The Family in Theological Perspective*; Moxnes (ed.), *Constructing Early Christian Families* and Osiek and Balch, *Families in the New Testament World.* For a very favourable review of Moxnes (ed.) see Trevor J. Burke, 'Review of H. Moxnes, ed., *Constructing Early Christian Families: Family as Social Reality and Metaphor*', *EvQ* 71 (1999), pp. 280–84.

example, Dale Martin has examined methodological considerations for constructing ancient families by challenging the work of Saller and Shaw.[12] Nevertheless, Beryl Rawson, although recognising certain aspects of Martin's work, has critiqued his methodology for understanding ancient families.[13] Study of the Jewish family in the Graeco-Roman period is in its infancy, as is direct study of the Christian family.[14] Consequently this area remains relatively unexplored for the educated elite in the Corinthian church.[15]

This chapter completes the development of my education model by considering, and incorporating, essential aspects of education, family, and society. I shall start by referring to Graeco-Roman society thus assisting readers to avoid an anachronistic and ethnocentric reading of 'society', as if Paul's world was a modern western democracy. Next, I introduce Paul's family language and associated studies on ancient families. The chapter then investigates: literacy in ancient society, education and parental responsibilities, education and genealogy, education as a status-determinant, child education and labour, infant prodigies, and youth in politics. The analysis of these areas allows a more sensitive discussion on the educated elite in 1 Corinthians and prepares for the application of my model in chapters 5 and 6.

2. *Ancient Society*

In my Introduction, I outlined the importance of reading theory, reading scenarios and the need for considerate readers to make themselves aware of the first-century world. Here, I continue along the same lines. Indeed, Bruce Malina and Richard Rohrbaugh explain the importance of so reading ancient texts in their comment on the synoptic gospels:

12. Dale B. Martin, 'The Construction of the Ancient Family: Methodological Considerations', *JRS* 86 (1996), pp. 40–60. He challenges the methodology, and hence conclusions, of the article: Richard Saller and Brent Shaw, 'Tombstones and Roman Family Relations in the Principate: Civilians, Soldiers and Slaves', *JRS* 74 (1984), pp. 124–56.

13. Beryl Rawson, '"The Family" in the Ancient Mediterranean: Past, Present and Future', *ZPE* 117 (1997), pp. 294–96. She notes that the articles in the 1996 issue of the *Journal of Roman Studies* 86, witness the development of recent 'family' studies in Roman social history (p. 294).

14. Osiek, 'The Family in Early Christianity', pp. 8–9.

15. Helpful studies on Paul and father imagery include: Eva Marie Lassen, 'The Use of the Father Image in Imperial Propaganda and 1 Corinthians 4:14–21', *TynBul* 42 (1991), pp. 127–36, and her 'The Roman Family: Ideal and Metaphor'; Joubert, 'Managing the Household'; Anthony A. Myrick, '"Father" Imagery in 2 Corinthians 1–9 and Jewish Paternal Tradition', *TynBul* 47 (1996), pp. 163–71.

> The distance between ourselves and the Bible is *social* as well as temporal and conceptual. Such social distance includes radical differences in social structures, social roles, values and general cultural features. In fact it may be that such social distance is the most fundamental distance of them all. It may have had a greater impact on our ability to read and understand the Bible than most of what has preoccupied scholarly attention to date.[16]

They continue to focus on this 'social distance' by making the central distinction between the modern industrial period and the New Testament, which is set in an 'agrarian society'. This does not simply mean 'agricultural' but indicates a pre-industrial society embracing all people preceding the industrial revolution. Here both the rural peasant and the city-dweller, without contact with the soil, are 'agrarian'. By contrast Malina and Rohrbaugh see both modern manufacturers and farmers as 'industrialized'.[17] Space prevents further discussion but readers unaware of these issues would benefit from reading the contributions in Jerome Neyrey (ed.) *The Social-World of Luke Acts*.[18] Moreover, James Arlandson has devised a useful figure showing the relationships between wealth, status and power among the various population groups in the Roman empire from the Emperor to the governing classes and urban elite right down to the expendables of society.[19] His model improves earlier models because it attempts to show how wide the social gap was between the elite and all others.

If we turn our focus to first-century Corinth then helpful descriptions of the ancient society can be found in, for example, Chow, Horrell, Thiselton and Clarke.[20] Andrew Clarke clearly identifies the issues, stating, 'One of the major problems facing the interpreter of first-century sources, not least the texts which comprise the New Testament, is the hermeneutical gap which inevitably exists between the languages and beliefs of today's society and those of the distant Graeco-Roman world'.[21] His in-depth study provides five chapters on specific first-century institutions to assist readers in understanding Graeco-Roman society. In Part I Leadership in Graeco-Roman

16. Bruce J. Malina and Richard L. Rohrbaugh, *Social-Science Commentary on the Synoptic Gospels* (Minneapolis, MN: Fortress Press, 1992), p. 2. See also their comments on 'Reading Scenarios', pp. 10–11.

17. Malina and Rohrbaugh, *Social-Science Commentary*, pp. 2–3.

18. Neyrey (ed.), *The Social World of Luke-Acts*. On agrarian society see pp. 154–60.

19. Arlandson, *Women, Class and Society in Early Christianity*, p. 22, Figure 1. His following pages describe the figure clearly.

20. Chow, *Patronage and Power*; Horrell, *Social Ethos*; Thiselton, *First Epistle*; Clarke, *Serve the Community*.

21. Clarke, *Serve the Community*, p. 5. This is in chapter 1 in his second section 'Mind the Gap', where he warns about the assumptions, which can catch the unwary, and evidence that is now challenging scholars' opinions. His first section addresses 'The Social Context of the New Testament'.

Society, he addresses leadership in the: Graeco-Roman City (with political and religious structures, and leading figures), Roman Colony and City, Voluntary Associations, Family and Household and finally, Jewish Synagogues.[22] He is able to conclude from these five contexts, that in each case:

> It is clear that a similar economy of honour and status widely operated. Graeco-Roman society was highly stratified, and at all levels of community life people recognized and elevated the *status quo* whereby those of comparatively greater rank and social standing received due deference and honour. Since such principles of leadership permeated structures at so many different levels of community life, it is reasonable to assume that these dynamics will have impinged significantly on the lives of all in Graeco-Roman society of the first century, whether rich or poor, pagan or Christian.[23]

First-century Graeco-Roman society is certainly not a modern western democracy; rather it is more like an oligarchy.[24] Clarke's analysis evaluates family and household and we must now consider this area while remembering that first-century Corinth existed in a society that was considerably different to that of twenty-first-century western democracies.

3. *Paul and Family*

Families, of course, were situated in Graeco-Roman society. Therefore we need to discover something about these ancient families to see where responsibilities for education lay. In 1 Corinthians we read of Paul's fictive family but also about actual family situations (e.g. 1 Cor. 7 on marriage issues). However, my study is developing an ancient education model in the context of the educated elite and so this chapter seeks to locate education within the family in Graeco-Roman society. My focus is necessarily limited to education and family.

Terrance Callan provides a useful overview of Paul's references to parents and children, which he complements with a consideration of their cultural context in antiquity, before attempting a psychological analysis of Paul.[25] He considers the relevant passages in the Corinthian correspon-

22. These are chapters 2–6 respectively. Thus his work provides a detailed discussion on Graeco-Roman society before he engages in Part II with 'Leadership in the Christian Community'.

23. Clarke, *Serve the Community*, pp. 146–47.

24. Clarke, *Serve the Community*, p. 145. As Clarke notes, the democracy of the classical city-states was replaced by a system in which the local elites held authority.

25. Terrance Callan, *Psychological Perspectives on the Life of Paul: An Application of the Methodology of Gerd Theissen* (Studies in the Bible and Early Christianity, 22; Lewiston, Queenston and Lampeter: The Edwin Mellen Press, 1990), chapter 4 'Parent and Child'.

dence and provides a foundation for interpreting 1 Corinthians, but limited space restricts his examination of the passages in-depth. Thus there is no attempt to relate the family language to the social-status schisms and the elite in 1 Corinthians, although his work has merit in its overview of Paul and provides a basis for further investigation of Paul's family language in 1 Corinthians.

In his examination of Paul's kinship terminology, Bossman observes that at first glance family and kinship appear to be a universal phenomenon, but later he remarks that although 'biological generation' is shared when we consider kinship there exists a wide range of meanings attached to the term.[26] Moreover, he notes the difference between biological and fictive kinship in Paul's kinship terminology:

> We immediately recognize that Paul's relationships with those to whom he writes are not indeed biological, but something we can conveniently term 'fictive' or 'pseudo' kinship. Accordingly, whatever social variation in kinship that Paul's kinship system held, the fictive kinship he enunciates in his letters likely assumes something similar.[27]

This sensible comment should assist in a sensitive reading of Paul's letters, for Bossman warns that in the biblical world kinship units are substantial different from, or even conflict with current 'American "family values"' (either imagined or real).[28]

Bossman's study is, like Callan's, an overview of Paul and therefore displays the same strengths and weaknesses. In his analysis of Paul's use of 'father' he comments on 1 Cor. 4.14–17, 'he uses both father and mother ... to describe his relation to the communities with whom he corresponds in the role of its superior. He contrasts father with a mere guide and suggests a higher role he plays as father'.[29] After citing 1 Thess. 2.7–8 (Paul as a mothering nurse) he states, 'In neither case does Paul wield power so much as he lays claims to his status, his corresponding honor, and the weight of his teaching'. In 1 Thess. 2.9–12 Paul is an exhorting and encouraging father and this leads Bossman to conclude, after these three references, Paul's father-role:

> Is one of instruction, encouragement, and reinforcement rather than one that is authoritative, powerful, or punitive as one might assume from true patriarchy. One can infer from such a definition that the family is built less around the father's authority than around the father's teaching

26. Bossman, 'Paul's Fictive Kinship Movement', p. 163.
27. Bossman, 'Paul's Fictive Kinship Movement', p. 163.
28. Bossman, 'Paul's Fictive Kinship Movement', p. 164.
29. Bossman, 'Paul's Fictive Kinship Movement', p. 164.

> and nurturing, roles typical of maternal uncles, who had no real authority but served precisely these functions.[30]

Yet this conclusion may be premature because he merges texts from two different letters, and situations, while assuming that Paul uses the same facets of his father image in both.[31] Bossman has not introduced the context of the social-status divisions in 1 Corinthians and overlooks Paul's challenge on power and his threat of coming with a rod (1 Cor. 4.18–21).

In her article, Carolyn Osiek examines 'family values' and biblical values within the context of antiquity.[32] Nevertheless, while having much of value in providing a historical situation for understanding 1 Corinthians, her work does not specifically investigate the fictive family in Paul's letter. Her book, with David Balch, is an excellent source on the family in the ancient world and deals with the historical situation of early Christianity.[33] Although not offering any specific models for ancient education they do usefully address education, learning and the family using four tracts from Plutarch.[34] In chapter 6 they summarise Paul's comments on children:

> In his painful debates with the Corinthians about apostleship and status, he uses a parental analogy: 'Children ought not to lay up for their parents, but parents for their children' (2 Cor. 12:14b). Already in the first epistle, he had admonished them as his 'beloved children' (1 Cor. 4:14), insisting that they might have many guardians in Christ, but not many fathers (v. 15). Paul regrets that he could not address the Corinthians as adults, but only as 'babes in Christ' (1 Cor. 3:1–2), a passage O. Larry Yarbrough illuminates by observing that men (usually freedmen) sometimes played significant roles in tending children in the Greco-Roman world.[35]

They, however, do not wish to conclude Paul's ethic of parenthood from the metaphors he uses.[36] Yet their description of ancient education is valuable for its shows differences between modern and ancient education in a family context. Moreover, they include two references to the gymnasium. First, they observe that students in the gymnasium used

30. Bossman, 'Paul's Fictive Kinship Movement', p. 165.

31. See John M.G. Barclay, 'Thessalonica and Corinth: Social Contrasts in Pauline Christianity', *JSNT* 47 (1992), pp. 49–74, for a discussion on their different social situations.

32. Osiek, 'The Family in Early Christianity'.

33. Osiek and Balch, *Families in the New Testament World*.

34. Osiek and Balch, *Families in the New Testament World*, pp. 68–74, on Greco-Roman Education.

35. Osiek and Balch, *Families in the New Testament World*, pp. 156–57; citing O. Larry Yarbrough, 'Parents and Children in the Letters of Paul', in White and Yarbrough (eds.), *The Social World of the First Christians: Essays in Honor of Wayne A. Meeks* (Minneapolis, MN: Fortress Press, 1995), pp. 126–41.

36. Osiek and Balch, *Families in the New Testament World*, p. 157.

exercises (breathing and singing) before tackling texts.[37] Second, they refer to the process of swaddling babies at birth (recommended by doctors). Soranus (early second century AD) recommended where, how, and how long, bandages should be applied to restrict movement. They note, 'Each day nurses would also reshape the head, nose and a boy's penis, which would later be seen at baths and at the gymnasium'.[38] And, of course, during Greek athletics.

In another study, James Francis comments that any theological discussion on the family should take account of children and so he explores the theme of children and the imagery of childhood.[39] He usefully notes that the concept of childhood is recent:

> Childhood is a social artefact, not a biological category ... if we take the word 'children' to mean a special class of people between the ages say of seven and seventeen, who require special forms of nurturing and protection, and who are believed to be qualitatively different from adults, then there is ample evidence that children have existed for less than four hundred years.[40]

'Childhood', he notes, is a great invention from the Renaissance.[41] Furthermore, in his discussion on the social background of the New Testament, he briefly remarks:

> Because children are thought of as essentially adults in the making, childhood tends to be contrasted with adulthood. At root a child is thought of as weak in mind, that is, deficient in 'logos' ... Just like barbarians, children with their faltering speech, are non-participants in the adult rational world. Echoes of this outlook appear in the New Testament, e.g., Paul at 1 Cor 3.1ff likens his readers to babes in their lack of understanding (cf. Hebrews 5.13), and at 1 Cor 13.11–12 adulthood is contrasted with childhood as the stage of entering into maturity of understanding.[42]

37. Osiek and Balch, *Families in the New Testament World*, p. 71. They cite Plutarch's tract 'On Music'.

38. Osiek and Balch, *Families in the New Testament World*, p. 66. They cite from Soranus, *Gyn*. II.15, 42.

39. James Francis, 'Children and Childhood in the New Testament', in Barton (ed.), *The Family in Theological Perspective*, pp. 65–85 (65).

40. Francis, 'Children and Childhood in the New Testament', p. 66.

41. Francis, 'Children and Childhood in the New Testament', p. 66.

42. Francis, 'Children and Childhood', pp. 70–71. He notes Wiedemann's suggestion 'that Paul here may be echoing a definite stage in a child's life when games and toys were set aside, as reflected in many so-called "dedication poems" (p. 71). He cites, Thomas Wiedemann, *Adults and Children in the Roman Empire* (London: Routledge, 1989), p. 152.

These observations are useful in understanding Paul but, because of the necessarily brief analysis, they neither consider the social context of Paul's disputes nor develop childhood within an ancient education model.

In *Children in the Early Church*, William Strange discusses children in the New Testament world with a focus on children and the Gospels.[43] His examination of children in the epistles includes a few references in 1 Corinthians, where he mentions Paul's role of 'father' and others (teachers/leaders) as *paidagogoi*.[44] But this is the nearest that he comes to mentioning education in 1 Corinthians.

The essays in Moxnes' *Constructing Early Christian Families* present comprehensive, well-documented and recent, insights into the social structures of the New Testament world.[45] Moxnes' opening essay examines families and what we mean by 'family' but although he looks at the relationships of parents and children the issue of education remains undiscussed.[46] Lassen ably explains the Roman family but does not discuss education.[47] This essay has common elements with her earlier article on the Roman father image in 1 Cor. 4.14–21 and both are helpful in investigating Paul's use of the term father.[48] Nevertheless, they are not directly applicable to developing my education model.

Bruce Winter's analysis of a student (Neilus) among the Alexandrian sophists provides a window on the first-century sophistic movement in Alexandria and its impact on an advanced student of παιδεία (*paideia*).[49] He describes the student, his slave and his father. Neilus had a wealthy background and his father paid for the boy's education. This illustrates the important connection in antiquity between family and education.

All these studies have much that is commendable and contribute to our understanding of 'family' in the New Testament world. Nevertheless, apart from Winter, they lack detailed discussion on 1 Corinthians and do not use any education model associated with 'family' to interpret Paul's letter. However, despite this they do provide a social context for 'family'. Osiek

43. William A. Strange, *Children in the Early Church: Children in the Ancient World, the New Testament and the Early Church* (Carlisle: Paternoster Press, 1996).

44. Strange, *Children in the Early Church*, pp. 67–69.

45. Moxnes (ed.), *Constructing Early Christian Families*.

46. Halvor Moxnes, 'What is Family? Problems in Constructing Early Christian Families', in Moxnes (ed.), *Constructing Early Christian Families*, pp. 13–41.

47. Lassen, 'The Roman Family: Ideal and Metaphor'.

48. Lassen, 'The Use of the Father Image'.

49. Winter, *Philo and Paul*, chapter 1 'A student among the Alexandrian sophists'. See my discussion of Winter's work in chapter 2.

sums up what 'family' meant in the Mediterranean region in the imperial period:

> Households and family units included children, slaves, unmarried relatives, and often freedmen and freedwomen or other renters of shop or residential property. The easy access between commercial and domestic space in the surviving archaeological material attests to this, as does the literary evidence. All, including slaves, seem to have participated in family religious festivals. Household ownership and management was not restricted to a single nuclear group and its dependencies; there are known examples of houses owned and occupied by brothers, for instance, presumably each with his own dependants. Women headed households, too, both singly and with other women. Therefore, it would seem that, in spite of the strictly patriarchal legal structure of families, there was a great deal of variety in the composition of actual households (οἰκίαι, *domus*). Family and household in our meanings of the word are not necessarily to be equated with their ancient counterparts.[50]

She appears to describe a wealthy family. This foundational material permits the further development of an ancient education model.

Fortunately, recent specific works on the family in its first-century environment have rectified the earlier deficit in scholarly attention. For example, Scott Bartchy and Reidar Aasgaard have addressing siblings in Paul's thinking.[51] Trevor Burke has also written important works on the first-century family.[52] And Andrew Clarke, as we saw above, considers families in antiquity.[53] Clarke investigates the father's role in the household (as leader, and in relationship to sons, slaves and household religion). Thus his work assesses the father's role as leader but does not consider education, the focus of my study.

Trevor Burke's book *Family Matters* is a socio-historical study in which he focuses on kinship metaphors in 1 Thessalonians. Following his earlier article 'Pauline Adoption: a Sociological Approach' he sensitively reads

50. Osiek, 'The Family in Early Christianity', p. 11.

51. S. Scott Bartchy, 'Undermining Ancient Patriarchy: The Apostle Paul's Vision of a Society of Siblings', *BTB* 29 (1999), pp. 68–78; Reidar Aasgaard, ' "Role Ethics" in Paul: The Significance of the Sibling Role for Paul's Ethical Thinking', *NTS* 48 (2002), pp. 513–30, and his *'My Beloved Brothers and Sisters!' Christian Siblingship in Paul* (JSNTSup, 265; London and New York: T & T Clark International, 2004). Time restraints meant I was unable to read his book before my book went to press.

52. Trevor J. Burke, 'Pauline Adoption: a Sociological Approach', *EvQ* 73 (2001), pp. 119–34; *Family Matters*; 'Paul's Role as "Father" to his Corinthian "Children" in Socio-Historical Context (1 Corinthians 4:14–21)', in Burke and Elliott (eds.), *Paul and the Corinthians*, pp. 95–113.

53. Clarke, *Serve the Community*, pp. 79–101. This is chapter 5 ' Leadership in the Family and Household'.

Paul's language in its socio-historical context. Thus his work is valuable for my study of ancient education. Although his work focuses on 1 Thessalonians, which has a different social location to 1 Corinthians, his book is valuable on two accounts.[54] First, his extensive analysis of Jewish and non-Jewish sources provides a rich mine of information that can be applied to other Pauline letters (including 1 Corinthians). Second, his application to 1 Thessalonians provides a model for how his material is used in interpreting Paul's letter.

In his chapter 1 'Background and Context' Burke discusses the neglect of the family in the gospels and Pauline letters even though his letters are 'replete with familial terminology'.[55] He asks what relationship exists between the ancient family, as a social institution and reality, and Paul's understanding of the Christian family. Then he examines family terminology with a brief summary of research followed by examining metaphors and meaning. Paul's metaphors depend upon social realities so Burke argues, correctly, that it is necessary to examine the ancient family to identify 'dominant meanings'. He thus launches into a fruitful investigation of the ancient family. The relationship between parents and children is investigated in chapters 2 and 3, followed by chapter 4 on brotherly relations.

In his chapter on the Jewish evidence, Burke examines Philo, Pseudo-Phocylides and Josephus.[56] This is followed by a chapter on the non-Jewish evidence. Here he considers: Aristotle (*c.* 384–322 BC), Plutarch (*c.* 50–120 AD) and the Stoics (Seneca, Musonius Rufus, Epictetus and Hierocles).[57] Each chapter is divided into, first, 'Parents' Responsibilities towards their Children' and second, 'Children's Responsibilities towards their Parents'. In 'Parents' Responsibilities' Burke discusses Jewish and non-Jewish sources under sub-headings: procreation, hierarchy, authority, nurture and care, affection, example, and education. In 'Children's Responsibilities' Burke again discusses both sets of sources using the headings of: reciprocation, honour, obedience, care, and affection. Thus within parental responsibilities for children Burke includes the importance of education.

What are the implications of Burke's analysis for my study? From his examination of literary and non-literary evidence he determines 'the normal social expectations of parents and children in the ancient

54. On the social contrasts see Barclay, 'Thessalonica and Corinth: Social Contrasts in Pauline Christianity', pp. 49–74.

55. Burke, *Family Matters*, p. 3.

56. Burke, *Family Matters*, pp. 36–59. This is chapter 2 'Parents and Children in the Ancient World: Jewish Evidence'.

57. Burke, *Family Matters*, pp. 60–96. This is chapter 3 'Parents and Children in the Ancient World: Non-Jewish Evidence'.

world'.[58] One particular discovery is that the sources indicate authors (Jewish and Graeco-Roman) have the same family values, they do not provide different viewpoints.[59] On education he does note that the *content* of education might vary with the sources but the duty on fathers, Jewish and non-Jewish, is to provide this for their children. He considers that what is so remarkable about depictions of family life is not difference but similarities. Family values and expectations among Jews are 'entirely comparable with, and hardly distinguishable from, those of Graeco-Roman society'.[60]

Thus scholarship is now addressing the family in Graeco-Roman society. Burke's work agrees with my doctoral work when I assessed the importance of the connection between education, families and society. I shall now engage with particular aspects starting with literacy in ancient society.

4. *Literacy in Ancient Society*

Joanna Dewey remarks, on scholars' evaluations of developing Christianity, that they, 'have on the whole assumed that the first-century media world functioned much as our modern print media world does, giving priority to logical linear thinking and to written texts'.[61] Commentators on 1 Corinthians often discuss Paul's 'readers' assuming that virtually all Christians could read, but Dewey's 'hypothesis is that Christianity began as an oral phenomenon in a predominately oral culture within which the dominant elite were literate and made extensive use of writing to maintain hegemony and control'.[62] Her article draws upon William Harris' *Ancient Literacy* to examine literacy, textuality and orality in the Pauline traditions.[63] She recognises that schooling had to be paid for by the family and there was virtually no public support for mass education.[64] This link between education and literacy needs investigation.

58. Burke, *Family Matters*, pp. 95–96 (95), for his overall conclusion on chapters 2 and 3. He does not determine how the expectations actually worked in practice because he admits this could be quite different to the assumptions associated with the expectations.

59. Burke, *Family Matters*, p. 95. He notes that at the start of the study we might have expected different viewpoints from Jewish and non-Jewish sources but the outcome has shown the opposite result – they agree.

60. Burke, *Family Matters*, p. 96. Burke, 'Paul's Role as "Father"', pp. 104–5, also mentions the expectations that parents, especially fathers, would educate their children.

61. Joanna Dewey, 'Textuality in an Oral Culture: a Survey of the Pauline Traditions', *Semeia* 65 (1994), pp. 37–65 (37).

62. Dewey, 'Textuality in an Oral Culture', p. 38.

63. Harris, *Ancient Literacy*.

64. Harris, *Ancient Literacy*, p. 42.

Chapter 3 presented the gymnasium as a social location for education and identified how this would be applicable to residents at Corinth in the first century AD. To integrate this model further with the social world of New Testament I start with Marc Kleijwegt's study. His interest is not in the technicalities of education, e.g. buildings or particular subjects, but rather in education's social character.[65] Thus Kleijwegt asks an essential question for ancient education when he asks what its objectives were.[66] This is a crucial question for investigating the educated elite in the Corinthian church.

Kleijwegt discusses four different, but related, aspects of education: (a) the scale of illiteracy in the ancient world, (b) education as a status-determinant, (c) whether ancient people recognised the psychological differences between children, e.g. between an eight-year old and a fifteen-year old, (d) preferences for infant prodigies (i.e. those having adult characteristics). All these have an impact on my model for 1 Corinthians.

First, who received education in ancient society? Strange, while recognising that the level of education for a child varied according to status, means and location, briefly examines some evidence and concludes, 'So literacy in the first century AD, though not universal, stretched far down the social scale, and we must therefore assume that schooling of some form was part of the childhood experience of many inhabitants of the Empire'.[67] However, Strange shows no knowledge of Harris' work, *Ancient Literacy*, and although he cites Kleijwegt he appears unfamiliar with his discussion.[68] How many were 'many'? Can we be more precise?

The Corinthian believers wrote to Paul who replied with 1 Corinthians.[69] However, unlike a modern western society, such as Great Britain, where most adults are literate what do we know about literacy in Corinth? How many in the church were literate or illiterate? Members of the church at Corinth are not like the members of a church in modern western democracies, where education is funded by the state, and the vast majority of adults can read and write. Even most junior school children can read and write to some extent. In the ancient world, however, was literacy widespread? I address this wider context before focusing on the situation of the Corinthian Christians.

65. Kleijwegt, *Ancient Youth*, chapter 4 'Youth and education in ancient society', p. 75.

66. Kleijwegt, *Ancient Youth*, p. 75.

67. Strange, *Children in the Early Church*, p. 25. His evidence includes: the papyri from Egypt, Pompeian inscriptions, the Roman army, Pliny's slaves and schoolteachers who were slaves or freedmen.

68. Strange, *Children in the Early Church*, p. 26. He cites Kleijwegt, *Ancient Youth*, pp. 76–83, to show that access to schools in the New Testament may have been limited to those living in large cities both in the Greek East and the Latin West.

69. See chapter 1 for my discussion on the integrity of 1 Corinthians.

Kleijwegt notes the widely held view by ancient historians that in the ancient world most people could at least write their own name, and read it, i.e., they had basic literacy.[70] But he observes that both Harris and Duncan-Jones have shown in detail that this view is an illusion.[71] Kleijwegt comments that Marrou assumes that all freeborn children attended school. However, he observes that although this 'classic' on ancient education world has influenced others, he notes that Harris regards the assumption as utterly improbable.[72]

Even in democratic classical Athens the authorities did not provide state-financed education for most citizens and in the Hellenistic era public education financed by a city was unusual.[73] Kleijwegt notes that when we read about elementary education in city-schools it is rich benefactors who provide these, e.g. at Teos and Miletus.[74] For example, a benefactor from Roman Xanthos in Lycia (mid-second century AD) made benefactions including that 'He educates and nourishes all the children of the citizens, having accepted their charge in person for 16 years'. This benefactor also provided benefactions for other groups/works, e.g. to the Xanthians for the gymnasium with bath 45,000 denarii and to the people of Myra for the peristyle of the gymnasium and its mosaics/columns 56,000 denarii.[75]

In the imperial era, Marrou believes every important town had a school for elementary education, grammar and also rhetoric but Kleijwegt asks where the evidence is for this.[76] In the Greek East, during the imperial period, Kleijwegt remarks that Jones understands that provisions for public elementary education were absent, and Jones suggests, 'in the majority of cities the first stage of education was left to private enterprise and was not even subject to public control'.[77] Kleijwegt reviews the situation in the Latin West and notes that the situation is more complicated than in the Greek East, but again there is no evidence for state supported education.[78]

In conclusion, Kleijwegt comments that public schools existed on a small scale because education was considered a private issue. Hence,

70. Kleijwegt, *Ancient Youth*, p. 76.

71. Kleijwegt, *Ancient Youth*, p. 76. Harris, *Ancient Literacy*; R.P. Duncan-Jones, 'Age-rounding, Illiteracy, and Social Differentiation in the Roman Empire', *Chiron* 7 (1977), pp. 333–53, and his 'Age-rounding in Greco-Roman Egypt', *ZPE* 33 (1979), pp. 169–77.

72. Kleijwegt, *Ancient Youth*, p. 76 n. 2; citing W.V. Harris, 'Literacy and Epigraphy I', *ZPE* 52 (1983), pp. 87–112 (99).

73. Kleijwegt, *Ancient Youth*, pp. 78–79.

74. Kleijwegt, *Ancient Youth*, p. 79.

75. André Balland, *Fouilles de Xanthos*, Vol. 7, *Inscriptiones d'époque impériale du Létoon* (Paris: Klincksieck, 1981), n. 67, pp. 185–214.

76. Kleijwegt, *Ancient Youth*, p. 80.

77. Kleijwegt, *Ancient Youth*, p. 80; citing Jones, *The Greek City*, p. 223.

78. Kleijwegt, *Ancient Youth*, pp. 80–83.

benefactors were needed or parents grouped together to finance teachers. However elite children were educated at home (normal during antiquity) or by a teacher whom the father chose to educate his children. He regards it as unremarkable that in Ps-Plutarch's writing on educating children there is no mention of a school as an institution. Rather, parents had to pay for a child's education, selecting pedagogue and teachers with care. Ps-Plutarch's comments address the wealthy although he admits, in principle, that they should include the poor. However, as Kleijwegt notes, if they are too poor and cannot educate their children Ps-Plutarch regards this as just hard luck.[79]

Kleijwegt thus shows that the provision of education was family, not state, directed. It depended on the wealth, and will, of parents. Although he states that elite children were educated at home later he notes that they were also educated as ἔφηβοι in the gymnasium.[80] His discussion describes the situation in the New Testament period.

The Greek papyri from Egypt show with reasonable clarity the literacy of different social groups and Harris comments:

> Most of the males of the 'gymnasium' class – essentially the Greek townsmen who possessed some substantial property and were the sons of other such persons – were literate. A few, however, belonged to the intermediate group of the 'slow writers,' such as a fisherman – fortunate to be in the gymnasium class – who is attested in a document of the year 99. These men formed an elite which made a real effort to maintain its own Greekness. In the towns and large villages a certain number of artisans (some of whom belonged to the gymnasium class) were literate, but many others were not, so that, for instance, every one of the master weavers who appears in apprenticeship contracts is said to be illiterate.[81]

Yet Harris notes that no member of the gymnasium class is known to have been illiterate until 285 AD, although some women in families of the gymnasium class were illiterate.[82] Harris' cardinal question, whether conclusions drawn from the papyri have any value for the rest of the

79. Kleijwegt, *Ancient Youth*, p. 83; citing Ps-Plutarch, *The Education of Children* (*De liberis educandis*). His chapter 11 addresses education of poor children. Arlandson, *Women, Class and Society in Early Christianity*, pp. 95–96, discusses Plutarch's view on the poor and comments, 'His conclusion that poor people do not formally educate their children or perhaps do not even make an attempt to do this reflects not only his upper-class perspective but also historical reality. Throughout the Greek East children of poor commoners, such as urban day laborers, did not receive an adequate education, if at all, if only because they could not afford it' (p. 96).

80. Kleijwegt, *Ancient Youth*, pp. 90–101. The ephebes were boys.

81. Harris, *Ancient Literacy*, pp. 276–77.

82. Harris, *Ancient Literacy*, p. 277 n. 502 and pp. 279–80. Harris, p. 280 n. 519, cites *P.Oxy*. xxxviii. 2858 (171 AD) for women who were illiterate.

Greek world, leads him to remark, 'But nothing that is known about Greek schools outside Egypt would lead us to suppose that under the Roman Empire they had a significantly greater impact than the schooling we know of from the papyri'.[83]

Teresa Morgan's study of literate education in Egypt, with its 'core and periphery' model, identifies that the number of children who received more than the 'basic "core" education' was always low.[84] She notes that the number of literary texts (written on papyrus) from many authors and the presence of highly cultured people in certain towns may give the impression of high literacy but she is pessimistic about literacy in the cities. She cautions against being too optimistic on both the numbers of literates or their culture.[85]

New Testament scholars are now beginning to show awareness of this restriction in literacy. Thus Richard Rohrbaugh discusses literacy and schools for Syria-Palestine in the first century and recognises, 'There is general agreement among social historians that two to four percent of the population in agrarian societies could read, or read *and* write, and that the vast majority of these lived in the cities'.[86] Moreover, Dewey's article examines 'Literacy and Orality in the Pauline Tradition,' including the situation at Corinth.[87] She concludes that people who have had 'some literacy' probably carried Paul's letters to the churches. If Phoebe performed Paul's letter to the Roman church then, Dewey concludes, 'she was probably literate'. She is reasonably certain, on the basis of occupations, that Luke the physician and Erastus (Rom. 16.23) were literate. Lydia may have been literate (or employed literate slaves) and Crispus (Acts 18.8; 1 Cor. 1.14) may also have been literate. She thinks that the tentmakers Prisca and Aquila were not literate.[88] For those wealthy enough to own houses for the lodging of Paul, and others, and the gathering of the church, Dewey believes that 'literacy is a possibility but not a necessity for them. Even if literacy was high among this group, the overall literacy of the Pauline congregations would remain low'.[89] I agree.

83. Harris, *Ancient Literacy*, p. 281.

84. Morgan, *Literate Education*, p. 72.

85. Morgan, *Literate Education*, p.73.

86. Richard L. Rohrbaugh, 'The Social Location of the Marcan Audience', *BTB* 23 (1993), pp. 114–27 (115). He sees this as especially important for an understanding of Mark's audience.

87. Dewey, 'Textuality in an Oral Culture', pp. 47–56. See also Lucretia B. Yaghjian, 'Ancient Reading', in Rohrbaugh (ed.), *The Social Sciences and New Testament Interpretation*, pp. 206–30, for a contribution from The Context Group.

88. Dewey, 'Textuality in an Oral Culture', p. 50.

89. Dewey, 'Textuality in an Oral Culture', p. 50. See also her article 'From Storytelling to Written Text: The Loss of Early Christian Women's Voices', *BTB* 26 (1996), pp. 71–78. She notes, 'Access to manuscripts and their contents requires formal education and money, both

It is reasonable to conclude that literacy in first-century Corinth among the Corinthian Christians, like that elsewhere, was restricted to a small proportion of the population. However, it was a privilege enjoyed by the educated elite. Although there were benefactors in Corinth, as elsewhere, no evidence demonstrates that they supported the education of children (and any gymnasia – as the benefactor in Roman Xanthos did).[90] Education was a family responsibility, but many were unable to purchase it. Let us then examine the relationship between education and parental responsibilities.

5. *Education and Parental Responsibilities*

Kleijwegt observes the views of Plutarch on education and the responsibilities of parents.[91] Winter also helpfully discusses the relevance of Plutarch and his visits to Corinth in the late seventies, the beginning of the nineties and the early second century AD.[92] He was present during the Isthmian Games where he mixed with important friends of high social status, including Herodes Atticus.[93] Plutarch, 'recorded the activities of the sophists at the Isthmian Games, particularly the highly competitive spirit engendered between themselves and amongst their pupils. Plutarch also confirms their social status and exalted position in the life of Corinth'.[94] Although Winter cites Plutarch's *Moralia*, he does not discuss his work *The Education of Children*.[95]

Here Plutarch begins with what advantages free-born children should enjoy 'to give them a sound character when they grow up,' and he comments:

of which were limited to the few upper-class males and their retainers in a patriarchal culture such as the Roman empire' (p. 74). As manuscripts proliferated, Dewey observes that the oral tradition was 'recorded by the few relatively high-status literate men' (p. 74).

90. For benefactors and Corinth see Chow, *Patronage and Power*. He cites no evidence for educational patronage at Corinth. Benefactors are recorded in Kent, *Corinth: The Inscriptions, 1926–1950*, pp. 20–22.

91. Kleijwegt, *Ancient Youth*, p. 83. See the previous citation. He speaks of Ps-Plutarch.

92. Winter, *Philo and Paul*, pp. 8, 63, 67, 110, 114, 141–4, 189–90, 232.

93. Winter, *Philo and Paul*, pp. 141–43.

94. Winter, *Philo and Paul*, p. 232.

95. Winter, *Philo and Paul*, cites *De. Lib. Ed.* but he does not comment on it (pp. 26–27 n. 25). For this essay see: Plutarch, *Moralia* I (trans. Frank Cole Babbitt; LCL; London: William Heinemann Ltd; New York: G.P. Putnam's Sons, 1927). Despite appearing in the *Moralia*, Babbitt comments that it is generally believed that the essay on *The Education of Children* cannot be by Plutarch (p. 3). Nevertheless, Babbitt notes that the essay 'is interesting in itself, since it reflects in many ways the educational conditions of the time'.

> It is perhaps better to begin with their parentage first; and I should advise those desirous of becoming fathers of notable offspring to abstain from random cohabitation with women; I mean with such women as courtesans and concubines. For those who are not well-born, whether on the father's or the mother's side, have an indelible disgrace in their low birth, which accompanies them throughout their lives, and offers to anyone desiring to use it a ready subject of reproach and insult.[96]

Honourable birth is considered 'A goodly treasure,' and children of distinguished parents are 'full of exultation and pride'.[97] To avoid begetting children fond of wine the father must not beget them when drunk.[98] Paul also discusses the issue of noble birth (1 Cor. 1.26–31) in the context of God's calling and community conflict.

According to Plutarch, mothers preferably ought to feed and nurse their own children.[99] Slaves are to be chosen with care 'so that the children may not be contaminated by barbarians and persons of low character'.[100] When children reach the age of needing παιδαγωγοί these must be chosen with great care, and not slaves taken in war, barbarians or unstable people.[101] Unfortunately, he adds, it was common practice for slaves who were wine-bibbers, gluttons and useless for anything to be chosen as παιδαγωγοί. Most importantly, teachers should be hired who are scandal-free, impeachable in manners, and in experience the best available.[102] Paul uses the image of pedagogues in 1 Cor. 4.15 when he contrasts his unique position as father with the vast number of παιδαγωγοί available to the Corinthians.

Fathers are repeatedly addressed, and some admonished, for their selection of teachers. For example, some fathers, 'deserve utter contempt, who, before examining those who are going to teach, either because of ignorance, or sometimes because of inexperience, hand over their children to untried and untrustworthy men'.[103] 'Many fathers, however, go so far in their devotion to money as well as in animosity toward their children, that in order to avoid paying a larger fee, they select as teachers for their children men who are not worth any wage at all – looking for ignorance, which is cheap enough'.[104] For fathers who have badly brought up and badly educated their sons Plutarch provides a tragic description of their

96. Plutarch, *Mor*. 1A–1B.
97. Plutarch, *Mor*. 1B–1D.
98. Plutarch, *Mor*. 1D–2A.
99. Plutarch, *Mor*. 3C–D.
100. Plutarch, *Mor*. 3F–4A.
101. Plutarch, *Mor*. 4A–4B.
102. Plutarch, *Mor*. 4B–4C.
103. Plutarch, *Mor*. 4C.
104. Plutarch, *Mor*. 4F.

sons' vices once they become adults.[105] He sums up (he calls it an oracle rather than advice):

> The beginning, the middle, and end in all these matters is good education and proper training (ἀγωγὴ ... παιδεία); and it is this, I say, which leads on and helps towards moral excellence and towards happiness. And, in comparison with this, all other advantages are human, and trivial, and not worth our serious concern. [106]

The other advantages are: good birth, wealth, repute, beauty, health, and strength. 'But learning (παιδεία), of all things in this world, is alone immortal and divine'.[107] He advises 'people to make nothing of more immediate importance than the education of their children (παιδεία τῶν τέκνων)'.[108] In conclusion, we are told fathers are to be an example so that children by looking at their fathers' lives may be discouraged from evil and mothers are to follow the example of Eurydice (an Illyrian and barbarian) who took up education for her children's benefit.[109] Osiek and Balch note here that the author's challenge is an extreme example, comparable with the exemplary mother in 4 Maccabees.[110] Thus Plutarch demonstrates the supreme importance of παιδεία with the essential responsibility required of both parents. Fathers are rebuked for failure. Education is a family matter.

The Alexandrian Jew Philo also explains the family orientation of education in his commentary on the Fifth Commandment:

> Further, who could be more truly called benefactors (εὐεργέται) than parents in relation to their children? First, they have brought them out of non-existence; then, again, they have held them entitled to nurture and later to education (παιδείας) of body and soul, so that they may have not only life, but a good life. They have benefited the body by means of the gymnasium (γυμναστικῆς) and the training there given, through which it gains muscular vigour and good condition and the power to bear itself and move with an ease marked by gracefulness and elegance. They have done the same for the soul by means of letters and arithmetic and geometry and music and philosophy as a whole which lifts on high the mind lodged within the mortal body and escorts it to the very heaven and shews it the blessed and happy beings that dwell therein, and creates in it an eager longing for the unswerving ever-

105. Plutarch, *Mor.* 5B–C.
106. Plutarch, *Mor.* 5C.
107. Plutarch, *Mor.* 5E.
108. Plutarch, *Mor.* 6A.
109. Plutarch, *Mor.* 14A–C.
110. Osiek and Balch, *Families in the New Testament World*, p. 69.

> harmonious order which they never forsake because they obey their captain and marshal.[111]

H.A. Harris uses this passage as evidence for the Greek education that the devout Jew Philo, had himself enjoyed.[112] Alan Mendelson also cogently argues that Philo's education was in the Greek gymnasium and included both physical and intellectual training.[113] This passage emphasises, in the important language of the benefactor, the primary nature of parents in the education process.[114]

The Roman educator Quintilian also details parental responsibility in the education of their children. His *Institutio Oratoria* was dedicated to his friend Marcellus Victorius for assistance in the education of his young son Geta who showed talent.[115] He wants a father to have, from the boy's birth, the highest aspirations for his son and in this case he will be more careful for his education.[116] On parents' education Quintilian wants both parents, 'as highly educated as possible,' and gives examples of educated women.[117] However, even parents who have unfortunately not received 'a good education' should not use that as a reason for neglecting their son's education but, rather, should show greater attentiveness in assisting their children.[118] Moreover, wise parents will make their first objective to choose a teacher of the highest character for teaching the boy at home. These three important 'education' sources demonstrate parental responsibilities for the education of children in antiquity. These concern the children of the elite

111. *Philo, Spec. Leg.* 2.229–230. In *Dec.* 106–120, Philo also addresses the fifth commandment. He states, 'we see that parents by their nature stand on the border-line between the mortal and immortal side of existence, the mortal because of their kinship with men and other animals through the perishableness of the body; the immortal because the act of generation assimilates them to God the generator of the All' (p. 107). Moreover, Philo remarks, 'For parents are the servants of God (θεοῦ γὰρ ὑπηρέται) for the task of begetting children, and he who dishonours the servant also dishonours the Lord', cf. 1 Cor. 4.1 ὡς ὑπηρέτας Χαριστοῦ, 'servants of Christ' (p. 119).

112. Harris, *Trivium, Greek Athletics and the Jews*, p. 91.

113. Mendelson, *Secular Education in Philo of Alexandria*. See especially pp. 28–33 and my chapter 3.

114. On the language of benefaction and euergetism see Stephan J. Joubert, 'One Form of Exchange or Two? "Euergetism," Patronage, and Testament Studies', *BTB* 31 (2001), pp. 17–25.

115. Quintilian, *The Institutio Oratoria of Quintilian*, Vol. I (trans. H.E. Butler; LCL; London: William Heinemann; New York: G.P. Putnam's Sons, 1921), I. Pr. 6. His work is dated in the first century AD.

116. Quint., *Inst.* I.1.1.

117. Quint., *Inst.* I.1.6.

118. Quint., *Inst.* I.1.7.

as Kleijwegt noted for Plutarch, yet Plutarch also lays responsibility upon poor parents.[119]

R.A. Kearsley provides a Greek inscription of a civic benefactor of the first century in Kyme (Asia Minor) where, in the honorific decree from the city of Kyme, Kleanax's considerable actions are detailed.[120] Regarding his family, Kearsley comments that in the cities of Western Asia Minor families established roles as benefactors throughout consecutive generations. Kleanax, as benefactor, shows the family role in giving a public banquet for his daughter's marriage.[121] In the decree attention focuses on Kleanax's son:

> Kleanax trained and encouraged his son to follow his own practice of goodwill toward the city...The city focuses especially on the son indicating that in him especially lies its chief hope of the continuation of the family's generosity. The fact that Kleanax's son bears the name Sarapion, which is also the name of his grand-father, serves to underline the strong sense of continuity already remarked on in *l*.5. Sarapion is shown to have embarked on this public career already even while his father was still an active office-holder of the city and the possibility exists that the boy was in fact still a minor and that Kleanax acted in his name... Regardless, the text makes clear... the son had already made his mark in his own name. Decrees have been passed in his honour by the city and it has awarded him the epithet φιλοπάτορ (lover of his father) in recognition of the way he was carrying on the family tradition.[122]

Kleanax is honoured for considering his son's education but, moreover, this family responsibility has 'provided for the people a man worthy of his family'.[123] Beneficence was not limited to the Greek East but existed in

119. Kleijwegt, *Ancient Youth*, p. 83, referring to *Moralia*, 8E-F. Plutarch admits that his propositions should include, in principle, the poor. But if they cannot afford their children's education that it just unfortunate.

120. R.A. Kearsley, 'A Civic Benefactor of the First Century in Asia Minor', in Llewelyn and Kearsley, *New Documents Illustrating Early Christianity*, 7, no. 10, pp. 233–41. She dates the inscription as somewhere between 2 BC and 2 AD (p. 236).

121. Kearsley, 'A Civic Benefactor of the First Century', p. 237.

122. Kearsley, 'A Civic Benefactor of the First Century', pp. 237–38.

123. Kearsley, 'A Civic Benefactor of the First Century', p. 234. Kearsley translates, 'And for this reason also the *prytanis* Kleanax is worthy of praise and honour, (namely) that when a handsome son became his, he took thought for the boy's education in letters (τᾶς ἐν τοῖς λόγοις ἀγώγας), and provided for the people a man worthy of his family, Sarapion (by name), and a protector and helper, one who in many ways has already displayed zeal toward the city through his own manly deeds; a father-loving man and meriting also that by public consent this name should be added, a man whose affection for his father is attested also by public decree for all time; for all these reasons the people approving Kleanax the *prytanis* praise him who has continuously maintained goodwill toward the people' (pp. 234–35). Amongst his benefactions he gave a banquet to 'the victorious athletes in the sacred games'.

Rome where it was particularly developed by Augustus. Although a tradition of euergetism was practised in the Greek cities during the Hellenistic period, certain actions of benefactors were 'specifically due to Roman rule and the consequent desire of the civic elites to imitate their political masters'.[124] This inscription supports the literary evidence on parental responsibilities for children's education. Here it is publicly recognised by Graeco-Roman society.

Honorific inscriptions insist upon the return of honour being commensurate with the benefactions bestowed.[125] Harrison notes that this is apparent in *SEG* XI 948 (first century AD).[126] Here the people in Cardamylae behave reciprocally to honour Poseidippos, their benefactor. Their decree gave him front seats in the theatre, first place in procession and the privilege of eating in public festivals: 'And (it was resolved) to set up this decree on a stone stele in the most conspicuous place in the gymnasium, while the ephors make the solemn procession to the building without hindrance'. Reciprocity terminology carefully displays the incentives for the benefactor and the beneficiary.

However, Harrison comments, 'This ideology of reciprocity embraced household relations as much as the civic arena. The popular philosophers urged the reciprocation of parental benefaction by their progeny'.[127] Harrison sees that Paul uses the traditional reciprocity motif in Graeco-Roman benefactor ideology in 1 Tim. 5.4 for children to make a return for their parents.[128] The philosopher 'Hierocles gives this doctrine of the pious reciprocation of parental favour its fullest and finest exposition'.[129] In discussing Paul's use of this traditional motif in 1 Tim. 5, Harrison observes that these 'theological contours of Paul's thought' have a counterpart in the larger Graeco-Roman world.[130] He observes that

124. Kearsley, 'A Civic Benefactor of the First Century', p. 239, where she uses S.R.F. Price, *Rituals and Power: the Roman Imperial Cult in Asia Minor* (Cambridge: Cambridge University Press 1984), pp. 89–90.

125. J. R. Harrison, 'Benefactor Ideology and Christian Responsibility for Widows', in Llewelyn, *New Documents Illustrating Early Christianity*, 8, no. 7, pp. 106–16 (114).

126. Harrison, 'Benefaction Ideology and Christian Responsibility for Widows', p. 114.

127. Harrison, 'Benefaction Ideology and Christian Responsibility for Widows', p. 114. His citations include: Dio Chrysostom, *Or.* 12.42–43 and Plutarch *Mor.* 479F.

128. This argument is, of course, rather weak for scholars who do not accept the Pauline authorship of 1 Timothy. Nevertheless, Paul uses similar language in 2 Cor. 12.14 where he says that it is the responsibility of parents to provide for their children. He is the parent and the Corinthians are his children.

129. Harrison, 'Benefaction Ideology and Christian Responsibility for Widows', p. 114. Harrison, p. 115, cites Hierocles, 'How to Conduct Oneself Toward One's Parents' (*Stob.* 3.52). Hierocles states that parents are the images of the gods, domestic gods, benefactors, kinsmen, creditors, lords and the warmest of friends.

130. Harrison, 'Benefaction Ideology and Christian Responsibility for Widows', p. 115.

Pythagoras 'reminds the young men at the gymnasium of Kroton that they owed their parents gratitude as benefactors: "Our parents alone are the first in benefactions (εὐεργεσίαις), even before our birth, and ancestors are responsible for all the achievements of their descendants" '.[131]

Thus, child education and parental responsibilities were essentially linked in antiquity. Philo established this link in education at the gymnasium. Plutarch's education also includes gymnasium aspects, 'It is not proper, either, to overlook the exercise of the body, but we should send the children to the trainer's and cultivate adequately this side of education with all diligence, not merely for the sake of gracefulness of body but also with an eye to strength; for sturdiness of body in childhood is the foundation of a hale old age'.[132]

Nevertheless, his ideal is training in the contests of war (using the javelin and bow) and hunting, rather than to become 'fleshy athletes'.[133] Finally, Quintilian includes physical exercise, 'I will not blame even those who give a certain amount of time to the teacher of gymnastics. I am not speaking of those, who spend part of their life in rubbing themselves with oil and part in wine-bibbing, and kill the mind by over-attention to the body: indeed, I would have such as these kept as far as possible from the boy whom we are training'.[134] He allows training in motion for the benefit of gestures in oratory but these are limited to the years of boyhood.[135] Here Quintilian displays a dislike for gymnastic training although he admits that an orator should move his body in a fashion derived from both martial and gymnastic exercises.[136] Thus the essential connection between parents and child education embraces Greek gymnasium education and the Roman education specified by Quintilian. Moreover, the language of parents and children may display that of the Graeco-Roman benefactor ideology.

This section agrees with the work of Burke who sees the father with particular responsibilities for the education of his children. In this respect, Raffaella Cribiore has provided an insightful discussion on the relationship between parents and students.[137] Her evidence includes letters between fathers and sons. She notes that one of the foremost concerns for upper-

131. Harrison, 'Benefaction Ideology and Christian Responsibility for Widows', p. 115; citing Iamblichus, *Vit. Pyth.* 38.

132. Plutarch, *Mor.* 8C.

133. Plutarch, *Mor.* 8D.

134. Quint., *Inst.* 1.11.15.

135. Quint., *Inst.* 1.11.16–19.

136. Quint., *Inst.* 1.11.18. Here he cites Cicero (*De Oratore* 59.220) who quotes Crassus, that the orator 'should learn to move his body in a bold and manly fashion derived not from actors or the stage, but from martial and even from gymnastic exercises (*sed ab armis aut etiam a palaestra*)'.

137. Cribiore, *Gymnastics of the Mind*, pp. 102–23. This is chapter 4 'Parents and Students'.

class parents was education because this was such a crucial factor for the child and the family. Great efforts and considerable finances were used to ensure success: 'Investment in education was a top priority for families who could afford it: it was planning for a family's future and for the parent's own well-being'.[138]

6. *Education and Genealogy*

The relationship between education and birth needs further examination because a person's genealogy could significantly affect educational opportunities. Llewelyn has helpfully discussed this for Roman Egypt in his review of an Oxyrhynchus *epikrisis* (*P.Mich.* XIV 676, dated 272 AD).[139] This papyrus is an *epikrisis* for admission to the gymnasium class. One component involves showing that the youth's ancestors (paternal and maternal) were members of the gymnasium class. This membership was traced back to the list made up in 4/5 AD and revised in 72/3 AD. Llewelyn helpfully explains its significance:

> After the latter date admission to the *gymnasium* seems to have been closed. The present *epikrisis* is declared by the boy's guardian. His father was no doubt dead. Theonis' genealogy is traced back on his father's side six generations to an *epikrisis* in 72/3 AD and on his mother's side by eight generations to two *epikriseis* in years 56/7 AD & 58/9 AD. It is usual for the father's genealogy to be traced further back than that of the mother.
>
> The condition that the youth's paternal and maternal ancestors belong to the *gymnasium* class was a strong incentive for marriage to be endogamous.[140]

Thus the urban elite group of 'those from the gymnasium' had to maintain records and submit proof of their genealogy over many generations for entrance to the gymnasium. The latest of the rolls was 72/3 AD but the initial registration went back to the time of Augustus. Thus at the time of writing 1 Corinthians this was an important issue. Llewelyn observes this in remarking, 'The *epikrisis* illustrates an ancient society's awareness of and care in guarding status and privilege. The context may be important for an understanding of Paul's treatment of status'.[141] After a discussion on

138. Cribiore, *Gymnastics of the Mind*, p. 123.

139. S.R. Llewelyn, 'The Preservation of Status and its Testing', in Llewelyn and Kearsley, *New Documents Illustrating Early Christianity*, 6, no. 17, pp. 132–40. Llewelyn notes, 'An *epikrisis* was conducted to ascertain an individual's status and thus the privileges to which he was entitled' (p. 135).

140. Llewelyn, 'The Preservation of Status and its Testing', pp. 136–37.

141. Llewelyn, 'The Preservation of Status and its Testing', p. 139.

status in 2 Cor. 11.22 and *peristasis* catalogues in 1 Cor. 4.6–13, he concludes:

> Such statements [Phil 3:5–8] by Paul which contrast the conventions of status and his experience in Christ show the tension within his own consciousness. In the *epikrisis* the boy's privileged status was traced back through several generations. His status afforded him social, political and educational advantages. Paul also was aware of the advantages afforded him by his birth and this was not negated by his experience in Christ.[142]

We must remember that Apollos, who was preferred by some at Corinth, was an Alexandrian. Communication occurred between Alexandrians and Corinthians. For example, Alexandrians of all ages (boys, youths and men) attended the games on a regular basis and are recorded in victor lists.[143] Thus Egyptian visitors to Corinth may have belonged to this hereditary class. However, A.H.M. Jones notes:

> In the Egyptian metropoleis, it is true, membership of the gymnasium was restricted to a hereditary class, comprising the best families of the town; but no similar rule is known elsewhere. Nevertheless it seems unlikely that the poorer citizens can in practice have often been able to put their children through the boys' and ephebes' course of training, which, even if no fees were demanded, involved many heavy incidental expenses.[144]

This first-century emphasis on genealogy continued in the second century AD. Cartledge and Spawforth observe that from the letter of Marcus Aurelius to the Athenians we now know 'that Greek cities in the second century, to guard against infiltration by persons of freedman descent, not uncommonly required proof of three generations of free birth (*trigonia*) from candidates for major magistracies'.[145] Nevertheless, at Sparta and Athens ambitious and well-connected persons of freedman stock evaded these restrictions. Moreover, we know that at Corinth freedmen held magistracies. However, significant wealth was required for office.[146] Lanci

142. Llewelyn, 'The Preservation of Status and its Testing', p. 140.

143. Meritt, *Corinth: Greek Inscriptions, 1896–1927*, no. 16, pp. 21–25. Meritt comments on the Isthmian Games, 'the large number of cities represented in these [victor] lists indicates the cosmopolitan character of the festival, at least in the first and second centuries A.D. In 3 A.D. all three of the boxing contests (boys, youths, and men) were won by Alexandrians, a fact which indicates that even the younger groups were rather well represented from various points in the Roman world. It is but natural, perhaps, that Corinthians predominate in the victor lists, especially in the more expensive competitions with horses' (p. 24).

144. Jones, *The Greek City from Alexander to Justinian*, p. 285.

145. Cartledge and Spawforth, *Hellenistic and Roman Sparta*, p. 160. Marcus Aurelius was emperor 161–180 AD.

146. Clarke, *Serve the Community*, p. 42.

observes that although Corinth's charter has not survived we do have the charter from the colony of Urso (Spain), which was founded a little earlier than Corinth. He notes that this Julian colony permitted freedmen (*liberti*) to be decurions.[147] Nevertheless, Donald Engels observes that although Caesar did initially permit freedmen to become duovirs in his colonies, Augustus later revoked this privilege and thereafter all duovirs were required to be free born.[148]

Sparta's social structure followed a pattern widespread in Greek cities during the Roman rule and Cartledge and Spawforth note the advances of freedmen. They argue that 'it appears that by the second century the Roman city's ephebic training, which one would normally expect to have been the preserve of free-born youths, was open no less than its magistracies to infiltration by well-connected persons of freedman stock'.[149] Some old families in Sparta were descended from the aristocracy of Classical Sparta and had spectacular pedigrees over tens of generations reaching back to the Bronze Age, 1250 BC.[150] Hereditary priesthoods were prominent and claimed descent from the deities they served, e.g., Poseidon, Dioscuri and Apollo.[151] The city's educational system the *agoge* was traced back to the mythical founder, the god Lycurgus.[152] Not only was the city a tourist attraction because of the practice of its ancient education system but also we saw in chapter 3 how Spartans were resident in Corinth and benefactors. Moreover, we saw how the family of Herodes Atticus was associated with Athens, Sparta and Corinth.

Further, as mentioned in chapter 3, fictive kinship ties existed between Jews and Spartans.[153] Martin Hengel notes that, 'Sparta was particularly attractive to the Jewish Hellenists so that at an early stage they constructed a primal relationship between Jews and Spartans'.[154] In 1 Macc. 12 the high priest Jonathon exchanges letters with the Spartan King Arius confirming that the Jews and Spartans are brothers and of Abraham's family. Thus bonds existed between Jews and Spartans. Consequently, Sparta was no

147. John R. Lanci, *A New Temple for Corinth: Rhetorical and Archaeological Approaches to Pauline Imagery* (Studies in Biblical Literature, 1; New York: Peter Lang, 1997), pp. 39 n. 19, 42 n. 56. For Urso he refers to *CIL* 2.5439 and the *Lex Coloniae Genetivae Juliae* 105.

148. Engels, *Roman Corinth*, p. 18.

149. Cartledge and Spawforth, *Hellenistic and Roman Sparta*, p. 167.

150. Cartledge and Spawforth, *Hellenistic and Roman Sparta*, pp. 163–64.

151. Cartledge and Spawforth, *Hellenistic and Roman Sparta*, pp. 164–65.

152. This connection is investigated by Kennell, *The Gymnasium of Virtue*.

153. Cartledge and Spawforth, *Hellenistic and Roman Sparta*, pp. 37, 85, 100, 114.

154. Hengel, *Judaism and Hellenism*, I.26. Hengel also notes that this legend of the affinity between the Jews and Spartans goes back to pre-Maccabean times (p. 72). He explains the similarities between their beliefs and notes, 'It is certainly no coincidence that Jason, author of the Hellenistic reforms in Jerusalem, ended his life in Sparta'.

isolated community but its educational system was admired by the elite, visited by tourists, and members of Herodes Atticus' family entered the ephebate. For a detailed discussion on genealogy and descent in Herod's family and Mediterranean kinship see the articles by Hanson.[155]

In conclusion, noble birth granted certain educational, and other, benefits. Slaves were excluded from attending the gymnasium, although freedmen managed on occasions to gain admission. Clarence Forbes comments, 'The stern exclusion of slaves from the pleasures and benefits of physical education was an ancient and enduring policy on which the Greeks presented a united front'.[156] Nevertheless, Forbes finds a few references to slaves involved in physical education but comments, 'Truly the penetration of slaves into physical education was pitifully slight and hedged by legal restrictions and disabilities'.[157]

7. *Education as a Status-Determinant*

The decree honouring Kleanax, discussed previously, shows the relationship between education, family and the political elite. Kleijwegt remarks that ancient education was essentially the privilege of the elite, citing Pleket who saw education as confirming the status quo of the small political elite.[158]

In the cities during the imperial period a mixture of political influence and an interest in education was normal. Kleijwegt observes that the same families provided the magistrates, priests, literary figures and artists.[159] He sees this illustrated by epigraphic references to *paideia* and he remarks that although *paideia* was used in praise during the Hellenistic period its use grew in imperial inscriptions. He observes that *paideia* is often but imperfectly translated as culture or education. However, he regards it as more than an intellectual quality because it included moral and affectionate associations. A text from Priene clearly demonstrates this

155. K. C. Hanson, 'The Herodians and Mediterranean Kinship: Part I: Genealogy and Descent', *BTB* 19 (1989), pp. 75–84; 'The Herodians and Mediterranean Kinship: Part 2: Marriage and Divorce', *BTB* 19 (1989), pp. 142–51; 'The Herodians and Mediterranean Kinship: Part III: Economics', *BTB* 20 (1990), pp. 10–21. For a general guide see also his 'BTB Readers Guide: Kinship', *BTB* 24 (1994), pp. 183–94.

156. Forbes, 'The Education and Training of Slaves in Antiquity', p. 354.

157. Forbes, 'The Education and Training of Slaves in Antiquity', p. 358.

158. Kleijwegt, *Ancient Youth*, p. 83; H.W. Pleket, 'Opvoeding in de Grieks-Romeinse wereld: een inleiding', *Lampas* 14 (1981), pp. 147–55 (150). He mentions also that Bowersock, *Greek Sophists in the Roman Empire*, has shown that famous second-century sophists were both wealthy and politically important men.

159. Kleijwegt, *Ancient Youth*, p. 84. He cites C. Panagopoulos, 'Vocabulaire et mentalité dans les Moralia de Plutarque', *DHA* 3 (1977), pp. 197–237 (226).

aspect, '"He has made of his whole life, as is natural for someone of cultural standing, a fine example of what good citizenship should be." Good citizenship and cultural education are directly intertwined'.[160] This is an important example of the value of education. Citizenship and culture are linked. According to Kleijwegt, *paideia* was an object of praise, a status-determinant. He notes that, approximately, two categories of people receive such praise: experienced politicians, and prematurely deceased members of noble families who were about to receive political distinction. However, the number of politicians praised is far less than the numbers of young people. He observes that 'A young man from Aphrodisias is said to have lived adorned by paideia and youthful modesty.... He unfortunately died prematurely, but he left his fortune ... to the people in order to pay for a gymnasiarchy and a stephanèphoria in his name.'[161] Further, another deceased young man (also from Aphrodisias) is praised for the same qualities.[162]

Kleijwegt discerningly asks whether these intellectual and moral qualities are mentioned because they lack other distinguishing qualities (e.g., political offices performed by them) or whether these qualities were necessary assets of politicians. He finds the latter more attractive and answers:

> In Greek inscriptions of the Hellenistic-Roman period mention of detailed family-relationships and family-prestige is ubiquitous. In most cases in which paideia is mentioned as an asset of young people, their lineage can be traced back to important noble families, prominent in the political activities of their cities. In some cases these young men have themselves already started on a political career.[163]

On the question of why *paideia* is mentioned in honorary inscriptions, he answers that it distinguishes people. The person honoured belongs to an identifiable prominent group and is distinguished from illiterates. Kleijwegt also observes that politics was competitive so *paideia* distinguished different aristocrats. To obtain honour and status people outdid competitors through donating money on benefactions. Similarly, education provided another realm for competition and distinguishing oneself.[164] Within the community conflict evident in 1 Corinthians *paideia* would be a reason for boasting.

160. Kleijwegt, *Ancient Youth*, p. 84. The text is *I.Priene* 117, 11. 56/7.
161. Kleijwegt, *Ancient Youth*, p. 85.
162. Kleijwegt, *Ancient Youth*, p. 85. *MAMA* VIII 482.
163. Kleijwegt, *Ancient Youth*, pp. 85–86.
164. Kleijwegt, *Ancient Youth*, p. 86.

Finally, Kleijwegt observes that a related aspect of education for determining status was education's inability to offer social mobility.[165] However, he does not mean it was impossible to climb in society via education. Indeed, Horace, the son of a freedman, was educated and reached the status of a knight.[166] But this was exceptional, and Kleijwegt notes that such mobility did confirm the hierarchical status quo. There was a complete adaptation to elite values. So Kleijwegt sees a strong connection between education and the aristocracy and he illustrates this with an inscription from Kyme (see above), 'The son of the prytanis Kleanax is sent out by his father to pursue his studies, in order that he will soon be a man of political distinction'.[167]

Thus education was a status-determinant in the competitive social atmosphere of the Hellenistic-Roman period. Social advancement through education was exceptional, rather than common, and even when this happened it helped reinforce the hierarchical status quo. These aspects of education must be recognised in an ancient education model rather than one assumed from a modern western education system. This aspect of status-determinant is not confined to education in the Greek gymnasium but is a common feature that applies to other forms of education. In this respect it is not unique to my education model.

Other classical scholars also affirm the role of education. For example, Raffaella Cribiore states, 'In antiquity, education served well the interests of the elite and the preservation of the hierarchical status quo'.[168] Within the Eastern World and particularly in Graeco-Roman Egypt she observes that cultural survival and identity preservation made education particularly stable. This was because 'the Greek minority felt the need to empower itself in its daily contacts with a "barbarian" majority. Education became a powerful agent for preserving "Greekness" by maintaining fixed linguistic and social boundaries, excluding almost any form of Egyptian culture, and concentrating on Greek values, language, and literacy'.[169] Although, Cribiore remarks, most Greeks in the East were neither born in Greece nor claimed recent descent they did regard themselves as exiles from Greece.

165. Kleijwegt, *Ancient Youth*, p. 87.

166. The first-century AD slave Epictetus, who became a philosopher, and had his own school can be added. See W.A. Oldfather's Introduction in: *Epictetus. The Discourses as Reported by Arrian, The Manual, and Fragments*, Vol. I (trans. W.A. Oldfather; LCL; London: William Heinemann; New York: G.P. Putnam's Sons, 1926).

167. Kleijwegt, *Ancient Youth*, p. 88. Referring to R. Hodot, 'Décret de Kymè en l'honneur du prytane Kléanax', *Journal of the Paul Getty Museum* 10 (1982), pp. 165–80 = *SEG* XXXII 1231.

168. Cribiore, *Gymnastics of the Mind*, p. 9.

169. Cribiore, *Gymnastics of the Mind*, p. 9.

They had a common spoken language and through education could connect with their ideal past.[170]

Teresa Morgan, furthermore, confirms the importance of education and status. Her study, like that of Cribiore, focuses on Egypt and the papyri. Nevertheless, she is at pains to point out that Egypt is not untypical and its evidence on education does not distort the remainder of the Graeco-Roman world.[171] Against the usual 'curricular model' of education Morgan shows how her 'core and periphery model' is able to explain the aims of education.[172] She observes that 'core and periphery' education fulfilled two social tasks particularly efficiently:

> It constituted a mechanism for the admission of cultural non-Greeks or non-Romans into Greek or Roman cultural groups, while simultaneously controlling the numbers admitted. And it maximized both the acculturation of learners and their differentiation from one another, producing a pool of people who shared a common sense and common criteria of greekness or romanness but who were placed in a hierarchy according to their cultural achievements.[173]

Morgan notes that the 'core' (which includes Homer) acculturates pupils while also differentiating them. However, the 'periphery' of education had many various literary texts which pupils and teachers could choose but the prevalence of competition (rather than examinations) meant that the 'dominant socio-cultural group' had expectations for acceptance by which pupils could distinguish themselves from among their peers by impressing people with their performances.[174]

170. Cribiore, *Gymnastics of the Mind*, p. 9.

171. Morgan, *Literate Education*, pp. 44–46. Her work shows that the content of Greek literate education is paralleled throughout the Graeco-Roman world. Although she admits the 'socio-cultural implications of education' would vary in different contexts (p. 45). Moreover, her study shows the content of education and what learners could receive from it. Yet, she recognises the complex question of what particular people *did* get out of it could be different – but she admits this needs another study (p. 47).

172. Morgan, *Literate Education*, pp. 33–39 (33), states that literate education, Hellenistic and Roman, started with reading and writing and moved on to reading authors (Greek and Latin), grammar, literary criticism ... rhetoric and philosophy.... This collection was called the *enkyklios paideia*. The 'curricular model' refers to structure: 'a set collection of exercises existed in a set order, and pupils did them all, diverging only at the end to become orators and philosophers' (p. 67). But her 'core and periphery model' has a core in three senses (that which most pupils learnt, what was learnt first and, for reading, what pupils practised longest). The 'periphery' includes all not in the 'core' but it is not homogenous (pp. 67–73).

173. Morgan, *Literate Education*, p.74. See her discussion on status and identity related to birth, wealth and culture. She examines two fourth-century AD pupils learning literature. Theophilos (probably a Christian), whose family attended the gymnasium, had a cultural advantage over Aurelios whose family probably did not attend the gymnasium or speak Greek at home.

174. Morgan, *Literate Education*, pp. 78–86 (86).

Moreover, Morgan comments on the different stages in education. Although learning grammar had a number of functions in education, it was when a pupil studied rhetoric that he moved from being a passive recipient to an active user of education. This transition 'was a vital marker of social status and power'.[175] Yet Morgan is willing to admit that rhetorical exercises found on papyrus are suitable for students who were likely to become 'bureaucratic middlemen in a variety of posts'.[176] They could take orders and transmit them without answering back their superiors. She notes the contrast with the traditional view where the intention is to produce an orator (e.g. in Quintilian). In her conclusion, she remarks that 'Many must have found themselves implicated, by having a degree of education, in a cultural and value-system which demanded that they respect the better-educated while it allowed the better-educated to regard them as ignorant or cognitively incapable'.[177] Finally, for a detailed discussion of Greek literature and elite activity in Rome see Charles McNelis, who recognises the relationship between *paideia*, social status and learning.[178]

Certainly, education in antiquity was different in many respects to the modern Western education system. Its importance as a status-determinant must be recognised. Access was not free, open and continuous for a fixed period, so some children would work.

8. *Child Education and Labour*

In the modern west children are required by law to attend school and restrictions control child labour. State schools provide free education and 'poor' families are supported by state finances. Thus all children, irrespective of social class, receive free education up to a minimum age. However, in antiquity there were considerable differences, regarding education and labour, between the children of the elite and other children. Thus in 1 Corinthians, Paul's metaphorical use of 'family language', must be understood through different family situations.

Keith Bradley discusses the place of child education and labour in the Roman world.[179] His study concludes:

175. Morgan, *Literate Education*, pp. 188, 198.

176. Morgan, *Literate Education*, p. 225.

177. Morgan, *Literate Education*, p. 272.

178. Charles McNelis, 'Greek Grammarians and Roman Society during the Early Empire: Statius' Father and his Contemporaries', *ClAnt.* 21 (2002), pp. 67–94.

179. Bradley, *Discovering the Roman Family*, pp. 103–24. He notes, 'This book is about the Roman family. Or better, given what I have said so far, it is about some aspects of family life in Roman antiquity. By *Roman* I mean pertaining to Rome in the central period of its history, roughly from 200 B.C. to A.D. 200, so that the term has a generic meaning and refers

> By modern standards, to reemphasize, children in Roman society were introduced through the medium of child labor to the adult world at early stages of their physical development and were conditioned to fulfill obligations that could be discharged fully only when their parents died. At the lower levels of society especially, the result was that the adult pattern of life was established under strong constraints. Whereas the paradigms for the children of the socially elite were predicated on the continuous enjoyment and exploitation of wealth, those for the children outside the ranks of the elite were governed by the expectation of constant hardship from which there was little respite.[180]

C.K. Williams argues that the main function of the new city of Corinth was to serve as a commercial centre.[181] Thus the city would provide ample opportunities for child labour. This social insight helps us to understand more fully Paul's metaphorical language of calling church members children. We must recognise the diversity of children's experience in ancient Corinth. While children from elite families received education other children would have worked. So some children would function in their work like adults. However, even in the area of education children could be considered as adults. We turn to this next and consider infant prodigies.

9. *Infant Prodigies*

The boundaries between adults and children were not as sharply marked in ancient society as they are in ours. Many children worked and were introduced into the adult world much earlier than in our society. Moreover, children were often portrayed, in inscriptions and literary texts, as adults (in contrast to Paul's portrayal of Corinthian adults as children). These infant prodigies, Kleijwegt defines, as young people with adult characteristics.[182] He notes:

> The absence of a specific feeling, based on psychological insights, for the differences between children, teenagers and young adults and the preference for precocious youths are of vital importance for

not merely to the city of Rome and its inhabitants but to any place and people imbued with Roman culture in a broad sense' (p. 4). He considers upper-class childhood with examples from the early life of Cicero's son Marcus and a portrait of Minicia Marcella from the Younger Pliny (*Ep.* 5.16) but then he asks, 'Paradigms of upper-class childhood can thus be safely established. But what of childhood in other sectors of Roman society?' (p. 106). Bradley examines the evidence on work performed by children outside the aristocracy with information pieced together from literary, legal and inscriptional sources.

180. Bradley, *Discovering the Roman Family*, pp. 118–19.

181. Williams II, 'Roman Corinth as a Commercial Center', pp. 31–46.

182. Kleijwegt, *Ancient Youth*, p. 75.

> analyzing the character of ancient education. They determine whether or not ancient society did know child-specific education as we know it.[183]

Because of the importance of the educated elite in 1 Corinthians, and Paul's fictive relationships, I examine Kleijwegt's viewpoint and introduce further references to support his conclusions.

Kleijwegt's catalogue addresses infant prodigies but he admits that these are not all infants, rather he includes teenagers and other youngsters because, 'in the ancient world society could be divided into young and old. The ideal-type of the infant prodigy can be used of anyone who is regarded as non-adult.'[184] This is an important distinction for Paul's metaphorical use of children and adults. If adults are portrayed by Paul as children, then what is Paul saying when in the social world the ideal-type of infant prodigy is used to portray children as adults? Is this a reversal process applied against those Corinthians who are educated and of high status?

Kleijwegt's discussion, using Roman and Greek evidence, demonstrates that their views on infant prodigies complement each other and show the same understanding. The young (irrespective of age) were expected to follow the example of adults including respecting the older generation.[185] For example, Pliny the Younger (*Ep*. 8.23.3) complains that young people do not respect their elders. In addition, Kleijwegt notes that this was a stereotype: the complaint is common in all periods of history. Pliny uses the stereotype to show the elegance of the respectful Junius Avitus. Betty Radice translates:

> And such moreover was his affectionate regard for me that he took me for his moral guide and mentor. This is rare in the young people of today, few of whom will yield to age or authority as being their superior. They are born with knowledge and understanding of everything; they show neither respect nor desire to imitate, and set their own standards.
>
> Avitus was not like this. His wisdom consisted in his belief that others were wiser than himself, his learning in his readiness to be taught. He always sought advice for his studies or his duties in life.[186]

There is a combination here of youth, wisdom, knowledge, authority and imitation that we find in 1 Corinthians. Pliny clearly gives his view on the opposite conduct.

183. Kleijwegt, *Ancient Youth*, pp. 75–76.

184. Kleijwegt, *Ancient Youth*, p. 123 n. 296.

185. Kleijwegt, *Ancient Youth*, p. 123.

186. Betty Radice, *The Letters of the Younger Pliny*, p. 231. Junius Avitus, a senator who took Pliny for his moral guide and mentor, had died.

Kleijwegt too ties education and elite families together with comments on the importance of maintaining family prestige. This could be achieved by ensuring a son was highly educated. Such education was the preserve of the elite who recognised its importance for retaining the status quo. Moreover, sons who completed higher education were not considered adolescents but Kleijwegt maintains, 'adult intellectuals'.[187]

Indeed, the common feeling was that childhood and adolescence warranted little interest. To grow up quickly was important: 'Childhood and adolescence had no additional value in themselves'.[188] He illustrates this from Kleiner, 'who pointed out that children who died prematurely are portrayed on funeral reliefs not as they were at their time of death, but as they would have been if they had lived on. She calls this a prospective (in contrast to a retrospective) view of life'.[189] Kleijwegt concentrates on the preference for precocious children in ancient society but notes that his work supplements previous work.[190]

In contrast to our society, that expects children to be children, Kleijwegt observes that the ancient world viewed the ideal child as not a child:

> In one person, the spontaneity and vitality of youth were combined with the wisdom and experience of mature age. The result was the Latin concept of the puer-senex and the Greek ideal of the παῖς τέλειος. It is highly significant that τέλειος in Greek means both 'perfect' and 'grown-up' or 'adult'. The young person transcends his own age, as it were, by a variety of characteristics, commonly associated with a more mature age.[191]

Many sources emphasise the intellectual qualities of a child or young man. These express the idea that we are interacting with an adult. Ancient people were able to treat young people as such but, as Kleijwegt remarks, this was limited and the time quickly arrived when people preferred to see him not as a child or adolescent but as a young adult. He cites a fine example of a child with adult features from the Younger Pliny (*Ep*. 5.16).[192] This important text describes a girl with the features of a woman, mentioning her wisdom, pedagogues and education.[193] Kleijwegt also

187. Kleijwegt, *Ancient Youth*, pp. 123–24.

188. Kleijwegt, *Ancient Youth*, p. 124.

189. D. Kleiner, 'Women and Family Life on Roman Funerary Altars', *Latomus* 46 (1987), pp. 545–55 (553).

190. Kleijwegt, *Ancient Youth*, p. 124 n. 307.

191. Kleijwegt, *Ancient Youth*, pp. 124–25.

192. Kleijwegt, *Ancient Youth*, p. 125.

193. Radice, *The Letters of the Younger Pliny*, p. 152, translates:

I am writing to you in great distress: our friend Fundanus has lost his younger daughter. I never saw a girl so gay and lovable, so deserving of a longer life or even a life to last for ever. She had not yet reached the age of fourteen, and yet she combined the wisdom of age and

mentions the Younger Pliny (*Ep*. 6.26) where Pliny congratulates Julius Servianus on his choice of Fuscus Salinator to marry his daughter.[194] Here the best qualities of each age coalesce in this educated person: innocence (childhood), kindness (youth) and gravity (old man).[195]

Kleijwegt notes the objection that Pliny describes the exceptional not the normal, ideal not reality, but he counters that epigraphic evidence indicates this ideal was both widespread and intense and this is likely to have shaped reality. Children are frequently recorded as having intellectual qualities that permit them to function as mature adults. These Greek and Roman inscriptions apply to children irrespective of age or gender.[196] For his extreme example, Kleijwegt cites an inscription from Rome of the deceased Kritiès (aged two and a half) but his intelligence, it said, should be compared to a person of grey wisdom.[197] Automenes from Athens (aged seven years) equalled an old man in *paideia*.[198] Hephaistion, an ephebe from Saittai (Lydia), had a good character and beautiful physique. He was esteemed because, although still young, he had a friendly tongue and a greybeard's reasoning ability.[199] The deceased boy Pistikos (aged nineteen) had absorbed all human knowledge. He notes the typical nature of these inscriptions 'youth is described as a stage of life already long passed, while according to our view Pistikos is still in his youth'.[200] An inscription from Tergeste mentions a young senator, 'Although he is still young, he has obliged his mother-city and especially the city-council to his person by these perfect benefactions, which befit an old man'.[201]

dignity of womanhood with the sweetness and modesty of youth and innocence. She would cling to her father's neck, and embrace us, his friends, with modest affection; she loved her nurses, her attendants and teachers, each one for the service given her; she applied herself intelligently to her books and was moderate and restrained in her play.

194. Kleijwegt, *Ancient Youth*, p. 126.

195. Radice, *The Letters of the Younger Pliny*, p. 176, translates:

He belongs to one of our noble families and his father and mother are both highly respected; while he himself is scholarly, well read, and something of an orator, and he combines a childlike frankness and youthful charm with mature judgement. Nor am I blinded by affection – I love him as dearly as his merits and regard for me deserve, but I have kept my critical powers.

196. Kleijwegt, *Ancient Youth*, p. 126.

197. Kleijwegt, *Ancient Youth*, p. 126. Kleijwegt dates this with – Third century AD?

198. Kleijwegt, *Ancient Youth*, p. 126. 3rd/4th century AD.

199. Kleijwegt, *Ancient Youth*, p. 126. He was not older than eighteen or nineteen. Dated 148–9 AD.

200. Kleijwegt, *Ancient Youth*, pp. 126–27. Inscription from Smyrna. Not dated but Kleijwegt adds: imperial period?

201. Kleijwegt, *Ancient Youth*, pp. 126–27. Dated between 138 and 161 AD.

Kleijwegt's further examples include a funeral text, from Caesarea (Mauretania), 'Marcia Rogata ... Cytisis, aged 15 years, ... months. She was pious and wise beyond her age, as though her mind was competing with the swift onset of death'.[202] Horsley notes a number of inscriptions (mostly Jewish), including children's epitaphs giving them adult functions and titles, e.g. *grammateus*, gymnasiarch, as well as noting an honorific inscription where two adolescent sons are portrayed as (adult) philosophers.[203] A Greek epitaph, from a Jewish catacomb in Rome, states, 'Here lies Gaianos, secretary, psalm-singer, lover of the Law. May his sleep be in peace'.[204] Horsley observes, 'Gaianos is the secretary of his synagogue congregation. While we know little in detail about the functions of such an official, almost certainly it is not to be equated with "scribe", the sense found most frequently in the NT'.[205] He notes that of the epitaphs in Rome containing this word, 'The striking feature of the list is the youthfulness of several of these people'. Although these titles may be given to deceased children as a family tribute, Horsley asks, if it could be 'that in the early Christian centuries a Jewish son inherited the role of secretary of his synagogue from his father, and was accorded the title in anticipation? Certain families in the synagogue at Rome may have been able to monopolise some of the offices'.[206] Again, Horsley notes that the problem of official titles accorded to children confronts us elsewhere. Horsley's examples are useful because they offer Jewish examples, which, although late, supplement Kleijwegt. Nevertheless, Kleijwegt develops the discussion to include questions raised by Horsley.

Kleijwegt notes, 'The Greek equivalent to the puer-senex was the παῖς τέλειος. In Greek texts the word τέλειος is used in the case of children mainly to give the impression that they have reached a certain degree of perfection, normally only reached by adults' so here, adult standards describe children.[207]

202. Kleijwegt, *Ancient Youth*, p. 127; citing G.H.R. Horsley, 'Wise beyond her years ...', in Horsley, *New Documents Illustrating Early Christianity*, 3, no. 13, pp. 46–47. The Latin text is dated in the first quarter of the second century AD. Horsley identifies the location as Mauretania but Kleijwegt gives Numidia. Horsley sees the text as memorable because of, 'its attribution to the deceased of the process of maturation quickened up in competition with its speed of fate'.

203. G.H.R. Horsley, *New Documents Illustrating Early Christianity: A Review of the Greek Inscriptions and Papyri Published in 1976*, 1 (North Ryde: Macquarie University, 1981), no. 13, p. 47.

204. G.H.R. Horsley, 'Epitaph for a Jewish Psalm-singer', in Horsley, *New Documents Illustrating Early Christianity*, 1, no. 74, pp. 115–17 (115). Dated 3rd/4th century AD.

205. Horsley, 'Epitaph for a Jewish Psalm-singer', p. 116.

206. Horsley, 'Epitaph for a Jewish Psalm-singer', p. 116.

207. Kleijwegt, *Ancient Youth*, p. 129.

Honorific inscriptions illustrate this. The people's assembly at Samos honoured Xenophon, 'a child by age, a perfect writer of histories'. A text from Olympia indicates maturity, 'Hellas that called me perfect, when it saw me, still a boy, grasp the virtue of the adult men'. This may refer to a young pankratiast who beat adults in the 'all-categories' game. The text for Titus Statilius Lamprias from Epidauros (who died aged eighteen) records, 'in his general education, modesty, insight and respect for his parents he has given perfect examples of his overbearing excellence'.[208]

Kleijwegt's conclusion remarks that as state-subsidized schooling was virtually non-existent many children were excluded from opportunities for education.[209] Moreover, he notes in the Hellenistic-Roman period the gap widened between those who received education and those who did not. Thus Kleijwegt observes:

> Pride in education was a privilege of the elite, viz. the senatorial, equestrian and municipal elite. Since politics was a game of competition, competition also ensued in the qualities attributed to politicians. In the imperial period a life of moral rectitude and a good education became something to be proud of. Pride of education thus operated on two levels: against the mass of illiterates and among the elite herself. Since access to education was a political factor, it resulted in imitation of or (as we have seen in the case of infant prodigies) in equation with adulthood rather than in a period of preparation for society.[210]

Second, he believes that ancient education totally lacked child-specific education. Courses could be followed together by παῖδες and ἔφηβοι. Thus Kleijwegt states, 'The purpose of ancient education was to present children as early as possible as adult intellectuals. Hence the stereotype of the puer-senex and the pais teleios,' and, 'The adult intellectual frequently found in literary and epigraphical sources presents the ideal-type of ancient education. Young men and children were presented as adults rather than as unripe adolescents'.[211]

Kleijwegt's work on infant prodigies provides a considerable insight to the ancient world of children and adults. When we read Paul's language of adults and children in 1 Corinthians the understanding developed by Kleijwegt provides the opportunity for a more sensitive reading of Paul's interaction with the community.[212]

208. Kleijwegt, *Ancient Youth*, pp. 129–130. The word τέλειος occurs in each inscription.

209. Kleijwegt, *Ancient Youth*, p. 131.

210. Kleijwegt, *Ancient Youth*, p. 127.

211. Kleijwegt, *Ancient Youth*, p. 132.

212. In 1 Cor. 2.6 Paul speaks of the mature/perfect before he addresses the Corinthians as infants in 1 Cor. 3.1.

10. *Youth in Politics*

Kleijwegt's contribution to understanding children and families continues with his analysis of texts that illustrate the close association between honours conferred on youngsters and their families' political achievements.[213] Consolation decrees display expectations concerning young members of the Greek civic elite. An ideology of young men/women, who were anticipated to achieve immense prestige as adults, honoured those who died prematurely. This shows the close link in honouring the deceased and the family's political achievements. However, Kleijwegt notes that this tradition of expectations is hard to find in Latin texts, and even the tradition of family office-holding is less emphasised. He summarises that the honoured deceased were expected to follow the family's example, but their youth was not as important as their social status. References to honours, processions and state-funerals show the city considered the loss as emotional not merely financial or political. Young members in elite families were expected to follow in the family footsteps. [214]

Thus expectations were one side of the political ideology. But what self-perception did the politician have and at what age did he or she begin their activity? From the texts Kleijwegt demonstrates, 'We should realize that benefactions and an ideal of moral rectitude were two aspects which were inseparable in the ideology of municipal politics', moreover, 'Moral rectitude was an essential aspect of the benefactor's behaviour'.[215] To raise the prestige of their families young children and adolescents were expected to start a political career early.

One Greek text from Sestos (Thrace), an honorific inscription for the benefactor Menas, dated 122 BC demonstrates the relationship of benefactor and city.[216] His greatest reputation as a benefactor was being gymnasiarch. In the second century BC the gymnasiarch trained the young men (ephebes and *neoi*), but to achieve prestige he spent money on embellishing the gymnasium building, he erected a marble statue, organised games and awarded prizes at his own expense. Menas' text begins by 'indicating that from his earliest youth he had felt that the highest degree of perfection to be reached by a citizen was to make oneself useful to one's city'.[217]

Kleijwegt's Greek sources show abundant benefactions in childhood. He notes a benefactor in Aphrodisias who has been gymnasiarch from early

213. Kleijwegt, *Ancient Youth*, p. 227.
214. Kleijwegt, *Ancient Youth*, p. 233.
215. Kleijwegt, *Ancient Youth*, p. 235.
216. Kleijwegt, *Ancient Youth*, pp. 237–40.
217. Kleijwegt, *Ancient Youth*, p. 237.

youth, following in the footsteps of his father and also grandfather. Tiberius Claudius Theophanes (from Stratonikeia) held priesthoods, was honoured as 'son of the city', and had, as a child, been gymnasiarch of the *neoi*.[218] Despite the rich Greek material Kleijwegt notes extreme difficult in finding parallels in Latin texts. Most have a late date but some date from the Principate. He concludes that there was a strong inclination towards the early introduction of children/adolescents into public life. Kleijwegt writes that youngsters were shown as adults and expected to perform in similar roles. Was this a common practice? Drawing on the inscriptions, he regards it as 'not untypical' because the texts display similar material forming a 'coherent series'. Thus the emphasis is not on the exceptional but normality.[219]

Again, Kleijwegt comments that elite sons and daughters were expected to start their political careers young. Public language addressed children/ adolescents as their parents' successors, not as children but as adults.[220] Elite politics, Kleijwegt claims, were to a considerable amount family matters. Kleijwegt effectively argues that children held offices. For example, he notes one text in second-century AD Stratonikeia identifies Thrasoon Leoon as high priest, gymnasiarch, and priest of Zeus Panamaros as well as of Zeus Chrysaorios. These positions were held, respectively, at the ages of 10, 11, 16 and 20 years.[221] Furthermore, a text identifies a fourteen-year-old who was a former gymnasiarch and had been *agoranomos*.[222]

Additionally, Kleijwegt comments on the popularity of athletic contests. Although the president of the contest (ἀγνωθέτης) was a particularly important and prestigious role, texts indicate that children performed this duty. For example, an inscription in Thyateira identified a Dionysius who is only a child (*pais*), yet he was *agonothetes* for the local games that celebrated the emperor and also the local god. He acted as referee and donated prizes. Moreover, he offered sacrifices for the city and invited dignitaries to dinner.[223] Kleijwegt sees that in offices where wealth and ceremonial tasks were particularly important children were equal to adults.[224] These were not nominal appointments for both children and adults performed the same functions. In a long section, Kleijwegt discusses

218. Kleijwegt, *Ancient Youth*, p. 244. He provides further examples.

219. Kleijwegt, *Ancient Youth*, p. 247.

220. Kleijwegt, *Ancient Youth*, p. 247.

221. Kleijwegt, *Ancient Youth*, p. 248.

222. Kleijwegt, *Ancient Youth*, p. 248. The text is from Epidauros. Kleijwegt describes the office of *agoranomos* (the market superintendent in Greek cities) and children holding the office (pp. 248–50).

223. Kleijwegt, *Ancient Youth*, pp. 251–52.

224. Kleijwegt, *Ancient Youth*, p. 253.

nominal office holding and argues, against earlier scholars, that youngsters participated in politics in their own right because parents wanted them to appear on the civic scene early.[225] This gave early prospects for a potential political career. What then was the situation in Corinth?

Glenn Bugh has evidence for this practice at Corinth in seven joined fragments:

> Gaius Curtius Benignus and Iuventia Hagne erected (this monument) to their son, Gaius Curtius Benignus Iuventianus [of the tribe - - -] (who was) *theocolus* of Jupiter Capitolinus, Imperial Priest of Neptune, *isagogeus* to the agonothetes, praenomen, nomen, - - - reiticus and Ti. Claudius Atticus and who was honoured by the *ordo* with the perquisites of *aedilis, duovir, duovir quinquennalis*, and *agonothetes*.[226]

He argues that the inscription can be dated not much earlier than the mid-90s AD. Iuventianus would have been a young man in the 90s and this is implied in the office of *isagogeus*. The *isagogeus* was a young man chosen by the *agonothete* to assist him in administering the Isthmian Games for that year. Moreover, it is possible that he was still a young man at the time of the dedication of the monument. The honours granted him may reflect the esteemed position of his parents. Bugh comments that backed by considerable family wealth he might have advanced quickly through the priestly offices and continued on to the grant of the municipal *ornamenta*.[227]

Geagan discusses the *isagogeis* of the imperial contests, which are attested for games under Tiberius and Trajan, and notes that Kent identified the proper name of the official as 'the *isagogeus* of the *agonothetes* so and so'.[228] He might go on to become *agonothetes* of the Isthmia and Caesarea but not of the imperial contests, and in possibly two instances he was a member of the same family of the *agonothetes*.[229] In

225. Kleijwegt, *Ancient Youth*, pp. 253–62.

226. Glenn R. Bugh, 'An Emendation to the Prosopography of Roman Corinth', *Hesp* 48 (1979), pp. 45–53 (46).

227. Bugh, 'An Emendation', p. 52 n. 30, adds, 'To be sure, family wealth is certainly the reason why a N. Popidius N. f. Celsinus, *age six*, was adlected into the *ordo* at Pompeii when he (i.e. his parents) rebuilt the Temple of Isis destroyed by the earthquake in A.D. 62: *CIL X*, 846'. Kleijwegt, *Ancient Youth*, p. 258, also cites this text, but adds that the child was the son of the rich freedman, N. Popidius Ampliatus, Kleijwegt suggests that the father could not rise in the society, but the son could. Therefore the benefaction by the son would allow his entrance into the municipal council.

228. Daniel J. Geagan, 'Notes on the Agonistic Institutions of Roman Corinth', *GRBS* 9 (1968), pp. 69–80, 72–74; Kent, *Corinth: The Inscriptions, 1926–1950*, p. 30 n. 32.

229. Geagan, 'Notes on the Agonistic Institutions', p. 74. A discussion on the relationship between the Isthmian and Caesarean Games is given by Elizabeth R. Gebhard, 'The Isthmian Games and the Sanctuary of Poseidon in the Early Empire', in Gregory (ed.), *The Corinthia in the Roman Period*, pp. 78–94 (86–89).

Kent no. 156 the Hieromnemones erected a monument to Aulus Arrius Proclus, whose offices included '*isagogeus* of the Tiberea Augusta Caesarea and agonothete of the Isthmian and Caesaraen Games'.[230] His presidency of the games was almost certainly 39 AD, which places his office of *isagogeus* earlier. Kent no. 173 has an *isagogeus* of a certain Cornelius who, Kent suggests, was probably the Cornelius Pulcher who was agonothete in 43 AD. Moreover, 'As the *isagogeus* was usually a comparatively young man, the posthumous monument was probably dedicated in the reign of Domitian'.[231]

Further, Kent no. 212, an inscription to Lucius Papius Venereus, records that he was an *isagogeus* and a *pyrophorus*. Kent comments:

> The inscription offers a good example of how a Corinthian rose through various local religious offices, for the text is a sort of priestly *cursus honorum* given in the ascending order. Papius' first office, probably held while he was still a boy, was that of assistant (cf. West, p. 67) to the agonothete Tiberius Claudius Anaxilaus, who was a Corinthian duovir during the reign of Nero .... His next office, *pyrophorus* at the Isthmian sanctuary, is recorded at Corinth for the first time in this inscription; the title *pyrophorus* occurs, however, in other parts of the Peloponnese, notably at Epidauros ... where doubtless illumination at night played an important role in the worship of Asklepios.[232]

Kent assumes that Papius was a youth in Nero's reign, so his career falls in the last half of the first century. The inscription is probably dated near 90 AD. Kent no. 213 (dated late-first or early-second century AD) also records an *isagogeus*. Kent no. 214 (undated) records a *pyrophorus* and then an *isagogeus*. Geagan remarks, 'There was also a *pyrophoros* of the Isthmia; he could be a child, and this was an early office in a liturgical *cursus honorum*. Two references are preserved for the Isthmia (Kent nos. 212, 214), and in both *cursus* a service as *isagogeus* is also preserved, although the sequence differs in each. His duties involved the bearing of the sacred fire'.[233] Both Kent no. 208 and no. 209 record an *isagogeus*. In Kent no. 208 Publius Puticius Rufus is *isagogeus* of the Caesarea Neronea and later *agonothete* of the Isthmian and Caesarea. Geagan suggests that

230. Kent, *Corinth: The Inscriptions, 1926–1950*, no. 156, pp. 73–74. Kent commented that the Hieromnemones seem to be 'a board of Corinthian officials with priestly functions whose duty was to supervise the Isthmian sanctuary' (p. 74). In effect they were priests of Poseidon and 'it seems probable that Arrius Proclus was a priest of Neptune at the Isthmia and ... a member ... of the Hieromnemones'. But Geagan, 'Notes on the Agonistic Institutions', p. 76, argues that they were connected with the Caesarea.

231. Kent, *Corinth: The Inscriptions, 1926–1950*, no. 173, pp. 79–80 (80).

232. Kent, *Corinth: The Inscriptions, 1926–1950*, no. 212, pp. 91–92 (92).

233. Geagan, 'Notes on the Agonistic Institutions', p. 76.

Kent no. 209 is a dedication to the *isagogeus* of the same person honoured in Kent no. 208.[234]

Finally, Geagan regards Kent's text of no. 224 as unsatisfactory.[235] This text, for Marcus Antonius Achaicus, records he was *agonothetes* of the [Nervanea Trajanea] of the Isthmian Games. Geagan notes that traces resembling a P. suggests the word *pyrophoros*. In Kent no. 134 M. Antonius Achaicus set up a monument (dated 102–114 AD) to Titus Prifernius Paetus, thus his office of *pyrophoros* would be in the first century. West nos. 82–85 also record an *isagogeus*.[236]

Antony Spawforth observes, 'It was not unknown... for adolescent or even infant scions of distinguished family to hold office: *cf.* Cn. Cornelius Pulcher of Epidauros, *agoranomos* and gymnasiarch at the age of four (*IG* IV^2 653)'.[237] Now Cn. Cornelius Pulcher was a provincial Greek notable, a patron of Corinth, Isthmian *agonothete* c. 41–47 (*SIG*^{3} 802) and a member of the famous Epidaurian family. He was grandfather of the Roman knight Cn. Cornelius Pulcher who was also a patron of Corinth (*PIR*^{2} C 1424).[238]

Kleijwegt shows that children may hold the office of *agoranomos*.[239] This office is attested in three epigraphical references at Roman Corinth where it refers to the traditional Greek office (an *agoranomia* of the Isthmian Games) and not the Roman aedileship. Geagan does not identify any of these as held by children.[240]

Thus the practice of young people holding office is attested in Roman Corinth for the period of Paul's mission work. Both the *isagogeus* and *pyrophorus* were held by young members of the elite and considered honourable enough to be included with their later offices and publicly displayed. They appear at the lower end of the *cursus honorum* but show young people starting off on the political ladder early. As an *isagogeus* the person assisted the agonothete (the top position on the *cursus honorum*) and thus was greatly honoured. In 1 Corinthians, Paul does not explicitly address any children, however, his fictive language, and interaction with the educated elite, is best read with this social situation in mind.

234. Geagan, 'Notes on the Agonistic Institutions', p. 79.

235. Geagan, 'Notes on the Agonistic Institutions', pp. 79–80.

236. Geagan, 'Notes on the Agonistic Institutions', pp. 78; West (ed.), *Corinth: Latin Inscriptions, 1896–1926*, nos. 82–85, pp. 66–71.

237. Antony J.S. Spawforth, 'The Appaleni of Corinth', *GRBS* 15 (1974), pp. 295–303 (297 n. 10).

238. Antony J.S. Spawforth, 'Roman Corinth: the Formation of a Colonial Elite', in Rizakis (ed.), *Roman Onomastics in the Greek East*, pp. 167–82 (174).

239. Kleijwegt, *Ancient Youth*, pp. 248–250; Geagan, 'Notes on the Agonistic Institutions', pp. 75–76.

240. Geagan, 'Notes on the Agonistic Institutions', p. 76.

11. *Summary*

In antiquity, education, family and society were closely aligned in a number of ways. Education itself was not state directed but family controlled. Nevertheless, the study of families is a fairly recent interest both in classical and biblical studies. This area remains relatively unexplored in the study of the educated elite in the Corinthian church. Scholars provide a first century social context for 'family' but this foundation needs to be built upon to construct an ancient education model for Paul's community.

Despite a widespread view that most people in the ancient world could read and write their own name (i.e., they were basically literate) Kleijwegt argues that Harris and Duncan-Jones reveal this is an illusion. Biblical scholars such as Rohrbaugh and Dewey now recognise that literacy was confined to the educated elite. From the evidence of occupations and house ownership, Dewey correctly concludes that the overall literacy of the Corinthian Christians was low. Without state-financed education its provision was a family responsibility, although benefactors may help in the provision of education. Parents were responsible for providing education as Plutarch, Philo and Quintilian show. Epigraphic evidence confirms this. Burke's work demonstrates these expectations. Moreover, Graeco-Roman benefactor language was used between parents and children. Furthermore, a civic benefactor who educated his son was praised for this because it equipped him to continue as a future benefactor, within his family, for the benefit of the people. Education and genealogy were linked. This is particularly illustrated by the *epikrisis* required in Egypt for membership of the gymnasium class.

In antiquity, education was a status-determinant and the relationship between education, family and politics was strong. Kleijwegt shows that παιδεία was used to distinguish one aristocrat from another in their competitive world. Moreover, lack of mobility through education maintained education as a status-determinant. Social advancement through education was exceptional rather than common and when this occurred it was predisposed to reinforce the hierarchical status quo.

While children of the elite enjoyed an education, many children were required by family constraints to work from an early age, as Bradley has shown. This requirement effectively prevented them from receiving a good education. Consequently, children's experiences exhibit considerable diversity. It is reasonable to hypothesise that their experience in Corinth would reflect that of the Empire. Certainly the thriving city of Corinth offered ample opportunities for work. This diversity of experience must be recognised in interpreting Paul's family language.

The boundaries between adult and child were not as sharply marked in many ways as they are in our society. Children were often portrayed in inscriptions and literary texts as adults. These child prodigies are portrayed by the stereotype of the *puer-senex* and παῖς τέλειος. Children are often presented as adult intellectuals. Furthermore, elite children often entered politics from an early age. Inscriptions from Corinth demonstrate this practice.

All these aspects need to be recognised in an ancient education model. They are wider than just considering education in the Greek gymnasium but they set education firmly in its family and societal context, from which we can achieve a more nuanced interpretation of the educated elite in 1 Corinthians. Consequently, this chapter draws together essential elements for understanding the community conflict Paul faced in 1 Corinthians.

12. *General Conclusion for Part II: Chapters 3 and 4*

Chapters 3 and 4 develop my ancient education model. In agreement with recent studies on education my model recognises diversity in ancient education against the earlier views expressed in histories of ancient education. Chapter 3 developed the model of the Greek gymnasium. Although first-century Corinth had as least one gymnasium we have little information on it apart from the archaeological finds. Nevertheless, gymnasia were ubiquitous in the Hellenistic and Roman periods. My model thus selects typical features of the gymnasia. Residents and visitors to first-century Corinth may have received gymnasium education in Corinth or elsewhere in the ancient world, e.g. in Egypt. This would apply to the Corinthian community (whether members or associates, e.g. benefactors). It is impossible, therefore, to be more precise by discussing individual gymnasia (even if we had the evidence) because we would also need to know which individuals attended them where, when, why, what they learnt and selected social aspects (which we do not know). Chapter 4 places my education model within Graeco-Roman society and family where the father was responsible for the education of his children. These features need to be held together in my model.

Part III

Application of the Ancient Education Model

Chapter 5

Application of the Model I

1. *Introduction*

This chapter begins to apply the insights of the ancient education model to examine three topics: Paul's Corinthian Household, Ancient Athletes (1 Cor. 9.24–27), and Nurses, Nutrition and Nurture (1 Cor. 3.1–4). Chapter 6 continues my application by investigating: Agriculture and Education (1 Cor. 3.5–9), Disciplining with the Rod (1 Cor. 4.21), The *Grammateus* (1 Cor. 1.20), Ancient Writing (1 Cor. 4.6) and Circumcision (1 Cor. 7.17–24). These are areas where the model advances our understanding of Paul's interaction with the Corinthian church. Paul's Corinthian Household is dealt with first because this sets the scene for the following topics. Ancient Athletes occurs next because this area is clearly connected with the Greek gymnasium and education. The remaining topics benefit from the application of the education model although they are not as obviously related to the educated elite as the subject of 'ancient athletes'. The examples do not exhaust the text; other passages would benefit from an analysis with an education model.[1] But to contain the study the selected texts must be limited.

The Greek gymnasium was not the total education system available to an elite child but it was an important aspect. After gymnasium education further studies might follow (in philosophy or rhetoric). Moreover,

1. In my MA dissertation, 'Pupils, Pedagogues and Paul: Education in the Greco-Roman World' (unpublished masters dissertation, University of Bristol, 1994), I examined: 'Do not go beyond what is written' (understood as a reference to learning to write), pedagogues, memory and imitation, talk or power, and discipline. The building imagery within 1 Cor. 3.10-15 would benefit from applying an educational model. J. Duncan M. Derrett, 'Paul as Master-Builder', *EvQ* 69 (1997), pp. 129–37 (130), comments on this verse, 'No one doubts, in the context, but that Paul is using foundation-laying not only as a metaphor (as at 1 Cor. 14:4) for the commencement of a religious community (used by Jesus himself at Mt. 16:18), but also the better-known metaphor of introductory teaching, a "foundation-course". Philo talks of an introductory exegesis upon which one can raise a structure by means of allegory as a master-builder's work, and such metaphors are acceptable'.

education conducted outside the gymnasium had many common features with gymnasium education and therefore it would be wrong to attempt to compartmentalise all aspects of ancient education. For example, literary education was taught at home, in schools and within the gymnasium, e.g. with grammarians. So we expect to see common features even if some of the elite did receive part or all of their education outside the gymnasium. My model is part of the diversity now recognised in studies on the history of ancient education. Thus I have a 'messy model' without sharp boundaries. Nevertheless, I contend that it is valuable for investigating the 'messy' ancient world in which the early Corinthian congregation lived and where sharp boundaries and straightforward definitions so appreciated by scholars and students did not always exist.

2. *Paul's Corinthian Household*

I begin by considering Paul's 'household'. Margaret Mitchell concludes her study with:

> It may surprise the reader that, in an investigation which so much stresses the factionalism at Corinth, no new comprehensive analysis of the names, composition, socioeconomic background and theological positions of the Corinthian parties is provided. This has been deliberate. My intention here has been to read *Paul's rhetoric of response to factionalism* against the background of Greco-Roman political texts which do the same thing. The tasks of historical reconstruction remain. This study provides some prerequisites, both positive and negative, for further investigations of the Corinthian parties.[2]

These points provide a foundation for proceeding.[3] Mitchell's investigation of 1 Cor. 1.10 (concerning 'divisions') establishes that this crucial verse 'is filled with terms which have a long history in speeches, political treatises and historical works dealing with political unity and

2. Mitchell, *Paul and the Rhetoric of Reconciliation*, p. 301.

3. Pogoloff, *Logos and Sophia*, pp. 89–90, too readily dismisses Mitchell's investigation when he argues her assumption that dissension is an issue in the 16 chapters is flawed. According to Pogoloff scholars must look for 'the particular situation'. Mitchell, p. 300, admits her study is devoted to the 'political nature' of 1 Corinthians but that is not to deny it is a 'religious document'. In 1 Corinthians Paul deals with *'practical ecclesiology'* using:

> Greco-Roman political terms and concepts for the society and the interrelationships of its members. This means that Paul in 1 Corinthians presents a viewpoint on the church as a *real political body* (even the local church) to which some Greco-Roman political lore, especially the call for concord, is directly applicable. Paul's intimate conception of the church as a family or household in need of harmony also is consistent with such Hellenistic analogues.

factionalism'.[4] Moreover, she notes that ἔριδες in 1.11 ('there are contentions [ἔριδες] among you' [repeated in 3.3]), is often found in Greek texts dealing with discord (domestic or political).[5] For the slogans in 1.12 she investigated, without success, philosophical texts to see if the formulae reflected slogans of adherence to teachers.[6] Nevertheless, she discovered that the genitive was most frequently used in both parent–child and master–slave relationships, and comments, 'That Paul interprets to the Corinthians the "slogans" as self-pronunciations, not of self-determined politicos, but of children and slaves, is shown definitively in 3:1–4; 6:19–20, and especially 7:23'.[7]

She argues that Paul does not quote actual Corinthian slogans but uses the rhetorical figure of 'impersonation'.[8] Thus she comments, 'While the Corinthians themselves may not have expressed their allegiances in this fashion, Paul interprets their factional activity as indicative, not of political sophistication, but of childishness, and renunciation of their precious freedom, through their alignment behind the various missionaries'.[9] When Mitchell considers references to factions in 1 Cor. 3 she notes the 'slogans' are repeated in 3.4 (cf. 3.21–23), and 'Paul compares the factionalists to silly children whose cries for superiority actually demonstrate their infantile dependence on their leaders'.[10] This comparison of contenders with children is frequent in literature advising concord. She cites Dio Chrysostom who uses this *topos*, 'and [if] it is not fitting even for private persons to squabble over them, much less cities of such importance, then let us not behave at all like foolish children who, ashamed lest they may seem to their fathers or mothers to be enraged without a cause, do not wish to make it up with one another lightly'.[11]

She notes other references to family images in such texts and observes that in chapters 3–4 Paul uses the images of the family and of building which Barton has stressed. 'First, he appeals for unity between household factions by representing the church to itself as *one household* with Paul himself as its father (4:14–21) and the members as brothers and sisters of one another'.[12]

4. Mitchell, *Paul and the Rhetoric of Reconciliation*, p. 79. See her section 'Political Terms in 1 Cor 1:10'.

5. Mitchell, *Paul and the Rhetoric of Reconciliation*, p. 81; citing LSJ, p. 689. In the section 'Political Terms and *Topoi* Introduced in 1 Cor 1:11–4:21'.

6. Mitchell, *Paul and the Rhetoric of Reconciliation*, p. 85.

7. Mitchell, *Paul and the Rhetoric of Reconciliation*, p. 85.

8. Mitchell, *Paul and the Rhetoric of Reconciliation*, pp. 84–86; citing Quint., *Inst*. 9.2.30.

9. Mitchell, *Paul and the Rhetoric of Reconciliation*, p. 86.

10. Mitchell, *Paul and the Rhetoric of Reconciliation*, p. 96.

11. Mitchell, *Paul and the Rhetoric of Reconciliation*, p. 96; citing *Or*. 38.21.

12. Mitchell, *Paul and the Rhetoric of Reconciliation*, p. 96 n. 186; citing Stephen C. Barton, 'Paul's Sense of Place: an Anthropological Approach to Community Formation in Corinth', *NTS* 32 (1986), pp. 225–46 (239).

However, Paul goes further. In the church he has a large elite (?) household.[13] Besides the freeborn, married and unmarried, there were slaves and possibly freed slaves (1 Cor. 7.21–24). He refers to himself as nurse/mother (1 Cor. 3.1–2), with Apollos he is a servant (1 Cor. 4.1–2), but he alone is their father (1 Cor. 4.15). Some are pedagogues (1 Cor. 4.15). The Corinthians are referred to as children. John Fitzgerald notes family terminology here but does not relate this to elite households.[14] However, Charles Wanamaker rejects Meggitt's critique of the 'new consensus' and argues that the Corinthian community is socially stratified with the majority of low status and some 'socially strong members'.[15] Moreover, Bruce Winter ably analyses the two 'underlays' of conflict and compromise in 1 Corinthians, which are the cause of problems in the congregation. He concludes his analysis by noting the highly personal nature of Paul's letter and observing, 'What is striking is that Paul makes his appeal on numerous occasions to the Christian community in familial terms addressing the recipients as brothers and sisters. His frequent use of this term reflects his view of Christians as the family of God who were in a primarily spiritual 'sibling' relationship with himself'.[16] On the complexity of ancient houses and families David Balch's recent article is particularly illuminating.[17] He notes that in his study, by focusing on the wealthiest houses, we learn that many books concluding that the 'early Pauline house churches were *necessarily* small and private are mistaken'.[18] Balch argues, 'that we as New Testament scholars should heed the conclusions of Andrew Wallace-Hadrill that Roman *domus* were 'housefuls' of persons unconnected by family ties, that there were massive social contrasts *within the domus* that many rich and poor (far more than 1% of the population) lived in the same spaces'[19]. Thus the diverse social standings in the Pauline fictive household appear to reflect real households. Paul's fictive family is a large household and Paul's intention may have been to give the impression that he is the father over an elite household.

In the secular sources, Plutarch discusses the use of nurses, the selection of slaves and pedagogues, and teachers in educating the children of the

13. See chapter 1 for my brief discussion on the number of members in the Corinthian church.

14. Fitzgerald, *Cracks in an Earthen Vessel*, pp. 117–19.

15. Charles A. Wanamaker, 'A Rhetoric of Power: Ideology and 1 Corinthians 1–4', in Burke and Elliott (eds.), *Paul and the Corinthians*, pp. 115–37 (126–27).

16. Winter, 'The "Underlays" of Conflict and Compromise in 1 Corinthians', pp. 139–55 (154). He notes that in 1 Corinthians Paul addresses them 20 times as 'brothers'/'sisters' and another 17 times he appeals to them in their own relationships, using the same term. This use here is more frequent than in any other of Paul's letters.

17. Balch, 'Rich Pompeiian Houses', pp. 27–46.

18. Balch, 'Rich Pompeiian Houses', p. 30.

19. Balch, 'Rich Pompeiian Houses', pp. 41–42.

wealthy.[20] Quintilian also discussed these aspects in the education of the ideal orator.[21] Furthermore, Ronald Hock convincingly argues, mainly from 1 Cor. 9 and 2 Cor. 11.7, that Paul was indeed socially from the upper classes and, 'By working at a slavish and demeaning trade Paul sensed a considerable loss of status, a loss that makes sense only if he were from a relatively high social class'.[22] Thus it seems that Paul would be familiar with these elite households from his own upbringing and possibly through receiving hospitality during his missionary work. The ancient education model developed addressed the elite household in chapter 4.

By presenting himself as the father in an elite household Paul can effectively meet the challenges of the educated elite who come from such households. In presenting the church as an elite household he incorporates those Christians who do not belong to such households and who have been marginalized. Although some may be slaves or freed slaves attached to elite households, nevertheless, they are not themselves members of the elite. Paul is adopting an inclusive approach as is evident by his stress throughout 1 Corinthians on all Christians.[23] He deals with the educated elite by metaphorically moving into their socially privileged area.

3. *Ancient Athletes: Importance, Imagery, Ideology and Identity (1 Corinthians 9.24–27)*

a. *Importance*

Paul's athletic imagery in 1 Cor. 9.24–27 is important, not only because of its form and function in 1 Cor. 9, but through its essential link with the gymnasium, education, social status and prizes. Biblical scholars recognise

20. Plutarch, *Mor.* 1.3C-5A. In *Mor.* 4A-B, on slaves, he notes, disapprovingly, the common practice of some persons of putting trustworthy slaves to manage farms or be house-stewards (οἰκονόμους), 'but any slave they find to be a wine-bibber and a glutton, and useless for any kind of business, to him they bring their sons and put them in his charge. But the good attendant (παιδαγωγὸν) ought to be a man of such a nature as was Phoenix, the attendant (παιδαγωγός) of Achilles', (4B). Similarities occur here with 1 Cor. 4.15; 11.20–22.

21. Quint., *Inst.* 1.1.4–5 (ideal nurses), 1.1.8 (ideal pedagogues), 1.1.10–11 (what to do if the ideal nurse and pedagogue cannot be found), elsewhere he discusses home and school education and suitable teachers.

22. Hock, 'Paul's Tentmaking and the Problem of His Social Class', p. 564.

23. For example, in 1 Cor. 1–2 Paul stresses the oneness of those who are being saved, in 1 Cor. 3 they are all God's field and building, in 1 Cor. 12 they all have gifts. Martin, *Corinthian Body*, p. 56, sees Paul's emphasis on 'all' Christians as one of the three recurring themes in 1 Cor. 1–4 and throughout the letter. See chapter 1 for my discussion on this aspect of Martin's work.

Paul's imagery here as derived from the Isthmian Games.[24] Moreover, Gordon Fee observes, 'The use of athletic metaphors such as these had a long history in the Greek philosophic tradition, to which Paul is undoubtedly indebted. Nonetheless, the usage and application are his own (perhaps based on his own personal observations of the athletes)'.[25] The Pauline scholar Victor Pfitzner notes, 'The Greek gymnasium is of interest not only in so far as it formed a centre where the agonistic ideals of Greek life were inculcated and fostered, but also because the education which it offered largely contributed to the popularization and extension of athletic imagery'.[26]

Athletics and education are essentially united through the gymnasium. Allen Kerkeslager opens his article with the comment, 'A Greco-Roman athlete's participation in any series of athletic games presupposed a long period of training in the gymnasium'.[27] Also A.H.M. Jones remarks that Greek culture had a characteristic feature in its emphasis on athletics.[28] Moreover, Michael Poliakoff makes the important observation that studying games and play is not a trivial issue because it reveals much about a society's 'character, values and priorities'.[29] Therefore Paul's use of athletic imagery should not be regarded as merely an interesting illustration. Rather, it is grounded within one of the characteristic features of Greek society and related to the gymnasium and education. In particular the Isthmian Games, and other games, were held by Corinth and clearly had an impact on the people and the Corinthian Christians.[30]

Fortunately, classicists have written widely on ancient athletics.[31] Earlier classical scholars had considerable influence within their own field, in the public's understanding of Greek athletics, and in biblical scholarship. This is evident in Pfitzner where he mentions the change and deterioration from Greek amateurism to professionalism.[32] Yet, David Young notes, 'The myth of Greek amateurism now permeates all studies of classical sport,

24. For example, Witherington, *Conflict and Community in Corinth*, p. 214, observes, 'He speaks of the Isthmian games'.

25. Fee, *First Epistle*, pp. 433–34.

26. Victor C. Pfitzner, *Paul and the Agon Motif: Traditional Athletic Imagery in the Pauline Literature* (NovTSup, 16; Leiden: E.J. Brill, 1967), p. 21.

27. Allen Kerkeslager, 'Maintaining Jewish Identity in the Greek Gymnasium: A Jewish "Load" in CPJ 3.519', *JSJ* XXVIII (1997), pp. 12–33 (12).

28. Jones, *The Greek City*, p. 279.

29. Poliakoff, *Combat Sports*, p. 1.

30. Geagan, 'Notes on the Agonistic Institutions'.

31. The vast amount of material in this area can be seen, for example, from Nigel B. Crowther 'Studies in Greek Athletics, Part I', *CW* 78 (1985), pp. 497–558, and 'Studies in Greek Athletics, Part II', *CW* 79 (1985), pp. 73–135.

32. Pfitzner, *Paul and the Agon Motif*, pp. 18, 187 n.2. Pfitzner's work is still used in biblical studies. For example, by Fee, *First Epistle*, pp. 175, 434, 435, 436, 438 etc., although Fee does not use his work uncritically.

even the most scholarly reference works'.[33] Young's work covers an important aspect to keep in mind throughout this section. Ancient Greek amateurism and professionalism were distorted by earlier classicists and misleadingly presented to a modern audience through the revived Olympic Games. Recent scholarship frequently deals with this issue because of its major impact on the social classes of those who could, or could not, compete in Greek games. Therefore their studies range from pre-classical times to the second century AD. This long time-frame is necessary to ensure that New Testament studies benefit from a sensitive understanding of social aspects among athletic competitors.[34] Intricately woven through Paul's imagery is the ideology of athletics, social status and prizes. But what is sport and athletics?

Poliakoff helpfully clarifies the meaning of both. In his book he defines sport and athletics:

> As activity in which a person physically competes against another in a contest with established regulations and procedures, with the immediate object of succeeding in that contest under criteria for determining victory that are different from those that mark success in everyday life (warfare, of course, being included as part of everyday life in antiquity).[35]

Sport requires an opponent(s) and a system that measures competitors' performances (using success and failure). Poliakoff's definition excludes some forms of combat. Thus a gladiator who fights an opponent (to kill or disable) and save himself is not involved in sport but a type of warfare for the benefit of spectators.[36] This is an important distinction, for in 1 Cor. 9.24–27 Paul uses athletic, not gladiatorial, imagery.

Pfitzner identifies the importance of Paul's athletic imagery. He notes Paul's relatively frequent use of this imagery compared to other metaphors and pictures. This use, he comments, is generally recognised as related to important motifs, but to discover and define these motifs has been problematical. He notes that to ascertain the imagery's importance (what he calls the 'picture of the Agon') one is met with:

33. David C. Young, 'How the Amateurs Won the Olympics', in Raschke (ed.), *The Archaeology of the* Olympics, pp. 55–75 (72). See also his book *The Olympic Myth of Greek Amateur Athletics* (Chicago: Ares Publishers, Inc., 1985).

34. See the brief comments by Poliakoff, *Combat Sports* who notes, 'To speak of amateurism in Greek sport is an inadmissable though common fiction' (p. 7).

35. Poliakoff, *Combat Sports*, p. 7. His study examines the three important forms of combat sports in the ancient world: boxing, wrestling and *pankration* (a combination of boxing and wrestling).

36. Poliakoff, *Combat Sports,* p. 7. For a discussion on gladiatorial combat see Erik Gunderson, 'The Ideology of the Arena', *ClAnt* 15 (1996), pp. 113–151.

> A *threefold task*: 1. the search for possible contemporary sources, or at least literary or non-literary parallels for the use of this picture, 2. the establishment of the manner, meaning, and purpose of Paul's use of the image, and 3. the ordering of the theological motif(s) suggested by the image in the thought of the Apostle.[37]

Pfitzner's detailed and valuable study is not limited to 1 Corinthians and scholars have used his study to provide light on Paul's thought. Nevertheless, since Pfitzner's early study, recent scholarship has identified social aspects in 1 Corinthians including the important issues of social status and the educated elite.[38] My examination of these areas advances the understanding of Paul's use of the *agon* motif in his letter.

Commentaries cite Pfitzner's major contribution to Pauline studies but this area now needs further study. David Horrell's study on the Corinthian letters only states that Paul may fail in the race and be disqualified is a connecting link with 10.1–13 and 9.24 turns to exhortation.[39] Dale Martin's study of slavery in Pauline Christianity, despite his extensive treatment of 1 Cor. 9, only makes very minor comments on this section.[40] In *The Corinthian Body* Martin does not consider this section.[41] This is an omission in a work on the body, especially as Jerome Neyrey had commented, 'Paul's attitude to the physical and its replication of the social body is never clearer than in the athletic metaphor he uses in 9:24–27'.[42] Similarly, Peter Gooch examines 1 Cor. 8–10 but omits 9.24–27.[43] This is surprising because he carefully examines the nature of idol-food in Corinth, and in the Graeco-Roman world, yet ignores the importance of the social context of the Isthmian Games for interpreting 1 Corinthians.

Clarence Glad's discussion of Paul and psychagogy examines 1 Cor. 8.1–13; 9.19–23; 10.24–11.1 but omits 9.24–27.[44] Nevertheless, as Thiselton observes, Glad makes a valuable contribution to understanding 1 Cor. 9.19–23 where Paul focuses on his strategy for the gospel. Thiselton notes that the verses provide 'a rhetorical climax' to Paul's argument in vv. 1–18 and here Glad's monograph makes a significant contribution.[45] So, for Thiselton,

37. Pfitzner, *Paul and the Agon Motif*, p. 1.
38. See my discussion in chapter 1.
39. Horrell, *Social Ethos*, pp. 199–205.
40. Martin, *Slavery as Salvation*, pp. 87, 129, 132, 199–200 n. 31. His last reference notes a passage in Dio Chrysostom (*Discourses* 3.83–85) 'where the good king is compared to an athlete who does not exercise in vain but attains his goals (cf. 1 Cor. 4.8 where the Corinthians are addressed as kings).
41. Martin, *Corinthian Body*.
42. Neyrey, 'Body Language in 1 Corinthians', p. 162.
43. Gooch, *Dangerous Food*.
44. Glad, *Paul and Philodemus*.
45. Thiselton, *First Epistle*, p. 699; Glad, *Paul and Philodemus*. See chapter 2 for my discussion of Glad's work.

Glad shows that Paul combines both 'strategy and stance'. First, Paul uses familiar Graeco-Roman traditions where educators (or 'wise people') demonstrate that, because of human diversity, there is a need for approaches that are both adaptive and flexible. Second, Paul appeals to the 'strong' to act according to their claim to be 'wise' and make due allowance for the 'weak' in various circumstances rather than pursue their own interests.[46]

Bruce Winter, in *Seek the Welfare of the City*, discusses '1 Corinthians 8–10 and the Isthmian Feasts'.[47] In his analysis Winter recognises that Paul's athletic imagery in 9.24–27 provides evidence that the Isthmian Games are the *Sitz im Leben* where the problem of idol-food arises and 'the issue in Paul's mind is the dining "rights" of Christian Roman citizens to attend the "several" feasts given by the President of the Games'.[48] In his later book, *After Paul Left Corinth*, Winter addresses this issue further, demonstrating the close relationship between the Federal Imperial Cult, the prestigious Isthmian Games and dining. Corinthian Christians had attended the feasts in the temple following personal invitations from the President of the Games. They had attempted a theological justification for their attendance (8.4). Thus Paul is addressing the 'strong' who are in great danger of falling and of detrimentally affecting the 'weak' Christians.[49]

In his discussion of the athletic metaphor, Roman Garrison concludes, its purpose 'is to call the Corinthians to the exercise of love demonstrated in self-control, an athletic self-denial of privilege and rights'. Paul is the model for imitation. He considers that the Corinthians would understand Paul's challenge because Cynics and Stoics had similar imperatives.[50] Garrison observes that, 'The truly wise man is described as an athlete, expected to train for the Olympic competition of life itself'.[51] His work uses citations from Stoics and Cynics to demonstrate Paul's imagery.

46. Thiselton, *First Epistle*, p. 699.

47. Winter, *Seek the Welfare of the City*, pp. 165–77 (173–74). This is chapter 9 'Civic Rights: 1 Corinthians 8–11:1'. He notes that feasts could occur in a gymnasium (p. 169). See my discussion in chapter 2 on the gymnasium as a venue for feasts.

48. Winter, *Seek the Welfare of the City*, p. 173. Winter states that the problem had not arisen when Paul was in Corinth and the reason may be because 'no games occurred during Paul's ministry in Corinth to which Christians who were Roman citizens were invited' (p. 173).

49. Winter, *After Paul Left Corinth*, pp. 269–86. This is chapter 12 'The Imperial Cult, the Games, and Dining in a Temple (1 Corinthians 8–10:21)'. Winter shows that feasts were part of the Isthmian festival.

50. Roman Garrison, *The Graeco-Roman Context of Early Christian Literature* (JSNTSup, 13; Sheffield: Sheffield Academic Press, 1997), p. 104. This is in chapter 9 'Paul's Use of the Athletic Metaphor in 1 Corinthians 9', pp. 95–104.

51. Garrison, *Graeco-Roman Context*, p. 96. He cites Epictetus, *Discourses* 1.24.1–2; 2.18.27–29; 3.10.8; 4.4.30.

Vernon Robbins addresses 1 Cor. 9, using it as an extended illustration in his explanation of socio-rhetorical criticism.[52] Robbins offers valuable detailed discussion on different textures in 1 Cor. 9 and thus interacts with 1 Cor. 9.24–27.[53] Starting from Robbins' recent books Margaret E. Dean provides an analysis of 1 Cor. 9.[54] She notes that when the passage was heard, these sounded syllables evoke a vast array of associations.[55] Dean shows repetition in the auditory dimension of the text is persuasive in a rhetorical context.[56] Amphilochios Papathomas has also examined Paul's *agon* motif in 1 Cor. 9.[57] More recently, Jerry Sumney, in a critical note, has examined 9.24–27 within Paul's argument.[58] These studies demonstrate a useful refocus on 1 Cor. 9.24–27 that serves to advance the groundwork provided by Pfitzner. My focus explores the educated elite.

From the 6th century BC the four Greek festivals at Olympia, Isthmia, Delphi and Nemea were recognised as the sacred crown games (the Panhellenic games). The festivals were dedicated to particular gods. The Isthmian Games were the responsibility of the city of Corinth. The chief deity of the Isthmian sanctuary was Poseidon. These games achieved international status and together they formed a circuit.

When the Isthmian Games were staged in 51 AD Paul was present in Corinth.[59] Many scholars believe that Paul refers to these games in 1 Cor. 9. Oscar Broneer reconstructs Paul's visit to the biennial Isthmian Games and believes that they played a contributing, possibly a decisive, role in Paul's choice of Corinth as his Greek missionary base.[60] Elizabeth Gebhard's review of the evidence argues that while the Isthmian

52. Vernon K. Robbins, *The Tapestry of Early Christian Discourse: Rhetoric, Society and Ideology* (London and New York: Routledge, 1996). In this work he brings together social-scientific and literary-critical approaches to explore early Christianity.

53. Robbins, *The Tapestry of Early Christian Discourse*, pp. 65–90 on 'Inner texture'; pp. 120–142 on 'Intertexture'; pp. 176–189 on 'Social and Cultural Texture'; pp. 220–235 on 'Ideological Texture'.

54. Margaret E. Dean, 'Textured Criticism', *JSNT* 70 (1998), pp. 79–91.

55. Dean, 'Textured Criticism', p. 82.

56. Dean, 'Textured Criticism', p. 83. She notes, 'Auditory signals alone cannot answer questions about a text's underlying social structures, cultural categories, or ideologies. But the analysis of aural patterns at the level of the syllable can uncover a composition's structure. It can also identify the textual phenomena which require interpretation and suggest how those phenomena are related' (p. 87).

57. Amphilochios Papathomas, 'Das agonistische Motiv 1Kor 9.24ff. im Spiegel zeitgenössischer dokumentarischer Quellen', *NTS* 43 (1997), pp. 223–41.

58. Jerry L. Sumney, 'The Place of 1 Corinthians 9:24–27 in Paul's Argument', *JBL* 119 (2000), pp. 329–33.

59. Jerome Murphy-O'Connor, 'The Corinth that Saint Paul Saw', *BA* 47 (1984), pp. 147–59 (149). The Isthmian Games were celebrated every 2 years in the spring.

60. Oscar Broneer, 'Paul and the Pagan Cults at Isthmia', *HTR* 64 (1971), pp. 169–87 (169). Broneer excavated Isthmia.

Games were returned to Corinthian control by 40 BC 'they were celebrated in the city of Corinth. The festival did not come to be held regularly at the Isthmian sanctuary until A.D. 50–60'.[61] Mika Kajava has also investigated when the Isthmian Games returned to the Isthmus and he proposes AD 43.[62] Thus both scholars argue for a mid-first-century date.

In Paul's time other games were also celebrated by the city.[63] The Corinthian Christians understood Paul's imagery, which used an important feature of Greek culture central to Corinth.[64] Archaeological discoveries show how the importance and imagery of Greek athletics was promoted through various meanings including amphorae, bases, coins, inscriptions and sculptures.[65] Athletes depicted include runners and boxers.

b. *Imagery*

1. Running. Paul's imagery in 1 Cor. 9.24–27 uses running and boxing from the Isthmian Games. In the foot races turning posts were provided for races longer than one stade.[66] There was no oval track. Starting gates ensured an equal start. Victor lists show separate events at the Isthmian Games for boys, youths, and men.

The presence of women contestants at Isthmia is confirmed by *SIG*^{3} 802 dated AD 47. Stephen Miller notes that the inscription was found at Delphi on a limestone statue base, which originally supported the statue of three sisters.[67] Their father Hermesianax, son of Dionysios, dedicated the

61. Gebhard, 'The Isthmian Games', p. 94. After Corinth's destruction (146 BC) they came under the control of nearby Sicyon.

62. Mika Kajava, 'When did the Isthmian Games return to the Isthmus? (Rereading Corinth 8.3.153)', *CPhil* 97 (2002), pp. 168–78. I am gratefully to Elizabeth Gebhard for bringing this article to my attention.

63. See Geagan, 'Notes on the Agonistic Institutions', for a discussion on the Isthmian, Caesarea and the Imperial Games. See Gebhard, 'The Isthmian Games', pp. 86–89, for the relationship of the Caesarea and the Isthmian Games. She states, 'it seems likely that: 1. the two sets of contests were held together; 2. the Isthmia usually preceded the Caesarea; 3. the Caesarea were often, but not always, celebrated in Corinth' (p. 87).

64. Garrison, *Graeco-Roman Context*, p. 103, concludes that '1 Cor. 9.24–26 echoes the themes and values of his contemporary culture' and he notes that Paul uses the language of other first-century AD teachers such as Philo.

65. See especially the catalogue in Tzachou-Alexandri, (ed.), *Mind and Body*, nos. 1–235, pp. 105–349. This beautifully illustrated coloured catalogue includes finds from the Bronze Age through to the Imperial Age.

66. Stade (*stadion* – one length of the stadium) about 190 m. For a description of the events see: Elisabeth Kakarouga-Stassinopoulou, Rosa Proskynitopoulou, and Stavroula Papadiamantopoulou-Kalliodi, 'The Events', in Tzachou-Alexandri (ed.), *Mind and Body*, pp. 97–104; Meritt, *Corinth: Greek Inscriptions, 1896–1927*, no. 16, pp. 21–25, and William R. Briers and Daniel J. Geagan, 'A New List of Victors in the Caesarea at Isthmia', *Hesp* 39 (1970), pp. 79–93.

67. Miller, *Arete*, no. 106, pp. 103–4. Miller provides a translation of the inscription.

statue to Pythian Apollo for his daughters (Tryphosa, Hedea and Dionysia). The father and his daughters held citizenship in Kaisarea Tralles, Athens and Delphi. This inscription, contemporary with Paul, specifically mentions the games in which the sisters won, including the Isthmian Games. Their victories included running in the *stadion* at the Pythian Games, Isthmian Games, Nemean Games and at Epidauros. The games are dated by the names of the *agonothetes*. Olivier Picard states, 'This inscription, dated to around AD 45 is one of the most explicit indications that young girls were involved in the great festivals (leaving aside the events for girls in the various cities, including Sparta)'.[68] Moreover, an inscription from Corinth for Lucius Castricius Regulus, states that he introduced a contest for girls.[69] So male and female victors exist from the first-century AD Isthmian Games. Corinthian coins depict athletes including runners and boxers. These are discussed below under boxing.

2. *Boxing*. Boxing, wrestling and *pankration* were the 'heavy' events, or combat sports, and had many similarities. Although these required different skills and tactics the Greeks saw them as related.[70] Often the same man excelled in more than one combat sport.[71] There were few rules, no time limit except nightfall and no ring. Divisions were by age (boys, youths and men), but not by weight. Thus combat sports favoured the large and strong.[72] H. A. Harris comments that, 'while no doubt small men

68. Picard, 'Delphi and the Pythian Games', p. 74. Further discussions in the literature show the presence of girls/women in athletics. See Nancy Serwint, 'The Female Athletic Costume at the Heraia and Prenuptial Initiation Rites', *AJA* 97 (1993), pp. 403–22, for citations of recent scholarship. Mary C. Sturgeon, 'The Corinth Amazon: Formation of a Roman Classical Sculpture', *AJA* 99 (1995), pp. 483–505 (495) discusses whether a statue from the Corinth Theatre in the first half of the second century AD was a female athlete, a victor's statue from a girl's race. But after reviewing the evidence she decides that the statue was an Amazon. See also Stephen V. Tracy and Christian Habicht, 'New and Old Panathenaic Victor Lists', *Hesp* 60 (1991), pp. 187–236, which show women victors who appear to have actually competed in equestrian events in the second century BC.

69. Kent, *Corinth: The Inscriptions, 1926–1950*, no. 153, pp. 70–73. The restored inscription is in Latin. Kent, p. 72, states that Regulus' public career was from about 10 BC to AD 23 and the text is dated to approximately AD 25, 'he expanded the program to include an athletic contest for girls'. He was *agonothete*. But see Gebhard, 'The Isthmian Games', pp. 87–88, who discusses Kent's restoration. The spacing could allow Cn. Publicius Regulus, who was a *duovir* in AD 50/51. He would be a contemporary of Paul's mission work in Corinth.

70. Unlike modern athletes who do not usually compete at a high level in both boxing and wrestling.

71. Poliakoff, *Combat Sports*, p. 8.

72. The ideological and ethical terms were also similar. Poliakoff, *Combat Sports*, remarks that, 'the athletes' ability to suffer in silence was proverbial' (p. 9). He mentions from Plutarch an ancient anecdote that Aeschylus, who observed the Isthmian Games, saw spectators cry out at the force of the punches but the boxer's training ensured he remained silent. Poliakoff,

wrestled and boxed with one another in palaestra and gymnasium, in open competition only the biggest had any chance of success'.[73] Poliakoff agrees that boxing, wrestling and *pankration* were the sphere of the strong and large competitors."[74] Dio Chrysostom, in his second Tarsic discourse, comments, 'For what is happening to you resembles what happens in the case of athletes when a smaller man contends against one much larger. For the larger man is not allowed to do anything contrary to the rules, but even if unwittingly he is guilty of a foul, he gets the lash; whereas nobody observes the smaller, though he does anything within his power'.[75] Smaller men could compete but clearly the larger man had an advantage. Although Timothy Carter's article on '"Big Men" in Corinth' offers a useful discussion on the rivalries of local leaders in 1 Corinthians he does not address the size of boxers.[76]

Competitors competed outdoors in the stadium. They attempted to get the sun behind them so it shone in their opponent's eyes. The Greeks considered boxing as the most challenging of the three heavy events. Poliakoff notes a first-century BC inscription (from the island of Thera) that praises a boxer, and begins 'A boxer's victory is gained in blood'. Poliakoff comments that he was both successful and tough. But ancient boxing did not only require brutality for victory it also 'required a high degree of skill and strategy in addition to courage and fortitude. But trauma has always been a given, an essential part of the sport, and the Greeks quite accurately viewed boxing as the most physically punishing and damaging of all athletic contests'.[77] Similarly, Finley and Pleket state that ancient boxing:

> Was the really tough sport. Leather thongs were wound tightly round the hands and wrists leaving the fingers free, and the originally soft

Combat Sports, comments, 'So Eurydamas of Kyrene in large measure won through his grim determination – his opponent hit him hard enough to break several of his teeth, but Eurydamas preferred to swallow them rather than spit them out and thereby inform his opponent that he had landed such a successful blow' (p. 9).

73. Harris, *Greek Athletes and Athletics*, p. 97.

74. Poliakoff, *Combat Sports*, p. 8.

75. *Or*. 34.13. This oration was delivered before a public gathering of the citizens of Tarsus. Dio Chrysostom lived AD 40 – *c*. 120.

76. Timothy L. Carter, '"Big Men" in Corinth', *JSNT* 66 (1997), pp. 45–71. Carter contests Neyrey, 'Body Language in 1 Corinthians', for his use of Mary Douglas's 'Grid and Group' matrix to analyse differing attitudes to the body in 1 Corinthians. He offers a different social situation analysis and concludes that in 1 Cor. 1–4; 9 Paul defends himself against the attacks of the local leaders. His analysis of 1 Cor. 9 uses Douglas's model and 'Big Men' based substantially on anthropological studies of tribes in New Guinea. He applies this to first-century Corinth. Thus he does not consider the size of boxers in Paul's athletic imagery in 1 Cor. 9.24-27.

77. Poliakoff, *Combat Sports*, p. 68. See his chapter V 'Boxing'.

> leather eventually gave way to hard, sharp thongs ... Blows were allowed with both the fist and open hand; few punches were prohibited. The two contestants fought on, without a break, until one or the other was either knocked out or raised his right hand as a sign of defeat.[78]

Thus the boxer required for success: size, strength, skill, strategy, stamina and courage.[79]

Ancient boxing contests had no rounds. The fighters might pause for breath but clinching was banned. The contenders fought until one either accepted defeat or was knocked out. Hazards and injuries were common in the sport. Thus Poliakoff notes vase paintings often show blood pouring from boxers' noses. In Artemidoros, dreaming of boxing meant a deformed face and blood-loss.[80] Texts refer to athletes who had lost their eyes.[81] Blows appear to have focused on the head (predominantly the nose, cheek and the jaw). When contests were particularly lengthy with closely matched contestants then the *klimax* procedure was used. Here each boxer took turns at standing stationary and received a punch from the opponent. This procedure continued until the contestant who endured the longest became the winner.[82] Ancient boxing was different in many significant ways to modern boxing.

Men, boys and youths had their own boxing events. Evidence for women's boxing is scanty, but not entirely absent. For example, Thomas Scanlon cites sources showing that Spartan females participated in athletics including wrestling, *pankration* and boxing.[83] But there is no evidence for female boxing at the Isthmian Games. However, Corinthian terracotta lamps and coins show boxers. Oscar Broneer shows a type XXII terracotta lamp no. 423 from Corinth, where 'on the discus is the figure of a boxer to right with the left hand advanced; he wears loin cloth and

78. M.I. Finley and H.W. Pleket, *The Olympic Games: The First Thousand Years* (London: Chatto & Windus Ltd, 1976), p. 39.

79. Poliakoff, *Combat Sports*, p. 9, notes that *kartereia* ('toughness' or 'endurance') is particularly prominent in ancient descriptions of combat sports (but it also occurs on other victors' monuments).

80. Artemidoros, *Interpretation of Dreams*, 1.61–62. Second century AD.

81. Poliakoff, *Combat Sports*, p. 87. His references, p. 174 n. 26, for eye injuries are Libanius 64.119 and Galen, *Protrept.* 12 (1.32 K., 124–25 M) and he comments, 'these texts refer to punching, which was a part of both *pankration* and boxing, not gouging (which would make the injury peculiar to *pankration*)'.

82. Kakarouga-Stassinopoulou, Proskynitopoulou, and Papadiamantopoulou-Kalliodi, 'The Events', p. 102.

83. Thomas F. Scanlon, '*Virgineum Gymnasium*: Spartan Females and Early Greek Athletics', in Raschke (ed.), *The Archaeology of the Olympics*, pp. 185–216 (185, 205). Propertius (3.14), *c.* 23 BC, mentions boxing.

boxing gloves but is otherwise nude'.[84] All Corinthian lamps of this type belong to the first century AD.[85] The same figure appears with his opponent on a type XXI lamp that is also first century.[86]

As I mentioned in chapter 1, coins excavated at Corinth show athletes, boxers and runners. These are small bronze coins without names of any duoviri or emperor. They have short legends and Greek subjects, e.g. Pegasus, Melicertes and Isthmus. One group has Poseidon's head (on the obverse) and athletes (on the reverse) including boxers, runners and a discus-thrower. Edwards infers that these coin-types were popular during Augustus' reign and attributes these athletic types to his reign.[87] Images show figures of boxers, athletes, runners and a discus-thrower.[88] No. 83 shows two naked boxers facing, and striking, each other. No. 84 also has two naked boxers facing each other but one appears to be falling over backwards. No. 85 shows one naked athlete standing and a naked runner crouched and ready to start. No. 86 displays a discus-thrower and finally, no. 87 shows an athlete running. Greek athletes competed naked.[89]

Room 'C' (the office of the *agonothetes*) in Corinth's South Stoa shows a first-century AD mosaic of a naked victorious athlete presenting himself to a goddess. He holds a victory palm and wears a wreath.[90] Moreover, a marble head of a young boy athlete (dated first/second century AD) has been found in the theatre at Isthmia. The size of the

84. Oscar Broneer, *Corinth: Terracotta Lamps* (ASCSA, 4.2; Cambridge, MA: Harvard University Press, 1930), no. 423, figure 97, p. 172.

85. Broneer, *Corinth: Terracotta Lamps*, p. 78.

86. Broneer, *Corinth: Terracotta Lamps*, pp. 76, 172. Broneer, p. 172, notes that this lamp is in the British Museum. It also appears to be from the Corinthian excavations. Also in the British Museum, and on display in August 1997, is a terracotta panel showing a scene in a palaistra. It is from Campania about the first century AD. The description comments, 'On the right is a statue of a victorious boxer, holding a palm-branch and a winner's ribbon. A boxing throng is bound on his left fist and forearm. On the pillar is a bust of Hermes, patron god of wrestlers; such monuments (*herms*) often stood in the gymnasium and palaistra'. The boxer is naked. Townley Collection, GR 1805.7–3.390, BM CAT Terracottas D 632.

87. Edwards, *Corinth: Coins, 1896–1929*, p. 7. The short legends include COR, CORIN, SE or COL.

88. Edwards, *Corinth: Coins, 1896–1929*, nos. 83–87, pp. 25–26 and Plate III.

89. James A. Arieti, 'Nudity in Greek Athletics', *CW* (1975), pp. 431–36. Gruen, *Diaspora*, p. 125, notes 'Philo praised the overseers of gymnastic contests for maintaining propriety by banning women spectators, lest they observe men stripping themselves to the nude' (Philo, *Spec. Leg.* 3.176). See also: Nigel B. Crowther, 'Nudity and Morality: Athletics in Italy', *CJ* 76 (1980–81), pp. 119–23; Nigel B. Crowther, 'Athletic Dress and Nudity in Greek Athletics', *Eranos* 80 (1982), pp. 163–68, and Michael L. Satlow, 'Jewish Constructions of Nakedness in Late Antiquity', *JBL* 116 (1997), pp. 429–54.

90. Broneer, *Corinth: The South Stoa*, pp. 107–10. The mosaic is shown in Plates 30–31 and Plan II. The inner panel is also shown as a coloured plate on p. 108. Plan XXI shows the location of Room 'C' with respect to the other rooms in the South Stoa. See my earlier discussion in chapter 1.

head indicates it belonged to a statue that was less than life-size. He wears a victor's pine crown. His facial features indicate that he was probably a victorious boxer. The iconography of ancient boxers shows them with damaged faces and ears.[91] Let us turn to winning and crowns.

3. *Winning and Crowns*. Athletic contests were widespread and popular in the Roman empire.[92] At the time of Paul victors in games could receive cash prizes, crowns with cash prizes, or simply crowns.[93] The 'Big Four' Games (i.e. the Olympic, Isthmian, Pythian [at Delphi] and Nemean Games) only gave crowns.[94] These were made of perishable material and at Isthmia during the time of Paul from pine and/or celery.[95] Moreover, although some games had first, second and third

91. Tzachou-Alexandri (ed.), *Mind and Body*, no. 127, pp. 236–37. For other statues of boxers see, in the above: no. 174 p. 286 (almost complete bronze statuette of a nude boxer from a shipwreck off Antikythera, 2nd century BC), no. 175 p. 287 (an arm from a bronze statue probably of a boy boxer, also from the shipwreck; the ship may have come from Pergamon where the statue probably occupied a public place (perhaps in a gymnasium), 2nd (?) century BC), no. 176 pp. 287–88 (bronze statuette of an oldish nude boxer of unknown providence, dated Hellenistic (?) period but possibly modelled on a 5th century BC sculpture), no. 219 pp. 328–330 (youthful boxer called Kyniskos, see no. 221), no. 221 pp. 330–32 (the base of bronze statue of the victorious boy boxer Knyiskos of Mantineia, providence Olympia, dated *c*. 460 BC and mentioned by Pausanias (6.4.11)), no. 230 pp. 340–43 (life-size bronze head from a statue of a bearded boxer from the sanctuary of Zeus at Olympia and dated *c*. 330 BC). No. 230 is of particular interest. The facial features clearly show a boxer: 'the flattened nose, protruding frontal bones and cauliflower ears all bear witness to the bruises and injuries received in a long pugilistic career' (p. 340). He is crowned with an olive-wreath. Drawing upon Pausanias' description (who says statues honouring victorious athletes were displayed at Olympia) this may have been Satyros who won at the Nemean Games (five times), the Pythian Games (twice) and in the Olympic Games (twice). No. 216 p. 326, is a marble fragment of a grave stele from Athens, dated 560–550 BC. It shows a mature bearded boxer with an almost flat eyeball, a curved nose (broken) and cauliflower ears. In the iconography of boxers these are considered characteristic features.

92. Antony J.S. Spawforth, 'Agonistic Festivals in Roman Greece', in Walker and Cameron (eds.), *The Greek Renaissance in the Roman Empire* (Bulletin Supplement, 55; London: Institute of Classical Studies, University of London, 1989), pp. 193–97.

93. H.W. Pleket, 'Games, Prizes, Athletes and Ideology: Some Aspects of the History of Sport in the Greco-Roman World', *Stadion* 1 (1975), pp. 49–89.

94. For discussions on these games see Klaus Herrmann, 'Olympia: The Sanctuary and Contests', in Tzachou-Alexandri (ed.), *Mind and Body*, pp. 47–68; Elizabeth R. Gebhard, 'The Sanctuary of Poseidon on the Isthmus of Corinth and the Isthmian Games', in Tzachou-Alexandri (ed.), *Mind and Body*, pp. 82–88; Olivier Picard, 'Delphi and the Pythian Games'; and, Stephen G. Miller, 'Nemea and the Nemean Games', in Tzachou-Alexandri (ed.), *Mind and Body*, pp. 87–96. See also Gebhard, 'The Isthmian Games'.

95. Oscar Broneer, 'The Isthmian Victory Crown', *AJA* 66 (1962), pp. 259–63, demonstrates that the crown was first pine (from the foundation of the games until the early 5th century BC) then celery (to the 2nd century BC) and finally pine and/or celery (to the 2nd century AD and perhaps later).

prizes, in the Isthmian Games only first prize was awarded. The status of these games was so great that people came from across the Graeco-Roman world to participate without any cash prizes. Stephen Miller notes the spread in the Hellenistic-Roman period of games that were based on the status of 'the old original four stephanitic games'.[96] These games were considered, 'in some sense', as equal or equivalent to these original games. Miller cites an inscription (found in Olympia and dated 2 BC) referring to games that Augustus established at Naples. This mentions contestants' ages, contests, crowns and registration of competitors. The *gymnasion* is mentioned as the location for certain activities. Athletes who failed to register correctly were fined and flogged (if they did not pay).

A Latin inscription from Corinth illustrates the prestige of winning in the games, 'To Lucius Papius Venereus, son of Lucius, of the tribe Amelia, (who served as) Isagogeus to the Agonothete Tiberius Claudius Anaxilaus, (was) pyrophorus of the Isthmian [sanctuary?], co-agonothete with Lucius Vibullius Pius of the Isthmian games, victor at the Nemean games, priest of Mars Aug[ustus?----]'.[97] Here Lucius Papius Venereus, a member of the educated elite, had his particular honours from the important roles he held in the games at Corinth and his priesthood displayed together with his victory at the Nemean games. His victory was important enough to display publicly with his other honours. Indeed, victor lists in Greek were displayed for all to see.[98] Pausanias (2.1.7) records that when he visited

96. Miller, *Arete*, no. 140, pp. 156–57 (56). The inscription, *IVO* 56.11–28, is very fragmentary. Boys under the age of 17 years were not allowed to participate but those 17–20 years old competed in the boys' category. Older contestants were entered in the men's category.

97. Kent, *Corinth: The Inscriptions, 1926–1950*, no. 212, p. 92. Kent sees the reference to the Isthmian Games as the 'Lesser Isthmian' Games. For my discussion on the *isagogeus* see chapter 4.

98. Benjamin Dean Meritt, *Corinth: Greek Inscriptions, 1896–1927* (ASCSA, 8.1; Cambridge, MA: Harvard University Press, 1931). No. 14, pp. 14–18 is a headless marble herm inscribed on three sides in Greek and found near the gymnasium. It is dated 3 AD and records the victors in the Isthmia Caesarea. It includes first the names of the consuls, then the *agonothete* (name now obliterated) and then the *hellenodikae* before the contests (for boys, youths and men). The pancratium contests for boys and youths were draws. The prize went to the god. The Vibulii, a well-known Corinthian family, are mentioned in the inscription. No. 15, pp. 18–21 is a marble triangular pedestal inscribed on three sides in Greek (dated late second century AD) also found near the gymnasium. It includes the *agonothetes* and then *hellenodikae* before the contests in three groups. First are trumpeters, heralds and musicians, second horse and chariot races and finally the individual athletic events in the Isthmian games. No. 16, pp. 21–25 is another victor list in Greek. The date of the inscription is 181 AD. With suitable restorations this follows nos. 14 and 15, being dated by an introductory formula that includes first the date by consuls, second the date by *agonothete* and finally dated by

Isthmia he saw the marble racecourse and inside Poseidon's sanctuary stood statues of athletes victorious in the Isthmian Games. Elsewhere some statues show victorious athletes crowning themselves. For example, a marble funeral statue from Athens (dated 150 AD) shows a naked athlete holding in his left hand a palm-leaf (indicating he is a victor). His right hand is lifted towards his head, with the victor's wreath, to crown himself.[99]

If athletes were to win and receive crowns then they needed to compete according to the rules. Paul uses this imagery in 1 Cor. 9.27 when he speaks about not being disqualified. Thiselton argues that in this verse Paul has abandoned his boxing imagery and therefore he misses the relationship of being disqualified from the athletic events.[100] Fee rightly sees 9.27 as continuing Paul's boxing metaphor with a contrast between the 'absurd boxer' in v. 26 and Paul 'boxing' with real purpose.[101] The mention of disqualification from obtaining the prize is also part of the athletic metaphor.[102] This image is used in 2 Tim. 2.5 'And in the case of an athlete, no one is crowned without competing according to the rules' (NRSV). Clarence Forbes has explained the importance of keeping to the rules in athletic competitions and the associated punishments for non-compliance.[103] More recently, Allen Kerkeslager has addressed problems with ancient athletes breaking rules and disqualification.[104]

I have considered the two individual events running and boxing in some detail because these are the ones Paul refers to in 1 Cor. 9.24–27. Moreover, as Paul also refers in these verses to winning and crowns I have discussed these also. However, did Paul spectate at these events when he was at Corinth or are his comments not based on direct experience as a

hellenodikae (ten in number). From these inscriptions Meritt provides a tentative list of the order of athletic events in the Empire for the Isthmian Games. No. 17, pp. 25–27 is very fragmentary but Meritt suggests this is also a victor list and no. 20, p. 29.

99. Tzachou-Alexandri (ed.), *Mind and Body*, no. 232, pp. 343–44. There is no indication of the games, or event, in which he was a victor. An athlete crowning himself is called an *autostephanoumenos*.

100. Thiselton, *First Epistle*, pp. 715–16. He does not take sufficient account of the demands of ancient boxing and the fact that boxers were sometimes killed in competition. See my discussion below.

101. Fee, *First Epistle*, pp. 438–39.

102. Fee, *First Epistle*, pp. 439–40.

103. Clarence Allen Forbes, 'Crime and Punishment in Greek Athletics', *CJ* 47 (1951/52), pp. 169–73, 202–3. I address this issue further in chapter 6. Although, Kerkeslager, 'Maintaining Jewish Identity in the Greek Gymnasium', p. 18 n. 22 cautions that Forbes' conclusion and interpretations must now be corrected from the more recent work by Young, *The Olympic Myth*.

104. Kerkeslager, 'Maintaining Jewish Identity', pp. 18–19.

spectator? Are there any substantial reasons why Paul would *not* spectate at the Isthmian Games? To answer 'Paul as a Jew would not spectate' is not convincing. As I demonstrated in chapter 3, drawing primarily on the work of John Barclay and Erich Gruen, some Jews in the ancient world were educated in the Greek gymnasium and this did not necessarily require them to abandon their Jewishness.[105] The devout Alexandrian Jew Philo, Paul's contemporary, was educated in the Greek gymnasium.[106] Gruen notes that Philo wrote primarily for Jewish readers and Philo's works show that he expected them to be familiar with athletic contests. Thus, Gruen observes that the philosopher Philo demonstrates intimate knowledge of athletic contestants and contests. He is a fervent fan who attended all forms of contest.[107] Philo speaks about the contrast of some athletes using artificial bulking up while others followed rigorous preparation.[108] Gruen also notes that Philo is specific in descriptions of heralds, referees, judges crowning people, and fastening wreaths on victors.[109] Moreover, Philo comments on boxers (both their tactics and brutality), pancratiasts, wrestlers runners and jumpers.[110] Finally, Gruen notes that Philo's analogies and similes used 'the imagery of athletic contests and physical training'.[111] Consequently, the devout Jew Philo demonstrates the whole-hearted engagement he enjoys with athletic events and his Jewish readers are expected to be similarly engaged. Paul's being a Jew is insufficient reason for him to eschew the Isthmian Games. So it is quite possible that Paul had first-hand experience of the Isthmian Games during his stay in Corinth. He would see winners being crowned.

c. *Ideology*

1. Victor Pfitzner. The term 'ideology' has two fundamentally different contemporary uses. David Horrell says it may be a neutral descriptive term that refers to any system of thought or belief, or a 'critical' conception linking ideology to maintaining asymmetric power relations (i.e. domination).[112] Scholars do not consistently maintain this distinction but

105. Barclay, *Jews in the Mediterranean Diaspora* and Gruen, *Diaspora*.

106. See my discussion in chapter 3.

107. Gruen, *Diaspora*, p. 125.

108. Gruen, *Diaspora*, p. 125. He cites Philo *Spec. Leg*. 2.91.

109. Gruen, *Diaspora*, p. 125. He cites Philo *Agr. 112–113; Vita Cont*. 43.

110. Gruen, *Diaspora*, p. 125. He cites Philo *Cher*. 81; *Agr*. 114 (boxers); *Omn. Prob. Lib*. 26, 110; *Somn*. 2.134, 1.145–146 (wrestlers and pancratiasts); *Deus Imn*. 75; *Agr*. 115, 177, 180; *Migr. Abr*. 133 (for sprinters and also jumpers).

111. Gruen, *Diaspora*, p. 125. See his extensive references to Philo in n. 150.

112. Horrell, *Social Ethos*, pp. 50–53 (50); citing. J.B. Thompson, *Studies in the Theory of Ideology* (Cambridge: Polity Press, 1984), p. 4. Thompson identifies these 'two fundamentally differing ways' (p. 3). Horrell follows the second concept 'as this seems to give the term a sharp and useful meaning, rather than an over-generalised one' (p. 51).

it is useful. Charles Wanamaker also usefully discusses ideology and 1 Cor. 1–4.[113] Like Horrell he focuses on the negative, rather than the neutral, concept of ideology.[114]

Pfitzner's study does not use the term ideology but in his section 'The Spirit and Ideals of Greek Athletics' he discusses three main features of Greek athletics:

1. The spirit of rivalry and self-assertion,
2. The nature of the games as holy,
3. The Greek gymnasium and its ideals, e.g. the ideal of perfection through training.[115]

Under 1., Pfitzner remarks, 'It is by no means insignificant that the public games assumed a central position in the life of the Greek peoples, for there was something intrinsic in the Greek "Lebensideal" itself which readily found expression in the games and in the whole sphere of athletics. The idea of developed competitive contest in sports is typically Greek'.[116]

The Greeks had as a key driving force for activity and self-assertion their character of contention and competition. Consequently, the word 'agon' was used for athletics, horse-racing and music contests, but also in war (for the people's struggle), and all kinds of contests in civic life.[117] The desire for fame is fundamental to the games and public life. In athletic contests fame and victory are the true goal of Greeks for these produce awe, admiration and remembrance (even after death). Pfitzner traces these thoughts back to the Homeric writings.

Under 2., Pfitzner argues that the early Greek games are commonly designated as holy and that even in the first centuries AD evidence shows that the religious significance of the games was not lost.[118] This is an important point that modern readers of the text may not appreciate. However, there is a need to distinguish between games that were designated as 'sacred' and those not so designated (see below).

Under 3., Pfitzner makes the essential connection between the Greek

113. Wanamaker, 'A Rhetoric of Power', pp. 115–37.

114. Wanamaker, 'A Rhetoric of Power', p. 117, follows John B. Thompson, *Ideology and Modern Culture* (Cambridge: Polity Press, 1990), in using 'only one criterion of negativity' for the concept of ideology: 'ideology and ideological phenomena involve symbolic meanings and forms which serve "*to establish and sustain relations of domination*"'. Wanamaker uses Thompson's criteria as tools for analysing how Paul's rhetoric operates, particularly in 1 Cor. 1–4, to re-establish/maintain his authority/domination over his converts but 'without suggesting that Paul intentionally sought to deceive the Corinthians while attempting to sustain his power to shape the community as its founder'.

115. Pfitzner, *Paul and the Agon Motif*, pp. 16–22.

116. Pfitzner, *Paul and the Agon Motif*, pp. 16–18.

117. Pfitzner, *Paul and the Agon Motif*, p. 16.

118. Pfitzner, *Paul and the Agon Motif*, pp. 19–20.

gymnasium, its ideals and the games.[119] Thus he remarks, 'The Greek gymnasium is of interest not only in so far as it formed a centre where the agonistic ideals of Greek life were inculcated and fostered, but also because the education which it offered largely contributed to the popularization and extension of athletic imagery'.[120] He notes that gymnasium life was a continual winning, or being defeated, a measuring of oneself against another. Superiority was an aim without being focused towards any practical use of the acquired strength and skill.

2. H.W. Pleket. Pleket observes that for the ideology of athletes, 'There is a clear ideological constant from the time of Pindar's athletes onwards'.[121] He notes a few essentials. First, 'relatively trivial values like physical beauty and strength receive due and constant attention'.[122] Two official interpretations of beauty existed. The young ephebe was a beautiful idealised product from the gymnasium (as the Heracles statues in the ephebic gymnasium demonstrate). Heracles was also the patron of the association of professional athletes. Pleket notes the prominence given to physical beauty was remarkable because boxing and *pankration* were associated with blood and injuries and to win unwounded was extraordinary.[123] Moreover, the 'manly and military values of sport' were emphasised. Keywords included 'ἀνδρεία (courage), πόνος (toil) and καρτερία (endurance)'.[124] With καρτερία the enduring athlete wants *to win or die*.[125] This 'philosophy' reaches from the 5th century BC to beyond the first century AD.[126] Pleket connects the value systems of Pindar and Hellenistic-Roman athletes through the gymnasium, noting that in Hellenistic-Roman gymnasium the route by which old values were transmitted was via the ephebes.[127]

He identifies the principal value in 'the everlasting *glory* of the victorious athlete', and observes the essential distinction between modern and ancient understandings of the Olympic Games. Thus, ' "To participate is more important than to win"... is probably the most un-Greek statement that can be made'.[128] Both literary and epigraphic sources confirm that victory

119. Pfitzner, *Paul and the Agon Motif*, pp. 21–22.

120. Pfitzner, *Paul and the Agon Motif*, p. 21.

121. Pleket, 'Games, Prizes, Athletes and Ideology', p. 74. Pindar's odes are fifth century BC.

122. Pleket, 'Games, Prizes, Athletes and Ideology', p. 75.

123. Pleket, 'Games, Prizes, Athletes and Ideology', p. 76.

124. Pleket, 'Games, Prizes, Athletes and Ideology', p. 76. Paul does not use these words in 1 Corinthians.

125. Pleket, 'Games, Prizes, Athletes and Ideology', p. 77. For further information see: Erich Segal, ' "To Win or Die": A Taxonomy of Sporting Attitudes', *JSH* 11 (1984), pp. 25–31.

126. Pleket, 'Games, Prizes, Athletes and Ideology, p. 76.

127. Pleket, 'Games, Prizes, Athletes and Ideology', p. 77.

128. Pleket, 'Games, Prizes, Athletes and Ideology', p. 79.

was simply not sufficient. Ancient athletes added 'surplus-value', additional features which amplified victories and verified achievements. This feature, Pleket argues, can be traced from a small group of archaic aristocratic victors to a large number of later aristocrats and even non-aristocrats. This was loudly proclaimed self-importance.

Finally, Pleket examines the current principal ideological problem, i.e. 'professionalism' versus 'amateurism'.[129] Currently we consider full professionals as those who devote all their time to sport and make a living from it. However, wealthy ancient athletes who devoted all their time to sport would accept the title 'professional' but would reject it if by definition it meant a man who derived his income from sport. It is true that before 50 BC there was an association of *professional* athletes.[130] But Pleket observes that not a single document states that members exercised a profession and derived a living from their sport. It is the critics who apply the term 'profession' to the athletes. The significance of this for ancient athletes, their counter-ideology and Paul's imagery is considered later.

3. Michael Poliakoff. In his valuable work on combat sports, Poliakoff observes, 'Among the unusual features of Greek sport, four aspects in particular make it different from the sports of most other societies. Viewed together, they are explicable only as manifestations of a deep and cultivated love for contest peculiar to the Greeks'.[131] Poliakoff uses sport in other cultures to highlight the contrast with Greece.[132] Ancient Greece was focused on contest and he identifies four unusual features:

1. Athletics were serious activities for Greeks, and achievement brought honor and status.[133] The seriousness of Greek athletics is seen in Greek literature, e.g. Homer and Pindar.[134] Athletic success brought honour and

129. Pleket, 'Games, Prizes, Athletes and Ideology', p. 80. See Young, *The Olympic Myth*, chapter VII 'The Truth **almost** Told', pp. 89–103 for his interaction with Pleket. He disagrees with aspects of Pleket's definitions of professionalism.

130. See H.W. Pleket, 'Some Aspects of the History of the Athletic Guilds', *ZPE* 10 (1973), pp. 197–227. Also see Poliakoff, *Combat Sports*, p. 20, who notes that athletes began organizing themselves into guilds before the first century BC. Through their guilds they attended to 'corporate interests'. He observes that initially there were two guilds, 'sacred victors' and 'athletes'. About mid second century AD these merged into one guild.

131. Poliakoff, *Combat Sports*, p. 105.

132. Poliakoff, *Combat Sports*, pp. 107–12.

133. Poliakoff, *Combat Sports*, p. 105.

134. Homer's *Odyssey* (8.145–49) where Odysseus is asked to join the contests and *Iliad* (23.667–75) where the boxer Epeios substitutes combat sport for victory on the battlefield. Homer was a school textbook and so the educated, at least, would be familiar with this. See Mary R. Lefkowitz, 'The Poet as Athlete', *JSH* 11 (1984), pp. 18–24, who says, 'The subject of the greatest surviving lyric poetry is not love nor death but athletic games' (p. 18). Homer's *Iliad c.* 750 BC, *Odyssey c.* 725 BC (see Miller, *Arete*, pp. 1, 14).

status for victors from individuals, families, and from the victors' native cities.

2. Winning was important, at times overwhelmingly so. Thus in some smaller athletic festivals, second, third and fourth places mattered. However in the four great Panhellenic Games only first place mattered.[135]

He notes that although some late Greek inscriptions mention with pride that an athlete's participated at Olympia the predominant obsession was to achieve victory.

Poliakoff explains that the Greeks valued recognition.[136] One reads of no-contest (*akoniti* 'without getting dusty') victories as proudly recorded.[137] The pankratiast Marcus Aurelius Asclepiades was so ferocious that after seeing him in the early rounds his remaining competitors defaulted. The victory inscription of Tiberius Claudius Marcianus reads, 'When he undressed, his opponents begged to be dismissed from the contest'.[138] Besides the recognition of winning at Olympia the Greek ambition went further to include the coveted title of *periodonikes*. Poliakoff explains the exceptional importance of this title:

> In the top rank were the games at Olympia and Delphi (Pythian festival), held every four years, and those at Corinth (Isthmian festival) and Nemea, held every two years. These were the period games, that is, the games of the four-year circuit (*periodos*), also known as sacred crown games, since at the festival sites the victors received only wreaths ... A man who won at all four festivals received the special title of *periodonikes*.[139]

A winner in wrestling and *pankration* at Olympia was a 'successor of Herakles'. Ancient athletes' inscriptions used *paradoxos* ('amazing') if they won in two different sports. There are athletes who were: 'undefeated', 'never caught in a waistlock', or 'never took a fall'.[140] Moreover, unique combinations of victories gained recognition. For example, one man Kleitomachos noted that he alone won all three combat events at the Isthmus. Others boasted using the pattern 'first from *x* to accomplish *y*' to claim the merit of being the first from their homeland to win an event. Poliakoff comments, 'The term *anephedros* ("winning without a bye") appears on some inscriptions as a particular sign of honor, testimony

135. Poliakoff, *Combat Sports*, p. 106.
136. Poliakoff, *Combat Sports*, p. 106.
137. Poliakoff, *Combat Sports*, p. 106.
138. Poliakoff, *Combat Sports*, p. 106. He won the wrestling at Antiocheia in Pisida (*IG* 14.1102).
139. Poliakoff, *Combat Sports*, p. 18.
140. Poliakoff, *Combat Sports*, p. 106.

to great endurance and stamina'.[141] This term was applied in the first/second century AD for the pankratiast Tiberius Claudius Rufus (from Smyrna) who fought for an Olympic crown until darkness against an opponent who had drawn a bye. The judges considered the competition a draw.[142] The Pauline scholar Savage also considers these competitive features of the Isthmian Games in his examination of the social setting of first-century Corinth.[143] He observes that in microcosm the games reflected, but with more intensity, the competitive nature of the first century and, 'the city of Corinth was so immersed in the games it also reflected the competition'.[144] But because his interest is elsewhere he does not apply this to 1 Cor. 9.24–27. Poliakoff's third point focuses on individuality.

3. Greek sport was, with only a few exceptions, a completely individual competition. There were teams of ballplayers but only in militaristic Sparta. Some cities sponsored team torch races for runners or riders. However, the victors did not gain the prestige received in the traditional athletics events.[145]

Poliakoff highlights a difference with the many team events in modern sports. Paul's references to running and boxing are individual events. Torch races at Corinth are known but these were religious events associated with sacrifice and not part of the traditional athletic events.[146] Finally, Poliakoff considers social class.

4. All social classes could participate in the agon. Even from an early date, within the archaic age, non-aristocrats participated in the Greek athletic festivals.[147]

This is of particular importance for two main reasons. First, the history of interpretation of ancient athletics has often been distorted over issues of

141. Poliakoff, *Combat Sports*, p. 21.

142. Poliakoff, *Combat Sports*, p. 127.

143. Timothy B. Savage, *Power Through Weakness: Paul's Understanding of the Christian Ministry in 2 Corinthians* (SNTSMS, 86; Cambridge: Cambridge University Press, 1996), pp. 44–45.

144. Savage, *Power through Weakness*, p. 45.

145. Poliakoff, *Combat Sports*, p. 107.

146. See Sharon Herbert, 'The Torch-Race at Corinth', in Del Chiaro (ed.), *Corinthiaca*, pp. 29–35, who discusses vases from the fifth and early fourth century BC, but these do not provide any new evidence on whether the race was a relay or occasionally an individual event. She notes that the torch race was not primarily an athletic event but a religious ritual where sacred fire was transferred from one altar to another. William R. Briers and Daniel J. Geagan, 'A New List of Victors in the Caesarea at Isthmia', *Hesp* 39 (1970), pp. 79–93 (91–93), discuss a second century AD torch-race at Corinth. It is unclear whether a team or a single runner ran this. But they note, 'Despite its inclusion in catalogues of victors, the torch race maintained a primarily religious purpose, that of transferring fire from a source to an altar as quickly as possible'.

147. Poliakoff, *Combat Sports*, p. 107. See the earlier discussion on amateurism and professionalism, and the long time period classical scholars use to establish the social classes

social class and amateurism versus professionalism. Second, recent interpretations of 1 Corinthians have identified social class as a major factor in understanding the letter.[148]

Poliakoff recognises that for non-aristocrats it was not easy to secure the leisure and money required for training but there was no law prohibiting participation.[149] Nick Fisher has also considered non-elite participation in sports in classical Athens. He too argues that non-elite participation occurred and suggests reasons for their involvement.[150] Thus Greek society permitted non-elite citizens access to athletic contests. Local athletic successes with prizes could make the training and travel costs to national festivals affordable.[151]

By examining participants in Greek combat sport in the archaic and classical periods through to later antiquity, Poliakoff shows that competitors came from the upper, middle and lower classes.[152] In the early days, Poliakoff comments that, it is unlikely competitors from the middle and lower classes were successful.[153] In Athens among the citizenry the lowest class, the *thetes*, did not receive ephebic training. Moreover, a youth of hoplite status who received some gymnasium training may still not have enough time or money for higher training. An inscription (*c.* 300 BC from Ephesus) requesting a subsidy shows that a Nemean victor from a poor family, despite substantial rewards from previous victories, could not afford the costs of training and travel for an Olympic entry.[154] Two other factors were important. First, not all festivals gave large prizes. Second, very many competitors, including fearsome athletes, may arrive at apparently obscure games. Thus the hopeful athlete could be badly beaten and leave empty-handed. Nevertheless, David Young, and Stephen Miller, both show how large prizes could be won. Young notes, 'A lad from a non-noble family who won a prize in a local event ... might use it to finance a

of the competitors. There is a contrast with those scholars who try to impose an artificial division between amateurism and professionalism that represents modern European thought rather than ancient distinctions.

148. See my discussion in chapter 1.

149. Poliakoff, *Combat Sports*, p. 107. Legends of early sports heroes do show humble origins, e.g. the boxer Glaukos of Karysos (Olympic winner in 520 BC) was a ploughboy. Although Poliakoff admits that the accounts have a mythological air they do show that Greeks did not consider victors with such origins 'unthinkable'.

150. Nick Fisher, 'Gymnasia and the Democratic Values of Leisure', in Cartledge, Millett and von Reden (eds.), *Kosmos*, pp. 84–104.

151. For a discussion on local games see: Kostas J. Gallis, 'The Games in Ancient Larisa: An Example of Provincial Olympic Games', in Raschke (ed.), *The Archaeology of the Olympics*, pp. 217–35.

152. Poliakoff, *Combat Sports*, pp. 117–33.

153. Poliakoff, *Combat Sports*, p. 131.

154. Poliakoff, *Combat Sports*, p. 131

trip to a larger festival, such as the Panathenaic games'.[155] Thus athletic success offered financial rewards.

After the fourth century BC people without family wealth may succeed through subsidies provided by the cities. In the Graeco-Roman period less affluent people were evident in athletic festivals. Poliakoff notes:

> A late second-century C.E. treatise on the interpretation of dreams noted that the middle-class woman who dreamed of giving birth to an eagle was fated to raise an outstanding athlete, while an upper-class woman or a poor woman could expect different progeny: what is implicit here is that professional sport was acquiring the reputation of being largely (but not exclusively) a middle-class phenomenon, for this group would be able, given the huge rewards to be had for success, to scrape together the capital necessary to get a promising child started in athletics.[156]

Harris argues, from epigraphic and literary evidence, that Tiberius Claudius Patrobius, a favourite of Nero, was a freedman yet he was an athletic victor.[157] He was a *periodonikes* as a wrestler whose victories included: Olympia and Isthmia, the Pythian Games and Nemea. Later antiquity shows subsidies for athletes, slaves competing, many festivals, and cash incentives for famous athletes to appear/compete and thus give status to a festival. Poliakoff concludes that the ancient sporting world:

> At least in its ideology and vocabulary – remains ennobled. Athletes assuredly competed for money, but consistently they received *dora* ('rewards'), like those the heroes of old received for their labors. Their guilds, notwithstanding the fact that they supervised a big business, fostered in them a sense of respect for one another and for their pursuit. One Kallikrates, according to the monument erected by his fellow athletes, 'has obtained with sweat and toil a glorious reputation' and was renowned 'among all men throughout the world because of the perfect wisdom that was the object of his dedicated effort'. The inscription continues, 'He took care of his soul'.[158]

The fact that all social classes could participate at the same level of opportunity (i.e., the educated elite did not have any competitive advantage over other social classes) in the agon is important for the mixed social classes in the Corinthian church and the impact of Paul's metaphor.

155. David C. Young, 'Panathenaic Prizes in the Classical Period (*IG* II^2 2311)', in Young, *The Olympic Myth*, pp. 115–27; Miller, *Arete*, pp. x-xi. Young, *The Olympic Myth*, p. 159.
156. Poliakoff, *Combat Sports*, pp. 131–32.
157. Harris, *Trivium*, p. 48.
158. Poliakoff, *Combat Sports*, pp. 132–33.

Nevertheless, Poliakoff and Pleket maintain that throughout Greek history the games were controlled by the ideology of the elite. Thus Poliakoff observes that although the practice in classical times whereby great athletes were treated as heroes was not continued later 'the status of the athletes remained high in later antiquity. Though clearly all social classes were free to enter the contests, it is also clear that throughout its history, sport in the Greek world claimed the attention and participation of the nobility and was moulded by its ideology'.[159] Similarly, Pleket remarks:

> By avoiding the words *techne* and *epitedeuma* the athletes avoided giving the impression that obtaining money through their sport was tantamount to professional work for one's daily bread. In its origin the world of athletics was dominated by aristocrats who introduced their value-system; members of the urban aristocracies continued to dominate, if not the sports, at any rate the ideology of sport.[160]

Here, the ideology of sport is related to avoiding the impression of obtaining money yet receiving prizes. Money is a major concern of Paul in 1 Cor. 9 and this ideology of athletics helps us to appreciate this aspect. It is not obvious to a modern reader but would be evident to the Corinthian Christians. Poliakoff's four features illustrate the underlying thoughts encapsulated in the apostle's athletic imagery. These provide a valuable supplement to Pfitzner's three main features of the *agon* ideology.

d. *Identity*

1. Function of 1 Corinthians 9. Paul's unified discussion on the issue of idol-food in chapters 8 and 10 seems disrupted by chapter 9. However, James Dunn notes the overlapping themes of 'authority/right' (*exousia* 8.9 and 9.4-6, 12, 18) and 'freedom' (*eleutheria*, 9.1, 19 and 10.29).[161] In chapter 9 Paul raises the issue of his financial support, and shows he has rights yet foregoes them. Dunn sees Paul's social behaviour as an example to the strong.[162]

But what is the function of 1 Cor. 9? The Pauline scholar Martin sees the chapter as 'Paul's fictitious defense, his apologia' but within 1 Cor. 8–10 it functions more to show his actions, not to just defend them, but as an example. The apology is a rhetorical ploy 'for the more immediate goal of establishing himself as a model for the strong. He gives up his right for the good of the weak; his manual labor, therefore, is an example to the strong

159. Poliakoff, *Combat Sports*, p. 129.
160. Pleket, 'Games, Prizes, Athletes and Ideology', p. 85.
161. Dunn, *1 Corinthians*, p. 60.
162. Dunn, *1 Corinthians*, p. 60.

of self-lowering. Social abasement is here one instance of giving up one's own interests for the sake of the other'.[163]

Similarly, Ben Witherington sees 1 Cor. 9 as a 'mock' self-defence.[164] He sees no indication here that many people gravely doubt Paul's apostleship and that Paul defends it. Rather: 'If he is defending anything it is his right as an agent of Christ to receive or refuse support'.[165] He correctly notes that the rhetorical questions in vv. 1–5 do assume the Corinthian believers agree. Accordingly, Paul is reasserting, not establishing, his rights here.

Charles Talbert's commentary sees 9.1–23 as Paul's example of foregoing rights for the benefit of others.[166] In 9.24–27 Talbert also sees Paul as an example for imitation by the Corinthians.[167] But he does not argue that Paul defends his apostleship. C.K. Barrett, however, sees Paul's apostolic rights under question because Paul is unlikely to have spent so long on this issue if they were not been challenged.[168] Fee's commentary too argues that Paul reasserts his apostleship (vv. 1–2) and the 'defense' is a passionate insistence on his rights before he explains his social behaviour: 9.1–27 is 'Paul's Apostolic Defense'.[169] Similarly, in the context of rejecting vv. 24–27 as serving primarily a paraenetic purpose, Pfitzner says Paul's concern is not, 'with impressing on his readers the necessity of a Christian moral Agon. Rather, his *immediate concern is to defend his apostolic actions* and the principle of self-negation demanded by his special office'.[170]

The polarity in scholarship is helpfully summarised by Horrell who notes that even when the unity of 1 Cor. 8–10 is recognised there still remains a debate over the purpose of chapter 9. Is the passage primarily an *example* where Paul does in fact establish his apostolic rights (ἐξουσία) to highlight that he gave these up to prevent a hindrance (ἐγκοπή) to the gospel? Or, is chapter 9 primarily Paul's *defence* because he has been criticised (possibly over his actions regarding idol-meat but definitely for failure to take the Corinthians' material provision)?[171] Here Horrell effectively argues that the text demands both dimensions should be taken seriously. He shows that Paul's conduct is an example to the strong *and* there

163. Martin, *Slavery as Salvation*, pp. 140–41.

164. Witherington, *Conflict and Community*, p. 203. He follows Mitchell, *Paul and the Rhetoric of Reconciliation*, p. 130.

165. Witherington, *Conflict and Community*, p. 203.

166. Talbert, *Reading Corinthians*, pp. 61–62. Talbert sees the area of concern as 'freedom and social responsibility' (p. 61).

167. Talbert, *Reading Corinthians*, p. 62. However, he divides chapter 9 so that the first component is 9.1–23 and the second component is 9.24–10.14.

168. Barrett, *First Epistle*, pp. 199–200.

169. Fee, *First Epistle*, pp. 392–94.

170. Pfitzner, *Paul and the Agon Motif*, p. 97.

171. Horrell, *Social Ethos*, p. 204–5.

is criticism of Paul's rejection of material support. There is a twofold explanation of this refusal. First, Horrell says that 'Paul rejects the support and patronage of certain relatively wealthy members of the Corinthian congregation'.[172] Second, Paul's acceptance of manual labour was a problem to some. Although he took on manual labour to reach the socially weak it is likely that this offended the strong who were called upon to imitate him.

Finally, Anthony Thiselton's commentary discusses 1 Cor. 9. He considers 9.1–27 as Paul's personal example of subordinating his rights for the overall good.[173] Thus, 'The argument about "rights" and "apostleship" simply runs parallel to Corinthian arguments about *their* "right to choose" (cf. 6:12; 8:1–13 . . .) in order *first to establish the validity of the "right"* so that Paul, in turn, *may choose to relinquish it where it threatens to harm the welfare of others*, or of the church as a whole'.[174] He convincingly draws upon rhetorical and sociological studies to support his position.[175] For the sociological studies he uses Marshall and Chow to demonstrate the obligations of friendship and patronage.[176] Paul would not wish to be indebted to a rich patron who would expect some return such as 'status, influence or leadership role within the church' if Paul could not repay in financial terms.[177] Thus Thiselton argues that a superficial reading of chapter 9 may indicate Paul defends his apostleship, however, Paul does not defend '*his apostleship as such*'.[178] I find this solution attractive. He also observes that Paul's 'sustained argument' is to provide his parallel with 'the strong' who use the arguments in 1 Cor. 8.1-13 as their reasons for eating food offered to idols.[179]

However, I now wish to consider further connections between 1 Cor. 9 (and especially 9.24–27) within 1 Cor. 8–10 and the whole letter. Jerry Sumney has critically reviewed where scholars place 1 Cor. 9.24–27 in Paul's argument and concludes 'Thus, 9:24–27 is best understood as the introduction to the stories that serve as the foundation for the instructions about sacrificed food in chapter 10, and not as the conclusion to Paul's

172. Horrell, *Social Ethos*, p. 213.

173. Thiselton, *First Epistle*, pp. 661–63. He notes that some scholars see the chapter as part of a separate letter to 8.1–13. However, he has ably defended the integrity of the letter in pp. 36–41. See my comments in chapter 1.

174. Thiselton, *First Epistle*, pp. 661–62. Emphasis in original.

175. Thiselton, *First Epistle*, pp. 662–63. For rhetorical studies he uses Mitchell, *Paul and the Rhetoric of Reconciliation*.

176. Thiselton, *First Epistle*, pp. 662–63. He uses Peter Marshall, *Enmity in Corinth: Social Conventions in Paul's Relations with the Corinthians* (Tübingen: J.C.B. Mohr [Paul Siebeck], 1987) and Chow, *Patronage and Power*.

177. Thiselton, *First Epistle*, pp. 662–63 (663).

178. Thiselton, *First Epistle*, p. 663.

179. Thiselton, *First Epistle*, p. 667.

presentation of himself as an example of giving up rights'.[180] I shall not address his arguments here but I do wish to include aspects that Sumney has not considered because his argument has largely overlooked the socio-historical context of the Isthmian Games. These issues need to be evaluated in reaching any conclusion.

2. Sacred Games. The Isthmian Games were sacred games (ἱεροι) so this provides a connection with the religious aspects of idols and temples in 1 Cor. 8–10. The linguistic connection is evident in 1 Cor. 9.13 τὰ ἱερὰ (the holy things) ... τοῦ ἱεροῦ (the temple) and 1 Cor. 10.28 ἱερόθυτόν (slain in sacrifice). Lanci notes that this connection goes back further to 1 Cor. 3.16–17 with Paul's image of the temple and the Corinthian congregation.[181]

Athletes may belong to a worldwide *collegium* or athletics guild as Paul, and the Corinthian believers, belong to a worldwide church.[182] The high status games attracted competitors (the elite and others) from across the Graeco-Roman world. The organisers of the games were those from the social elite. Thus Geagan notes that in the Greek cities one of the most burdensome liturgies was the *agonothesia*.[183] The *agonothetes* paid for, and managed, the contests. At Corinth they could add new contests and possibly change the order. His name appears on the victor lists where he is the eponymous official. The *agonothesia* gave its holder honours at both Isthmia and in the city and was included in the holder's *cursus honorum*. Other official positions in the games also honoured the holders from the social elite including children.[184]

180. Sumney, 'The Place of 1 Corinthians 9:24–27 in Paul's Argument', pp. 329–33.

181. Lanci, *A New Temple for Corinth*. Lanci effectively argues that Paul is not considering the Jerusalem Temple but temples in Corinth.

182. Pleket, 'Some Aspects of the History of the Athletic Guilds'. See also Miller, *Arete*, no. 150, pp. 168–69 on an interesting inscription. The inscription, *IG* XIV.747 (dated AD 107) discovered at Naples, gives the illustrious athletic career of Titus Flavius Archibius from Alexandria. It demonstrates that athletic guilds or unions existed and they honoured this particular athlete with the inscription identifying his considerable number of victories in various contests in different age categories spanning very many different locations/festivals. He is declared to be 'high priest for life of the entire *xystos*, victor incomparable'. Many victories are highlighted by the phrase 'the first of mankind to do so'. He competed in the combat sports: *pankration* and *pale* (wrestling). See also no. 149, pp. 167–68 which is a letter from Mark Antony (*P.Lond* 137, dated 33/32 BC) to the Greeks in Asia mentioning the '*Synodos* of Worldwide Winners of Sacred Games and Crowns'. A *synodos* is a union or guild. See further: Michael B. Poliakoff, 'Guilds of Performers and Athletes: Bureaucracy, Rewards and Privileges', *JRA* 2 (1989), pp. 295–98.

183. Geagan, 'Notes on the Agonistic Institutions', p. 69.

184. See the discussion in chapter 4 on children in Corinth holding positions. See D.R. Jordan and A.J.S. Spawforth, 'A New Document from the Isthmian Games', *Hesp* 51 (1982), pp. 65–68 (67), for their discussion on the board of magistrates (Ἑλληνοδίκαι) that officiated at Isthmia.

From this examination of the Isthmian Games we can identify aspects of Paul's use of the athletic metaphor in 1 Corinthians under three headings: social status, finance and education. First, the Isthmian Games permitted contestants from all social classes (with the possible exception of slaves) and included males and females. This mixed grouping is similar to the church. Contestants in physical competitions did not have any advantage even if they were elite (although the elite may have more resources available for preparation, travel, etc.). Nevertheless, the Games were organised, financed, and run, by the elite much as the educated elite in the Christian community as patrons apparently lead the church, or at least exercised some considerable influence (enough for Paul to address them at length in his letter).

Spectators supported the participants with devotion and enthusiasm, as it seems some in the church supported Christian leaders/teachers of their choice.[185] The educated Apollos, from Alexandria, is supported against Paul. Success in Greek games provided considerable opportunities for upward social mobility and acquired status.[186] It was a route by which one could enter the elite, with their value system, even if contestants started off from a comparatively lowly position.

Second, on finance, we have seen that athletes competed in the Isthmian Games for honour as no value prizes were given.[187] Spectators shared in the honour of their victors. Magistrates, such as the *agonothetes*, received honour for their generosity. They contributed materially, including the provision of feasts, without expecting a financial return, but they received their reward in honours. Honour discourse in the Corinthian correspondence has been discussed by David A. deSilva, who shows its prominence in 1 Corinthians.[188] However, he does not discuss 1 Cor. 9.24–27 although in an earlier article he recognises the honour inherent in athletic imagery, especially for minority groups.[189] Paul too argues that he has received a

185. See the enthusiasm of the crowd in Dio Chrysostom's *Or*. 9.14. This oration is supposedly an account by the Cynic philosopher Diogenes in the fourth century BC and his visit to the Isthmian Games. However, Oscar Broneer, 'The Apostle Paul and the Isthmian Games', *BA* 25 (1962), pp. 2–31 (18) notes that the details of the account are from his own time. In *Or*. 9.15–16 the victor tells Diogenes that he is the first in the stadion race and the swiftest Greek afoot.

186. I discuss the issue of social mobility and circumcision related to the Greek gymnasium in chapter 6.

187. Pleket, 'Games, Prizes, Athletes and Ideology', shows that some games did give value prizes.

188. David A. deSilva, '"Let the One Who Claims Honor Establish That Claim in the Lord": Honor Discourse in the Corinthian Correspondence', *BTB* 28 (1998), pp. 61–74.

189. David A. deSilva, '"Worthy of His Kingdom": Honor Discourse and Social Engineering in 1 Thessalonians', *JSNT* 64 (1996), pp. 49–79 (55–56). He notes, 'The use of contest or athletic imagery leads to the minority culture's appropriation of topics of courage or endurance, which are now made to serve minority cultural values' (p. 56).

reward in making the gospel free of charge (1 Cor. 9.18). His boast is in preaching free of charge (1 Cor. 9.15–18). That he receives no financial support, or reward, in the church from the Corinthian patrons is mirrored in their own Isthmian Games. He receives honour.

At the Isthmian Games athletes received crowns but if they competed in other games, elsewhere, everyone knew that they could receive value prizes, which may be significant.[190] When they returned from Corinth to their own cities they received financial rewards and privileges, as a right, for their victories in the Isthmian Games. Such freedom to participate in both crown games and prize (or gift) games was widely known. Similarly, Paul also can legitimately forgo financial support at Corinth even when he accepts support from churches in other cities. This implication would be evident to the educated elite, the patrons, whose support Paul has declined. But carefully constructed within the agonistic world was the idea of payment, or wages, and gifts. Athletes did not receive wages but gifts, as Pleket has shown. He comments, 'In its origin the world of athletics was dominated by aristocrats who introduced their value-system; members of the urban aristocracies continued to dominate, if not the sports, at any rage the ideology of sport'.[191] Moreover, '*Techne* was inferior; as a successful athlete one did not receive a *misthos* – that was reserved for trainers – but prizes or gifts'.[192]

Paul shows himself as an athlete and cleverly locates himself within this dispute. While some argued that athletes took wages, the athletes' counter-ideology was that they received gifts.[193] There were two perspectives. In the church Paul is criticised for not accepting material support and working with his hands. In 1 Cor. 9.17 Paul says he has a reward (μισθόν) and then asks (9.18), 'What then is my reward (ὁ μισθός)?' He rejects a financial reward just as successful athletes rejected a reward (μισθός). This was the athletes' counter-ideology. They accepted prizes or gifts. Paul offers his gospel free of charge – that is his reward. As a boxer who 'works' with his hands he offers an alternative viewpoint of his position. The charge that he is involved in demeaning work (a charge possibly brought by the elite) is effectively answered by his comparison with the Corinthians' Isthmian Games.

New Testament scholars, such as Dunn, Martin and Horrell, argue that in 1 Cor. 9, Paul is specifically addressing the 'strong' or educated elite. The biblical commentator Witherington notices that in 1 Cor. 9.23, 'Paul does not say he becomes strong to the strong, probably because it is

190. See the discussion in Papathomas, 'Das agonistische Motiv', pp. 226–28, and Pleket, 'Games, Prizes, Athletes and Ideology', pp. 54–71.

191. Pleket, 'Games, Prizes, Athletes and Ideology', p. 85.

192. Pleket, 'Games, Prizes, Athletes and Ideology', p. 85.

193. Pleket, 'Games, Prizes, Athletes and Ideology', p. 84.

"strong" Christians to whom he is directing many of his corrective remarks in this letter'.[194] In using the στάδιον race for his metaphor Paul selects the fastest running race. In using boxing imagery Paul shows himself as the strong man *par excellence*. This was the toughest of all the Greek athletic contests. A competitor at such a high level in the Isthmian Games required size, strength, skill, strategy, stamina and courage. Because there were no weight divisions (only age divisions: boys, youths and men) at this level of contest Paul would probably be understood to convey himself as a physically huge man. All this clearly portrays Paul as showing himself as one of the strong and thus speaking in particular to the strong Christians in order to reform their behaviour. In the games athletes needed to compete within the rules to avoid disqualification and the strong in the church needed to behave correctly. Witherington notes that Paul's boxing 'may well be an allusion to the Sophists, whom Philo calls shadow boxers, those who box with the air, i.e., with imaginary opponents. Cf. *Det.* 1.41f'.[195]

The individual nature of the events matches the competitive nature of some members in the church (the educated elite). But the fact that all social classes could participate at the same level of opportunity (i.e., the educated elite did not have any competitive advantage over other social classes) in the ἀγών is important for the mixed social classes in the church. Athletic conflict in Paul's imagery speaks to the situation of the community conflict.

Third, we shall consider education. Paul's metaphor has a direct impact on the educated elite who were educated in the gymnasium. Both the classicist Pleket and the Pauline scholar Pfitzner see the continuity between Greek gymnasium education and Greek athletics. Boys, ephebes, and men, trained, and competed, in the gymnasium as well as in games. In the Corinthian church the educated elite who were ephebes, or ex-ephebes, possibly *neoi*, had this intimate connection with the Isthmian Games and may have competed in them and/or other contests. They would, within their own 'educational institute', have met Isthmian competitors who were training in the gymnasium for the games.[196] Finally, the boasting of the victorious athletes of their success recalls the boasting of the elite throughout 1 Corinthians and Paul's response (e.g. 1 Cor. 1.31 'Let the one who boasts, boast in the Lord' [NRSV]). It is ironic that the 'weak'

194. Witherington, *Conflict and Community*, p. 213.

195. Witherington, *Conflict and Community*, p. 214 n. 37. He also cites with approval Winter, *Philo and Paul*, p. 177, who comments, 'The discipline and self-control which Paul exercises over his own appetites in vv. 23–27 contrast starkly with the self-indulgence of the sophists with their lifestyle which they clearly defended on philosophical grounds'.

196. James Wiseman assumes that the Isthmian athletes would train in the Corinthian gymnasium, as athletes did before the festivals at Olympia and Delphi. Personal communication. Reproduced by kind permission.

apostle Paul uses athletic imagery, particularly of the 'strong' boxer, to appeal to the educated elite.[197] As athletes competing to win exercised self-control in training, eating and drinking so the educated elite needed to respond likewise.

Finally, I wish to mention the work of Tim Whitmarsh on *paideia*. He discusses the reader in the Second Sophistic period.[198] He argues that to understand the role of *paideia* we must take account of the fundamental role of the reader. Thus, 'The literature in this period is ever playing to the most sophisticated audience, an audience willing to mull over minor insinuations and pore over details. To neglect this element is to impoverish our understanding not only of the texts, but also of the social function of *paideia*'.[199] Of course, Paul is able to use rhetorical techniques in his letter.[200] My point is that the first-century educated elite reading Paul's letter will be well aware of the implications of his athletic metaphor in his argument against them, much more so than most twenty-first century readers who are so distant from their world. These wise people will understand the 'wisdom' in Paul's argument even if they do not necessarily like it.

4. *Nurses, Nutrition and Nurture (1 Corinthians 3.1–4)*

This section considers 3.1–4 (infants, nurse and nutrition) and education. My focus is on the education of elite believers. As Winter has effectively argued the Corinthian congregation had been influenced by 'secular educational mores'.[201] Malherbe remarks on how Paul shaped the Thessalonian Christian community, 'It should now be evident that Paul's method of pastoral care had distinct similarities to the "pastoral care" of contemporary moral philosophers. The way Paul describes his activity, particularly his use of the images of nurse and father [1 Thess 2:7, 2:11], makes it clear that he consciously availed himself of their tradition of care'.[202]

197. See 1 Cor. 4.10, 'We are weak, but you are stong!' (NIV) and his comments in 2 Cor. 12.8; 13.4.

198. Tim Whitmarsh, 'Reading Power in Roman Greece: the *paideia* of Dio Chrysostom', in Too and Livingstone (eds.), *Pedagogy and Power*, pp. 192–213. Whitmarsh (p. 192 n. 3) explains that the 'Second Sophistic' covered the period 50–250 AD but he gives reasons why he dislikes the label. Winter, *Philo and Paul Among the Sophists* has demonstrated that this elitist sophistic movement was active in Paul's time.

199. Whitmarsh, 'Reading power', p. 212.

200. See, for example, David R. Hall, 'A Disguise for the Wise: ΜΕΤΑΣΧΗΜΑΤΙΣΜΟΣ in 1 Corinthians 4.6', *NTS* 40 (1994), pp. 143–49 and his book *The Unity of the Corinthian Correspondence*.

201. Winter, *After Paul Left Corinth*, p. 43.

202. Abraham J. Malherbe, *Paul and the Thessalonians: The Philosophic Tradition of Pastoral Care* (Philadelphia, PA: Fortress Press, 1987), p. 58. He also notes that there were distinct differences. Stanley Kent Stowers, *The Diatribe and Paul's Letter to the Romans*

In considering 1 Thess. 2 Malherbe argues that there are verbal and formal parallels between Paul and Dio Chrysostom, and between Paul and the Cynics. There were gentle Cynic philosophers, and he notes:

> It is not surprising that in ancient times the subject of gentleness should call to mind the figure of the nurse crooning over her wards. In addition to their physical attributes, the main qualification of nurses was that they were not to be irascible. That people remembered their nurses in this way is illustrated by the large number of tomb inscriptions that describe nurses affectionately as being kind. It became customary to contrast the harshness of a certain kind of *parresia* with gentle speech like that of a nurse who knows her charges.[203]

How does this assist in understanding 1 Cor. 3.1–4? Paul's image of a nurse uses the philosophical tradition but in the passage 'mere infants' (νηπίοις) is clearly pejorative. Fee comments that the word 'almost always has a pejorative sense, in contrast with being adult, and refers to thinking or behaviour that is not fitting'.[204] The 'mere infants' relates to the 'grown-ups' in 2.6. Fee notes that in antiquity it is common imagery, 'most often reflecting the theme of "progressing in understanding," i.e., moving from an elementary grasp of truth to a more mature knowledge of the deeper things of a system'.[205] However, he rejects this view arguing that Paul uses the pejorative sense here.

The relationship of infants/children and nurse in antiquity is one used in discussing the education of the elite, where it is not restricted to those educated in the gymnasium. Thus in his training of an orator Quintilian defines the family atmosphere in which the child should be reared:

> Above all see that the child's nurse speaks correctly. The ideal, according to Chrysippus, would be that she should be a philosopher: failing that he desired that the best should be chosen, as far as possible. No doubt the most important point is that they should be of good character: but they should speak correctly as well. It is the nurse that the child first hears, and her words that he will attempt first to imitate.[206]

(SBLDS, 57; Chico, CA: Scholars Press, 1981), has also conclusively demonstrated that in the diatribe Paul uses the same educational technique employed by the philosophers in the classroom instruction of their students.

203. Abraham J. Malherbe, '"Gentle as a Nurse": The Cynic Background to 1 Thess 2', in his *Paul and The Popular Philosophers* (Minneapolis, MN: Fortress Press, 1989), pp. 35–48 (43). Originally published as '"Gentle as a Nurse": The Cynic Background to 1 Thess ii', *NovT* 12 (1970), pp. 203–17.

204. Fee, *First Epistle*, p. 125.

205. Fee, *First Epistle*, p. 124. Fee, p. 124 n. 12, cites Epict., *Diss*. 2.16.39 and Philo, *Agr*. 9 (and refers to *Congr*. 19, *Omn. Prob. Lib*. 160) but does not make the connection with education.

206. Quint., *Inst*. 1.1.4–5. Chrysippus was the famous Stoic philosopher.

Plutarch, discussing children's education, prefers mothers to feed and nurse their children because of their greater affection, care and love:

> But the goodwill of foster-mothers and nursemaids is insincere and forced, since they love for pay. Nature too makes clear the fact that mothers should themselves nurse and feed what they have brought into the world, since it is for this purpose that she has provided for every animal which gives birth to young a source of food in its milk.[207]

If mothers cannot do this then foster-mothers/nurse-maids are acceptable to him, provided they are not randomly chosen. The best ones should be selected 'and, first of all, in character they must be Greek'.[208] Children's characters, like their bodies, are to be regulated from the beginning.[209]

So Paul uses maternal/nurse imagery here for in antiquity men could act as nurses, as Yarbrough and Bradley have demonstrated.[210] The New Testament scholar Paul Beasley-Murray sees Paul as mother but concludes that the emphasis is not so much on Paul's care for the Corinthians as their failure as believers to grow and develop in their faith.[211]

The image of milk and solid food was widely used in antiquity. Fee cites Epictetus: 'Are you not willing, at this late date, like children, to be weaned and to partake of more solid food?'[212] He also cites Philo, *Agr*. 9 on babes, milk, grown men and wheaten bread to illustrate 1 Cor. 3.1–4, but leaves their relationship undeveloped. In citing Epictetus he omits part of the quotation, which is, in full: 'Are you not willing, at this late date, like children, to be weaned and to partake of more solid food, and not to cry for mammies and nurses – old wives' lamentations?' He does not develop this within an education context.

Epictetus instructs his students. In speaking on true judgements he says, 'Children, indeed, when they cry a little because their nurse has left, forget their troubles as soon as they get a cookie. Would you, therefore, have *us* resemble children? No, by Zeus!'[213] They should not be influenced by a cookie but true judgements, which are: 'The things which a man ought to practise all day long, without being devoted to what is not his own, either comrade, or place, or gymnasia (γυμνασίοις), nay, not even to his own

207. Plutarch, *Mor*. 1.3C.

208. Plutarch, *Mor*. 1.3D-E.

209. Plutarch, *Mor*. 1.3E.

210. Yarbrough, 'Parents and Children in the Letters of Paul', pp. 132–33. Yarbrough builds his analysis on Bradley, *Discovering the Roman Family*, pp. 37–75 ('Child Care at Rome: The Role of Men').

211. Paul Beasley-Murray, 'Pastor, Paul as', in Gerald F. Hawthorne and Ralph P. Martin (eds.), *Dictionary of Paul and His Letters* (Downers Grove, IL and Leicester, England: InterVarsity Press, 1993), pp. 654–58 (656).

212. Fee, *First Epistle*, p. 124, n. 12; citing Epict., *Diss*. 2.16.39.

213. Epict., *Diss*. 2.16.26.

body; but he should remember the law [of God] and keep that before his eyes'.[214]

When Epictetus speaks of students not crying for their nurse and mammy, he asks them: 'In what respect are you superior to the man who weeps for a maid, if you grieve for a trivial gymnasium (γυμνασίδιον), a paltry colonnade, a group of youngsters, and that way of spending your time?'[215] This appears as a clear reference to their former experiences in the gymnasium before they took up philosophy. He talks to the poor man who longs for Athens and the Acropolis and asks if he will sit and cry as little children do.[216] Epictetus then asks the man about his schooling, what he heard and learned, why he recorded himself as a philosopher when he did no serious work in philosophy. He inquires, 'Can you image one of these men [Chrysippus, Socrates or Diogenes] crying or fretting because he is not going to see such-and-such a man, or such-and-such a woman, or to live in Athens or in Corinth, but, if it so happen, in Susa or Ecbatana?'[217]

He urges his students to endure, as men, the demands of studying philosophy away from home. His references to the gymnasia indicate that some students had studied there, including an introduction to philosophy, but they need to reform their current attitudes. Their previous education, for some at least, in the gymnasium, is compared with milk. The study of philosophy now is solid food. Thus a closer examination of the text reveals an education situation in Epictetus.

Quintilian also uses the milk image in an education context, when the boy has progressed from the teacher of literature to the teacher of rhetoric.[218] He does not expect a perfect style of narrative from the boys but comments, 'I have no objection to a little exuberance in the young learner. Nay, I would urge teachers too like nurses to be careful to provide softer food for still undeveloped minds and to suffer them to take their fill of the milk of the more attractive studies. For the time being the body may be somewhat plump, but maturer years will reduce it to a sparer habit'.[219]

The Jew Philo provides a more detailed use of the imagery in his treatise on 'The Preliminary Studies' covering the training of the mind by the

214. Epict., *Diss*. 2.16.27.

215. Epict., *Diss*. 2.16.29. Hock, 'The Workshop as a Social Setting for Paul's Missionary Preaching', p. 448 n. 50 observes, 'On the importance of the gymnasium as a social setting for intellectual discourse in the early empire, see Epictetus, *Diss*. 3.16.14; 4.1.113'.

216. Epict., *Diss*. 2.16.32–33.

217. Epict., *Diss*. 2.16.36.

218. Quint. *Inst*. 2.4.1.

219. Quint. *Inst*. 2.4.5.

school subjects.[220] After covering the teaching of grammar, music, rhetoric and dialectic, he comments:

> It is profitable then to take these and the like for our associates and for the field of our preliminary studies. For perhaps indeed it may be with us, as it has been with many, that through the vassals we shall come to the knowledge of the royal virtues. Observe too that our body is not nourished in the earlier stages with solid and costly foods. The simple and milky foods of infancy come first. Just so you may consider that the school subjects and the lore which belongs to each of them stand ready to nourish the childhood of the soul, while the virtues are grown-up food, suited for those who are really men.[221]

Now Philo received his boyhood education in the gymnasium and this constitutes the preliminary studies.[222] Philosophy is the grown-up food. His treatise is set in the allegorical form of the union of Abraham and Hagar and thus in a family context. His extensive discussion uses the family of Abraham to distinguish between the school subjects (Greek education) and philosophy.

Richard Horsley has investigated this language in Philo.[223] In his articles he compares Philo's imagery to Paul's in 1 Corinthians.[224] Although these are informative studies they suffer from failing to read Philo in his social and educational context. Thus Horsley sees Philo's language as one of religious status, spiritual elitism and soteriological status. He does not read Philo's contribution through his education in παιδεία, which he enjoyed through the Greek gymnasium. Consequently he misses the central issue that Philo is a member of the educated elite whose work is focused on the educated elite.

Susan Holman's study of the formation and feeding of the ancient newborn helpfully focuses on infants.[225] She notes, 'The ancient under-

220. For a comprehensive account of Philo and education see Mendelson, *Secular Education in Philo of Alexandria*. For the relevance of Philo to the study of 1 Corinthians, and especially the study of παιδεία and the sophists, see the convincing work of Winter, *Philo and Paul*.

221. Philo, *Congr*. 18–19. Colson and Whitaker note, 'The subject of the treatise is the training of the mind by the school subjects, the training being termed "mating," or "intercourse," because the union of Abraham with Hagar is the allegorical form in which it is set'. See also *Agr*. 8–9, covered earlier, for diets and education.

222. See the discussion in chapter 3 on Philo and the Greek gymnasium.

223. Richard A. Horsley, 'Pneumatikos vs. Psychikos'; 'Wisdom of Words and Words of Wisdom in Corinth'; '"How can some of you say that there is no resurrection of the dead?" Spiritual Elitism in Corinth', *NovT* 20 (1978), pp. 203–31.

224. See the earlier discussion on Horsley's work in chapter 1.

225. Susan R. Holman, 'Molded as Wax: Formation and Feeding of the Ancient Newborn', *Helios* 24 (1997), pp. 77–95. Her paper explores 'certain prescriptions, especially those of the second-century physician Soranus and the fourth-century medical writer

standing of infant character is frequently illustrated by the identification of babies with wax. The malleable properties of wax made it a common literary image in antiquity for describing the constructive character formation that began in infancy'.[226] Wax was a common metaphor for infant care from Plato onwards. This image was used with food as the formative tool so that both images 'evoke the deliberate physical formation of a good social or spiritual character'.[227] She continues, 'This formation required special attention during the early phases before the child became "firm". As long as it remained wax-like, the child could, like wax, be either "properly" formed or distorted, physically, socially and spiritually'.[228]

In conclusion, she captures the issues when she states:

> The social formation of the Roman infant began with the body of the well baby. The infant who could survive into childhood and adulthood began 'as wax,' unformed, yet malleable to external social forces. As Gourevitch and others have shown, these forces were effected by men and women in ancient society who, in the name of 'natural' and 'healthy' social formation, sought to distance the newborn as quickly as possible from its liminal and agitated neonatal state, by physical 'shaping' – ablutions, massage, swaddling – as well as by specific advice about feeding. The feeding regimes in these texts, defined in terms of gentle and sympathetic moderation, similarly reflect this concern with cultural formation.[229]

The advantage of Holman's study is the association of the two images, wax and feeding, in the formation of character. Feeding is not solely associated with physical well-being but, in antiquity, with social well-being and character formation. Instead of the Corinthians developing as they should from Paul's correct feeding they had failed to mature in their characters. Within the processes of swaddling, as I mentioned in chapter 4, was that, 'Each day nurses would also reshape the head, nose and a boy's penis, which would later be seen at baths and at the gymnasium'.[230]

This passage with nurse and nutrition uses language that would be recognised as educational by the elite, and non-elite, in the church. In Philo

Oribasius, about infant feeding in late antiquity' (p. 77). She examines these in relation to the 'real' infant. Holman notes, 'Although Oribasius never discusses the therapeutic treatment of sick infants, he preserves much of his predecessors' detailed advice about infant hygiene and diet' (p. 79).

226. Holman, 'Molded as Wax', p. 80.

227. Holman, 'Molded as Wax', p. 81.

228. Holman, 'Molded as Wax', p. 81.

229. Holman, 'Molded as Wax', p. 92.

230. Osiek, and Balch, *Families in the New Testament World*, p. 66; citing Soranus, *Gyn.* II.15, 42.

and Epictetus, milk represented the studies undertaken before philosophy, those taught in the gymnasium. Quintilian uses nutrition language within the school context. For those who apparently boasted in philosophy and criticised Paul for not giving them advanced instruction he uses a common education image to show them as relative beginners. This applies to their Christian lives but the image is used from education terminology in teaching the elite. Paul as mother/nurse by his nutrition and nurture socially moulds them as infants to develop a good spiritual and social character but they failed to mature.

5. *Summary*

The section 'Paul's Corinthian Household' argued that in the apostle's fictive language he is the father of a large elite household (the church). This inclusive strategy allows him to bring all the Christians together in a unity against the factionalism that is evident. By this technique he metaphorically enters the domain of the educated elite, into their socially privileged area. From here he tackles the problems they are causing.

A careful examination of the socio-historical context of the importance, imagery and ideology in 1 Cor. 9.24–27 has enabled us to investigate the identity of the Christians Paul is addressing. My analysis agrees with New Testament scholars who see Paul's references in 1 Cor. 9 as applying particularly to the strong. However, I advance the discussion by identifying the strong as the particular target of Paul's athletic imagery. The strong are in competition with Paul and the weak Christians in Corinth. Therefore Paul chooses an ancient, time-honoured, status scenario set at Corinth to address the strong. He uses the ideological status system of the elite to challenge their self-control. The educated elite in the church, those educated in the gymnasium, would feel the impact of Paul's position, particularly because of the intimate connection between the gymnasia and the Games. Community conflict is addressed through this conflict in Games and gymnasia.

The passage 1 Cor. 3.1–4 would be understood by the Corinthian community as references to Paul's missionary work and to education and social formation. For Philo and Epictetus milk can signify the Greek education received in the gymnasium while philosophy is the solid food. Quintilian uses the same imagery but related to divisions in the school curriculum. The passage demonstrates that Paul has acted correctly but the educated elite in the church have failed to mature.

The next chapter continues the application of the model to Paul's letter.

Chapter 6

Application of the Model II

1. *Agriculture and Education (1 Corinthians 3.5–9)*

In chapter 5 I considered three topics: Paul's Corinthian Household, Ancient Athletes (1 Cor. 9. 24–27) and Nurses, Nutrition and Nurture (1 Cor. 3.1–4). Chapter 6 investigates five more areas of interest: Agriculture and Education (1 Cor. 3.5–9), Disciplining with the Rod (1 Cor. 4.21), The *Grammateus* (1 Cor. 1.20), Ancient Writing (1 Cor. 4.6) and Circumcision (1 Cor. 7.17–24). These are areas where the model advances our interpretation of Paul's interaction with the Corinthian church. The first topic Agriculture and Education (1 Cor. 3.5–9) follows immediately after Nurses, Nutrition and Nurture (1 Cor. 3.1–4) and we will see the connection with education in both passages. In 3.5–9 (where Paul plants the seed, Apollos waters but God gives the increase) Paul continues with education language.

Andrew Clarke sees the artisan images of agriculture, and building (3.9–15) as 'non-status leadership vocabulary' and necessarily menial.[1] As chapter 1 shows, Clarke's study demonstrates elite leadership in the Corinthian church. In this context, Paul uses two images applied to himself and Apollos. Clarke notes that these images are significant because Paul 'disparages any self-exaltation. The emphasis throughout avoids elevating personal status, and instead concentrates on the function of the apostles'.[2] There is a focus on their tasks and both men working together. Paul's principles contrast with the practices of a secular leadership model that the elite in the church have used. Clarke's comments are helpful. More recently, Clarke has discussed Paul's 'agricultural, artisan and household imagery' in 1 Cor. 3–4, noting that Paul does not legitimize his position as leader using 'his own secular status or credentials' but his imagery inverts

1. Clarke, *Secular and Christian Leadership*, pp. 118–19. He says that in the agricultural image the menial tasks are watering and planting. God gives the growth. Thus the focus is on God not human leaders.

2. Clarke, *Secular and Christian Leadership*, p. 120.

social status and its significance.[3] Thus, Clarke sees that the above imagery may have been considered 'offensive to those within the Christian community who sought to base their own authority on such widely-held criteria as secular honour and status'.[4] He notes that this position is supported by Paul's use of irony in 1 Cor. 4.8–13 where he provides a contrast between 'the élitist view of leadership, adopted by some Corinthians' and the role of the apostles (the Corinthians are rich, kings, wealthy and wise, strong and honoured whereas the apostles are the opposite: scum and refuse).[5] These are valuable points.

Anthony Thiselton draws upon Clarke and Martin in also seeing social-statues issues and contrasting leadership models in these verses.[6] He identifies the Old Testament background here, commenting, 'The image of the people of God as a field draws on a well-known tradition concerning Israel, perhaps derived initially from Israel as God's vineyard (Isa 5:7; Ezek 36:9). Wolff offers extended examples of OT and Jewish pictures of the people of God as "planted by God"'.[7] Again, these are valuable observations. Considering the imagery in its Graeco-Roman context can extend these observations.

The agricultural image is also an educational image. Plutarch, after speaking of parentage and fathers not begetting children when they are drunk continues by speaking about education (ἀγωγῆς).[8] To produce right action he recognizes three things are required together: nature (the starting point), reason (λόγον, learning) and habit (constant practice, repetition). If one of these is missing then 'moral excellence' is deficient. He comments that nature devoid of learning is blind while learning devoid of nature is imperfect, and continues:

> Just as in farming, first of all the soil must be good, secondly, the husbandman (τὸν φυτουργὸν) skilful, and thirdly, the seed sound, so, after the same manner, nature is like to the soil, the teacher to the farmer, and the verbal counsels and precepts like to the seed. I should strenuously insist that all three qualities met together and formed a perfect union in the souls of those men who are celebrated among all mankind, – Pythagoras, Socrates, Plato, and all who have attained an ever-living fame.[9]

3. Clarke, *Serve the Community*, pp. 216–17.
4. Clarke, *Serve the Community*, p. 217.
5. Clarke, *Serve the Community*, p. 217.
6. Thiselton, *First Epistle*, pp. 296–301. He uses Clarke, *Secular and Christian Leadership*, and Martin, *The Corinthian Body*. Thiselton (p. 296) notes that Martin speaks of a 'status-reversal strategy'.
7. Thiselton, *First Epistle*, p. 302. He uses C. Wolff, *Der erste Brief des Paulus an die Korinther* (THKNT, 7; Leipzig: Evangelische Verlagsanstalt, 1996), p. 67.
8. Plutarch, *Mor.* 1.2A.
9. Plutarch, *Mor.* 1.2B–C.

Thus the farmer sowing seed is an image used of the teacher with his counsels and precepts. His farming image is concerned with learning and attaining moral excellence. On the power of diligence Plutarch remarks:

> A piece of land is good by nature, but without care it grows waste, and the better it is by nature, so much the more is it spoiled by neglect if it be not worked. Another piece is forbidding and rougher than land should be, but, if it be tilled, straightaway it produces noble crops. What trees if they are neglected do not grow crooked and prove unfruitful? Yet if they receive right culture, they become fruitful, and bring their fruit to maturity. What bodily strength is not impaired and finally ruined by neglect and luxury and ill condition? On the other hand, what weak physique does not show a very great improvement in strength if men exercise and train themselves (τοῖς γυμνασαμένοις και καταθλήσασι)?[10]

So he considers the care of the body in the gymnasium, or palaestra, like caring for a field and trees. On choosing teachers he asserts, 'For to receive a proper education (παιδείας) is the source and root of all goodness. As husbandmen (οἱ γεωργοὶ) place stakes beside the young plants, so do competent teachers with all care set their precepts and exhortations beside the young, in order that their characters may grow to be upright'.[11]

In 1 Cor. 3.9, 'you are God's field (γεώργιον),' refers to the Corinthians among whom Paul worked. The implication is that as a farmer/teacher Paul used tools. On this Plutarch states:

> In regard to education (παιδείας)... it is useful, or rather, it is necessary, not to be indifferent about acquiring the works of earlier writers, but to make a collection of these, like a set of tools in farming. For the corresponding tool of education is the use of books, and by their means it has come to pass that we are able to study knowledge at its source.[12]

Books are compared with farming tools. Besides the wealthy collecting books we saw that gymnasia may have their own libraries.[13] Thus Plutarch uses agricultural imagery to convey the task of educating children. Susan Holman comments on the formation of the infant to a socially conditioned citizen and notes that Plutarch considered infants 'more like a plant than an animal' until their naming.[14]

If we turn to Philo, we see that he uses an allegory on woman taking oaths and remarks:

10. Plutarch, *Mor*. 1.2E
11. Plutarch, *Mor*. 1.4C.
12. Plutarch, *Mor*. 1.8B.
13. See chapter 3.
14. Holman, 'Molded as Wax', p. 84. She cites *Quaest. Rom.* 102.288C. The naming was on day 8 for girls, day 9 for boys. See the discussion of her work in chapter 5.

> We should know, then, that nature's right reasoning has the functions both of a father and a husband, though the conceptions attached to each are different. It acts as a husband because it deposits the seed of virtue in the soul as in a fertile field. It acts as a father because its nature is to beget good intentions and noble and worthy actions, and then to foster its offspring with the water of the truths which education and wisdom (παιδεία και σοφία) abundantly supply.[15]

Again, Philo considers 'soul-husbandry' and states:

> But who else could the man that is in each of us be save the mind (νοῦς), whose place it is to reap the benefits derived from all that has been sown or planted? But seeing that for babes (νηπίοις) milk is food, but for grown men wheaten-bread, there must also be soul-nourishment, such as is milk-like suited to the time of childhood, in the shape of preliminary stages of school-learning (τῆς ἐγκυκλίου μουσικῆς), and such as is adapted to grown men in the shape of instructions leading the way through wisdom and temperance and all virtue. For these when sown and planted in the mind will produce most beneficial fruits, namely fair and praiseworthy conduct.[16]

The 'school-learning' is the education that Philo acquired in the gymnasium.[17] This passage and 1 Cor. 3 use the imagery of babes and agriculture. For Philo the outcome is suitable conduct which was a major failing at Corinth. Elsewhere Philo writes, 'Accordingly, they tell us that the men of old likened philosophical discussion with its threefold division to a field, comparing that part which deals with nature to trees and plants; that which deals with morality to fruits and crops, for the sake of which the plants exist; that part which has to do with logic to a fence enclosing it'.[18] Paul's image is simpler than this but Philo again shows the imagery of education and morality linked to agriculture.

The Roman educator Quintilian remarks on the need for special care, 'above all where boys are concerned to avoid a dry teacher, even as we avoid a dry and arid soil for plants that are still young and tender. For with such a teacher their growth is stunted and their eyes are turned earthwards, and they are afraid to rise above the level of daily speech'.[19] Elsewhere, he gives a detailed description of relationships between the

15. Philo, *Spec. Leg.* 2.29.

16. Philo, *Agr.* 9. Nevertheless, Philo here speaks of husbandry (tree planting) and distinguishes it from soil tilling which he regards as less worthy.

17. See Mendelson, *Secular Education in Philo of Alexandria*, pp. 2–3, 88 n. 14, on *enkyklios paideia* and this term as a synonym. See my chapter 3 for a discussion on Philo's gymnasium education.

18. Philo, *Agr.* 14. The translators Colson and Whitaker, p. 490, observe that this is a fundamental Stoic doctrine, which is given again in Diog. Laert. vii.40.

19. Quint., *Inst.* 2.4.8–9.

teacher, pupils, parents and seed. Learners are to love their teachers, regarding them as parents of their mind (not bodies), for this has benefits for the pupils (e.g. they will like listening to them, gladly attend school, accept correction without anger, seek the teacher's affection through devotion to studying). He then continues:

> For as it is the duty of the master to teach, so it is the duty of the pupil to show himself teachable. The two obligations are mutually indispensable. And just as it takes two parents to produce a human being, and as the seed is scattered in vain, if the ground is hard and there is no furrow to receive it and bring it to growth, even so eloquence can never come to maturity, unless teacher and taught are in perfect sympathy.[20]

This is in the context of the teacher of rhetoric. Although Quintilian's teaching is not based in the gymnasium he uses this to illustrate training the orator.[21] However, Teresa Morgan has shown that in literate education and the nurture of learning the image of the teacher as farmer with the pupil portrayed as the soil is common.[22]

In 1 Cor. 3.6–8 Paul planted and Apollos watered (3.6: Ἀπολλῶς ἐπότισεν). Watering is an education image in Philo.[23] The translators Colson and Whitaker comment:

> 'Watering' is so apt a figure of teaching, that Philo is soon showing us Hagar, who represents preliminary education, filling her water-skin from the well of knowledge, to give drink to the boy, who is the soul in its first cravings for instruction, that he may grow up to be an 'archer,' directing arguments with sure aim. But Philo hastens to give us the picture of Rebecca supplying the water of perfection to the servant of Abraham.[24]

Philo himself remarks, 'For he shows us Hagar filling a water-skin and giving the child drink (τὸ παιδίον ποτίζουσαν). Hagar represents imperfect training (μέση παιδεία), being handmaid of Sarah who represents perfect

20. Quint., *Inst*. 2.9.3.

21. For example, in *Inst*. 2.8.12–15, immediately preceding the above section, Quintilian compares training the orator to training a pancratiast. Specifically, he names Nicostratus, 'whom we saw when he was old and we were boys,' who was a champion in boxing and wrestling. In *Inst*. 2.7.3–4 he compares the teacher of oratory adopting his instruction to individual needs to 'an expert gymnast, when he enters a gymnasium full of boys, after testing body and mind in every way, is able to decide for what class of athletic contest they should be trained'.

22. Morgan, *Literate Education*, pp. 255–60. She cites Ps-Plutarch and Quintilian. Education is concerned with cognitive changes.

23. Philo, *Poster. C.* 130–132.

24. Philo, Vol. 2, 325.

virtue (τέλειας ἀρετῆς)'.[25] And again he writes, ' "Child" is the name he gives to the soul just beginning to crave after instruction, and now become to some extent engaged in learning. It is in accordance with this that the boy, when grown to manhood, becomes a sophist, for which Moses' name is "archer".'[26] Finally, Philo says, 'Rebecca is discovered watering her pupil (ποτίζουσα τὸν μαθητὴν) not with gradual progress like Hagar, but with perfection (τελειότητι)'.[27] Paul uses this educational language of watering for the educated Jew Apollos, from Alexandria, while the Alexandrian Jew Philo uses it in his analysis of Hagar and Rebecca. In both cases watering is teaching. In Philo it refers to both Hagar who gives 'imperfect training' (μέση παιδεία) in contrast with Rebecca who gives perfection.[28]

Thus all these sources compare education to agriculture. Paul sowing the seed is like the teacher. Apollos, who waters, is a teacher. Paul speaks of teaching the gospel and this conveys a clear message to the Corinthians, including the educated elite and reminds them of their education. For those not so educated, who could not look to their own education experience, they would still be able to understand the image.

What is the relationship of this section to the one examined in chapter 5, i.e. 1 Cor. 3.1–4 (Nurses, Nature and Nurture)? In following 1 Cor. 3.1–4 the educational imagery in 1 Cor. 3.5–8 of Paul planting and Apollos watering repeats with different imagery the emphasis on education. In both cases, as mother/nurse and farmer, Paul has behaved properly. The milk and seed were given but the result is disappointing. The educational imagery behind both figures would not be lost on the educated elite.[29] In fact, both passages link back to 1 Cor. 2 and its discussion on maturity and wisdom: 'Yet among the mature (ἐν τοῖς τελείοις) we do speak wisdom, though it is not a wisdom of this age or of the rulers of this age' (1 Cor. 2.6 [NRSV]). Moreover, when Paul concludes 1 Cor. 2.16 'But we have the

25. Philo, *Poster. C.* 130. For μέση παιδεία as education in the gymnasium see Mendelson, *Secular Education*, pp. 2–3, 88 n. 14, on *enkyklios paideia* and this term as a synonym.

26. Philo, *Poster. C.* 131.

27. Philo, *Poster. C.* 132.

28. In Philo, *Poster. C.* 132–141 Philo continues the imagery of water, drinking, education, pupils, and teachers.

29. See Vernon K. Robbins, *Exploring the Texture of Texts: A Guide to Socio-Rhetorical Interpretation* (Valley Forge, PA: Trinity Press International, 1996), p. 60, where he notes, 'An important argument for the existence of echo in a chapter of New Testament text has been Burton L. Mack's analysis of the use of *paideia* (instruction on how to live a successful life according to the values of Greek society) in Mark 4:1–34, the text on the planting of seeds'. Robbins comments, 'An "echo" is a word or phrase that evokes, or potentially evokes, a concept from cultural tradition. In other words, echo does not contain either a word or a phrase that is "indisputably" from one cultural tradition. Echo is subtle and indirect. One person may hear it while another does not, and the speaker may or may not have directly intended the echo to be there' (p. 60).

mind (νοῦν) of Christ' (NRSV) there is another link with education as Morgan's work illuminates when she shows the cognitive development that accompanied literate education in the ancient world.[30] She notes the enormous differential of both status and power that separated the educated and uneducated and occurs within *enkyklios paideia*. Morgan observes, 'The partially educated are described as being as far from the perfectly educated in information, behaviour, language and cognitive development as they are from the illiterate'.[31]

2. *Disciplining with the Rod (1 Corinthians 4.21)*

a. *Family Discipline*

Biblical commentators recognise that when Paul threatens to come to the Corinthians with a rod (ἐν ῥάβδῳ) in 1 Cor. 4.21 he talks of discipline.[32] Thus C.K. Barrett remarks, 'Is it to be a visit in which the mutual confidence of father and children is expressed in mutual love, or one in which the father must punish and discipline his children because they have disgraced the family?'[33] Gordon Fee sees this verse as a further use of the father-child metaphor, where Paul asks, 'Must I come as a father who has to mete out discipline? Or will you allow this letter and Timothy's coming to serve as the proper inducement to correcting your behavior?'[34] Similarly, Ben Witherington sees 4.21 as a father coming with a rod of discipline, but, drawing on Daube, he comments also that the rod (as a metaphor) could indicate a schoolmaster (either Jewish or Graeco-Roman).[35] Thiselton, however, states that ῥάβδος refers to the OT and LXX traditions and is the 'rod of correction' not the Hellenistic schoolmaster's whip (as the NIV translates).[36] Yet Thiselton does not explain his preference. Could it be both or even more? Brian Dodd argues that the rod could carry three images: parental discipline (continuing the earlier father motif), the shepherd's rod (Ps. 22.4, LXX) or the Roman imperial use of authority

30. Morgan, *Literate Education*, pp. 240–70. This is chapter 7 'All in the Mind: Images of Cognitive Development'.

31. Morgan, *Literate Education*, p. 270.

32. 1 Cor. 4.21 (NIV) reads, 'What do you prefer? Shall I come to you with a whip, or in love and with a gentle spirit?' Fee, *The First Epistle*, pp. 193 n. 49, prefers rod to the NIV's whip because the image is the 'rod of correction'. The NRSV has 'a stick'.

33. Barrett, *First Epistle*, pp. 118–19.

34. Fee, *First Epistle*, p. 193.

35. Witherington, *Conflict and Community*, p. 148 n. 32. For this he refers to D. Daube, 'Paul a Hellenistic Schoolmaster?' in R. Loewe (ed.), *Studies in Rationalism, Judaism, and Universalism in Memory of Leon Roth* (London: Routledge and Kegan Paul, 1966), pp. 67–71.

36. Thiselton, *First Epistle*, p. 378. He has ῥάβδος as staff, rod, or a stick.

using the father image.[37] He opts for Paul's use of a double image: parental discipline and the Roman image of father. Dodd admits that we cannot with certainty choose between the nuances but they nevertheless, emphasise his authority.

Clearly the verse fits in with Paul's fictive family language but the school image identified by Daube is worth further examination. Moreover, this is not the first use of the imagery of discipline, or judgment, for it occurs earlier in 1 Corinthians. David Kuck shows that 'the judgment language of 3:5–4:5 complements the overall theological perspective which Paul develops in 1 Cor. 1–4'.[38] In 4.15 Paul mentions that the Corinthians 'have ten thousand guardians (μυρίους παιδαγωγούς)' (NIV and NRSV). Unfortunately the NIV and NRSV translations fail to capture the role of the παιδαγωγός. However, some studies helpfully clarify the role.[39] The pedagogues were either household slaves, or freedmen, purchased or hired, whose role included supervision of children to ensure their physical protection and moral education.[40] Their role included the administration of discipline and this implication would be evident to the Corinthians.[41] This perspective should be recognised when Paul mentions discipline.

Moreover, Young observes, 'No youth went to the palaestra or gymnasium without his pedagogue. They were close at hand at athletic meetings. They went to lectures, and even occasionally gained an education themselves at the same time'.[42] Ronald Hock observes that, 'Epictetus ... advised his students, most of whom were persons of

37. Brian Dodd, *Paul's Paradigmatic 'I': Personal Example as Literary Strategy* (JSNTSup, 177; Sheffield: Sheffield Academic Press, 1999), p. 74. For the Roman image he uses Lassen, 'The Use of the Father Image'. Lassen, p. 136 n. 40, suggests that the rod may refer to one carried by a lector or even by Augustus (he is shown in a Corinthian statue as a magistrate with a rod).

38. David W. Kuck, *Judgment and Community Conflict. Paul's Use of Apocalyptic Judgment Language in 1 Corinthians 3:5–4:5* (NovTSup, 66; Leiden: E.J. Brill, 1992), p. 237.

39. Richard N. Longenecker, 'The Pedagogical Nature of the Law in Galatians 3:19–4:7', *JETS* 25 (1982), pp. 53–61; David J. Lull, '"The Law Was Our Pedagogue": A Study in Galatians 3:19–25', *JBL* 105 (1986), pp. 481–98; Norman H. Young, '*Paidagogos*: the Social Setting of a Pauline Metaphor', *NovT* 29 (1987), pp. 150–76, and 'The Figure of the Paidagogos in Art and Literature', *BA* 53 (1990), pp. 80–86. See also Bradley, *Discovering the Roman Family*, pp. 37–75 ('Child Care at Rome: The Role of Men').

40. Young, '*Paidagogos*', pp. 158–62. Conzelmann, *1 Corinthians*, p. 91, states that the pedagogue does not impart instruction and is distinguished from the διδάσκαλος. Fee, *First Epistle*, p. 185, also notes that the pedagogue was distinguished from the teacher. See my chapter 2 'Primary and Secondary Education in the Empire' where I discuss Alan Booth who recognises that the pedagogue was not a teacher but could still give some instruction to a child.

41. Young, '*Paidagogos*', pp. 162–64.

42. Young, '*Paidagogos*', pp. 164–65. He cites literary evidence and *SEG* 27 (1977): 66, which is the gymnasiarchal law discussed in chapter 3.

substance and status, that if circumstances required it, they should work; his recommendations were similar [to Plutarch's]: drawing water, escorting boys to and from school [παιδαγωγεῖν] and being a doorkeeper'.[43] Thus 4.21 should be read with awareness of Paul's strategy in 4.15 of assigning some, probably from the educated elite, to the position of pedagogues.[44]

Margaret Mitchell does not discuss the meaning of 4.21.[45] Dale Martin also omits a discussion on the verse.[46] Timothy Savage mentions the rod but does not discuss its meaning.[47] Similarly, Bruce Winter mentions this verse but does not discuss the significance of the rod, although he recognises that Paul is giving them a warning and choice.[48] However, in *After Paul Left* Corinth, Winter regards this as an apostolic rod of a father with the image of an 'imperial threat'.[49] Yet Paul's language of 'the stick' can be read within the social context of family, schools, gymnasia, and games.[50] Let us investigate these aspects.

In the family context, after discussing parents as benefactors who provide a gymnasium education for their children, Philo remarks that parents have authority over their children, not by chance:

> But [it] is awarded by the most admirable and perfect judgement of nature above us which governs with justice things both human and divine. And therefore fathers have the right to upbraid their children

43. Hock, 'Paul's Tentmaking and the Problem of His Social Class', p. 563; citing Epictetus *Diss*. 3.26.7. Hock also cites Plutarch's recommendation for those in financial straits.

44. Fee, *First Epistle*, p. 185 sees the reference to 'guardians' as referring to other teachers (including Apollos and Peter) but does not regard the term as an intended 'putdown' of them (father). Rather the metaphor, Fee notes, aims to distinguish Paul, with his unique relationship to them, from all the others. However, Clarke, *Serve the Community*, pp. 219–21 argues that some people may have also seen Apollos or Peter as a 'father'. He thinks that Paul's language allows this possibility.

45. Mitchell, *Paul and the Rhetoric of Reconciliation*, p. 334, gives references to 4.21 but in none of these does she discuss the significance of the 'rod'.

46. Martin, *The Corinthian Body*, pp. 85, 103, mentions the verse but does not discuss it.

47. Savage, *Power Through Weakness*, p. 67. He does, however, discuss this in the context of 2 Cor. 10.1 where it seems that the Corinthians accuse Paul of duplicity, of pretending to be one thing in letters that he is not in person. He deceives them into thinking that he is bold and strong when he is timid and meek. He threatens a rod (1 Cor. 4.21) but comes in weakness, fear and trembling (cf. 1 Cor. 2.3).

48. Winter, *Philo and Paul Among the Sophists*, p. 201.

49. Winter, *After Paul Left Corinth*, p. 160. He follows Lassen, 'The Use of the Father Image'.

50. Richard P. Saller, *Patriarchy, Property and Death in the Roman Family* (Cambridge Studies in Population, Economy and Society in Past Time, 25; Cambridge: Cambridge University Press, 1994), provides a very helpful overview of discipline and punishment. See his chapter 6 'Whips and words: discipline and punishment in the Roman household'. See also Catherine Atherton, 'Children, Animals, Slaves and Grammar', in Too and Livingstone (eds.), *Pedagogy and Power*, pp. 214–44 (224–26). She discusses physical discipline of children by teachers.

> and admonish them severely and if they do not submit to threats conveyed in words to beat and degrade them and put them in bonds.[51]

He states that parents' authority extends to the sentence of death but here they cannot act alone. Moreover, their authority over children is like that of a master over slaves.

Philo comments on the costs to parents for children's daily necessities until they are mature. They pay out far more than the cost of a slave for their children 'and for them to nurses, tutors (παιδαγωγοῖς) and teachers'.[52] Furthermore, he states that children who do not respect their parents (who he regards as seniors, instructors, benefactors, rulers and masters) deserve blame, disgrace and punishment. Rather, for children, 'Honour therefore, he [Moses] says, next to God thy father and thy mother, who are crowned with a laurel of the second rank assigned to them by nature, the arbitress of the contest'.[53]

The context is of observing the fifth commandment to honour your parents. Elsewhere, speaking of praise, which may appear negative but has the intention of giving blessing, Philo writes, 'This is obviously the custom of proctors, of home tutors (παιδαγωγῶν), schoolmasters, parents, seniors, magistrates, laws: all of these by reproaches, and sometimes by punishments, effect improvement in the souls of those they are educating (παιδευομένων)'.[54] Philo calls the father 'right reason' and the mother 'education' (παιδεία) or 'the lower learning of the schools'. These two stand as parents to children, 'and it is good and profitable to obey them'.[55]

51. Philo, *Spec. Leg.* 2.231–232. Note also *Jos.* 74, where Philo writes, 'He who does not gladly receive improving advice must to be consistent censure parents and guardians and teachers and all persons in charge, because they reprimand and sometimes even beat their own children or orphan-wards or pupils, though really it is against all morality to call such treatment evil-speaking or outrage instead of friendliness and benevolence'.

52. Philo, *Spec. Leg.* 2.233.

53. Philo, *Spec. Leg.* 2.234–235. Here he uses athletic imagery. In *Dec.* 106–120 (107) Philo also writes on honouring parents, 'we see that parents by their nature stand on the border-line between the mortal and immortal side of existence, the mortal because of their kinship with men and other animals through the perishableness of the body; the immortal because the act of generation assimilates them to God, the generator of the All'.

54. Philo, *Migr. Abr.* 116. The translators Colson and Whitaker note on 'proctors', 'The translation supposes that Philo is alluding to the Athenian office of σωφρονισταί, officials appointed to look after the morals of the Ephebi in general and particularly in the gymnasia. Philo certainly often introduces special Attic terms from his reading. But it is at least as probable that the word here means "moral censors" in general, and sums up the various forms of guardianship which follow' (pp. 198–99). Mendelson, *Secular Education* notes Colson's remarks but from Marrou's comment, that this office functioned under the Empire, he writes, 'This remark raises the possibility that Philo is alluding to the *sophronistes* not as an Athenian functionary, but as a contemporaneous official of the local gymnasium' (p. 31). He cites Marrou, *A History of Education in Antiquity*.

55. Philo, *Ebr.* 33–34.

Corporal punishment for children was widespread although some spoke against this practice. For example, Plutarch is against beatings for disciplining children. Rather, they should be directed to good practice by encouragement and reason and definitely, 'not by blows or ill-treatment, for it surely is agreed that these are fitting rather for slaves than for the free-born; for so they grow numb and shudder at their tasks, partly from the pain of the blows, partly from the degradation'.[56] For freeborn children he wants praise and reproof to be used as motivators to suitable behaviour. However, the fact that Plutarch speaks against corporal punishment demonstrates that parents used this in disciplining their children. Atherton also notes these comments from Ps-Plutarch and observes that, similarly, Quintilian disagrees with corporal punishment for freeborn children.[57]

John Pilch's research on the physical punishment of boys (approved in Sirach and Proverbs) shows the culture of the ancient Mediterranean world.[58] He uses a social-scientific model based on empirical research by Peter S. Cook, which aims to help non-Mediterranean readers to interpret biblical texts on boys and girls. Pilch notes two styles of parenting: the trusting cooperative style and, in contrast, the distrustful and directive style.[59] The 'basic distrust' model of parenting style applies to the ancient world. But Pilch remarks that the two styles are never actually found in the pure state there are intermediate types, which reflect in varying degrees each style.[60] Yet the 'basic distrust' model helps illuminate biblical texts.

56. Plutarch, *Mor*. 8F-9A.

57. Atherton, 'Children, Animals, Slaves and Grammar', p. 225. However, she notes that ancient education theory supported the use of force with children. She concludes, 'Children stand halfway between animals and adults, and must be treated in a way which combines the methods of instruction appropriate to both these groups – physical force, gentle encouragement, threats and rewards – but never rational persuasion, the supreme goal of élite education, and the reserve of adults alone' (p. 244).

58. John J. Pilch, '"Beat His Ribs While He Is Young" (Sir 30:12): A Window on the Mediterranean World', *BTB* 23 (1993), pp. 101–13.

59. Pilch, '"Beat His Ribs"', pp. 102–3. He states, 'Cultures like that of the mainstream United States which view human nature as basically neutral or good favor a style of parenting that trusts that youngsters will behave appropriately if simply instructed or kindly guided. Parents undertake the training, development, and disciplining of youngsters in a cooperative spirit with the youngster' (p. 102). Here the child is considered a 'partner' in the parental responsibility of caring. However, 'In contrast, cultures like that of the first century Mediterranean world which view human nature as a blend of good and evil tendencies favor a parenting style based on lack of trust in the youngster. One never knows when the evil tendencies will erupt into evil deeds. For this reason the parenting style is highly directive and relies on physical punishment as a major strategy both for controlling the youngster and teaching the youngster self-control'. See his Figure 1 for a comparison of parenting styles.

60. Pilch, '"Beat His Ribs"', p. 103.

Sirach's poem (30.1–13), which advises a father on how to raise a well-behaved and respectful son, states, 'Bow down his neck in his youth and beat his ribs while he is young, lest he become stubborn and disobey you and you have sorrow of soul from him' (v. 12).[61] Moreover, Pilch sees Sirach reflecting his culture perfectly when he writes, 'lashes and discipline are at all times wisdom' (22.6).[62] Thus, Pilch comments on Proverbs:

> The rod is an acceptable and recommended instrument for disciplining children (Prov 13:24; 22:15; 23:13–14; 29:15. 19 [*sic*]). At the same time, the parent is cautioned about the risk of killing the child with extreme physical punishment (Prov 19:18; 23:13–14). Particularly noteworthy is the Sage's expression of a peculiar combination of values to which contemporary western anthropologists call special attention: the cultural fusion of love with physical punishment and the infliction of pain.[63]

These texts show that physical punishment (sometimes severe) was a normal mode of raising boys. Pilch concludes that this 'basic distrust' model of 'fathering' is a key value in the ancient Mediterranean culture'.[64]

Pilch notes that Sirach and Proverbs concern 'sons' and are addressed to males in a male-orientated society; there is no instruction for women.[65] Elsewhere, Pilch comments on the Proverbs passages noting the failure of translations (e.g. the NRSV) that use inclusive language. These 'distort and misrepresent the emic position' that concerns boys, and not girls, receiving physical punishment, 'something neither the Bible nor Mediterranean culture would permit'.[66] Among his conclusions Pilch remarks that tolerance of pain was not made a virtue but this way of raising boys, 'was the most suited to the *values and social structure* of the Mediterranean society in which Jesus lived as a[n adult] male'.[67]

In a later article Pilch, reviews Cook's model (which highlighted the fact that severe physical punishment produced adult males trained to suffer in silence) as a heuristic tool for analysing Proverbs and Sirach.[68] He noted that fresh research in the 1970s 'casts doubt on the alleged causal

61. Pilch, '"Beat His Ribs"', p. 103.
62. Pilch, '"Beat His Ribs"', p. 103.
63. Pilch, '"Beat His Ribs"', p. 103.
64. Pilch, '"Beat His Ribs"', p. 103.
65. Pilch, '"Beat His Ribs"', p. 104.
66. John J. Pilch, 'Family Violence in Cross-Cultural Perspective: An Approach for Feminist Interpreters of the Bible', in Brenner and Fontaine (eds.), *A Feminist Companion to Reading the Bible*, pp. 306–23 (308). The passages for disciplining young boys are: Prov. 13.24; 19.18; 22.15; 23.13–14; 29.15, 17.
67. Pilch, '"Beat His Ribs"', pp. 110–11.
68. John J. Pilch, 'Death with Honor: The Mediterranean Style Death of Jesus in Mark', *BTB* 25 (1995), pp. 65–70.

connection between child-training and adult personality'.[69] He then introduces the Cultural Ideology Model based on McClelland's research where:

> His **cultural ideology** model proposes that a culture's ideology – namely, its norms and values reinforced by maintenance systems – is the central determining factor of adult personality and child-rearing practices. In other words, an honor-driven culture designates adult males who suffer in silence as honorable cultural heroes and then shapes its child-rearing procedures accordingly to contribute to the production of adult males. The key difference in this model is that many more elements than endurance of physical pain and suffering enter into the image of an honorable adult male.[70]

While it is not necessary to consider Pilch's application of this model to Jesus' death, nevertheless, his conclusions are relevant for 1 Cor. 4.21. He notes that ancient child-rearing practice alone does not explain why adult males silently suffered pain and death (i.e. without complaint):

> Rather, the ideology – that is, history, tradition, norms, and values – of ancient Mediterranean culture appear to be the more influential force for defining honorable adult male personality and behavior and for designating suitable child-rearing techniques for training a person in the requisite beliefs, values and behaviors.[71]

Thus discipline should be seen within the whole of first-century AD Mediterranean culture.

Finally, Pilch has developed a model for investigating family violence in the Hebrew Bible.[72] He has seven different categories identifying and clustering 'cultural factors conducive to family violence,' although Pilch admits that these may or may not be present in the Hebrew Bible.[73] He cites Levinson's classification of family violence according to state of life.[74] Under 'childhood' harsh socialization techniques include beating and a separate category exists for corporal punishment in schools. Under 'adolescence (puberty)' painful initiation rites include whippings and again a category of harsh socialization techniques. In the list, both aggressor and victim are family members.

69. Pilch, 'Death with Honor', p. 66.
70. Pilch, 'Death with Honor', p. 67.
71. Pilch, 'Death with Honor', p. 70.
72. Pilch, 'Family Violence in Cross-Cultural Perspective', p. 319. This is based on Straus's research on wife-abuse.
73. Pilch, 'Family Violence in Cross-Cultural Perspective', p. 319.
74. Pilch, 'Family Violence in Cross-Cultural Perspective', pp. 311–12.

In conclusion, Paul's use of the rod operates within the child-rearing patterns employed by families in the ancient world. It was a technique approved in the Hebrew Bible and acceptable in Graeco-Roman culture.

b. *Schools, Gymnasia and Games*

André Lemaire notes that in agreement with Ancient Near East tradition the relationship of teacher/pupil or master/disciple is expressed metaphorically in terms of the relationship of 'father' to 'son'.[75] He says that this way of teaching should not be misunderstood as if the biological father was teaching everything to his children. Although in 'biblical tradition, parents were responsible for the general education of their children, it is however clear that most of the references to "father" in wisdom books such as Proverbs, Qoheleth, and Sirach are to be understood as references to a teacher'.[76] Nevertheless, Pilch reads these references in Proverbs and Sirach as a father, as does Michael Fox who comments on Proverbs 1–9 that the situation is a father teaching his son, 'As in almost all instructional wisdom, the father is the speaker. There is no justification for the common assumption that the speaker is a schoolteacher, Even if these chapters were used in schools (which is merely a conjecture), the persona is a father'.[77]

This difference in viewpoint demonstrates the close relationship of father/teacher. Alan Moss, however, argues that wisdom is parental teaching in Proverbs.[78] He states, 'personified Wisdom's image as a teacher adds to the effect of the teaching parents' words,' and, 'Wisdom speaks as a superlative and authoritative teacher, and what she has to say lends weight to the message of the parents speaking within the household'.[79] This contrasts with modern western culture where a distinct line is drawn between parents and teachers in public and private schools. Abraham Malherbe notes, on Paul's paternal exhortation (1 Thess. 2.11–12) that it was standard for students to receive exhortation from a moral teacher who acts as their father and regards the pupils as his children, 'The teacher's relationship with his hearers transcended natural family relationships'.[80] Epictetus comments in his lectures on the Cynic, who does not marry or have children, 'Man, the Cynic has made all mankind his children; the men among them he has as sons, the women as daughters; in that spirit he

75. André Lemaire, 'Education (Ancient Israel)', in Freedman (ed.), *The Anchor Bible Dictionary*, Vol. 2, pp. 305–12 (311). He cites P. Nel, 'The Concept of "Father" in the Wisdom Literature of the Ancient Near East', *JNSL* 5 (1977), pp. 53–66.

76. Lemaire, 'Education (Ancient Israel)', p. 311.

77. Michael V. Fox, 'Ideas of Wisdom in Proverbs 1–9', *JBL* 116 (1997), pp. 613–33 (620).

78. Alan Moss, 'Wisdom as Parental Teaching in Proverbs 1–9', *HeyJ* 38 (1997), pp. 426–39.

79. Moss, 'Wisdom as Parental Teaching in Proverbs 1–9', p. 432.

80. Malherbe, *Paul and the Thessalonians*, p. 56. He cites his own work, 'Exhortation in First Thessalonians', *NovT* 25 (1983), pp. 243–45.

approaches them all and cares for them all. Or do you fancy that it is in the spirit of idle impertinence he reviles those he meets? It is as a father he does it, as a brother, and as a servant of Zeus, who is Father of us all'.[81] As we saw above, Philo also compares parents to teachers so the connection is very close and Paul appears to be using both images together. He is their teacher and father. This intimacy of roles is important in 1 Corinthians because of the conflict caused by devotion to particular Christian teachers and Paul's portrayal of himself as the Corinthians' father.[82]

Alan Booth's comprehensive considerations discuss discipline in schools.[83] He shows that for ancient education both Greek and Roman literature have a multitude of references to corporal punishment and, 'Learning and whipping become almost synonymous'.[84] He notes that in the *gnomai* attributed to Menander, which were used as sentences for copying in schools, we read, 'The man who is not flogged is not educated (παιδεύεται)'.[85] Booth has no doubts 'that descriptions of the irascible, whip-wielding teacher have elements of a literary commonplace, but there is sufficient evidence to show that teacher with his rod is no mere literary fiction'.[86] Various implements were used for inflicting punishment besides the rod (ῥάβδος).[87]

Booth admits that ancient people were not completely devoid of a more humane educational psychology but he cautions us about thinking that there was any replacement of physical coercion by milder educational approaches.[88] This doctrine of mildness was established in the first century AD, but corporal punishment continued in use, and later antiquity has many references.[89] Thus Booth comments that there are far more references to punishment than to reward:

81. Epictetus, *Diss*. 3.22.81–82. Compare here 'servant of Zeus' (ὑπηρέτης τοῦ Διός) with 1 Cor. 4.1 'servants of Christ' (ὑπηρέτας Χριστοῦ).

82. Fee, *First Epistle*, p. 128, captures this in his exegesis of 3.5–17. 'Their quarreling represents the old ways – living as mere humans. At issue, however, is not simply quarreling. This was just addressed in 3:1–4 with polemic and irony. At issue is their radically misguided perception of the nature of the church and its leadership, in this case especially the role of the teachers'. For an analysis of the Corinthians' leadership see Clarke, *Secular and Christian Leadership* and *Serve the Community*.

83. Alan D. Booth, 'Punishment, Discipline and Riot in the Schools of Antiquity', *EMC* 17 (1973), pp. 107–14.

84. Booth, 'Punishment, Discipline and Riot', p. 107.

85. Booth, 'Punishment, Discipline and Riot', p. 107. Paul cites from Menander's *Thais* in 1 Cor. 15.33, 'Bad company corrupts character,' (NIV). See Fee, *First Epistle*, pp. 772–73.

86. Booth, 'Punishment, Discipline and Riot', p. 108.

87. Booth, 'Punishment, Discipline and Riot', p. 112 n. 4.

88. Booth, 'Punishment, Discipline and Riot', p. 108.

89. Booth, 'Punishment, Discipline and Riot', p. 109.

> At the most, milder methods existed alongside corporal chastisement, but they did not replace it. Educational theorists might disparage the use of corporal punishment, but there appears to have been a breakdown between theory and practice. Rejection of the rod became a virtue of the ideal teacher, but the practical preceptor kept the whip in his hand.[90]

Consequently, Paul's threat of the rod is understandable in a first-century AD school context because in antiquity the standard technique used for student control (by teachers and government) was physical punishment. 'The evidence suggests that there was a constant level of pain associated with learning though theorists might advocate milder discipline, while moralists lamented a decline in severity'.[91]

Greeks provided schools in the palaestra and the gymnasium. Plato (*Lysis* 203a-211a) gives an example of a Greek palaestra used as a school.[92] Socrates, on his way from the Academy (the gymnasium) calls in and sees the boys and young men. In a conversation with Lysis, they discuss education, trust and Lysis' parents who, although they love him, yet restrain him through his *paidagogos*, who controls him by taking him to his teacher (*didaskalos*) who also controls him. Stephen Miller notes that laws were enacted to govern conduct in the gymnasium and this was not restricted to Athens, '*for conduct in the* gymnasion *seems to have been a frequent and widespread concern in antiquity*'.[93] Miller cites Aischines for gymnasium regulations included those which covered the teachers and supervision of *paidagogoi*.[94] The Laws stated, 'The *didaskaloi* of the *paides* shall not open the *didaskaleia* before sunrise, and they shall close them before sunset. Except for the son, brother, or son-in-law of the *didaskalos*, no one over the age of the *paides* is to enter when the *paides* are within. Anyone who disobeys and enters is to be punished with death'.[95] Moreover, the *gymnasiarchos* was not to permit anybody above the age limit to enter in the *Hermaia*, for 'The *gymnasiarchos* who allows this and does not exclude an overage person from the *gymnasion* is to be subject to the law about the ruination of the freeborn'.[96] An inscription from Teos details the conditions of employment for the faculty of the *palaistra*. This

90. Booth, 'Punishment, Discipline and Riot', p. 108.
91. Booth, 'Punishment, Discipline and Riot', p. 111.
92. Miller, *Arete* no. 123, pp. 124–31. Dated *c*. 386 BC.
93. Miller, *Arete*, no. 124, pp. 131–32 (131). The italics are Miller's.
94. Miller, *Arete*, no. 124, p. 131. Aischines, *Against Timarchos* 9–12. Miller notes 'Aischines claims that Timarchos' moral conduct disqualifies him from participation in public life, including the right to bring suit against anyone (and especially Aischines himself, of course). One area of legal prohibition which Aischines presents shows that laws were enacted to govern conduct in the *gymnasium*' (p. 131). Dated 345 BC.
95. Miller, *Arete*, no. 124, p. 132.
96. Miller, *Arete*, no. 124, p. 132.

includes the appointment of 'three grammar teachers who are to teach the *paides* and the girls'.[97]

In chapter 3 I discussed the stele with the 'gymnasiarchal law' and it is appropriate to examine aspects of this further.[98] When the γυμνασίαρχος takes office he swears that he will be γυμνασίαρχος according to the law. Concerning the νεανίσκοι Miller translates, 'All the regulars in the *gymnasion* are obliged to obey whomever the *gymnasiarchos* selects as leader just as if he were the *gymnasiarchos*. If not, the *gymnasiarchos* is to flog the disobedient one with a switch, and to fine the other boys.'[99]

Concerning the παῖδες we read, 'The *neaniskoi* are not to annoy the *paides* nor to natter at them, and the *gymnasiarchos* is to fine and punish transgressions of these restrictions'.[100] The γυμνασίαρχος 'is also to be in charge of flogging the *paides* who misbehave and the *paidagogoi* who are not free, and of fining those who are free'.[101] On those who are not to enter the γυμνάσιον, Miller translates, 'No slave is to disrobe in the *gymnasion*, nor any freedman, nor their sons, nor cripples, nor homosexuals, nor those engaged in commercial craft, nor drunkards, nor madmen'.[102] The γυμνασίαρχος is subject to a financial penalty if he knowingly permits any of these to be oiled. Any who talk back to the γυμνασίαρχος are to be fined and any who strike the γυμνασίαρχος in the γυμνάσιον are also to be fined.

Forbes cites a Pergamene inscription, 'Agias, when gymnasiarch, put aside all his other affairs, and, thinking his watchful presence in the gymnasium most desirable, never neglected anything in his oversight of the discipline of the ephebi and *neoi*; with an austere loathing for evil, he made provision for the observance of good order and good behaviour around the gymnasium'.[103] This especial obligation of the gymnasiarch to preserve

97. Miller, *Arete*, no. 125, pp. 132–33 (132). Translation of *SIG*^{3} 578, dated third century BC. Note that Miller's translation refers to the *gymnasiarchos* and the *gymnasion* rather than the *palaistra*. See his definition of *gymnasion* (incorporating a covered and uncovered track), p. 213, and *palaistra* (wrestling school), p. 219. He states, 'Technically, it [*gymnasion*] should be kept distinct from the *palaistra* although the two buildings were often physically connected' (p. 213). See my discussion in the appendix on the terminology.

98. Miller, *Arete*, no. 126, pp. 133–38. Miller provides a translation of *SEG* 27.261, dated before 167 BC (Beroia in Macedonia).

99. Miller, *Arete*, no. 126, p. 135. Miller, p. 218, notes that *neaniskoi* were young men, or youths, older than the *paides*, and in their mid to late teens. A more detailed discussion is provided by Forbes, *Neoi*, pp. 61–67. The term had a wide variation in meaning. It could refer to ephebes or *neoi*.

100. Miller, *Arete*, no. 126, p. 135.

101. Miller, *Arete*, no. 126, p. 135. Thus a παιδαγωγός, although often a slave, may not be one.

102. Miller, *Arete*, no. 126, p. 135.

103. Forbes, *Neoi*, p. 24. The inscription is *Ath. Mitt.* xxxiii (1908), 380, No. 2, *c*. 133 BC (Forbes, p. 9).

good order and behaviour among the νέοι, and his fulfilment of this, is praised in nine inscriptions from five different cities. He states, 'The gymnasiarch's oversight of the discipline and education (ἀγωγὴ και παιδεία) of the *neoi* is mentioned at Sestos and repeatedly at Pergamum'.[104] Kleijwegt also notes the responsibility of the gymnasiarch in maintaining order and good behaviour.[105] Miller's translation of *IG* II^2.1006 mentions the discipline that the ephebes maintained and the *kosmetes* showed his authority and dignity while maintaining discipline.[106] In Plutarch's *Life of Antony* we read of Antony, 'He left the insignia of his command and went forth carrying the wands of a gymnasiarch (τῶν γυμνασιαρχικῶν ῥάβδων), in a Greek robe and white shoes, and he would take the young combatants by the head and separate them'.[107] Thus ῥάβδος here illustrates the attire for a gymnasiarch and shows his authority. At Sparta ephebes were flogged but this unusual contest was considered an honour and not a punishment for inappropriate behaviour.[108]

G.H.R. Horsley comments on the gymnasiarchal law from Beroia that for New Testament studies it has no 'particular relevance' but it has items with philological interest in this area.[109] The text is relevant to my study on the gymnasium. Horsley notes one philological point for 1 Cor. 4.21:

> ὑπὸ τὴν ῥάβδον μαστιγούτω (B. 9: the verb again at B. 22, 70, 99) – for ῥάβδος as a rod for punishment see LSJ, s.v., 7; for the metaphorical use in the NT note 1 Cor. 4.21, ἐν ῥ. ἔρχεσθαι. Three of the occurrences of μαστιγόω in the text refer to beating for disobedience; at B. 70 μ. is a way of punishing those who cheat in athletic competition (for this usage see BAGD, s.v., 1 ad fin.).[110]

The term ῥάβδος is used. The connection with 1 Cor. 4.21 is significant in the context of gymnasium education and the reference to cheating in athletic competition.[111]

104. Forbes, *Neoi*, p. 25.

105. Kleijwegt, *Ancient Youth*, pp. 261–62. He cites Forbes for support but adds that in the Hellenistic-Roman period the Greek terms used for these virtues became widespread. They invaded daily speech, the language of socio-political life and the benefactor's behaviour.

106. Miller, *Arete*, no. 128, pp. 140–45 *IG* II^2.1006 is dated 122 BC.

107. Plutarch, *Ant.* 33.4.

108. See Kennell, *The Gymnasium of Virtue*, pp. 70–83 for an explanation of this endurance contest.

109. G.H.R. Horsley, 'A Gymnasiarchal Law from Beroia', in *New Documents Illustrating Early Christianity*, 2, no. 82, pp. 104–5 (4).

110. Horsley, 'A Gymnasiarchal Law from Beroia', p. 105.

111. In 1 Cor. 9.24 Paul warns the Corinthians about not being disqualified in the Isthmian Games.

At Beroia the gymnasiarch is responsible for organising the *Hermaia* and maintaining discipline.[112] Miller translates, 'The *gymnasiarchos* is responsible for flogging and fining those who disrupt the games and those who do not compete legally in the games, as well as anyone who sells a victory'.[113] Punishment was used at international and local athletic competitions. For example, Miller records an inscription found at Olympia but referring to games that Augustus established at Naples.[114] Athletes had to be registered in a prescribed manner. Anyone not complying was fined or flogged (if they did not pay) by the *agonothetes*. Clarence Forbes gives a useful discussion on punishment in Greek Athletics.[115] Moreover, Allen Kerkeslager also briefly discusses the issue of disqualification of athletes and the punishments they could receive and cautions that Forbes' work needs updating.[116]

Epictetus warns his students about approaching things thoughtfully and he speaks about the demands of winning an Olympic victory. In the contest you 'sometimes dislocate your wrist, sprain your ankle, swallow quantities of sand, take a scourging (μαστιγωθῆναι); yes, and then sometimes get beaten along with all that'.[117] The scourging was for any foul committed. In his discourse on the calling of a Cynic he tells his students they are engaged in an Olympic contest:

> In the Olympic games it is not possible for you merely to be beaten and then leave; but in the first place, you needs must disgrace yourself in the sight of the whole civilized world, not merely before the men of Athens, or Lacedaemon, or Nicopolis; and in the second place, the man who carelessly gets up and leaves must needs be flogged, and before he is flogged he has to suffer thirst, and scorching heat, and swallow quantities of wrestler's sand.[118]

Here Oldfather comments that the flogging 'would probably be reserved for the person who failed to appear finally in the lists, since everyone had to have a month's preliminary training on the spot, during which time those who had entered would suffer the inconveniences described

112. Miller, *Arete*, p. 214, notes that this was an athletic festival dedicated to Hermes.

113. Miller, *Arete*, no. 126, p. 137.

114. Miller, *Arete*, no. 140, pp. 156–57 (156). The inscription, *IVO* 56.11–28, is very fragmentary. It was mentioned in chapter 5 and is dated 2 BC.

115. Clarence A. Forbes, 'Crime and Punishment in Greek Athletics', *CJ* 47 (1951/52), pp. 169–73, 202–03.

116. Kerkeslager, 'Maintaining Jewish Identity in the Greek Gymnasium', p. 18. He notes that Forbes' interpretation and conclusions need updating from Young, *The Olympic Myth of Greek Amateur Athletics*.

117. Epict., *Diss*. 3.15.3.

118. Epict., *Diss*. 3.22.52. Oldfather, p. 130 n. 1, notes that 'Epictetus idealizes them somewhat in this discourse, regarding them as a kind of perfected wise men'.

here'.[119] But it may refer to the person who leaves during the preliminary bouts in the contest. Epictetus refers to the Cynic's pattern of life, 'he must needs be flogged like an ass, and while he is being flogged he must love the men who flog him, as though he were the father or brother of them all'.[120] His students do not behave like that, if flogged, but Epictetus says of the Cynic, 'And is he not persuaded that whatever of these hardships he suffers, it is Zeus that is exercising (γυμνάζει) him?'[121]

Dio Chrysostom in his Rhodian oration comments, 'It is just as if a person, in trying to persuade an athlete to give up and forego the crown for the price of a piece of silver, should say to him: 'Do you not see yonder man, the one who is being scourged, just in front of you, because he dropped out of the contest'.[122] Finally, 2 Clement, written to the Corinthian church, mentions the punishment associated with athletic contests. He exhorts, using athletic imagery, the Corinthians to strive in the contest of life, 'We must remember that if he who takes part in the contest for a corruptible prize be detected in unfairness, he is flogged, taken up, and thrown off the course. What do you think? What shall he suffer who cheats in the contest for that which is incorruptible?'[123] 'Inscribed lead tablets demonstrate that athletes were disqualified from the Isthmian Games but do not mention other punishments.[124] Kent no. 228 is a fragment from a marble three-sided prism-shaped post. The three faces are inscribed in Greek and the stone is from a victor list in the Isthmian Games. Although the stone gives little information, fortunately it does record 'one or more athletes who were disqualified'.[125] Paul warns the Corinthian congregation, in the context of the Isthmian Games, about his desire not to be disqualified for the prize (1 Cor. 9.24–27).

Thus discipline was administered by father and teacher. School discipline was harsh and often brutal. In the gymnasium, ephebes, *neoi*

119. Epict., *Diss*. 3.22.52. Oldfather, pp. 148–49 n. 1.

120. Epict., *Diss*. 3.22.54.

121. Epict., *Diss*. 3.22.55–56. Epictetus also refers to the Olympic scourging in the *Encheiridion*, or Manual, which is the compilation made by Arrian from the *Discourses*. See Oldfather, pp. 507–9.

122. Dio., *Or*. 31.119. Cohoon and Crosby, p. 122 n. 2, clarify the implication, 'It's scourging for you too if you drop out'.

123. *2 Clement* 7.4–5 in *The Apostolic Fathers*, Vol. 1 (trans. Kirsopp Lake; LCL; London: William Heinemann and New York: The Macmillan Co., 1912).

124. See Jordan and Spawforth, 'A New Document from the Isthmian Games', pp. 65–68, and Jordan, 'Inscribed Lead Tablets from the Games in the Sanctuary of Poseidon', pp. 111–26.

125. Kent, *Corinth: The Inscriptions, 1926–1950*, no. 228, p. 98. It was found in a cavern of the fountain of Lerna. Kent dates the text to the second century AD (third quarter).

and other persons, including pedagogues, may receive physical punishment from the gymnasiarch for various reasons, as well as during particular competitions in the gymnasium (e.g., the *Hermaia*). In the Corinthian gymnasium excavated by Wiseman the inscription on the unpublished herm shows that such contests occurred there.[126] It is reasonable to conclude from the evidence elsewhere that a disciplined regime would operate for the ephebes, and others, in the Corinthian gymnasia and other first-century AD gymnasia. Athletes competing in important festivals such as the Isthmian Games may also receive punishment. All these images would be familiar experiences to the educated elite in the Corinthian church.

Paul's imagery is multifaceted, he appears to operate primarily as a father, and teacher, but within the sphere of education as a gymnasiarch, and possibly as a judge, one of the Hellendonikai, at the Isthmian Games.[127] These roles are not mutually exclusive for elite fathers did perform important public roles in Corinth, as elsewhere in the Graeco-Roman world.[128] Moreover, in his letter the apostle Paul portrays himself with multiple images: mother/nurse, farmer, master architect, servant/slave, father, and athlete.[129]

c. *Philo and* Paideia

Thomas Conley investigates the use of παιδεία in Philo's works and notes that when it does not merely mean 'punishment' or 'chastisement' παιδεία tends to address both intellectual capital ('learning') and also moral discipline.[130] Conley says, both images exist in the image of παιδεία as the 'rod' – ῥάβδος.[131] For example, Philo writes on Gen. 38.18, 'A mind bent on purchasing that fairest possession, piety, gave a pledge in the form of three securities', one of these 'a staff' (ῥαβδοῦ) was 'straight and unbending

126. See the discussion in chapter 3.

127. Jordan and Spawforth, 'A New Document from the Isthmian Games', p. 67, discuss the Hellenodikai. They also note from a second century AD inscription from Isthmia (*IG* IV, 203) that in the reconstruction of the sanctuary's gymnasium, following an earthquake, the new building included rooms for examining the athletes before they were admitted as competitors.

128. Although beyond our period, this is clearly illustrated by stele 1465, dated 212/13 AD (on display in the National Archaeological Museum, Athens, in March 1997). This honours the Athenian *kosmetes* Aurelius Dositheos who is represented as being crowned by two ephebes who are his sons.

129. See 1 Cor. 3.1–2,5–9,10–11; 4.1; 4.14–15; 9.19; 9.24–27.

130. Thomas Conley, '*General Education*' *in Philo of Alexandria* (Hermeneutical Studies in Hellenistic and Modern Culture, 15; Berkeley: Center for Hermeneutical Studies in Hellenistic and Modern Culture, 1975), p. 4. He provides a detailed discussion on education in Philo.

131. Conley, '*General Education*', p. 4.

discipline παιδείαν), on which it is an advantage to lean'.[132] Here the staff supports learning. However, we read. 'The rod is the symbol of discipline (παιδεία), for there is no way of taking to heart warning and correction, unless, for some offences one is chastised and brought to a sense of shame'.[133] Both meanings appear when Philo comments on Deut. 21.20, 'by the addition of "this" they [the parents of the son] shew that they have other sons, strong-willed and self-controlling, who obey the injunctions of right reason and instruction (λογοῦ και παιδείας)'.[134] Conley warns that in Philo the semantic range of paideia should be kept in mind whether it is used in the general sense or in the phrase ἐγκύκλιος παιδεία.[135]

Elsewhere, when Philo comments on Gen. 38 he asks, 'Whose is the staff (ῥάβδος), that is the firmly planted, the unshaken, the unbending, the admonition, the chastening, the discipline (παιδεία); the sceptre, the kingship! Whose are they? Are they not God's alone?'[136] Philo also cites Prov. 3.11–12, 'My son despise not the discipline of God (παιδείας θεοῦ), nor faint when thou art rebuked by Him, for whom the Lord loveth He rebukes and scourges every son he receiveth'.[137] So in Philo παιδεία and ῥάβδος are used together to convey education and discipline. David Winston comments that παιδεία, 'which may mean either intellectual discipline or training of the will by moral precepts and by the control of a superior, is used in both these senses by Plato'.[138]

d. *The* Paideia *Model of Affliction*

Susan Garrett investigates 2 Cor. 12.7–10 using models of affliction to understand Paul's thorn.[139] She argues that Paul combines components from the cross/resurrection model of God's mode of action with two cultural models of affliction, which she labels the Job model and the παιδεία (or discipline) model.[140] Research, she states, shows alternative, and conflicting, models can govern experience in a culture:

> In Jewish culture of the late Second Temple era, an alternative to the 'Job model' of affliction envisioned suffering as a pedagogical process.

132. Philo, *Fug.* 150.
133. Philo, *Poster. C.* 97.
134. Philo, *Mut. Nom.* 206.
135. Conley, '*General Education*', p. 5.
136. Philo, *Mut. Nom.* 135. This deals with the same text as *Fug.* 150 above.
137. Philo, *Congr.* 177.
138. David Winston, 'Response', in Conley, '*General Education*', pp. 18–20 (18).
139. Susan R. Garrett, 'Paul's Thorn and Cultural Models of Affliction', in White and Yarbrough (eds.), *The Social World of the First Christians: Essays in Honor of Wayne A. Meeks* (Minneapolis, MN: Fortress Press, 1995), pp. 82–99.
140. Garrett, 'Paul's Thorn and Cultural Models', p. 85. She says the 'cultural models' are socially transmitted, taken-for-granted mental representations of the world (p. 84).

(In Greek contexts παιδεία could be understood as *education* or even *culture* in an idealized sense – and was often personified as such – but, as here, it could also be viewed as the learned *discipline* that makes one a cultured person.)[141]

In the παιδεία model God, as father, tests his children to discipline them. This model sees suffering as part of God's purpose (e.g. correction or improvement). Garrett sees this model in Wis. 3.1, 4–6. However, Heb. 12.3–11 clearly illustrates the model. After quoting Prov. 3.11–12 (which, Garrett notes, is a fundamental text for this cultural model) Heb. 12.7–8 states, 'Endure hardship as discipline [παιδείαν]; for God is treating you as sons. For what son is not disciplined [παιδεύει] by his father? If you are not disciplined [παιδείας] (and everyone undergoes discipline), then you are illegitimate children and not true sons' (NIV). Garrett correctly observes God's discipline. However, discipline also comes from human fathers. The author continues, 12.9, 'Moreover, we have all had human fathers who disciplined [παιδευτὰς] us,' and 12.10, 'Our fathers disciplined [ἐπαίδευον] us'.

She notes the widespread assumption in both Wisdom and Hebrews, 'that *successful endurance of tests of affliction makes one acceptable to God*'.[142] Moreover, she observes that, 'The Lord's commendation in the present (2 Cor. 10:18) anticipates approval at the judgment (cf. 1 Cor. 4:5)'.[143] She comments that 1 Cor. 11.27–32 shows Paul's familiarity with the παιδεία model and affliction. Sickness and death reflect God's judgment on the Corinthian Christians for unholy conduct. They need to examine themselves so they behave in an appropriate manner and do not incur God's judgment.[144] Yet Garrett observes in the current situation, 'Paul explains, "when we are judged, we are being disciplined (παιδευόμεθα) by the Lord so that we may not be condemned along with the world"' (11.32).[145] She sees the affliction as clearing away their impurities like the refiner's fire, although she does not connect this with 1 Cor. 3.13–15.

Her study, though focused on Paul's thorn in 2 Cor. 12.7–10, is valuable because she demonstrates that Paul is familiar with, and uses, the παιδεία model of affliction. The human father in Heb. 12.7 is relevant to 1 Cor. 4 where Paul is the father disciplining the Corinthian children. Garrett remarks that in the παιδεία model, 'God tests the righteous through affliction as a way of chastising or disciplining them in preparation for judgment'.[146]

141. Garrett, 'Paul's Thorn and Cultural Models', pp. 91–92.
142. Garrett, 'Paul's Thorn and Cultural Models', p. 93.
143. Garrett, 'Paul's Thorn and Cultural Models', p. 93.
144. Garrett, 'Paul's Thorn and Cultural Models', p. 93.
145. Garrett, 'Paul's Thorn and Cultural Models', p. 93.
146. Garrett, 'Paul's Thorn and Cultural Models', p. 97.

Moreover, 1 Clement also applies this model of affliction to the Corinthian church:

> Let us receive correction (παιδείαν) which we make one to another is good and beyond measure helpful, for it unites us to the will of God. For the holy word says thus: 'With chastisement did the Lord chastise me (Παιδεῦων ἐπαίδευσέν), and delivered me not over unto death; for whom the Lord loveth he chasteneth (παιδεύει) and scourgeth (μαστιγοῖ) every son whom he receiveth'.[147]

Thus in 4.21 Paul's language of the 'rod of correction' is intimately bound with the παιδεία model of God's correcting activity. The verse speaks directly to those who are puffed up (4.20) and overconfident in their talk (λογός). These elite are those likely to be educated in the gymnasium. Their Greek παιδεία as a status-determinant is cleverly applied against their activities as Paul draws upon images of discipline from the gymnasium and games. He thus overturns their glory in their education by threatening to apply punishment because they are in the wrong. If they want wisdom he gives it to them! The more education they received the more they would have been exposed to physical punishment. The rod is a suitable response to the educated elite, for in 1 Cor. 2 there appears to be a concern and criticism that they have not received appropriate level teaching.

3. *The* Grammateus *(1 Corinthians 1.20)*

a. *The Triad*

In 1 Cor. 1.10–17 Paul criticises the Corinthians' attitude of exclusive attachment to leaders in the Church (Paul, Apollos and Cephas, who are mentioned again in 2.5–9,21; 4.6). In 1.18–2.10 Paul criticises secular figures of influence: 1.20 (the wise, scholar/scribe, philosopher), 1.26 (the wise, the influential, those of noble birth), 2.8 (the rulers of this age). Undoubtedly, *inter alia*, these secular figures are from the educated elite, moreover, some will have received a gymnasium education. With the exception of the first triad the others are categories not individuals.

Mitchell briefly reviews 1.20 before opting for Lightfoot's explanation as the most plausible: σοφός is the Greek 'wise man,' γραμματεύς the Jewish counterpart, and συζητητὴς is 'a general expression comprehending both'.[148] She remarks:

147. *1 Clem.* 56.2–4. He cites Ps. 118.18 and Prov. 3.12. See also *1 Clem.* 56.5–6, 56.16 for chastisement language. In *1 Clem.* 56.16 God is the good father who chastises so that the Corinthians 'may obtain mercy through his holy chastisement'.

148. Mitchell, *Paul and the Rhetoric of Reconciliation*, p. 88; citing J.B. Lightfoot, *Notes on Epistles of St. Paul from Unpublished Commentaries* (London and New York: Macmillan, 1895), p. 159.

> Specifically, the term [συζητητὴς] encompasses all the disputants, whether Greek or Jewish. This is confirmed by the rest of the argument wherein only a two-part distinction is made, between Greek and Jew (1:22–24). Thus the anomalous term συζητητὴς chosen by Paul in 1:20 may be seen as another reference to the behavior of the factionalists within the community.[149]

Bruce Winter observes that E.A. Judge 'believes that the three terms refer to three main contemporary types of tertiary scholars'.[150] Similarly Gordon Fee, in his commentary, sees the questions as probably referring to the '"wise ones" of the ancient world' and states, 'The Greek word *grammateus* is that used among Jews for their rabbis, the teachers of the law (cf. the Gospels where it was traditionally translated 'scribe'; hence the KJV for this passage: 'Where is the scribe?'); it is simply not found among Greeks for their scholars or teachers'.[151] Fee, adds, 'In ordinary Greek vocabulary it refers to a civic officer, e.g., the "town-clerk" of Acts 19:35. See BAGD; cf. Lightfoot, 159'.[152] So Fee sees the triad as various wise ones who belong to this present age, which has been judged by God.

Stephen Pogoloff examines the triad but particularly the *grammateus*.[153] He sees σοφός as a generic term for a Greek or Jew 'who claims to be humanly wise,' noting that, 'This is borne out by the following terms which refer to scholars of both the Jewish and Hellenistic worlds'.[154] The third term he understands as a 'disputant' or 'debater': 'Thus, the συζητητὴς, in the context of Paul's rhetoric about rhetoric, most naturally refers to the rhetorician skilled at declamation and extemporaneous courtroom displays. Increasingly, such persons were called sophists, and were sought by all status seekers as prizes'.[155]

He agrees with Fee that 'it [*grammateus*] is simply not found among Greeks for their scholars or teachers'.[156] However, Pogoloff also comments, 'Among Greeks and Hellenists, it is a very frequent term for clerk or secretary, including titles of town officials with considerable status. However, this translation would not fit into the list: "Where is the wise man, where is the secretary, where is the debater of this age?"'[157] He establishes the meaning as a Jewish scholar. But his objection on

149. Mitchell, *Paul and the Rhetoric of Reconciliation*, p. 88.

150. Winter, *Philo and Paul*, p. 188 n. 46; citing Judge, 'The Reaction Against Classical Education in the New Testament', p. 11.

151. Fee, *First Epistle*, p. 71.

152. Fee, *First Epistle*, p. 71 n. 14.

153. Pogoloff, *Logos and Sophia*, pp. 160–72 for the *grammateus*.

154. Pogoloff, *Logos and Sophia*, p. 158.

155. Pogoloff, *Logos and Sophia*, p. 160.

156. Pogoloff, *Logos and Sophia*, p. 160; citing Fee, *First Epistle*.

157. Pogoloff, *Logos and Sophia*, p. 160 n. 103.

translation lacks force because the translation itself is the source of the difficulty. Today 'clerk or secretary' usually conveys a responsible but fairly low status job without much influence. A better modern equivalent, conveying a more exalted and powerful position may be the secretary of a large company. Nevertheless, this is inadequate in some respects. The ancient influential position of secretary could be an elite position in the city held by the wealthy, influential, and those of noble birth. They would be intelligent and well educated. Moreover, Pogoloff too readily rejects the status links of γραμματεύς. It is highly likely, in view of the status issues in the letter, that Paul chooses a word for the Jewish scholar that also has powerful status meanings.

Ben Witherington remarks on Paul's use of *skandalon* as something scandalous:

> To make his point, in v. 19 Paul partially quotes Isa. 29:14 from the LXX, with his own modifications. Whereas in the original there is reference to political leaders and their counselors, Paul in v. 20 refers to the sage (whether Jewish or Gentile), the expert in the law (the Jewish scribe), and the debater or Sophist (who liked to bat around concepts abstractly, declaiming on this or that subject).[158]

He refers to Pogoloff, for the identification of the debater as a sophist, but first comments, '*Grammatikoi* in Isaiah does not correspond to *grammateus* here. *Grammateus* can hardly have its non-Jewish meaning here of "secretary" as in Acts 19:35. It may be, therefore, that Paul uses terms to include all those considered wise according to two different cultural orientations'.[159] However, Witherington gives no reasons for his rejection of 'secretary' and he does not consider γραμματεύς in its social context.

Winter reviews scholars' views on the triad in 1.20.[160] He argues that, 'as the σοφός and γραμματεύς are discussed in verses 20–25, so the activity of the sophists and orators as the debaters of this age is reflected in the argument in verses 26–31'.[161] He notes that a survey of terms in 1.26 (wise, powerful and noble-birth) among first-century authors shows that, 'they are commonly applied to the ruling class of eastern cities'.[162] Moreover, based on the literary evidence Winter concludes that 1 Cor. 1.26 does refer to the Corinthian ruling class, where orators and sophists originated.[163] Winter cites the catalogue of Corinthian inscriptions that clearly show that orators

158. Witherington, *Conflict and Community*, p. 109.
159. Witherington, *Conflict and Community*, p. 109 n. 8.
160. Winter, *Philo and Paul*, pp. 187–88.
161. Winter, *Philo and Paul*, p. 189.
162. Winter, *Philo and Paul*, p. 189.
163. Winter, *Philo and Paul*, p. 191.

contributed to Corinth's political life and would have been regarded as those among the powerful, well-born and wise.[164] He argues that the sophists were well educated. However, he does not discuss γραμματεύς, apart from remarking that H.A.W. Meyer thought it meant Jewish scribes. Andrew Clarke has γραμματεύς as 'scholar'.[165] Thus where γραμματεύς is discussed scholars often accept scribe/scholar rather than 'secretary'.

Gregory Snyder has reviewed the role of scribes as textual experts.[166] He recognises that *grammateus* was often equivalent to 'secretary' and could refer to the 'town clerk' (Acts 19.35) but he cautions, 'just as there is no guarantee that the secretary of the local Elks club must be highly erudite to hold the post, so it was in antiquity'.[167] Nevertheless, following his discussion Snyder observes, 'While some have argued that scribes were of secondary importance, I believe that they performed a crucial service in their capacity as text-brokers and that such people might well have held a *de facto* monopoly on access to texts and traditions that governed people's behaviors'.[168] This is an important point. These were literate people with crucial roles. Pogoloff's case for the reading of Jewish scribe is well argued, but is this the whole story? Thiselton helpfully sees that the Jewish and Graeco-Roman meanings, respectively, of '*teacher of the law* or *expert*' and 'secretary' or 'clerk' can be combined. Thus, allowing this blend 'we might translate *person of letters* ... or, perhaps less controversially, **expert**'.[169]

b. *The* Grammateus *and Gymnasia*

Fragments with γραμματεύς occur in Corinth, but these are reconstructed from a few letters, and are not informative. Ronald Stroud discusses a small fragment of marble found on the foundations of Temple K. Line 2 which reads - - - -γρα]ṃματέως[- - -. The lettering probably belongs to the second century B.C.[170] He says that in line 2 the title of the official is not

164. Winter, *Philo and Paul*, p. 191. However, the three inscriptions are later than Paul and dated in the second century AD. See Kent, *Corinth: The Inscriptions, 1926–1950*, no. 226, p. 97; no. 264, pp. 106–7; no. 307, p. 121. The first two are dated in the reign of Antoninus Pius (138–161 AD). No. 226 is the third quarter of the second century, no. 264 is a little after the middle of the second century. No. 307 is dated near the end of the second century. Nevertheless, they provide valuable evidence.

165. Clarke, *Secular and Christian Leadership*, p. 115.

166. H. Gregory Snyder, *Teachers and Texts in the Ancient World: Philosophers, Jews and Christians* (London and New York: Routledge, 2000), pp. 181–88.

167. Snyder, *Teachers and Texts in the Ancient World*, p. 185.

168. Snyder, *Teachers and Texts in the Ancient World*, p. 188.

169. Thiselton, *First Epistle*, p. 164. He suggests that for today we may use a term such as '*the professional*'.

170. Ronald S. Stroud, 'Greek Inscriptions at Corinth', *Hesp* 41 (1972), pp. 198–217 (199).

certain but both γραμματεύς and ὑπογραμματεύς appear at the beginning of decrees found at Corinth.[171] The title here is in the genitive case and stood near the beginning of the decree. The form [γρα]μματέως indicates *koine* which among decrees found at Corinth has usually been taken as evidence for a non-Corinthian origin. Stroud remarks, 'Until clear evidence is available for the use of *koine* in firmly identifiable Corinthian decrees, it is best to regard the present text as originating in another Greek city which officially recognised some special service from Corinth'.[172] The inscription from Corinth in Thomas R. Martin is late Imperial and uninformative.[173] Meritt no. 7 is an undated fragmentary restoration.[174] Kent no. 46 (b) is a decree referring to an arbitration board associated with Argos.[175] It refers to judges and their secretary. The inscription appears to be pre–44 BC. The paucity of evidence from Corinth is disappointing, but does indicate that the term occurs within the history of Corinth.

O.W. Reinmuth considers a 1st century BC ephebic inscription from Athens in which the secretary is mentioned as honoured.[176] Reinmuth also discusses a general decree honouring the *epheboi*, the *kosmetes* and the instructors of the *epheboi, c.* 186/5 BC.[177] Wreaths are shown for the *grammateus* and *hyperetes.*[178] In the scale of importance there is the *paidotribes, grammateus* and then *hyperetes.* Stephen Tracy examines an Athenian ephebic decree, where the instructors' list has *grammateus* mentioned with 6 types of instructors and his name is recorded in 2 of the 5 dated periods.[179] Thus in the Hellenistic period, in at least Athens, the *grammateus* was an ephebic instructor in the gymnasium. Nevertheless, as Tracy admits the evidence for instructors at this time is thin and fragmentary.[180]

Clarence Forbes describes the functionaries in the Athenian ephebeia and notes that before the empire this included 'the secretary (γραμματεύς),

171. He notes that Γραμματεύς, Kent [*sic*, Meritt], no. 8, is a doubtful example, and refers to the discussion of Sterling Dow, 'Corinthiaca', *HSCP* 53 (1942), pp. 89–119 (111–12). See ὑπογραμματεύς in line 1 of Corinth Inventory I 2649, an unpublished fragment from the excavations of 1965 northwest of Temple E in J.K. Anderson, 'Corinth: Temple E Northwest, Preliminary Report, 1965', *Hesp* 46 (1977), pp. 1–12 (11).

172. Stroud, 'Greek Inscriptions at Corinth', pp. 199–200.

173. Thomas R. Martin, 'Inscriptions at Corinth', *Hesp* 46 (1977), pp. 178–98.

174. Meritt, *Corinth: Greek Inscriptions, 1896–1927*, no. 7, pp. 7–8.

175. Kent, *Corinth: The Inscriptions, 1926–1950*, no. 46 (b) pp. 14–15.

176. O.W. Reinmuth, 'The Ephebic Inscription, Athenian Agora I 286', *Hesp* 24 (1955), pp. 220–39 (238).

177. O.W. Reinmuth, 'Ephebic Texts from Athens', *Hesp* 30 (1961), pp. 8–22.

178. O.W. Reinmuth, 'Ephebic Texts from Athens', p. 13.

179. Stephen V. Tracy, 'Greek Inscriptions from the Athenian Agora: Third to First Centuries B.C.', *Hesp* 51 (1982), pp. 57–64. The decrees with the *grammateus* named are dated *c.* 180 and 171/0 BC.

180. Tracy, 'Greek Inscriptions from the Athenian Agora', p. 60.

who kept the records, and the servant (υπηρέτης), whose duties were not told, but are not hard to conjecture'.[181] Under the empire one of the notable changes was the increased complexity of the organisation with 'As many as twenty-five instructors and functionaries ... sometimes set over the ephebi'.[182] In the second century AD Forbes observes that the ephebic secretary often had an assistant.[183] Moreover, 'Among all these officials ... there was an understanding as to the rank and degree of importance,' thus an under-secretary may become a secretary.[184] Nevertheless, over time some teachers were discontinued and new ones introduced so no one list covers all periods 'and besides, some officials, such as the secretary, were very differently rated at different times'.[185] Forbes remarks that at Tegea, where a gymnasium is not attested but ephebic training was conducted in the palaestra, there was a college secretary.[186] An Athenian early second-century AD herm for the *kosmetes* Helidoros was dedicated, and paid for, by ephebes and instructors, including the *grammateus*. This herm appears to be from the local Gymnasium of Diogenes.[187] So here the *grammateus* is an instructor in an Athenian gymnasium and wealthy enough to contribute to the cost of the herm. He is mixing with those of high social status (ephebes and *kosmetes*).

Thus the role of secretary existed for the ephebeia in the gymnasium and so was associated with elite education. Forbes also shows that 'the governing and executive personnel of an association of *neoi* in any city consisted of three men; gymnasiarch, secretary, and treasurer'.[188] He observes that the *neoi* in Pergamum were so numerous and important that they sometimes needed three or four secretaries.[189] Thus secretaries served ephebes and *neoi*.

181. Forbes, *Greek Physical Education*, p. 141.

182. Forbes, *Greek Physical Education*, p. 164.

183. Forbes, *Greek Physical Education*, p. 166.

184. Forbes, *Greek Physical Education*, pp. 169–70.

185. Forbes, *Greek Physical Education*, p. 170. The information board, 'The Diogeneion Gymnasium and the Stelai of Kosmetai and Ephebes,' on display in Room 31A at the National Archaeological Museum, Athens (March 1997) refers to second and third century AD honorific inscriptions. These note the titles of official trainers and include the *grammateus*.

186. Forbes, *Greek Physical Education*, pp. 191–92. Tegea in Arcadia (Peloponnese) created its ephebeia in the second century BC and it lasted until the third century AD. See chapter VII 'The Remainder of Greece and the Greek World' for Forbes' examination of physical education and the ephebeia.

187. Tzachou-Alexandri (ed.), *Mind and Body*, no. 85, pp. 192–94. On its location see no. 86 pp. 193–94 (194), the herm of the *kosmetes* Sosistratos (with the same location) and the note that the office of *kosmetes* 'was one of the highest distinctions of Athenian society'.

188. Forbes, *Neoi*, pp. 34–38 (38).

189. Forbes, *Neoi*, p. 35.

Finally, B.D. Meritt comments on part of a marble stele dated *c.* 58–65 AD, 'This is part of a prytany decree honouring the phyle Aigeis, to which the deme Erchia belonged. The treasurer of the prytaneis was named first in the register.... He and the secretary, as the more important officers, were named in the decree with patronymics as well as demotics, the other officers with demotics only'.[190] Thus γραμματεύς was used in the Greek East before and after Paul wrote 1 Corinthians, even if the inscriptional evidence for Corinth is poor.

c. *The* Grammateus, *Government and Gymnasiarchs at Ephesus*

This section examines the status and importance of the term ὁ γραμματεύς through the situation in Ephesus. R.A. Kearsley identifies persons holding the office of secretary in the late first and early second century at Ephesus where Paul worked.[191] During the riot in Ephesus, 'some of the officials of the province (τῶν 'ασιαρχῶν), friends of Paul, sent him a message begging him not to venture into the theatre,' (Acts 19.31). The commentator F.F. Bruce observes, 'Their friendly relations with Paul show that the imperial policy at this time was not hostile to the spread of Christianity, and that the more educated classes did not share the antipathy to Paul felt by the more superstitious populace'.[192] Michael Bullmore, in his study of 1 Corinthians, noting this, and other passages in Acts, states, 'Some weight is added to the general argument that Paul was growing increasingly familiar with Greco-Roman culture by the fact that he grew increasingly familiar with Greeks and Romans of high social standing'.[193] Philip Harland also notes the Christian connections with elites in Luke-Acts.[194]

Acts 19.35 states, 'The city clerk (ὁ γραμματεύς) quietened the crowd,' and Bruce observes, 'The "town-clerk" or executive officer who published the decrees of the Demos was an Ephesian, not a Roman official, but as the most important native official of the provincial capital, he was in close touch with the Roman authorities, who would hold him responsible for the riotous assembly'.[195]

Moreover, Bullmore argues for the impact of Ephesus on Paul's stay:

> It might, at first, be surmised that since this visit to Ephesus took place after Paul's visit to Corinth anything learned there would not have

190. B.D. Meritt, 'Greek Inscriptions', *Hesp* 29 (1960), pp. 1–77.

191. Kearsley, 'Some Asiarchs of Ephesos'.

192. F.F. Bruce, *The Acts of the Apostles: The Greek Text with Introduction and Commentary* (Leicester: Inter-Varsity Press, 2nd ed., 1976), p. 366.

193. Bullmore, *St. Paul's Theology of Rhetorical Style*, p. 190 n. 77.

194. Philip A. Harland, 'Connections with Elites in the World of the Early Christians', in Blasi, Duhaime and Turcotte (eds.), *Handbook of Early Christianity: Social Science Approaches*, pp. 385–408 (405).

195. Bruce, *The Acts of the Apostles*, p. 367.

> affected Paul's manner of preaching in Corinth. However, it is during his stay in Ephesus that Paul writes his first letter to the Corinthians in which the passage which interests us occurs. Thus Ephesus could wield its influence in Paul's formulation of his reflections on his preaching at Corinth. And Ephesus had some rhetorical influence to wield.[196]

Kearsley's article is significant because she considers the Salutaris document, dated 104 AD, which is 'among the earliest epigraphic references to the presence of asiarchs in Ephesus and is unlikely to date more than fifty years after the allusion to them in Acts 19:31'.[197] Moreover, she gives a brief survey of four named asiarchs in Ephesus who are the closest in time to its early Christians community where Paul lived and also worked.[198] Although Kearsley is primarily concerned with the asiarchs, I focus on the γραμματεύς.

She notes that Ti. Claudius Aristio was *archiereus* of Asia for 88/89 AD, provincial high priest in 89/90 AD and asiarch in 92/93 AD, and observes that from this date:

> Aristio played an active role in the administration of the city. Two inscriptions of that year record that he held one of the eponymous magistracies of Ephesos, the *grammateia* of the *demos*; and in both cases Aristio is simultaneously named asiarch (*I.Eph.* II.461, 508). One of these two inscriptions is known to have come from the base of a statue found in a large building complex known now as the Harbour Gymnasium; and dedications on several other statue bases from there should probably also be restored with Aristio's name as *grammateus* of the *demos* (*I.Eph.* IV.1128, 1129, 1129a).[199]

Kearsley comments that Aristio contributed to the construction of the gymnasium.[200] At that time he was holding another eponymous office of the city, the prytany and was simultaneously asiarch. It seems his office of prytany preceded that of *grammateus*. Aristio was also, at some point, gymnasiarch (probably of the Harbour Gymnasium after its completion). After 92/93 AD he continued as a leading figure in Ephesus, held public offices and engaged in philanthropic activity. He supervised the construction of the Celsus library.

A contemporary of Aristio was T. Flavius Pythio (asiarch in 104/05 AD), who also served as *grammateus* of the *demos* but holding office twice. In his second term as secretary he was concurrently asiarch. In 115/16 AD

196. Bullmore, *St. Paul's Theology of Rhetorical Style*, pp. 188–89.

197. Kearsley, 'Some Asiarchs of Ephesos', p. 48. She notes that currently these are the earliest securely-dated, and named, asiarchs in relation to the Christian community.

198. Kearsley, 'Some Asiarchs of Ephesos', p. 49.

199. Kearsley, 'Some Asiarchs of Ephesos', p. 49.

200. Kearsley, 'Some Asiarchs of Ephesos', p. 50.

he was *archiereus* of the city's imperial cult. On six occasions he shared, with his wife, the office of gymnasiarch.

In 115/16 AD the third asiarch, Pythio's son, T. Flavius Aristoboulos was both *grammateus* of the *demos* and asiarch. In 116/17 AD he was *prytanis* in Ephesus.[201] The fourth asiarch P. Vedius Antoninus is documented as *prytanis* (sometime between 93–103 AD). In 117/18 he is *grammateus* of the *demos* for the second time and asiarch at the time of the dedication of the Temple of Hadrian. A later inscription to his son reveals that Antoninus had also been gymnasiarch, panegyriarch of the Great Epheseia and the Pasitheia.

Kearsley notes for all four asiarchs 'the very strong link between the highest city magistracies, like the *grammateus* of the *demos*, and the asiarchy'.[202] She also mentions the *grammateus* 'of the temples of Asia in Ephesos' who is an administrative official.[203] Moreover, in *I.Eph.* Ia.27.220–46, dated 104 AD, Kearsley shows the secretary of the council (*boule*) and the secretary of the *synedrion* of the gerousia as responsible for the distribution of money to the council and *synedrion* respectively from the Salutaris foundation.[204] Kearsley notes, 'The secretary of the gerousia is given the power to make a distribution to them provided that they have registered with him in advance. The money they were given was to be used to buy supplies for the sacrifice on the birthday of Artemis'.[205]

Thus in the late first/early second century the term 'secretary' was used for different civic and sacred officials at Ephesus. On the importance of the γραμματεύς of the *demos* in the Roman period and his relation to other officials Kearsley refers to A.H.M. Jones.[206] He comments that administration of the city included considerable clerical work and that over time the position grew in importance 'in the Roman period he, either alone or supported by the principal magistrates, very frequently moves decrees and takes the lead in council and assembly: it will be recalled it was the clerk of the city who dealt so firmly with the riotous and unconstitutional assembly at Ephesus which Demetrius the silversmith provoked'.[207] Thus Jones clearly indicates the importance of the office. Kearsley notes the epigraphic

201. Kearsley, 'Some Asiarchs of Ephesos', p. 51.

202. Kearsley, 'Some Asiarchs of Ephesos', p. 53.

203. Kearsley, 'Some Asiarchs of Ephesos', p. 55.

204. Kearsley, 'Some Asiarchs of Ephesos', pp. 46–48. The lines occur in the inscription (the Salutaris document) recording the perpetual foundation of C. Vibius Salutaris, a Roman *eques* who had been an imperial procurator, but was also a citizen of Ephesus and a member of its council. Kearsley says, 'Such perpetual endowments (which differed from a testamentary bequest in that the benefits commenced during the lifetime of the donor) were not uncommon in the Greek East during the early Roman empire' (p. 47).

205. Kearsley, 'Some Asiarchs of Ephesos', p. 48.

206. Kearsley, 'Some Asiarchs of Ephesos', p. 53.

207. Jones, *The Greek City*, pp. 238–39.

evidence for women carrying civic burdens, including that of γραμματεύς, although this was much more rarely held than positions such as gymnasiarch and *agonothete*.[208] Thus the γραμματεύς was an important official and a civic leader.

In conclusion, scholarship has often not accepted the reading of 'secretary' for γραμματεύς but considers the term as referring to a scholar or Jewish scribe. My study shows that the γραμματεύς was a part of the Greek gymnasium and associated with ephebic education and the *neoi*. Tracy includes him among the instructors of the ephebeia although the particular texts are Hellenistic and restricted to Athens. The second-century AD Athenian herm for the *kosmetes* Helidoros was dedicated, and paid for, by ephebes and instructors, where the *grammateus* is an instructor in the gymnasium. In the empire the office of secretary included civic and sacred positions. At Ephesus it was one of the two eponymous magistracies and of considerable importance in civic leadership and status. The post may be held concurrently with other civic positions. A man may hold the office of γραμματεύς with gymnasiarch.

Thus in reading/hearing γραμματεύς in 1 Cor. 1.20 the Corinthians may well have thought of civic leaders, instructors in the gymnasia and scholar/scribe. When they came to 1.26, which Winter identifies as civic leaders in Corinth, this initial acceptance would be reinforced. On reaching 1 Cor. 2.8 this would again be confirmed for the passage shows the ignorance of the world rulers who crucified Christ.[209] The reading of γραμματεύς as a leader is also consistent with 1.19 where Paul cites Isa. 19.12 which refers to earthly leaders. Consequently, in the context of 1 Cor. 1.20 γραμματεύς speaks of the well-educated elite. This appears to be the class of the educated elite in the Corinthian church.

4. *Ancient Writing (1 Corinthians 4.6)*

a. *Fitzgerald's and Talbert's View*

This difficult verse has caused much debate and despair because of the meaning of μὴ ὑπὲρ ἃ γέγραπται ('Nothing beyond what is written'; NRSV).[210] Gordon Fee reflects on this situation, 'But on this matter we must finally plead ignorance. Here is a case where the apostle and his readers were on a wavelength that will probably be forever beyond our ability to pick up'.[211] Biblical scholars identify six main options: (a) the text is corrupt, (b) the

208. Kearsley, 'Women in Public Life', p. 26.

209. See Thiselton, *First Epistle*, pp. 233–39, 245–48 on 1 Cor. 2.8 for this verse referring to earthly rulers but not necessarily constrained by just referring to human rulers.

210. The NIV translates: 'Do not go beyond what is written'.

211. Fee, *First Epistle*, p. 169.

meaning is obscure: it probably refers to the Old Testament, either in general, or to passages in ch. 1–3, (c) it is a saying or slogan, (d) the text is unintelligible, (e) it is a warning to the socially elite against overstepping the limits of human knowledge set by God, (f) it refers to the ancient practice of learning to write.[212] Both John Fitzgerald and Charles Talbert understand 'Do not go beyond what is written' as a reference to learning to write.

I consider recent views on 1 Cor. 4.6 and their response, if any, to Fitzgerald's suggestion.[213] Mitchell comments:

> Fitzgerald's hypothesis, that it refers to the ancient mode of tracing letters for learning the alphabet is ingenious but not readily anchored in this particular context in 1 Cor 1–4. Nor is it clear how this domestic image fits with the conflict expressed in the parallel clause ἵνα μὴ εἷς ὑπερ τοῦ ἑνὸς φυσιοῦσθε κατὰ τοῦ ἑτέρου. I take the phrase as a reference back to the scripture quote (3:21; cf. 1:31), an interpretation which receives further support by the established parallelism of καυχᾶσθαι and φυσιοῦσθαι as Paul's caricatured description of Corinthian factionalism.[214]

Thus she rejects Fitzgerald's view because she cannot locate it in the context of 1 Cor. 1–4 or sees how the domestic image fits in with the conflict in the parallel clause: then you will not take pride in one man against another. But both objections can be answered.

Chow believes that the ὑπερ ... κατὰ should be taken as 'for ... against' so, 'It seems best to see Paul as referring to the Corinthians' preference of one teacher to another, namely, Apollos against Paul'.[215] Elsewhere, Chow sees 4.6 as referring to the proud and the 'puffed-up' who are behind the divisions in the church.[216] Apart from this he does not discuss Fitzgerald's argument for 4.6, although he shows awareness of his work.

Pogoloff's study on the rhetorical situation in 1 Corinthians has a short contribution on 4.6 but he does not discuss Fitzgerald's argument. He sees

212. Recently, Thiselton, *First Epistle*, pp. 352–55 has given seven options. His seventh point considers that it may refer to the 'childishness' of those who are addressees. He cites Ebner that it refers to children who cannot read letters correctly or trace properly. However, he rejects Ebner's view.

213. Fitzgerald, *Cracks in an Earthen Vessel*, pp. 122–27. Although Talbert, *Reading Corinthians*, p. 8, makes the same suggestion, scholars associate the view on 'writing' with Fitzgerald, who builds his case on Plato, *Prt.* 320C-328D, where the sophist Protagoras gives a speech claiming that virtue can be taught, and Seneca's *Ep.* 94. Talbert uses the same two passages but without the detailed discussion which Fitzgerald develops.

214. Mitchell, *Paul and the Rhetoric of Reconciliation*, p. 220 n. 183.

215. Chow, *Patronage and Power*, p. 103 n. 3. He names scholars to support his view.

216. Chow, *Patronage and Power*, pp. 131, 138.

the Corinthians as puffed up over leaders.[217] Savage mentions 4.6 but does not consider, or show awareness of, Fitzgerald's suggestion.[218] He refers to Legault 'for a tidy summary of the views'.[219] But Legault's article is dated and Savage does not cite more recent discussion in, for example, Fee, Talbert and Fitzgerald.[220] Indeed he is content to observe, 'that since this phrase appears throughout Paul as a formula introducing OT citations, it probably refers here to the five scriptural quotations which Paul has already cited in I Corinthians 1–3'.[221]

Winter considers 1 Cor. 4.6 but does not discuss the interpretation of the verse.[222] One reference refers to Fee for a summary of the discussion on 4.6.[223] Ben Witherington believes, 'Paul is suggesting that the way the Corinthians should evaluate their teachers is by following the OT models'.[224] But he adds, 'I would not rule out J. T. Fitzgerald's novel suggestion in *Cracks in an Earthen Vessel*, pp. 123–27, that the phrase in question means 'stay within the lines,' the advice of a teacher to a young pupil learning how to write. The point then would be in this case to follow the lines of the example set by Paul and Apollos and not go beyond them'.[225] Thus Witherington seems semi-persuaded by Fitzgerald's argument.

Raymond Pickett gives his support to Fitzgerald's suggestion.[226] He remarks:

> This background is significant in light of the fact that Paul presents the Corinthians as children (3.1–3) and uses a rhetorical term to characterize his own teaching. The parallel is even more striking when the Protagoras quotation is read in its larger context. The predominant theme of *Prt.* 320C-28D is moral education, and the imagery of children learning to draw by means of a model serves as an illustration of moral guidance. The virtues are learned by imitating those whose lives exemplify them. Since the Corinthians are still immature, Paul provides them with a model to imitate.[227]

217. Pogoloff, *Logos and Sophia*, p. 222.
218. Savage, *Power Through Weakness*, pp. 7, 58–9, 136, 161.
219. Savage, *Power Through Weakness*, p. 59 n. 17.
220. A. Legault, 'Beyond the Things which are Written (1 Cor. iv.6),' *NTS* 18 (1971), pp. 227–31.
221. Savage, *Power Through Weakness*, p. 59.
222. Winter, *Philo and Paul*, pp. 11, 174, 179, 193, 196–202.
223. Winter, *Philo and Paul*, p. 198 n. 81; citing Fee, *First Epistle*, pp. 167–69.
224. Witherington, *Conflict and Community*, p. 141.
225. Witherington, *Conflict and Community*, p. 141 n. 15.
226. Raymond Pickett, *The Cross in Corinth: The Social Significance of the Death of Jesus* (JSNTSup, 143; Sheffield: Sheffield Academic Press, 1997), pp. 78–80.
227. Pickett, *The Cross in Corinth*, p. 80.

Thus Pickett gives unqualified support to Fitzgerald's interpretation. Talbert already adheres to Fitzgerald's view, while Witherington seems semi-persuaded.

The recent discussion of J. Ross Wagner is very useful in areas but omits any discussion of Fitzgerald.[228] Wagner states, 'Paul's enigmatic phrase μὴ υπὲρ ἃ γέγραπται is best understood as a reference to a *particular* Scriptural admonition – one he has already cited (1:31) and to which he has subsequently alluded (3:21) – namely, "Let the one who boasts, boast in the Lord".'[229] He argues, from verbal and thematic links, that the source of Paul's thought in 1.31 is 1 Sam. 2.10, the Song of Hannah, which resounds 'with the theme of the reversal of human pride'.[230] Although he sees the call to boast as a strong call for unity and the end of factionalism nowhere does Wagner consider the educated elite.[231] But he admits ignorance on the origin of the slogan when he concludes:

> It is generally recognized that Paul is quoting a slogan here, the source of which was probably familiar both to Paul and to the Corinthians. The important question for our purposes is not, however, the origin of the slogan, but its meaning in the context of 1 Corinthians. Whether Paul has borrowed it or coined it, we have seen strong reasons to believe that he employs it here as a call to obey the Scriptures, namely the Scripture quoted in 1.31.[232]

It is a pity that Wagner remains unaware of Fitzgerald's and Talbert's work because an understanding of the origin of the slogan provides a profitable route for investigation of the factionalism and the educated elite.

James C. Hanges has recently discussed the views on 1 Cor. 4.6 and notes that the problem can be described according to the two fundamental presuppositions assumed: either (1) the present text cannot be interpreted, or (2) the text makes sense as it stands.[233] He rightly rejects emendation before examining views on understanding the text in its wider cultural

228. J. Ross Wagner, '"Not Beyond the Things which are Written": A Call to Boast Only in the Lord (1 Cor 4.6)', *NTS* 44 (1998), pp. 279–87.

229. Wagner, '"Not Beyond the Things which are Written"', p. 280.

230. Wagner, '"Not Beyond the Things which are Written"', p. 284. He sees Paul echoing in 1 Cor. 1.18-31 the wider context of the text from 1 Kgdms 2.10 (1 Sam. 2.10) which he quotes in 1 Cor. 1.31 'with or without Jer 9.22–3 in mind'. Wagner compares the Greek in Jer. 9.22 and 1 Kgdms 2.10 as sources for Paul's citation.

231. Wagner, '"Not Beyond the Things which are Written"', p. 287. Earlier, p. 283, he argues the Corinthians are creating factions in the church but shows no awareness of the educated elite.

232. Wagner, '"Not Beyond the Things which are Written"', p. 287.

233. James C. Hanges, '1 Corinthians 4:6 and the Possibility of Written Bylaws in the Corinthian Church', *JBL* 117 (1998), pp. 275–98 (275).

context. He mentions, but rejects, 'B. Fiore's proposal that Paul's phrase is an allusion to the common experience of school children who are taught to write correctly by tracing over paradigmatic figures supplied by their teachers'.[234] He notes Kuck's qualified agreement and recognises Fitzgerald's detailed defence of this hypothesis but he fails to engage with Fitzgerald, contenting himself with rejecting weaknesses in Fiore's argument.[235] His paper argues that the verse refers to writing, but concludes with a 'plausible hypothesis':

> That the referent of the phrase ἃ γέγραπται is a foundational document of the Corinthian church, a public document (i.e., open to all members of the community) modelled on the kind of cult bylaws that would have been familiar to every member of the church, in which Paul had laid out those guidelines and principles which he felt necessary for the group's prosperity.[236]

His plausible proposal, while interesting, suffers from an inability to overthrow the ancient writing viewpoint of Fitzgerald *et al*, which also fits within my educational model. Hanges does not relate his proposal to the educated elite.

Finally, Ronald Tyler independently reached the same conclusions as Benjamin Fiore and John Fitzgerald that this text refers to learning to write.[237] He remarks, 'Paul refers to a pedagogical conception which his hearers would recognize from their early education. They would recall their earliest experiences when, as children, they learned to write, and a person who could not write would know the image from the pedagogy of the time'.[238] Thus Tyler agrees with earlier scholars on the education context and concludes:

> This interpretation of 1 Cor 4:6 fits the context and the moment of the relationship between teacher and student just as it does in the passages quoted from Seneca, Plato, and Quintilian. The familiar image of not going above or below the line when writing was available to them. It fits the theological, ethical, and rhetorical context in which Paul develops

234. Hanges, '1 Corinthians 4:6', pp. 281–82; citing B. Fiore, *The Function of Personal Example in the Socratic and Pastoral Epistles* (AnBib, 105; Rome: Biblical Institute Press, 1986), pp. 165–66.

235. Hanges, '1 Corinthians 4:6', p. 281; citing Kuck, *Judgment and Community Conflict*, p. 213 and Fitzgerald, *Cracks in an Earthen Vessel*, pp. 123–28. Kuck remarks, 'The most likely possibility, however, is that the phrase refers to the ancient practice of training children to write by having them trace the outline of letters drawn by the teacher' (p. 213).

236. Hanges, '1 Corinthians 4:6', p. 298.

237. Ronald L. Tyler, 'First Corinthians 4:6 and Hellenistic Pedagogy', *CBQ* 60 (1998), pp. 97–103 (97 n. 1).

238. Tyler, 'First Corinthians 4:6', p. 101.

his argument within the total context of childhood language in 1 Corinthians. Finally, this interpretation satisfies.[239]

In antiquity learning to write may be taught at home, school or the gymnasium.[240] However, very many children and adults would be unable to write or have only a basic proficiency.[241] The educated elite would be able to write well and their children would learn the skill. To put adults back to learning to write is an action of reversal which opposes the ideology of the elite shown by Kleijwegt with the *puer-senex* and παῖς τέλειος. Here elite children are portrayed as 'adult intellectuals'.[242] If children of the elite are depicted as adult intellectuals Paul here portrays adult intellectuals as children. The illiterates in the church would not interpret this verse as a put-down for them, because they would not have learnt this skill, but they would understand its impact. For those people in between the elite and very poor who would have received some education the reference would be readily understood.[243] As discussed in chapter 4 literacy was restricted. While elite children were being educated in the gymnasium, or elsewhere, non-elite children would often be either employed or in apprentice contracts. So within the social context of 1 Corinthians this text is directed at the educated elite and functions to deflate them.

Finally, one objection could be raised on the relationship between the elite and writing: other people, such as slaves, may be able to write. Myles McDonnell has adequately answered this objection. After her discussion, she concludes on elite Romans, 'If only because of its importance to the elite, the ability to write in one's own hand, therefore, like the ability to read, almost certainly carried social prestige, a prestige that was diminished no more by the presence of professional scribes, than that of reading was diminished by literate slaves'.[244]

b. *Isis and Hermes*

1 Cor. 4.6 may be understood in the context of the invention of writing. G.H.R. Horsley discusses a Greek text from Maroneia (Macedonia) which

239. Tyler, 'First Corinthians 4:6', p. 103. He cites Seneca *Ep*. 94.51, Plato *Prt*. 326D, and Quint., *Inst*. 1.1.27–29. Both Seneca and Quintilian are first-century AD sources for this technique of learning to write.

240. For ephebes' literacy and their practice of writing see *IG* II^2.1006, dated 122 BC, for the decree from Athens. Translation in Miller, *Arete*, no. 128, pp. 140–45 (143).

241. See chapter 4 for the earlier discussion of literacy in my model.

242. See the discussion in chapter 4.

243. For a discussion on those in the 'middle' of elite and non-elite see Jongkind, 'Corinth in the First Century AD'.

244. McDonnell, 'Writing, Copying and Autograph Manuscripts in Ancient Rome', p. 491. She agrees that professional scribes may copy documents but sees this as very different to what the elite did (p. 490).

is a personalised aretalogy of Isis.[245] He comments, 'On palaeographic grounds this is the earliest of extant aretalogies of Isis'.[246] The translation, *ll.*23–24, reads, 'She with Hermes discovered writing; and of this writing some was sacred for initiates, some was publicly available for all'.[247] Horsley comments, 'Isis as the inventor of writing with Hermes is a notion common to other aretalogies'.[248]

A text from Kyme (Asia Minor), reads: 'Isis am I, the ruler of every land. I was educated by Hermes and I invented with Hermes sacred and public writing in order that everything might not be written in the same script'.[249] Scholars identify the importance of the Isis cult in the Graeco-Roman world.[250] For Corinth, J.H. Kent records an inscription, which may be contemporary with Paul: *Isi et Serapi v(ovit) G(aius) Julius [S]yr[us]*, 'Gaius Julius Syrus dedicated (this column) to Isis and Serapis'.[251] Horsley cites an inscription, from a stele of Isis and Sarapis, and remarks, 'This text provides the first evidence of an official and organised cult of the Egyptian gods in Megalopolis, and disproves the view based on previously

245. G.H.R. Horsley, 'A Personalised Aretalogy of Isis', in Horsley, *New Documents Illustrating Early Christianity*, 1, no. 2, pp. 10–21. A personalised aretalogy is a text in praise of a god. Horsley, p. 12, notes that this is one of a small group of Greek texts which praise Isis. The inscription is *SEG* 821 (dated second half of the second century/first half of the first century BC). In the literary tradition only one incomplete example (Diodorus Siculus 1.27) survives. But four other inscriptions have been found and appear to be from a common source in Egypt. The opening lines of *I.Kyme* 41 state that the inscription was a copy of an original set up in the temple of Hephaistos (= Ptah) in Memphis. Horsley observes, 'This small group of texts forms part of a larger body of aretalogies, invocations and hymns for various gods – especially Egyptian ones – which survive from places as far apart as Africa and Asia Minor, on papyri ... on stone, and in our literary sources (most notably Apuleius *Metamorphoses* 11.5.1–5). These texts span about 400 years, II/I-III/IV' (p. 12).

246. Horsley, 'A Personalised Aretalogy of Isis', p. 11.

247. Horsley, 'A Personalised Aretalogy of Isis', p. 11. Horsley, p. 13, notes, that the aretalogies are a Greek interpretation of Isis.

248. Horsley, 'A Personalised Aretalogy of Isis', p. 16.

249. Horsley, 'A Personalised Aretalogy of Isis', p. 19. *I.Kyme* 41 (*ll.* 5–7), dated first/second century AD.

250. See Sharon Kelly Heyob, *The Cult of Isis Among Women in the Graeco-Roman World* (Études Préliminaires aux Religions Orientales dans L'Empire Romain, 51; Leiden: E.J. Brill, 1975) and R.E. Witt, *Isis in the Graeco-Roman World* (n.p.: Thames and Hudson, 1971).

251. Kent, *Corinth: The Inscriptions, 1926–1950*, no. 57, p. 33. Here Kent states, 'There were two temples of Isis and two of Serapis in Roman Corinth, all of them situated on the lower north slope of Acrocorinth (Pausanias 2.4.6), but the above text is the first epigraphical confirmation of the existence of the cults in Corinth. In line 2 the single letter V probably represents *v(ovit)*, though *v(ivens)* is also possible. The dedicator, C. Julius Syrus, is unknown. The lettering suggests a date near the middle of the first century after Christ'.

known inscriptions that devotion to Isis and Sarapis in the Peloponnese was only of a personal nature'.[252]

In New Testament studies, Elisabeth Schüssler Fiorenza connected Isis devotees to the problems of hair and head-covering in 1 Cor. 11.2–16.[253] R.E. Witt argues that the language of 1 Cor. 13 demonstrates Paul's familiarity with the Isiac religion.[254] Moreover, Richard Oster also shows important connections between Isis and 1 Corinthians.[255] The family concerns of Isis were important and are discussed by Heyob and Witt. The aretalogies demonstrate this interest. This understanding of Isis in 1 Cor. 4.6 merges with Paul's family language.

In the texts cited by Horsley, Hermes is the inventor of writing. Marrou notes that in the gymnasium inventory discovered on Delos there were 'forty-one Hermes in the same gymnasium'.[256] Barclay discusses the Jews who were ephebes in the city of Cyrene.[257] In the two lists of ephebes with Jewish names (late first century BC and the first century AD [3/4 AD]) each list is dedicated to the gods of the gymnasium, Hermes and Heracles. Thus the reference to writing in 1 Cor. 4.6 may have been connected by the elite in the church, those educated in the gymnasium, with the gods Isis and Hermes.

Within the education model, 1 Cor. 4.6 can be understood with Fitzgerald, and other scholars, as a reference to learning to write. There is no need to despair as Fee does. Mitchell's objection that she cannot locate it in the context of 1 Cor. 1–4, or see how the domestic image fits in with the conflict in the parallel clause: 'then you will not take pride in one man against another', can be answered. The context of 1 Cor. 1–4 is the educated elite and Paul's household imagery. Education is a privilege, and a source of boasting, for an elite family. The father, at least, is literate and elite children learn to write. To indicate that the educated elite need to

252. G.H.R. Horsley, 'Standing on Sacred Ground', in Horsley, *New Documents Illustrating Early Christianity*, 4, no. 25, pp. 105–12 (110). The Greek inscription is dated to the second century AD. The stele addresses the requirements for entering the sanctuary.

253. Elisabeth Schüssler Fiorenza, *In Memory of Her: A Feminist Theological Reconstruction of Christian Origins* (London: SCM Press, 1983), p. 227.

254. Witt, *Isis*, chapter xix 'The Pauline View', pp. 255–68. For example, he states, 'The triad of Christian virtues, Faith, Hope and Love, so eloquently praised in *Corinthians*, is introduced in such a way as to suggest that the writer of what is obviously an aretalogy is taking a close look at contemporary cults. He mentions the gift of tongues, a gift on which much stress is laid in the New Testament. The followers of Isis held that she controlled the various tongues, "dialects", that prevailed in the world' (p. 263).

255. Oster, 'Use, Misuse and Neglect of Archaeological Evidence in Some Modern Works on 1 Corinthians'. He considers Egyptian cults and religious celibacy as a background to 1 Cor. 7.1-5.

256. Marrou, *A History of Education in Antiquity*, pp. 392–93.

257. Barclay, *Jews in the Mediterranean Diaspora*, pp. 234–35.

behave like one learning to write is a put-down. They would be proud of their education that separated them socially from the non-elite in the church (cf. 4.7 where they boast over gifts). In Paul's reference to writing they would grasp the imagery which recognises their social advantages but cleverly uses this against them. This figure then further reinforces the previous statements on their childlikeness and their education.

Finally, Laurence Welborn has persuasively argued that in 1 Cor. 1–4 Paul is portraying himself in the role of the 'fool'. After noting Paul's language that Greeks seek wisdom (1.22) Welborn remarks, 'Those who embraced Hellenism, whether of Greek nationality or not, participated in a learned culture thorough philosophy, rhetoric and art as represented in the gymnasium, the assembly and the theatre'.[258] He thus finds Paul's use of the image of the 'fool' (μωρία) as derived from the Greek world of the theatre and the fool's role in the mime. Welborn notes that the very common meaning that most Greek readers in Paul's day (especially the learned) would see is the social type of 'the lower class buffoon'.[259] Welborn argues that Paul was labelled as a fool (in contrast to Apollos), but he gladly accepted this role like other intellectuals who used this strategy in the early empire. Thus he concludes that Paul used this familiar Greek image to write to the 'wealthy and cultured' Corinthian Christians, 'The fool that you laugh at in the mime of life, whose grotesque suffering is the source of amusement, whose death on a cross is a welcome reminder of what it is like to belong to the upper class – educated, unmaimed, independent – this crucified fool is the Son of God'.[260] Thus Paul is able to use this Greek image of 'fool' effectively with the educated. Welborn's argument coheres with the arguments I use in the application of my model. Paul knows his world well and uses his knowledge effectively in engaging with the educated elite.

5. *Circumcision (1 Corinthians 7.17–24)*

The final topic that I shall address in applying my ancient education model to the educated elite is the topic of circumcision. In 1 Cor. 7.18 Paul asks, 'Was anyone at the time of his call already circumcised? Let him not seek to remove the marks of circumcision' (NRSV). This issue is directly related to the Greek gymnasium and Greek athletics where men competed nude.[261]

258. Laurence L. Welborn, 'Μωρὸς γένεσθω: Paul's Appropriation of the Role of the Fool in 1 Corinthians 1–4', *BibInt* X (2002), pp. 420–35.

259. Welborn, 'Μωρὸς γένεσθω, p. 424.

260. Welborn, 'Μωρὸς γένεσθω, p. 434–35.

261. See, for example, Arieti, 'Nudity in Greek Athletics', cited earlier (ch. 5 n. 90) and my chapter 5.

Public exposure of the marks of circumcision may produce an unfavourable reaction and cause embarrassment. What could Jewish men do? We saw in chapter 3 that even devout Jews in the ancient world attended the Greek gymnasium. Moreover, this could be a route to social mobility. Would they have the marks of circumcision removed by an operation? Bruce Winter discusses this practice of epispasm (the operation for removing the effects of circumcision). He concludes that the evidence is clear:

> The purpose of reversing circumcision related to social standing in the Roman empire, and not simply to ridicule that might be experienced in the public baths or the gymnasium. The reason for young Jewish men, (presumably shared by their parents), wanting them to participate in the latter was not solely connected with athletics. It had to do with their status as *ephebi* and the career opportunities that higher education opened for them. Financial success and social status in the Roman world were much coveted, but Jewish Christians of the Diaspora were precluded by Paul from surrendering their national identity for personal advantage.[262]

These comments help to locate Paul's instruction in the world of the gymnasium.

Brad Braxton has more recently investigated, in detail, the connection of circumcision with both the gymnasium and the synagogue.[263] In his chapter 3 'Circumcision in the Greco-Roman World' he examines the reality of circumcision plus metaphorical and allegorical uses of the term. He uses this analysis in his exegesis of 1 Cor. 7.17–24 and notes that in Corinth there were probably many circumcised people but in all probability the passage refers to Jews.[264] He observes that Paul uses the 'technical medical term' (epispasm) for reversing circumcision. Why would a Jew wish the marks removed? The first option, according to Braxton, is so that the person would not be embarrassed while in the gymnasium he was exercising nude or relaxing in the baths. The second option is that the person wished to renounce his ethnicity and be assimilated into either Greek or Roman ethnicity.[265] Braxton draws upon the work of Allen

262. Winter, *Seek the Welfare of the City*, pp. 146–52 (152). In his chapter 8 'Social Mobility', Winter explores the background of (I) removal of the marks of circumcision, (II) seeking manumission, and (III) voluntary selling of oneself into slavery. He argues that in the three instances, 'the reason for doing this was to secure enhanced social status, with its attendant financial advantages' (p. 147). He concludes, 'Those Christians who yearned to join the "class" of the "wise, mighty and well-born" whose significance was most visible in the public place were forbidden to do so [by Paul]' (p. 164).

263. Braxton, *The Tyranny of Resolution*.

264. Braxton, *The Tyranny of Resolution*, p. 165.

265. Braxton, *The Tyranny of Resolution*, p. 166.

Kerkeslager who discusses a discourse in the gymnasium related to athletics and the reasons why someone might be disqualified from competing. It includes reference to a Jewish load, which refers to circumcision.[266] He cites Kerkeslager, 'Our text presents the rather ironic image of a Jew whose very devotion to an expression of Greek identity [i.e. gymnasium] makes his Jewish identity all the more inescapably obvious'.[267] After a useful discussion on the gymnasium and *ephebeia* as important features in the social life of the Graeco-Roman world Braxton sees that a Jewish man might wish to climb the social ladder. Removing the marks of circumcision via epispasm might provide the access to assist him.[268] Braxton sees in 1 Cor. 7.17–24 that a man may also wish to receive circumcision for full admission to the synagogue. He therefore observes that for Paul both actions are equivalent.[269] Braxton rightly asks a number of important questions including, 'Did the fledgling Christian community have enough tradition and stability to compete with the attractions of the gymnasium and the synagogue?'[270] His study reads Paul's passage sensitively in its first-century AD context and is a valuable contribution to my study. In his chapter's conclusions, Braxton writes, 'Two institutions, undoubtedly conspicuous features of the Corinthian landscape, came clearly into our view, the gymnasium and the synagogue. The weakness of my reading is one that is endemic to all socio-historical and social scientific exegesis. My reading depends substantially upon imaginative hypothesis'.[271] Nevertheless, I think that Braxton and Winter have clearly shown how in this passage Paul is addressing a current social issue which is access to the Greek gymnasium. Their studies, therefore, are embraced within my model.

It is true that Braxton's work assumes the presence of the gymnasium in Corinth when Paul wrote 1 Corinthians. He does not attempt to demonstrate its presence or cover in detail typical features of the gymnasium, although he helpfully addresses the *ephebeia* and social mobility. I trust that my study has been able to adequately address these gaps and support his argument.

266. Braxton, *The Tyranny of Resolution*, p. 167–68. He uses Kerkeslager, 'Maintaining Jewish Identity in the Greek Gymnasium'. Kerkeslager argues the text he discusses is dated between 20 BC to 41 AD (pp. 29–32).

267. Braxton, *The Tyranny of Resolution*, p. 169; citing Kerkeslager, 'Maintaining Jewish Identity in the Greek Gymnasium', p. 33.

268. Braxton, *The Tyranny of Resolution*, p. 169.

269. Braxton, *The Tyranny of Resolution*, p. 174–75.

270. Braxton, *The Tyranny of Resolution*, p. 175.

271. Braxton, *The Tyranny of Resolution*, p. 176.

6. *Summary*

In 'Agriculture and Education' (1 Cor. 3.5–9) I discussed how Paul's imagery refers to both the missionary work of establishing the church, and education, to speak directly to the educated elite. 'Disciplining with the Rod' (1 Cor. 4.21) appears to be a multifaceted image where Paul is the father and teacher. Beyond this I identified the discipline in the gymnasium and games. Here Paul is not explicit but appears to be acting as a gymnasiarch and athletics official. The educated elite as ephebes, or ex-ephebes, would recognise this imagery, as would other community members. The imagery is one of παιδεία as education, culture and discipline. Paul's emphasis, contra the educated, is not on success but their failure.

In 'The *Grammateus*' (1 Cor. 1.20) we saw how Pauline scholars sometimes restrict this to scholar/scribe. But the Corinthians would not see such a restriction. The γραμματεύς in the empire might be a civic leader of considerable status and this is consistent with Paul's criticism of these leaders in 1 Cor. 1–2 and of the educated elite in the Corinthian community. He may also be associated with both the ephebes and *neoi* in the gymnasium, as an instructor or within some other role. In the examples of civic leaders at Ephesus a person could be the *grammateus* and hold other important offices, such as gymnasiarch.

In contrast to the confusion evident in scholarship on 1 Cor. 4.6 the reference to ancient writing is particularly applicable to the educated elite for they were literate and their children would be educated. Most people in antiquity were illiterate. To tell them that they needed to learn to write again is Paul's deflationary technique for those who were accomplished in this area. In her major work on 1 Corinthians, Margaret Mitchell objects that she cannot see how this domestic image fits with the conflict expressed in not taking pride in one man against another. But this difficulty is resolved by the recognition that education was a status-determinant. Moreover, it is not entirely a domestic image for writing was taught away from home in schools and gymnasia. Those educated as ephebes would certainly be proud of their παιδεία. It is a reversal of the ideology of the elite identified by Kleijwegt with the *puer-senex* and παῖς τέλειος when elite children where often portrayed as adult intellectuals.

Finally, Paul's discussion in 1 Cor. 7.18, on not removing the marks of circumcision, can be read as a reference to Jews attending the gymnasium. The operation of epispasm may assist them in climbing the social ladder. Paul speaks against this practice.

In conclusion, my application of the ancient education model to these five topics, though not exhaustive, shows how the model offers valuable insights. It provides a coherent picture of Paul speaking to the church as a parent in a household. There is an emphasis on education and status. Yet the overall picture painted is one in which lack of maturity is evident and status reversal is portrayed. The educated elite are depicted, using the insights from Kleijwegt with the stereotype of the *puer-senex* and παῖς τέλειος, not as adult intellectuals, but as children who are still immature, and learning to write. In his discussion of the triad Paul shows the failure of the educated. The Corinthian educated elite appear to have failed just as worldly leaders have failed to understand God's ways revealed in the crucified Christ. Paul offers them more education and wisdom when he offers them the choice of the rod! Paul's discussion on not removing the marks of circumcision is located in circumcised Jewish men attending the gymnasium, which offered a route for social mobility. Removing the marks may enhance their access and chances for climbing the social ladder.

CONCLUSION

My study examines the educated elite in 1 Corinthians within their Graeco-Roman context. Contemporary New Testament exegetes demonstrate the important role of social-status disputes in the community conflicts that Paul addresses in his letter. These opponents occupy the apostle's attention throughout his correspondence. Pauline scholars frequently identify them as the 'educated elite' and seek to understand their interaction with Paul and the non-elite Christians. In their research they offer various social situations for understanding the mode of education and the mentality of these elite.

My social-scientific methodology reconstructs an ancient education model for the educated elite in first-century Corinth. This explicit model is an ancient education model, i.e., an education system that was used in antiquity. Modern Western educational systems are substantially different, in many ways, from those in the first-century eastern Mediterranean world where Paul is engaging his readers/hearers. Consequently, it is essential to carefully construct, from the data available, an accurate model of the Corinthian elite in Paul's community in order to be sensitive readers of his discourse.

The approach adopted considers claims that Corinth was a 'Roman' city, and therefore unrelated to Greek culture, as flawed. Although Corinth was a Roman colony this does not require New Testament scholars to purge, or ignore, its Greek culture. The constructed model recognises the city's Greek inheritance, and social environment, which the Christian community knew. It offers a different approach to the traditional three-stage, or two-stage, education models that scholars have uncritically applied to Corinth without understanding the limits of these models. Pauline scholarship frequently understands education as operating in uniformity, termed 'Graeco-Roman education.' This has resulted in oversight of the relevance of the Greek gymnasium where Greek *paideia* and physical education were taught. My work reflects the more recent recognition that ancient education had diversity.

In New Testament times, the Greek gymnasium was an exclusive education centre catering for the elite. Greeks, Romans, and Jews frequented the institution. The case of the Jew Philo, and others of his social class, demonstrate that loyal Jews could receive this valued education, which consisted of both intellectual and physical training. However, education was not provided free by the state and entrance to the gymnasium was restricted mainly to elite males. Within this structure, ephebic education was particularly valued, but youths and men continued to attend the gymnasia after they had completed ephebic training. Athletes trained in the gymnasium.

This education model exhibits features applicable to a more sensitive understanding of 1 Corinthians that previous models have overlooked. Moreover, the developed model includes the important social context of family, and society, in ancient education and provides a broader platform than previous models for examining the elite in Paul's letter. This social-scientific model is able to incorporate the insights from previous rhetorical studies in 1 Corinthians by Stephen Pogoloff, Duane Litfin, and Michael Bullmore, because rhetoric was taught in gymnasium education. Moreover, philosophers taught in the gymnasium, so elite Corinthian Christians would be familiar with various teachings even if they did not choose to study philosophy at the tertiary level.

The centrality of the gymnasia in Greek society is evident and the elite in the Corinthian church would value this education. The presence of the excavated gymnasium in Corinth shows that the Corinthians valued, and used, this institution. Furthermore, the circumstantial evidence for ephebic education in this civic gymnasium is good. In addition, mobility in the empire would ensure that elite males, educated in the gymnasia, would be resident in Corinth. It is reasonable to conclude that the educated elite in the church, whether Jews or gentiles, had access to and enjoyed a gymnasium education similar to other Corinthian elite families. Even youths and men were involved in the gymnasia, particularly its physical activities. But they could also attend visiting lectures. This analysis agrees with Bruce Winter's study that Paul's opponents in 1 and 2 Corinthians were those educated in Greek *paideia*. However, it differs from his analysis by focusing on acquiring *paideia* through gymnasium education and particularly ephebic training.

The application of the model to eight areas in 1 Cor 1–4; 7 and 9 demonstrates how it provides a more nuanced understanding of Paul's interaction with the educated elite. Suitable conclusions throughout the study mean it is superfluous to again summarise the outcome of the analysis. I show that throughout these passages Paul, as father, is concerned with treating them as children and disciplining them, in order that they reform their ways. Paul demonstrates familiarity with Greek *paideia* as education, culture and discipline. In the passages examined, Paul uses education language that would be familiar to the Corinthian Christians, especially to those who had received, and boasted, in their education as a status-determinant. The issue of circumcision appears related to social mobility via the gymnasium.

Like the secular educated elite Paul identifies in 1 Cor. 1–2, who fail to understand God's plan, the Corinthian elite had failed and boasted in their own achievements, rather than in Christ's. Their attitude and behaviour had caused conflict in the community. In the city they may be successful but in the church they are failures.

My analysis agrees with contemporary New Testament scholarship that sees social stratification within the church as a major factor in the community conflict. Paul cleverly speaks to a dual audience, both the educated elite and the non-elite, in 1 Corinthians. He uses the rhetorical strategy of status reversal in addressing the elite. This is evident when Paul opposes the ideology of the elite with his use of the *puer-senex* and παῖς τέλειος terminology identified by Kleijwegt.

Paul requires a radical reorientation from the elite who glory in their ephebic education. They cannot transfer the cultural values of *paideia* learnt in the gymnasium with its intellectual and physical conflict, set within its religious tradition, to their new faith. God's work through Christ has overthrown the understanding of the educated elite leaders of this age. The elite Corinthian Christians need to accept a new perspective, as children they need to learn from their father to behave in appropriate ways that do not cause factionalism in the community. Ephebic education, with its time-honoured status, as an elite system was in conflict with the ethos of the Pauline ἐκκλησία. Conflict in gymnasium and games, and education as a status-determinant, ran counter to the weakness that the apostle Paul portrays to the elite.

It is ironic that the weak Paul has to contend with the socially strong, the intellectual and physical athletes, and get them to adopt another perspective from the values they had learnt and cherished in their gymnasium education. The widespread use of body language in 1 Corinthians reflects the Greek gymnasium as an important institution with its elite ephebic education and exercise.

APPENDIX
TERMINOLOGY: THE GYMNASIUM AND THE PALAESTRA

John Townsend, discussing the role of the gymnasium in education during the Graeco-Roman period, remarks, 'The typical gymnasium generally contained a sand-covered courtyard (palaestra) for physical exercises and a stadium. In addition, the complex included a lecture hall and hot and cold baths, as well as rooms for storing oil and dust, for working out on the punching bag and for massage.'[1] His explanation states that the gymnasium contained both a palaestra and a stadium.

However, Frederick Beck comments that it is necessary to distinguish the palaestra from the gymnasium, which had as an essential feature a running track, and normally a public palaestra was included among its facilities. Yet, he notes, palaestrae could exist independently of the gymnasium.[2] On this issue Donald Kyle observes:

> Most scholars agree that the fully developed Greek gymnasium was a public facility for physical education, controlled by municipal officials and open to all citizens. A standard feature of any *polis*, the gymnasium consisted of a running track (*dromos*) and a wrestling ground (*palaestra*). With the addition of areas for changing, storage and bathing, the gymnasium was able to accommodate the many types of activity involved in Greek athletics and gymnastics.[3]

Kyle discusses problems of approach and terminology, including clarification of the terms 'gymnasium' and 'palaestra'. He notes that the etymological distinction between palaestra, as a ground where men wrestle, and the gymnasium, as a place where men strip naked for exercise, did not apply by classical times when the general distinction was between 'palaestra' as a wrestling school and 'gymnasium' as a gymnastic facility.[4] Even ancient sources, especially late Greek and Latin authors,

1. Townsend, 'Education (Greco-Roman Period),' p. 313.
2. Frederick A.G. Beck, *Greek Education 450 – 350 B.C.* (London: Methuen & Co Ltd, 1964), pp. 90–91.
3. Kyle, *Athletics in Ancient Athens*, p. 64.
4. Kyle, *Athletics in Ancient Athens*, p. 66.

unfortunately used the terms vaguely or interchangeably. This has resulted in modern confusion and debate. Kyle comments:

> Among scholars, Gardiner tries to distinguish between the gymnasium as a place and the *palaestra* as a building. Forbes argues that *palaestrae*, as wrestling schools for boys, were private, while gymnasia were large public edifices. The best discussion, that by Delorme, suggests that the ancients saw the terms as interchangeable, and that the only viable distinction is architectural. A gymnasium, comprising a *dromos* for track and field events plus a *palaestra* for contact sports, was a complete athletic facility; a *palaestra*, when it existed independently, could accommodate only contact sports. *Palaestrae* could be public or private, and could be used by men or boys.[5]

Furthermore, Stephen Glass considers the relationship of the gymnasium and palaestra and notes certain textbook distinctions:

1. The gymnasium is a public complex; the palaestra a private one.
2. The palaestra is intended to serve *paides*; the gymnasium is reserved for older groups.
3. The palaestra is a specialized and distinctive structure which is an integral part of any gymnasium but which can be an independent entity. A gymnasium cannot exist, however, without a palaestra.[6]

After examining the literary and epigraphic evidence for each distinction, Glass remarks:

> This would seem to indicate that the palaestra in a gymnasium tended to lose that nominal identity which it possessed as an independent structure.
>
> Structurally, then, a palaestra with facilities for running is a gymnasium. But even that description is something of an oversimplification in that these added facilities must have served not only runners but also those field events – discus and javelin – requiring more open space than a simple palaestra could provide.[7]

Thus Glass appears to reach similar conclusions to Kyle.[8]

5. Kyle, *Athletics in Ancient Athens*, pp. 66–67; citing E.N. Gardiner, *Greek Athletic Sports and Festivals* (London: Macmillan, 1910), pp. 467–68; Forbes, *Greek Physical Education*, pp. 76–82; Delorne, *Gymnasion*, p. 266.

6. Stephen L. Glass, 'The Greek Gymnasium: Some Problems', in Raschke (ed.), *The Archaeology of the Olympics*, pp. 155–73 (162).

7. Glass, 'Greek Gymnasium', p. 165.

8. See the short entry by Richard Allan Tomlinson, 'Palaestra', in Hornblower and Spawforth (eds.), *The Oxford Classical Dictionary*, p. 1099. He comments, 'The distinction is one of usage, rather than form.'

Clive Foss discusses inscriptions referring to the 'Αλειπτήριον (*aleipterion*) in Greek gymnasia and baths to identify the meaning of the term.[9] In earlier times it was a room where the body was anointed with oil.[10] Yet, he detects a change in meaning by the imperial period:

> With the establishment of the *pax romana* and the great current of cultural influences between east and west, the Greek gymnasium and baths underwent considerable change. The two gradually came to be combined into one monumental complex, the *thermae*. This incorporated an elaborate bathing establishment with the manifold aspects of the gymnasium: exercise, education, worship and social functions.[11]

On the texts known, Foss proposes that the word *aleipterion* be understood to mean the whole building or complex not just one room although he recognised that imperial texts could be discovered in which *aleipterion* may be just an 'anointing-room'.[12]

What was the situation for Roman Corinth? Jane Biers has examined the nine known baths in Roman Corinth and her Figure 18.1 'Plan of Corinth with locations of the Roman baths', shows them as distinct from the excavated gymnasium (which is located north of the forum near the city wall and next to the Asklepieion).[13] The earliest known Roman baths are Augustan (repaired in the first-century A.D.), others were built in the first or second centuries A.D. and the latest baths are assigned to the fifth and sixth centuries. The gymnasium is separate and not part of these bathing complexes.

9. Foss, ''Αλειπτήριον', pp. 217–26.
10. Foss, ''Αλειπτήριον', p. 222.
11. Foss, ''Αλειπτήριον', p. 222.
12. Foss, ''Αλειπτήριον', p. 226.
13. Jane Biers, '*Lavari est vivere*: Baths in Roman Corinth', in Williams and Bookidis (eds.), *Corinth: Corinth, The Centenary 1896–1996*, pp. 303–19 (304). She notes that there may be a tenth bath and two more Roman Baths were discovered after the Centennial symposium (p. 317). See my discussion in chapter 3 of the excavated Corinthian gymnasium.

Bibliography

Aasgaard, Reidar, 'Brotherhood in Plutarch and Paul: Its Role and Character', in Moxnes (ed.), *Constructing Early Christian Families'*, pp. 166–82.

—' "Role Ethics" in Paul: The Significance of the Sibling Role for Paul's Ethical Thinking', *NTS* 48 (2002), pp. 513–30.

—'*My Beloved Brothers and Sisters! Christian Siblingship in Paul* (JSNTSup, 265; London and New York: T & T Clark International, 2004).

Anderson, J.K., 'Corinth: Temple E Northwest, Preliminary Report, 1965', *Hesp* 46 (1977), pp. 1–12.

Arieti, James A., 'Nudity in Greek Athletics', *CW* (1975), pp. 431–36.

Arlandson, James Malcolm, *Women, Class and Society in Early Christianity: Models from Luke-Acts* (Peabody, MA: Hendrickson Publishers, 1997).

Asmis, Elizabeth, 'Basic Education in Epicureanism', in Too (ed.), *Education in Greek and Roman Antiquity*, pp. 209–39.

Atherton, Catherine, 'Children, Animals, Slaves and Grammar', in Too and Livingstone (eds.), *Pedagogy and Power*, pp. 214–44.

Attridge, Harold W., 'Review of Clarence E. Glad, *Paul and Philodemus: Adaptability in Epicurean and Early Christian Psychagogy', JBL* 116 (1997), pp. 376–77.

Bagnall, Roger and Peter Derow (eds.), *The Hellenistic Period: Historical Sources in Translation* (Oxford: Blackwell Publishing, 2nd edn, 2004).

Balch, David L., 'Rich Pompeiian Houses, Shops for Rent, and the Huge Apartment Building in Herculaneum as Typical Spaces for Pauline House Churches', *JSNT* 27 (2004), pp. 27–46.

Balland, André, *Fouilles de Xanthos*, Vol. 7, *Inscriptiones d'époque impériale du Létoon* (Patis: Klincksieck, 1981), pp. 185–214.

Barbour, Ian G., *Myths, Models and Paradigms: A Comparative Study in Science and Religion* (New York: Harper & Row, 1974).

Barclay, John M.G., 'Thessalonica and Corinth: Social Contrasts in Pauline Christianity', *JSNT* 47 (1992), pp. 49–74.

—'Paul among Diaspora Jews: Anomaly or Apostate?' *JSNT* 60 (1995), pp. 89–120.

—*Jews in the Mediterranean Diaspora: From Alexander to Trajan (323 BCE – 117 CE)* (Edinburgh: T. & T. Clark, 1996).

—'Poverty in Pauline Studies: A Response to Steven Friesen', *JSNT* 26 (2004), pp. 363–66.

Barnett, P.W., 'Paul, Apologist to the Corinthians', in Burke and Elliott (eds.), *Paul and the Corinthians*, pp. 313–26.

Barrett, C.K., *The New Testament Background: Selected Documents* (London: SPCK, 1956).

—*The First Epistle to the Corinthians* (London: A. & C. Black, 2nd edn, 1971).

—'Sectarian Diversity at Corinth' in Burke and Elliott (eds.), *Paul and the Corinthians*, pp. 287–302.

Barrett, Stanley R., *A Student's Guide to Theory and Method* (Toronto: University of Toronto Press, 1996).

Bartchy, S. Scott, 'Undermining Ancient Patriarchy: The Apostle Paul's Vision of a Society of Siblings', *BTB* 29 (1999), pp. 68–78.

Barton, Stephen C., 'Paul's Sense of Place: an Anthropological Approach to Community Formation in Corinth', *NTS* 32 (1986), pp. 225–46.

—(ed.), *The Family in Theological Perspective* (Edinburgh: T. & T. Clark, 1996).

—'Social Values and Structures', in Evans and Porter (eds.), *Dictionary of New Testament Background*, pp. 1127–34.

Baslez, M.-F., 'Citoyens et non-citoyens dans l'Athènes imperiale au Ier et au IIe siècles de notre ère', in Walker and Cameron (eds.), *The Greek Renaissance in the Roman Empire*, pp. 17–36.

Baur, Ferdinand Christian, 'Die Christuspartei in der korinthischen Geneinde, der Gegensatz des paulinischen und petrinischen Christentums in der ältesten Kirche, der Apostel Petrus in Rom', *Tübinger Zeitschift für Theologie* 4 (1831), pp. 61–206.

Beasley-Murray, P., 'Pastor, Paul as', in Hawthorne and Martin (eds.), *Dictionary of Paul and His Letters*', pp. 654–58.

Beck, in Hornblower and Spawforth (eds.), *The Oxford Classical Dictionary*.

Beck, Frederick A.G., *Greek Education 450 – 350 B.C.* (London: Methuen & Co Ltd., 1964).

Beck, Frederick A.G., and Rosalind Thomas, 'Education, Greek', in Hornblower and Spawforth (eds.), *The Oxford Classical Dictionary*, pp. 506–9.

Benko, Stephen and John J. O'Rourke (eds.), *The Catacombs and the Colosseum* (Valley Forge, PA: Judson Press, 1971).

—*Early Christianity: The Roman Empire as the Setting of Primitive Christianity* (London: Oliphants, 1972).

Berding, Kenneth, 'The Hermeneutical Framework of Social-Scientific Criticism: How much can Evangelicals get involved?' *EvQ* 75 (2003), pp. 3–22.

Betz, Hans Dieter, 'The Problem of Rhetoric and Theology according to the Apostle Paul', in Vanhoye (ed.), *L'Apôtre Paul: Personnalité, Style et Conception du Ministère*, pp. 16–48.

Biers, Jane, '*Lavari est vivere*: Baths in Roman Corinth', in Williams and Bookidis (eds.), *Corinth: Corinth, The Centenary 1896–1996*, pp. 303–19.

Billows, Richard, 'Cities', in Erskine (ed.), *A Companion to the Hellenistic World*, pp. 196–215.

Bitzer, Lloyd F., 'Functional Communication: A Situational Perspective', in White (ed.), *Rhetoric in Transition*, pp. 21–38.

Blasi, Anthony J., Jean Duhaime and Paul-André Turcotte (eds.), *Handbook of Early Christianity: Social Science Approaches* (Walnut Creek, CA: Altamira Press, 2002).

Blumenfeld, Bruno, *The Political Paul: Justice, Democracy and Kingship in a Hellenistic Framework* (JSNTSup, 210; Sheffield: Sheffield Academic Press, 2001).

Boardman, John, Jasper Griffin and Oswyn Murray (eds.), *The Oxford History of the Classical World* (Oxford and New York: Oxford University Press, 1986).

Bohak, Gideon, 'Recent Trends in the Study of Greco-Roman Jews', *CJ* 99 (2003/04), pp 195–202.

Bonner, Stanley F., *Education in Ancient Rome: From the Elder Cato to the Younger Pliny* (London: Methuen & Co Ltd., 1977).

Bonz, Marianne P., 'The Jewish Community of Ancient Sardis: A Reassessment of Its Rise to Prominence', *HSCP* 93 (1990), pp. 343–59.

Booth, Alan D., 'Punishment, Discipline and Riot in the Schools of Antiquity', *EMC* 17 (1973), pp. 107–14.

—'Elementary and Secondary Education in the Roman Empire', *Florilegium* 1 (1979), pp. 1–14.

—'The Schooling of Slaves in First-Century Rome', *TAPA* 109 (1979), pp. 11–19.

Bossman, David M., 'Paul's Fictive Kinship Movement', *BTB* 26 (1996), pp. 163–71.

Bowen, James, *A History of Western Education*. Vol. 1. *The Ancient World: Orient and Mediterranean 2000 B.C. – A.D. 1054* (London: Methuen & Co Ltd., 1972).

Bowersock, G.W., *Greek Sophists in the Roman Empire* (Oxford: Clarendon Press, 1969).

Bradley, Keith R., *Discovering the Roman Family: Studies in Roman Social History* (New York and Oxford: Oxford University Press, 1991).

Braxton, Brad Ronnell, *The Tyranny of Resolution. I Corinthians 7:17–24* (SBLDS, 181; Atlanta, GA: Society of Biblical Literature, 2000).

Brenner, Athalya and Carole R. Fontaine (eds.), *A Feminist Companion to Reading the Bible: Approaches, Methods and Strategies* (Sheffield: Sheffield Academic Press, 1997).

Briers, William R., and Daniel J. Geagan, 'A New List of Victors in the Caesarea at Isthmia', *Hesp* 39 (1970), pp. 79–93.

Broneer, Oscar, *Corinth: Terracotta Lamps* (ASCSA, 4.2; Cambridge, MA: Harvard University Press, 1930).

—*Corinth: The South Stoa and Its Roman Successors* (ASCSA, 1.4; Princeton, NJ: The American School of Classical Studies at Athens, 1954).

—'The Apostle Paul and the Isthmian Games', *BA* 25 (1962), pp. 2–31.

—'The Isthmian Victory Crown', *AJA* 66 (1962), pp. 259–63.

—'Paul and the Pagan Cults at Isthmia', *HTR* 64 (1971), pp. 169–87.

Brown, William P., *Character in Crisis: A Fresh Approach to the Wisdom Literature of the Old Testament* (Grand Rapids and Cambridge, UK: Eerdmans, 1996).

Brown, Colin (ed.), *The New International Dictionary of New Testament Theology* (4 vols.; Exeter: Paternoster; Grand Rapids, MI: Regency Reference Library, rev. edn, 1986).

Bruce, F.F., *The Acts of the Apostles: The Greek Text with Introduction and Commentary* (Leicester: Inter-Varsity Press, 2nd edn, 1976).

Bugh, Glenn R., 'An Emendation to the Prosopography of Roman Corinth', *Hesp* 48 (1979), pp. 45–53.

Bullmore, Michael A., *St. Paul's Theology of Rhetorical Style: An Examination of 1 Corinthians 2:1–5 in the Light of First-Century Rhetorical Criticism* (San Francisco: International Scholars Publications, 1995).

Burke, Trevor J., 'Review of H. Moxnes, ed., *Constructing Early Christian Families: Family as Social Reality and Metaphor', EvQ* 71 (1999), pp. 280–84.

—'Pauline Adoption: a Sociological Approach', *EvQ* 73 (2001), pp. 119–34.

—'Paul's Role as "Father" to his Corinthian "Children" in Socio-Historical Context (1 Corinthians 4:14–21)', in Burke and Elliott (eds.), *Paul and the Corinthians*, pp. 95–113.

—*Family Matters: A Socio-Historical Study of Kinship Metaphors in 1 Thessalonians* (JSNTSup, 247; London and New York: T & T Clark International, 2003).

Burke, Trevor J., and J. Keith Elliott (eds.), *Paul and the Corinthians: Studies on a Community in Conflict. Essays in Honour of Margaret Thrall* (NovTSup, 109; Leiden: Brill, 2003).

Büyükklolancı, Mustafa and Helmut Engelmann, 'Inschriften aus Ephesos', *ZPE* 86 (1991), pp. 137–44.

Callan, Terrance, *Psychological Perspectives on the Life of Paul: An Application of the Methodology of Gerd Theissen* (Studies in the Bible and Early Christianity, 22; Lewiston, Queenston and Lampeter: The Edwin Mellen Press, 1990).

Carter, Michael, 'A *Doctor Secutorum* and the *Retiarius* Draukos from Corinth', *ZPE* 126 (1999), pp. 262–68.

Carter, Timothy L., '"Big Men" in Corinth', *JSNT* 66 (1997), pp. 45–71.

Cartledge, Paul, and Antony Spawforth, *Hellenistic and Roman Sparta: A Tale of Two Cities* (London and New York: Routledge, 1989).

Cartledge, Paul, Paul Millett and Sitta von Reden (eds.), *Kosmos: Essays in Order, Conflict and Community in Classical Athens* (Cambridge: Cambridge University Press, 1998).

Casarico, L., 'Donne ginnasiraco', *ZPE* 48 (1982), pp. 117–23.

Chamoux, François, *Hellenistic Civilization* (trans. Michel Roussel in cooperation with Margaret Roussel; Oxford: Blackwell Publishing, 2003).

Cheung, Alex T., *Idol Food in Corinth: Jewish Background and Pauline Legacy* (JSNTSup, 176; Sheffield: Sheffield Academic Press, 1999).

Chow, John K., *Patronage and Power: A Study of Social Networks in Corinth* (JSNTSup, 75; Sheffield: JSOT Press, 1992).

Chrimes, K.M.T., *Ancient Sparta: A Re-examination of the Evidence* (Manchester: The University Press, 1949).

Cimok, Fatih, *Pergamum* (Istanbul: A Turizm Yayinlari, 1999).

Clarke, Andrew D., 'Another Corinthian Erastus Inscription', *TynBul* 42 (1991), pp. 146–51.

—*Secular and Christian Leadership in Corinth: A Socio-Historical and Exegetical Study of 1 Corinthians 1–6* (AGJU, 18; Leiden: E.J. Brill, 1993).

—*Serve the Community of the Church: Christians as Leaders and Ministers* (First-Century Christians in the Graeco-Roman World; Grand Rapids, MI and Cambridge, UK: Eerdmans, 2000).

Clarke, Donald Lemen, *Rhetoric in Greco-Roman Education* (New York: Columbia University Press, 1957).

Clarke, M.L., *Rhetoric at Rome: A Historical Survey* (London: Cohen & West, 1953).

—*Higher Education in the Ancient World* (London: Routledge & Kegan Paul, 1971).

Clay, Diskin, 'A Gymnasium Inventory from the Athenian Agora', *Hesp* 46 (1977), pp. 259–67.

Coffield, Frank and Bill Williamson (eds.), *Repositioning Higher Education* (Buckingham: SRHE and Open University Press, 1997).

Cohoon and Crosby.

Collins, John J., *Jewish Wisdom in the Hellenistic Age* (The Old Testament Library; Louisville, KY: Westminster John Knox Press, 1997).

Conley, Thomas, *'General Education' in Philo of Alexandria* (Hermeneutical Studies in Hellenistic and Modern Culture, 15; Berkeley: Center for Hermeneutical Studies in Hellenistic and Modern Culture, 1975).

Connolly, Joy, 'The Problems of the Past in Imperial Greek Education', in Too (ed.), *Education in Greek and Roman Antiquity*, pp. 339–72.

Conzelmann, Hans, *1 Corinthians* (trans. James W. Leitch; Hemeneia; Philadelphia: Fortress Press, 1975).

Corbeill, Anthony, 'Education in the Roman Republic: Creating Traditions', in Too (ed.), *Education in Greek and Roman Antiquity*, pp. 261–87.

Couslan, J.R.C., 'Athletics', in Evans and Porter (eds.), *Dictionary of New Testament Background*, pp. 140–42.

Craffert, Pieter F., 'Relationships between Social-Scientific, Literary, and Rhetorical Interpretation of Texts', *BTB* 26 (1996), pp. 45–55.

Cribiore, Raffaella, *Gymnastics of the Mind: Greek Education in Hellenistic and Roman Egypt* (Princeton and Oxford: Princeton University Press, 2001).

—'The Grammarian's Choice: The Popularity of Euripides' *Phoenissae* in Hellenistic and Roman Education', in Too (ed.), *Education in Greek and Roman Antiquity*, pp. 241–59.

Crowther, Nigel B., 'Nudity and Morality: Athletics in Italy', *CJ* 76 (1980–81), pp. 119–23.

—'Athletic Dress and Nudity in Greek Athletics', *Eranos* 80 (1982), pp. 163–68.

—'Studies in Greek Athletics, Part I', *CW* 78 (1985), pp. 497–558.

—'Studies in Greek Athletics, Part II', *CW* 79 (1985), pp. 73–135.

Dahl, Nils A., 'Paul and the Church at Corinth according to 1 Corinthians 1:10–4:21', in Farmer, Moule and Niebuhr (eds.), *Christian History and Interpretation*, pp. 313–35.

Daube, D., 'Paul a Hellenistic Schoolmaster?' in Loewe (ed.), *Studies in Rationalism, Judaism, and Universalism in Memory of Leon Roth*, pp. 67–71.

Davis, James A., *Wisdom and Spirit: An Investigation of 1 Corinthians 1.18–3.20 Against the Background of Jewish Sapiential Traditions in the Greco-Roman Period* (Lanham, MD: University Press of America, 1984).

Dean, Margaret E., 'Textured Criticism', *JSNT* 70 (1998), pp. 79–91.

Del Chiaro, Mario A. (ed.), *Corinthiaca: Studies in Honor of Darrell A. Amyx* (Columbia: University of Missouri Press, 1986).

Delorme, Jean, *Gymnasion. Étude sur les monuments consacrés à l'éducation en Grèce (des origines à l'Empire romain)* (BEFAR, 196; Paris: E. De Boccard, 1960).

Derrett, J. Duncan M., 'Paul as Master-builder', *EvQ* 69 (1997), pp. 129–37.

deSilva, David A., '"Worthy of His Kingdom": Honor Discourse and Social Engineering in 1 Thessalonians', *JSNT* 64 (1996), pp. 49–79.

—'"Let the One Who Claims Honor Establish That Claim in the Lord": Honor Discourse in the Corinthian Correspondence', *BTB* 28 (1998), pp. 61–74.

—*Honor, Patronage, Kinship & Purity: Unlocking New Testament Culture* (Downers Grove, IL: InterVarsity Press, 2000).

Dewey, Joanna, 'Textuality in an Oral Culture: a Survey of the Pauline Traditions', *Semeia* 65 (1994), pp. 37–65.

—'From Storytelling to Written Text: The Loss of Early Christian Women's Voices', *BTB* 26 (1996), pp. 71–78.

Dickie, M., 'Παλαιστρίτης/"palaestrita": Callisthenics in the Greek and Roman Gymnasium', *Nikephoros* 6 (1993), pp. 118–20.

Dillery, John, 'Ephebes in the Stadium (not the Theatre): *Ath. Pol.* 42.4 and *IG* II^2.351', *ClQ* 52 (2002), pp. 462–70.

Dio Chrysostom, Vol. III (trans. J.W. Cohoon and H. Lamar Crosby; LCL; London: William Heinemann Ltd; Cambridge, MA: Harvard University Press, 1946).

—Vol. IV (trans. H. Lamar Crosby; LCL; London: William Heinemann Ltd; Cambridge, MA: Harvard University Press, 1946).

Dodd, Brian, *Paul's Paradigmatic 'I': Personal Example as Literary Strategy* (JSNTSup, 177; Sheffield: Sheffield Academic Press, 1999).

Dow, Sterling, 'Corinthiaca', *HSCP* 53 (1942), pp. 89–119.

—'The Athenian *Epheboi*; Other Staffs, and the Staff of the *Diogeneion*', *TAPA* 91 (1960), pp. 381–409.

Downing, F. Gerald, *Cynics, Paul and the Pauline Churches* (London and New York: Routledge, 1998).

—'Paul's Drive for Deviants', *NTS* 49 (2003), pp. 360–71.

Duncan-Jones, R.P., 'Age-rounding, Illiteracy, and Social Differentiation in the Roman Empire', *Chiron* 7 (1977), pp. 333–53.

—'Age-rounding in Greco-Roman Egypt', *ZPE* 33 (1979), pp. 169–77.

Dunn, James D.G., *1 Corinthians* (New Testament Guides; Sheffield: Sheffield Academic Press, 1995).

—'Who Did Paul Think He Was? A Study of Jewish-Christian Identity', *NTS* 45 (1999), pp. 174–93.

Dutch, R.S., 'Pupils, Pedagogues and Paul: Education in the Greco-Roman World' (unpublished masters dissertation, University of Bristol, 1994).

Edwards, Katharine M., *Corinth: Coins, 1896–1929* (ASCSA, 6; Cambridge, MA: Harvard University Press, 1933).

Elliott, John H., *A Home for the Homeless: A Sociological Exegesis of 1 Peter, Its Situation and Strategy* (London: SCM Press, 1982).

—*Social-Scientific Criticism of the New Testament* (London: SPCK, 1995).

Engels, D., *Roman Corinth: An Alternative Model for the Classical City* (Chicago and London: The University of Chicago, 1990).

Epictetus, *The Discourses as Reported by Arrian, The Manual, and Fragments* (trans. W.A. Oldfather; LCL; 2 vols.; London: William Heinemann and New York: G.P. Putnam's Sons, 1926).

Eriksson, Anders, '"Women Tongue Speakers, Be Silent": A Reconstruction Through Paul's Rhetoric', *BibInt* 6 (1998), pp. 80–104.

Erskine, Andrew (ed.), *A Companion to the Hellenistic World* (Blackwell Companions to the Ancient World, Ancient History; Oxford: Blackwell Publishing, 2003).

Esler, Philip F., 'Glossolalia and the Admission of Gentiles into the Early Christian Community', *BTB* 22 (1992), pp. 136–42.

—*The First Christians in their Social Worlds: Social-Scientific Approaches to New Testament Interpretation* (London: Routledge, 1994).

—'Review of David G. Horrell, *The Social Ethos of the Corinthian Correspondence. Interests and Ideology from 1 Corinthians to 1 Clement*', *JTS* 49 (1998), pp. 253–60.

—'Introduction: Models, Context and Kerygma in New Testament Interpretation' in Esler (ed.), *Modelling Early Christianity*, pp. 1–20.

—'Models in New Testament Interpretation: A Reply to David Horrell', *JSNT* 78 (2000), pp. 107–13.

—(ed.), *Modelling Early Christianity: Social-Scientific Studies of the New Testament in Its Context* (London and New York: Routledge, 1995).

Evans, Craig A. and Stanley E. Porter (eds.), *Dictionary of New Testament Background* (Downers Grove, IL and Leicester, England: InterVarsity Press, 2000).

Eyben, Emiel, *Restless Youth in Ancient Rome* (trans. Patrick Daly; London: Routledge, 2nd rev. edn, 1993).

Fagan, Garrett G., 'Gifts of *gymnasia*: A Test Case for Reading Quasi-technical Jargon in Latin Inscriptions', *ZPE* 124 (1999), pp. 263–75.

Farmer, William Reuben, Charles Francis Digby Moule and Richard Reinhold Niebuhr (eds.), *Christian History and Interpretation: Studies Presented to John Knox* (Cambridge: Cambridge University Press, 1967).

Farrington, Andrew, 'Imperial Bath Buildings in South-West Asia Minor', in Macready and Thompson (eds.), *Roman Architecture in the Greek World*, pp. 50–59.

Fee, Gordon D., *The First Epistle to the Corinthians* (NICNT; Grand Rapids: Eerdmans, 1987).

Feldman, L.H., *Jew and Gentile in the Ancient World.* Attitudes and Interactions from Alexander to Justinian (Princeton: Princeton University Press, 1993).

Fentress, E. (ed.) *Romanization and the City: Creation, Transformation, and Failures* (JRA Suppl., 38; Portsmouth: R.I.: *Journal of Roman Archaeology*, 2000).

Finley, M.I., and H.W. Pleket, *The Olympic Games: The First Thousand Years* (London: Chatto & Windus Ltd., 1976).

Fiore, B., *The Function of Personal Example in the Socratic and Pastoral Epistles* (AnBib, 105; Rome: Biblical Institute Press, 1986).

Fisher, Nick, 'Gymnasia and the Democratic Values of Leisure', in Cartledge, Millett and von Reden (eds.), *Kosmos*, pp. 84–104.

Fitzgerald, John T., *Cracks in an Earthen Vessel: An Examination of the Catalogues of Hardships in the Corinthian Correspondence* (SBLDS, 99; Atlanta, GA: Scholars Press, 1988).

Forbes, Clarence Allen, *Neoi: A Contribution to the Study of Greek Associations* (Philological Monographs, 2; Middletown, CT: The American Philological Association, 1933).

—'Expanded Uses of the Greek Gymnasium', *CPhil* 40 (1945), pp. 32–42.

—'Crime and Punishment in Greek Athletics', *CJ* 47 (1951/52), pp. 169–73, 202–3.

—'The Education and Training of Slaves in Antiquity', *TAPA* 86 (1955), pp. 321–60.

—*Greek Physical Education* (New York and London: The Century Company, 1929. Reprint, New York: AMS Press, 1971).

Ford, Andrew, 'Sophists Without Rhetoric: The Arts of Speech in Fifth-Century Athens', in Too (ed.), *Education in Greek and Roman Antiquity*, pp. 85–109.

Forsell, Renée, 'The Argolid Countryside in the Roman Period', in Ostenfeld (ed.), *Greek Romans and Roman Greeks*, pp. 64–69.

Foss, Clive, ''Ἀλειπτήριον', *GRBS* 16 (1975), pp. 217–26.

Fox, Michael V., 'Ideas of Wisdom in Proverbs 1–9', *JBL* 116 (1997), pp. 613–33.

Francis, James, 'Children and Childhood in the New Testament', in Barton (ed.), *The Family in Theological Perspective*, pp. 65–85.

Freedman, David Noel (ed.), *The Anchor Bible Dictionary* (6 vols.; New York: Doubleday, 1992).

Friesen, Steven J., 'Poverty in Pauline Studies: Beyond the So-called New Consensus', *JSNT* 26 (2004), pp. 323–61.

Furnish, Victor Paul, *The Theology of the First Letter to the Corinthians* (New Testament Theology; Cambridge: Cambridge University Press, 1999).

Gallis, Kostas J., 'The Games in Ancient Larisa: An Example of Provincial Olympic Games', in Raschke (ed.), *The Archaeology of the Olympics*, pp. 217–35.

Gardiner, E.N., *Greek Athletic Sports and Festivals* (London: Macmillan, 1910).

Gardiner, E. Norman, *Athletics of the Ancient World* (Oxford: Clarendon Press, 1930).

Garrett, Susan R., 'Sociology (Early Christianity)', in Freedman (ed.), *The Anchor Bible Dictionary*, Vol. 6, pp. 89–99.

—'Paul's Thorn and Cultural Models of Affliction', in White and Yarbrough (eds.), *The Social World of the First Christians*, pp. 82–99.

Garrison, Roman, *The Graeco-Roman Context of Early Christian Literature* (JSNTSup, 13; Sheffield: Sheffield Academic Press, 1997).

Geagan, Daniel J., 'Notes on the Agonistic Institutions of Roman Corinth', *GRBS* 9 (1968), pp. 69–80.

Gebhard, Elizabeth R., 'The Sanctuary of Poseidon on the Isthmus of Corinth and the Isthmian Games', in Tzachou-Alexandri (ed.), *Mind and Body*, pp. 82–88.

—'The Isthmian Games and the Sanctuary of Poseidon in the Early Empire', in Gregory (ed.), *The Corinthia in the Roman Period*, pp. 78–94.

Gebhard, Elizabeth R., and Matthew W. Dickie, 'The View from the Isthmus, ca. 200 to 44 B.C.', in Williams and Bookidis (eds.), *Corinth: Corinth, The Centenary 1896–1996*, pp. 262–78.

Gill, David W.J., 'The Importance of Roman Portraiture for Head-Coverings in 1 Corinthians 11:2–16', *TynBul* 41 (1990), pp. 245–60.

—'In Search of the Social Élite in the Corinthian Church', *TynBul* 44 (1993), pp. 323–37.

—'Macedonia', in Gill and Gempf (eds.), *The Book of Acts in Its Graeco-Roman Setting*, Vol. 2, pp. 397–417.

Gill, David W.J., and Conrad Gempf (eds.), *The Book of Acts in Its Graeco-Roman Setting*, Vol. 2 (The Book of Acts in Its First Century Setting; Grand Rapids: Eerdmans; Carlisle: Paternoster, 1994).

Glad, Clarence E., *Paul and Philodemus: Adaptability in Epicurean and Early Christian Psychagogy* (NovTSup, 81; Leiden: E.J. Brill, 1995).

Glass, Stephen L., 'The Greek Gymnasium: Some Problems', in Raschke (ed.), *The Archaeology of the Olympics*, pp. 155–73.

Gooch, Peter D., *Dangerous Food. 1 Corinthians 8–10 in Its Context* (Studies in Christianity and Judaism, 5; Waterloo, ON: Wilfred Laurier University Press, 1993).

Gottwald, Norman K. (ed.), *The Bible and Liberation: Political and Social Hermeneutics* (Maryknoll, NY: Orbis Books, 1983).

Grant, R., *Paul in the Roman World: The Conflict at Corinth* (Louisville, KY: Westminster/John Knox, 2001).

Gregory, Timothy E., 'The Roman Bath at Isthmia: Preliminary Report 1972–1992', *Hesp* 64 (1995), pp. 279–313.

—(ed.), *The Corinthia in the Roman Period* (JRA Supp., 8; Ann Arbor, MI: Journal of Roman Archaeology, 1993).

Griffith, Mark, ' "Public" and "Private" in Early Greek Institutions of Education', in Too (ed.), *Education in Greek and Roman Antiquity*, pp. 23–84.

Grosheide, F.W., *The First Epistle to the Corinthians* (NICNT; Grand Rapids, MI: Eerdmans, 1953).

Gruen, Erich, S., *Diaspora: Jews Amidst Greeks and Romans* (Cambridge, MA and London: Harvard University Press, 2002).

— 'Jews and Greeks', in Erskine (ed.), *A Companion to the Hellenistic World*, pp. 264–79.

Guijarro, Santiago, 'The Family in First-Century Galilee', in Moxnes (ed.), *Constructing Early Christian Families*, pp. 42–65.

Gunderson, Erik, 'The Ideology of the Arena', *ClAnt* 15 (1996), pp. 113–51.

Gwynn, Aubrey, *Roman Education from Cicero to Quintilian* (Oxford: Clarendon, 1926).

Habicht, Christian, *Athens from Alexander to Antony* (trans. Deborah Lucas Schneider; Cambridge, MA and London: Harvard University Press, 1997).

—'Roman Citizens in Athens (228–31 B.C.)', in Hoff and Rotroff (eds.), *The Romanization of Athens*, pp. 9–17.

Hall, David R., 'A Disguise for the Wise: ΜΕΤΑΣΧΗΜΑΤΙΣΜΟΣ in 1 Corinthians 4.6', *NTS* 40 (1994), pp. 143–49.

—*The Unity of the Corinthian Correspondence* (JSNTSup, 251; London and New York: T & T Clark International, 2003).

Hammond, N.G.L., and H.H. Scullard (eds.), *The Oxford Classical Dictionary* (Oxford: Clarendon Press, 2nd edn, 1970).

Hanges, James C., '1 Corinthians 4:6 and the Possibility of Written Bylaws in the Corinthian Church', *JBL* 117 (1998), pp. 275–98.

Hanson, K.C., 'The Herodians and Mediterranean Kinship: Part I: Genealogy and Descent', *BTB* 19 (1989), pp. 75–84.

—'The Herodians and Mediterranean Kinship: Part 2: Marriage and Divorce', *BTB* 19 (1989), pp. 142–51.

—'The Herodians and Mediterranean Kinship: Part III: Economics', *BTB* 20 (1990), pp. 10–21.

—'BTB Readers Guide: Kinship', *BTB* 24 (1994), pp. 183–94.

Harland, Philip A., 'Connections with Elites in the World of the Early Christians', in Blasi, Duhaime and Turcotte (eds.), *Handbook of Early Christianity: Social Science Approaches*, pp. 385–408.

Harris, Gerald, 'The Beginnings of Church Discipline: 1 Corinthians 5', in Rosner (ed.), *Understanding Paul's Ethics*, pp. 129–51.

Harris, Harold Arthur, *Greek Athletes and Athletics* (London: Hutchinson & Co Ltd., 1964).

—*Sport in Greece and Rome* (London: Thames and Hudson, 1972).

—*Trivium, Greek Athletics and the Jews* (eds. I.M. Barton and A.J. Brothers; Cardiff: The University of Wales Press, 1976).

Harris, William V., *Ancient Literacy* (Cambridge, MA and London: Harvard University Press, 1989).

—'Literacy and Epigraphy I', *ZPE* 52 (1983), pp. 87–112.

Harrison, J.R., 'Benefaction Ideology and Christian Responsibility for Widows', in Llewelyn, *New Documents Illustrating Early Christianity*, 8, no. 7, pp. 106–16.

Hawthorne, Gerald F., and Ralph P. Martin (eds.), *Dictionary of Paul and His Letters* (Downers Grove, IL and Leicester, England: InterVarsity Press, 1993).

Hedrick Jr., Charles W., 'The American Ephebe: The Ephebic Oath, U.S. Education, and Nationalism', *CW* 97 (2004), pp. 384–407.

Hendrix, Holland, 'Benefactor/Patron Networks in the Urban Environment: Evidence from Thessalonica', *Semeia* 56 (1991), pp. 39–58.

Hengel, Martin, *Judaism and Hellenism: Studies in Their Encounter in Palestine During the Early Hellenistic Period* (2 vols.; trans. John Bowden; Philadelphia, PA: Fortress Press; London: SCM Press, 1974).

—*Jews, Greeks and Barbarians: Aspects of the Hellenization of Judaism in the Pre-Christian Period* (trans. John Bowden; London: SCM Press, 1980).

—*The 'Hellenization' of Judaea in the First Century After Christ* (London: SCM Press and Philadelphia: Trinity Press International, 1989).

Herbert, Sharon, 'The Torch-Race at Corinth', in Del Chiaro (ed.), *Corinthiaca*, pp. 29–35.

Herrmann, Klaus, 'Olympia: The Sanctuary and Contests', in Tzachou-Alexandri (ed.), *Mind and Body*, pp. 47–68.

Heyob, Sharon Kelly, *The Cult of Isis Among Women in the Graeco-Roman World* (Études Préliminaires aux Religions Orientales dans L'Empire Romain, 51; Leiden: E.J. Brill, 1975).

Hock, Ronald F., 'Paul's Tentmaking and the Problem of His Social Class', *JBL* 97 (1978), pp. 555–64.

—'The Workshop as a Social Setting for Paul's Missionary Preaching', *CBQ* 41 (1979), pp. 438–50.

Hodot, R., 'Décret de Kymè en l'honneur du prytane Kléanax', *Journal of the Paul Getty Museum* 10 (1982), pp. 165–80.

Hoff, Michael C., and Susan I. Rotroff (eds.), *The Romanization of Athens* (Oxbow Monograph, 94; Oxford: Oxbow Books, 1997).

Holman, Susan R., 'Molded as Wax: Formation and Feeding of the Ancient Newborn', *Helios* 24 (1997), pp. 77–95.

Holmberg, B., *Paul and Power: The Structure of Authority in the Primitive Church as Reflected in the Pauline Epistles* (Lund: Gleerup, 1978).

Hooker, M.D., ''Beyond the Things which are Written': An Examination of 1 Cor. iv.6', *NTS* 10 (1963), pp. 127–32.

—'Beyond the Things that are Written? St Paul's Use of Scripture', *NTS* 27 (1981), pp. 295–309.

Hornblower, Simon, and Antony J.S. Spawforth, 'Epheboi' in Hornblower and Spawforth (eds.), *The Oxford Classical Dictionary*, pp. 527–28.

Hornblower, Simon, and Antony Spawforth (eds.), *The Oxford Classical Dictionary* (Oxford: Oxford University Press, 3rd edn, 1996).

Horrell, David G., 'Review of Peter D. Gooch, *Dangerous Food: 1 Corinthians 8–10 in Its Context*', *JTS* 46 (1995), pp. 279–82.

—'Review of Dale B. Martin, *The Corinthian Body*', *JTS* 47 (1996), pp. 624–29.

—*The Social Ethos of the Corinthian Correspondence. Interests and Ideology from 1 Corinthians to 1 Clement* (Studies of the New Testament and Its World; Edinburgh: T. & T. Clark, 1996).

—'Models and Methods in Social-Scientific Interpretation: A Response to Philip Esler', *JSNT* 78 (2000), pp. 83–105.

—'Social Sciences Studying Formative Christian Phenomena: A Creative Movement', in Blasi, Duhaime and Turcotte (eds.), *Handbook of Early Christianity*, pp. 3–28.

—'Domestic Space and Christian Meetings at Corinth: Imaging New Contexts and the Buildings East of the Theatre', *NTS* 50 (2004), pp. 349–69.

Horsley, G.H.R., *New Documents Illustrating Early Christianity*, 1: *A Review of the Greek Inscriptions and Papyri Published in 1976* (North Ryde: Macquarie University, 1981).

—*New Documents Illustrating Early Christianity, 2: A Review of the Greek Inscriptions and Papyri Published in 1977* (North Ryde: Macquarie University, 1982).

—*New Documents Illustrating Early Christianity, 3: A Review of the Greek Inscriptions and Papyri Published in 1978* (North Ryde: Macquarie University, 1983).

—*New Documents Illustrating Early Christianity, 4: A Review of the Greek Inscriptions and Papyri Published in 1979* (NSW: Macquarie University, 1987).

—'A Personalised Aretalogy of Isis', in Horsley, *New Documents Illustrating Early Christianity*, 1, no. 2, pp. 10–21.

—'Epitaph for a Jewish Psalm-singer', in Horsley, *New Documents Illustrating Early Christianity*, 1, no. 74, pp. 115–17.

—'A Gymnasiarchal Law from Beroia', in Horsley, *New Documents Illustrating Early Christianity*, 2, no. 82, pp. 104–5.

—'Wise beyond her years ...', in Horsley, *New Documents Illustrating Early Christianity*, 3, no. 13, pp. 46–47.

—' "... in memory of her" ', in Horsley, *New Documents Illustrating Early Christianity*, 4, no. 2, pp. 10–17.

—'Dearer than my mother...', in Horsley, *New Documents Illustrating Early Christianity*, 4, no. 9, pp. 33–35.

—'Standing on Sacred Ground', in Horsley, *New Documents Illustrating Early Christianity*, 4, no. 25, pp. 105–12.

'Review of Sjef van Tilborg, *Reading John in Ephesus*', *JTS* 49 (1998), pp. 265–73.

Horsley, Richard A., 'Pneumatikos vs. Psychikos: Distinctions of Spiritual Status Among the Corinthians', *HTR* 69 (1976), pp. 269–88.

—'Wisdom of Words and Words of Wisdom in Corinth', *CBQ* 39 (1977), pp. 224–39.

—' "How can some of you say that there is no resurrection of the dead?" Spiritual Elitism in Corinth', *NovT* 20 (1978), pp. 203–31.

—'Gnosis in Corinth: 1 Corinthians 8.1–6', *NTS* 27 (1980), pp. 32–51.

Hurd J., John C., *The Origin of 1 Corinthians* (London: SPCK, 1965).

Janowitz, Naomi, 'Rethinking Jewish Identity in Late Antiquity', in Mitchell and Greatrex (eds.), *Ethnicity and Culture in Late Antiquity*, pp. 205–19.

Jones, A.H.M., *The Greek City from Alexander to Justinian* (Oxford: Clarendon Press, 1940).

—*The Greek City from Alexander to Justinian* (Oxford: Clarendon Press, 2nd ed., 1979).

Jones, A.H.M., and P.J. Rhodes, 'Liturgy, *Greek*', in Hornblower and Spawforth (eds.), *The Oxford Classical Dictionary*, p. 875.

Jones, C.P., 'Atticus in Ephesus', *ZPE* 124 (1999), pp. 89–94.

Jongkind, Dirk, 'Corinth in the First Century AD: The Search for Another Class', *TynBul* 52 (2001), pp. 139–48.

Jordan, David R., 'Inscribed Lead Tablets from the Games in the Sanctuary of Poseidon', *Hesp* 63 (1994), pp. 111–26.

Jordan, D.R., and A.J.S. Spawforth, 'A New Document from the Isthmian Games', *Hesp* 51 (1982), pp. 65–68.

Joubert, Stephan J., 'Managing the Household: Paul as *Paterfamilias* of the Christian Household Group in Corinth', in Esler (ed.), *Modelling Early Christianity*, pp. 213–23.

—'One Form of Exchange or Two? "Euergetism," Patronage, and Testament Studies', *BTB* 31 (2001), pp. 17–25.

Judge, Edwin A., 'The Reaction Against Classical Education in the New Testament', *JCE* 77 (1983), pp. 7–14.

Kajava, Mika, 'When did the Isthmian Games Return to the Isthmus? (Rereading Corinth 8.3.153)', *CPhil* 97 (2002), pp. 168–78.

Kakarouga-Stassinopoulou, Elisabeth, Rosa Proskynitopoulou, and Stavroula Papadiamantopoulou-Kalliodi, 'The Events', in Tzachou-Alexandri (ed.), *Mind and Body*, pp. 97–104.

Kasher, A., 'The Jewish Attitude to the Alexandrian Gymnasium in the First Century A.D.', *AJAH* 1 (1976), pp. 148–61.

Kaster, Robert A., 'Notes on "Primary" and "Secondary" Schools in Late Antiquity', *TAPA* 113 (1983), pp. 323–46.

—'Controlling Reason: Declamation in Rhetorical Education at Rome' in Too (ed.), *Education in Greek and Roman Antiquity*, pp. 317–37.

Kearsley, R.A., 'Some Asiarchs of Ephesos', in Horsley, *New Documents Illustrating Early Christianity*, 4, no. 14, pp. 46–55.

—'Women in Public Life', in Llewelyn and Kearsley, *New Documents Illustrating Early Christianity*, 6, no. 3, pp. 24–27.

—'A Civic Benefactor of the First Century in Asia Minor,' in Llewelyn and Kearsley, *New Documents Illustrating Early Christianity*, 7, no. 10, pp. 233–41.

—'Women in Public Life in the Roman East: Iunia Theodora, Claudia Metrodora and Phoebe, Benefactress of Paul', *TynBul* 50 (1999), pp. 189–211.

—'Ephesus and Sardis Compete for the Cult of Caracalla', in Llewelyn, *New Documents Illustrating Early Christianity*, 9, no. 12, pp. 27–31.

Kennedy, George A., *Classical Rhetoric and Its Christian and Secular Traditions from Ancient to Modern Times* (Chapel Hill: University of North Carolina, 1984).

Kennell, Nigel M., *The Gymnasium of Virtue: Education and Culture in Ancient Sparta* (Chapel Hill, NC and London: The University of North Carolina Press, 1995).

Kent, John Harvey, *Corinth: The Inscriptions, 1926–1950* (ASCSA, 8.3; Princeton, NJ: The American School of Classical Studies at Athens, 1966).

Ker, Donald P., 'Paul and Apollos – Colleagues or Rivals?' *JSNT* 77 (2000), pp. 75–97.

Kerkeslager, Allen, 'Maintaining Jewish Identity in the Greek Gymnasium: A Jewish "Load" in CPJ 3.519' *JSJ* XXVIII (1997), pp. 12–33.

King, Fergus F., 'Eating in Corinth: Full Meal or Token Meal?' *IBS* 19 (1997), pp. 161–73.

Kinman, Brent, '"Appoint the Despised as Judges!" (1 Corinthians 6:4)', *TynBul* 48 (1997), pp. 345–54.

Kinneavy, James L., *Greek Rhetorical Origins of Christian Faith: An Inquiry* (Oxford: Oxford University Press, 1987).

Klaus, Herrmann, 'Olympia: The Sanctuary and Contests', in Tzachou-Alexandri (ed.), *Mind and Body*, pp. 47–68.

Kleijwegt, Marc, *Ancient Youth: The Ambiguity of Youth and the Absence of Adolescence in Greco-Roman Society* (Dutch Monographs on Ancient History and Archaeology, 8; Amsterdam: J.C. Gieben, Publisher, 1991).

Kleiner, D., 'Women and Family Life on Roman Funerary Altars', *Latomus* 46 (1987), pp. 545–55.

Klutz, Todd E., 'Re-Reading 1 Corinthians after *Rethinking "Gnosticism"*', *JSNT* 26 (2003), pp. 193–216.

König, Jason, 'Favorinus' *Corinthian Oration* in its Corinthian Context', *PCPS* 47 (2001), pp. 141–71.

Kreitzer, L.J., 'Coinage: Greco-Roman', in Evans and Porter (eds.), *Dictionary of New Testament Background*, pp. 220–22.

Kuck, David W., *Judgment and Community Conflict. Paul's Use of Apocalyptic Judgment Language in 1 Corinthians 3:5–4:5* (NovTSup, 66; Leiden: E.J. Brill, 1992).

Kyle, Donald G., *Athletics in Ancient Athens* (Leiden: E.J. Brill, 1987).
Lake, Kirsopp (trans.), *The Apostolic Fathers*, Vol. I (LCL; London: William Heinemann; New York: The Macmillan Co., 1912).
Lampe, Peter, 'The Eucharist: Identifying with Christ on the Cross', *Int* 48 (1994), pp. 36–49.
Lanci, John R., *A New Temple for Corinth: Rhetorical and Archaeological Approaches to Pauline Imagery* (Studies in Biblical Literature, 1; New York: Peter Lang, 1997).
Lane Fox, Robin, *Pagans and Christians* (London and Harmondsworth: Viking, 1986).
—'Hellenistic Culture and Literature' in Boardman, Griffin and Murray (eds.), *The Oxford History of the Classical World*, pp. 338–64.
Lassen, Eva Marie, 'The Use of the Father Image in Imperial Propaganda and 1 Corinthians 4:14–21', *TynBul* 42 (1991), pp. 127–36.
—'The Roman Family: Ideal and Metaphor', in Moxnes (ed.), *Constructing Early Christian Families*, pp. 103–20.
Lefkowitz, Mary R., 'The Poet as Athlete', *JSH* 11 (1984), pp. 18–24.
Legault, A., 'Beyond the Things which are Written (1 Cor. iv.6), *NTS* 18 (1971), pp. 227–31.
Lemaire, André, 'Education (Ancient Israel)' in Freedman (ed.), *The Anchor Bible Dictionary*, Vol. 2, pp. 305–12.
Levi, Peter, *Atlas of the Greek World* (Oxford: Phaidon, 1984).
Lewis, Naphtali, 'The New Evidence on the Privileges of the Gerousiasts of Ephesos', *ZPE* 131 (2000), pp. 99–100.
Lightfoot, J.B., *Notes on Epistles of St. Paul from Unpublished Commentaries* (London and New York: Macmillan, 1895).
Lim, T.H., ''Not in Persuasive Words of Wisdom, But in the Demonstration of the Spirit and Power' (I Cor. 2:4)', *NovT* 29 (1987), pp. 137–49.
Litfin, Duane, *St. Paul's Theology of Proclamation: 1 Corinthians 1–4 and Greco-Roman Rhetoric* (SNTSMS, 79; Cambridge: Cambridge University Press, 1994).
—'Review of Michael A. Bullmore, *St. Paul's Theology of Rhetorical Style: An Examination of 1 Corinthians 2:1–5 in the Light of First-Century Rhetorical Criticism', JBL* 116 (1997), pp. 568–70.
Livingstone, Niall, 'The Voice of Isocrates and the Dissemination of Cultural Power', in Too and Livingstone (eds.), *Pedagogy and Power*, pp. 263–81.
Llewelyn, S.R., 'The Epitaph of a Student Who Died Away from Home', in Llewelyn, *New Documents Illustrating Early Christianity*, 8, no. 8, pp. 117–21.
—'The Sale of a Slave-Girl: The New Testament's Attitude to Slavery', in Llewelyn and Kearsley, *New Documents Illustrating Early Christianity*, 6, no. 6, pp. 48–55.
—'The Preservation of Status and its Testing', in Llewelyn and Kearsley, *New Documents Illustrating Early Christianity*, 6, no. 17, pp. 132–40.
—*New Documents Illustrating Early Christianity*, 8: *A Review of the Greek Inscriptions and Papyri Published in 1984–85* (NSW: Macquarie University; Grand Rapids and Cambridge, UK: Eerdmans, 1997).

— *New Documents Illustrating Early Christianity*, 9: *A Review of the Greek Inscriptions and Papyri Published in 1986–87* (NSW: Macquarie University; Grand Rapids and Cambridge, UK: Eerdmans, 2002).

Llewelyn, S.R., and R.A. Kearsley, *New Documents Illustrating Early Christianity*, 6: *A Review of the Greek Inscriptions and Papyri Published in 1980–81* (NSW: Macquarie University, 1992).

—*New Documents Illustrating Early Christianity*, 7: *A Review of the Greek Inscriptions and Papyri Published in 1982–83* (NSW: Macquarie University, 1994).

Loewe, R. (ed.), *Studies in Rationalism, Judaism and Universalism in Memory of Leon Roth* (London: Routledge and Kegan Paul, 1966).

Longenecker, Richard N., 'The Pedagogical Nature of the Law in Galatians 3:19–4:7', *JETS* 25 (1982), pp. 53–61.

Lucian, Vol. III (trans. A.M. Harmon; LCL; London: William Heinemann and New York: G.P. Putnam's Sons, 1921).

Lull, David J., '"The Law Was Our Pedagogue": A Study in Galatians 3:19–25', *JBL* 105 (1986), pp. 481–98.

Macready and Thompson (eds.), *Roman Architecture in the Greek World.*

Malherbe, Abraham J., '"Gentle as a Nurse": The Cynic Background to 1 Thess ii', *NovT* 12 (1970), pp. 203–17.

—*Social Aspects of Early Christianity* (Philadelphia, PA: Fortress Press, 2nd edn, enl., 1983).

—'Exhortation in First Thessalonians', *NovT* 25 (1983), pp. 243–45.

—*Paul and the Thessalonians: The Philosophic Tradition of Pastoral Care* (Philadelphia, PA: Fortress Press, 1987).

—*Paul and The Popular Philosophers* (Minneapolis, MN: Fortress Press, 1989).

Malina, Bruce J., 'The Social Sciences and Biblical Interpretation', in Gottwald (ed.), *The Bible and Liberation*, pp. 11–25.

—'Reading Theory Perspective: Reading Luke-Acts', in Neyrey (ed.), *The Social World of Luke-Acts*, pp. 3–23.

—*The Social World of Jesus and the Gospels* (London and New York: Routledge, 1996).

Malina, Bruce J., and Richard L. Rohrbaugh, *Social-Science Commentary on the Synoptic Gospels* (Minneapolis, MN: Fortress Press, 1992).

Marrou, H.-I., *A History of Education in Antiquity* (trans. George Lamb; London and New York: Sheed and Ward, 1956).

—*Histoire de l'éducation dans l'antiquité* (Paris, 1965).

—*A History of Education in Antiquity* (trans. George Lamb; London and New York: Sheed and Ward, 1956. Second Impression, 1977).

Marsh, Clive, '"Who are you for?" 1 Corinthians 1:10–17 as Christian Scripture in the Context of Diverse Methods of Reading', in Burke and Elliott (eds.), *Paul and the Corinthians*, pp. 157–76.

Marshall, Peter, *Enmity in Corinth: Social Conventions in Paul's Relations with the Corinthians* (Tübingen: J.C.B. Mohr [Paul Siebeck], 1987).

Martin, Ralph P., *2 Corinthians* (WBC, 40; Waco, TX: Word Books, 1986).

Martin, Dale B., *Slavery as Salvation: The Metaphor of Slavery in Pauline Christianity* (New Haven and London: Yale University Press, 1990).

—'Tongues of Angels and Other Status Indicators', *JAAR* 59 (1991), pp. 547–89.

—'Social-Scientific Criticism', in McKenzie and Haynes (eds.), *To Each Its Own Meaning*, pp. 103–19.

—*The Corinthian Body* (New Haven and London: Yale University Press, 1995).

—'The Construction of the Ancient Family: Methodological Considerations', *JRS* 86 (1996), pp. 40–60.

Martin, Thomas R., 'Inscriptions at Corinth', *Hesp* 46 (1977), pp. 178–98.

McDonnell, Myles, 'Writing, Copying and Autograph Manuscripts in Ancient Rome', *ClQ* 46 (1996), pp. 469–91.

McKenzie, Steven L., and Stephen R. Haynes (eds.), *To Each Its Own Meaning: An Introduction to Biblical Criticisms and Their Application* (London: Geoffrey Chapman, 1993).

McNelis, Charles, 'Greek Grammarians and Roman Society During the Early Empire: Statius' Father and His Contemporaries', *ClAnt* 21 (2002), pp. 67–94.

Meeks, Wayne A., *The First Urban Christians: The Social World of the Apostle Paul* (New Haven and London: Yale University Press, 1983).

—*The First Urban Christians: The Social World of the Apostle Paul* (New Haven and London: Yale University Press, 2nd edn, 2003).

Meggitt, Justin J., 'Meat Consumption and Social Conflict in Corinth', *JTS* 45 (1994), pp. 137–41.

—*Paul, Poverty and Survival* (Studies of the New Testament and Its World; Edinburgh: T. & T. Clark, 1998).

Mendelson, Alan, *Secular Education in Philo of Alexandria* (Monographs of the Hebrew Union College, 7; Cincinnati, OH: Hebrew Union College Press, 1982).

Meritt, Benjamin Dean, *Corinth: Greek Inscriptions, 1896–1927* (ASCSA, 8.1; Cambridge, MA: Harvard University Press, 1931).

Meritt, B.D., 'Greek Inscriptions', *Hesp* 29 (1960), pp. 1–77.

Millar, Fergus, 'Review of L.H. Feldman, *Jew and Gentile in the Ancient World. Attitudes and Interactions from Alexander to Justinian*', *CR* 45 (1995), pp. 117–19.

Miller, Stephen G., *Arete: Greek Sports from Ancient Sources* (Berkeley, Los Angeles and Oxford: University of California Press, 2nd edn, 1991).

—'Nemea and the Nemean Games', in Tzachou-Alexandri (ed.), *Mind and Body*, pp. 87–96.

Mitchell, Alan C., 'Rich and Poor in the Courts of Corinth: Litigiousness and Status in 1 Corinthians 6.1–11', *NTS* 39 (1993), pp. 562–86.

Mitchell, Margaret M., *Paul and the Rhetoric of Reconciliation: An Exegetical Investigation of the Language and Composition of 1 Corinthians* (Louisville, KY: Westminster/John Knox Press, 1992).

Mitchell, Stephen, 'Festivals, Games, and Civic Life in Roman Asia Minor', *JRS* 80 (1990), pp. 183–93.

—'Ethnicity, Acculturation and Empire in Roman and Late Roman Asia Minor', in Mitchell and Greatrex (eds.), *Ethnicity and Culture in Late Antiquity*, pp. 117–50.

Mitchell, Stephen and Geoffrey Greatrex (eds.), *Ethnicity and Culture in Late Antiquity* (London: Duckworth; Swansea: The Classical Press of Wales, 2000).

Moretti, Jean-Charles, 'Le gymnase de Délos', *BCH* 120 (1996), pp. 617–38.

Morgan, Teresa, *Literate Education in the Hellenistic and Roman Worlds* (Cambridge Classical Studies; Cambridge: Cambridge University Press, 1998).
—'Literate Education in Classical Athens', *ClQ* 49 (1999), pp. 46–61.
—'A Good Man Skilled in Politics: Quintilian's Political Theory', in Too and Livingstone (eds.), *Pedagogy and Power*, pp. 245–62.
—'Legal Instructions in Classical Athens', in Too (ed.), *Education in Greek and Roman Antiquity*, pp. 111–32.
Morris, Leon, *The First Epistle of Paul to the Corinthians* (Grand Rapids, MI: Eerdmans; Leicester: Intervarsity Press, 2nd edn, 1985).
Moss, Alan, 'Wisdom as Parental Teaching in Proverbs 1–9', *HeyJ* 38 (1997), pp. 426–39.
Moxnes, Halvor, 'Introduction', in Moxnes (ed.), *Constructing Early Christian Families*, pp. 1–9.
—'What is Family? Problems in Constructing Early Christian Families', in Moxnes (ed.), *Constructing Early Christian Families*, pp. 13–41.
—(ed.), *Constructing Early Christian Families: Family as Social Reality and Metaphor* (London and New York: Routledge, 1997).
Muir, J.V., 'Education, Roman', in Hornblower and Spawforth (eds.), *The Oxford Classical Dictionary*, pp. 509–10.
Munck, Johannes, *Paul and the Salvation of Mankind* (London: SCM Press, 1959).
Murphy-O'Connor, Jerome, *St. Paul's Corinth: Texts and Archaeology* (Good News Studies 6; Wilmington, DE: Michael Glazier, Inc., 1983).
—'The Corinth that Saint Paul Saw', *BA* 47 (1984), pp. 147–59.
—*Paul: A Critical Life* (Oxford: Clarendon Press, 1996).
Myrick, Anthony A., ' "Father" Imagery in 2 Corinthians 1–9 and Jewish Paternal Tradition', *TynBul* 47 (1996), pp. 163–71.
National Committee of Inquiry into Higher Education, *Higher Education in the Learning Society* (London: HMSO, 1997).
Nel, P., 'The Concept of "Father" in the Wisdom Literature of the Ancient Near East', *JNSL* 5 (1977), pp. 53–66.
Neyrey, Jerome H., 'Body Language in 1 Corinthians: The Use of Anthropological Models for Understanding Paul and His Opponents', *Semeia* 35 (1986), pp. 129–70.
—(ed.), *The Social World of Luke-Acts: Models for Interpretation* (Peabody, MA: Hendrickson Publishers, 1991).
Newton, Derek, *Deity and Diet: The Dilemma of Sacrificial Food at Corinth* (JSNTSup, 169; Sheffield: Sheffield Academic Press, 1998).
Nightingale, Andrea Wilson, 'Liberal Education in Plato's *Republic* and Aristotle's *Politics*', in Too (ed.), *Education in Greek and Roman Antiquity*, pp. 133–73.
Nijf, Onno M. van, *The Civic World of Professional Associations in the Roman East* (Dutch Monographs on Ancient History and Archaeology, 17; Amsterdam: J.C. Gieben, Publisher, 1997).
Nolland, John, 'Review of *The Social World of Luke-Acts: Models for Interpretation*, edited by Jerome H. Neyrey', *EvQ* 66 (1994), pp. 81–87.
Noy, D., 'Inscriptions and Papyri: Jewish', in Evans and Porter (eds.), *Dictionary of New Testament Background*, pp. 539–41.

Oakes, Peter, 'Review of Philip F. Esler, ed., *Modelling Early Christianity. Social-scientific Studies of the New Testament in its Context*', *JTS* 49 (1998), pp. 281–84.

—'Constructing Poverty Scales for Graeco-Roman Society: A Response to Steven Friesen's "Poverty in Pauline Studies"', *JSNT* 26 (2004), pp. 367–71.

Ober, Josiah, 'The Debate Over Civic Education in Classical Athens', in Too (ed.), *Education in Greek and Roman Antiquity*, pp. 175–207.

Oldfather, W.A. (trans.), *Epictetus: The Discourses as Reported by Arrian, The Manual, and Fragments*, Vol. I (LCL; London: William Heinemann; New York: G.P. Putman's Sons, 1926).

Oliver, James H., 'Arrian in Two Roles' in *The Civic Tradition and Roman Athens*, pp. 66–75.

Oliver, James H., 'Arrian and the Gellii of Corinth', *GRBS* 11 (1970), pp. 335–37.

—*The Civic Tradition and Roman Athens* (Baltimore and London: The John Hopkins University Press, 1983).

Osiek, Carolyn, 'The Family in Early Christianity: "Family Values" Revisited', *CBQ* 58 (1996), pp. 1–24.

Osiek, Carolyn, and David L. Balch, *Families in the New Testament World: Households and House Churches* (The Family, Religion, and Culture; Louisville, KY: Westminster John Knox Press, 1997).

Ostenfeld, Erik Nis (ed.) with the assistance of Karin Blomqvist and Lisa Nevett, *Greek Romans and Roman Greeks: Studies in Cultural Interaction* (ASMA, III; Aarhus: Aarhus University Press, 2002).

Oster, Richard E., 'Use, Misuse and Neglect of Archaeological Evidence in Some Modern Works on 1 Corinthians', *ZNW* 83 (1992), pp. 52–73.

Padgett, Alan, 'Paul on Women in the Church: The Contradictions of Coiffure in 1 Corinthians 11.2–16', *JSNT* 20 (1984), pp. 69–86.

Panagopoulos, C., 'Vocabulaire et mentalité dans les Moralia de Plutarque', *DHA* 3 (1977), pp. 197–237.

Papathomas, Amphilochios, 'Das agonistische Motiv 1Kor 9.24ff. im Spiegel zeitgenössischer dokumentarischer Quellen', *NTS* 43 (1997), pp. 223–41.

Pausanias, *Description of Greece*, Vol. I (trans. W.H.S. Jones; LCL; London: William Heinemann Ltd; New York: G.P. Putnam's Sons, 1918).

Pearson, Birger Albert, *The Pneumatikos-Psychikos Terminology in 1 Corinthians: A Study in the Theology of the Corinthian Opponents of Paul and Its Relation to Gnosticism* (SBLDS, 12; Missoula, MT: Scholars Press, 1973).

Pearson, B.W.R, 'Gymnasia and Baths', in Evans and Porter (eds.), *Dictionary of New Testament Background*, pp. 435–36.

Pfitzner, Victor C., *Paul and the Agon Motif: Traditional Athletic Imagery in the Pauline Literature* (NovTSup, 16; Leiden: E.J. Brill, 1967).

Philo, *Works* (ed. F.H. Colson; 12 vols.; Cambridge, MA: Harvard University Press; London: Heinemann, 1929–53).

—Vol. IV (trans. F.H. Colson and G.H. Whitaker; LCL; Cambridge, MA: Harvard University Press; London: William Heinemann Ltd., 1932).

—Vol. VI (trans. F.H. Colson; LCL; Cambridge, MA: Harvard University Press; London: William Heinemann Ltd., 1935).

—Vol. VII (trans. F.H. Colson; LCL; Cambridge, MA: Harvard University Press; London: William Heinemann Ltd., 1937).

—Vol. IX (trans. F.H. Colson; LCL; London: William Heinemann Ltd; Cambridge, MA: Harvard University Press, 1941).

Picard, Olivier, 'Delphi and the Pythian Games', in Tzachou-Alexandri (ed.), *Mind and Body*, pp. 69–81.

Pickett, Raymond, *The Cross in Corinth: The Social Significance of the Death of Jesus* (JSNTSup, 143; Sheffield: Sheffield Academic Press, 1997).

Pilch, John J., '"Beat His Ribs While He Is Young" (Sir 30:12): A Window on the Mediterranean World', *BTB* 23 (1993), pp. 101–13.

—'Death with Honor: The Mediterranean Style Death of Jesus in Mark', *BTB* 25 (1995), pp. 65–70.

—'Family Violence in Cross-Cultural Perspective: An Approach for Feminist Interpreters of the Bible', in Brenner and Fontaine (eds.), *A Feminist Companion to Reading the Bible*, pp. 306–23.

Pleket, H.W., 'Some Aspects of the History of the Athletic Guilds', *ZPE* 10 (1973), pp. 197–227.

—'Games, Prizes, Athletes and Ideology: Some Aspects of the History of Sport in the Greco-Roman World', *Stadion* 1 (1975), pp. 49–89.

— 'Opvoeding in de Grieks-Romeinse wereld: een inleiding', *Lampas* 14 (1981), pp. 147–55.

Plutarch, *Moralia* I (trans. Frank Cole Babbitt; LCL; London: William Heinemann Ltd; New York: G.P. Putnam's Sons, 1927).

—*Moralia* II (trans. Frank Cole Babbitt; LCL; London: William Heinemann Ltd; New York: G.P. Putnam's Sons, 1928).

Pogoloff, Stephen M., *Logos and Sophia: The Rhetorical Situation of 1 Corinthians* (SBLDS, 134; Atlanta, GA: Scholars Press, 1992).

Poliakoff, Michael B., *Combat Sports in the Ancient World: Competition, Violence and Culture* (New Haven and London: Yale University Press, 1987).

—'Guilds of Performers and Athletes: Bureaucracy, Rewards and Privileges', *JRA* 2 (1989), pp. 295–98.

Porter, Stanley E., 'Inscriptions and Papyri: Greco-Roman', in Evans and Porter (eds.), *Dictionary of New Testament Background*, pp. 529–39.

Price, S.R.F., *Rituals and Power: the Roman Imperial Cult in Asia Minor* (Cambridge: Cambridge University Press 1984).

Quintilian, *The Institutio Oratoria of Quintilian*, Vol. I (trans. H.E. Butler; LCL; London: William Heinemann; New York: G.P. Putnam's Sons, 1921).

Radice, Betty, *The Letters of the Younger Pliny* (London: Penguin Books, reprinted 1969).

Raschke, Wendy J., 'Images of Victory: Some New Considerations of Athletic Monuments', in Raschke (ed.), *The Archaeology of the Olympics*, pp. 38–54.

—(ed.), *The Archaeology of the Olympics: The Olympics and Other Festivals in Antiquity* (Madison, WI and London: The University of Wisconsin Press, 1988).

Rawson, Beryl, '"The Family" in the Ancient Mediterranean: Past, Present and Future', *ZPE* 117 (1997), pp. 294–96.

Reinmuth, O.W., 'The Ephebic Inscription, Athenian Agora I 286', *Hesp* 24 (1955), pp. 220–39.

—'Ephebic Texts from Athens', *Hesp* 30 (1961), pp. 8–22.

Renfrew, Jane M., 'Food for Athletes and Gods: A Classical Diet', in Raschke (ed.), *The Archaeology of the Olympics*, pp. 174–81.

Richardson, Peter, 'Judgment in Sexual Matters in 1 Corinthians 6:1–11', *NovT* 25 (1983), pp. 37–58.

Ridgeway, Brunilde Sismondo, 'Sculpture from Corinth', *Hesp* 50 (1981), pp. 422–48.

Rizakis, A.D. (ed.), *Roman Onomastics in the Greek East: Social and Political Aspects: Proceedings of the International Colloquium Organized by the Finnish Institute and the Centre for Greek and Roman Antiquity, Athens 7–9 September 1993, Meletemata* 21 (1996).

Robbins, Vernon K., *Exploring the Texture of Texts: A Guide to Socio-Rhetorical Interpretation* (Valley Forge, PA: Trinity Press International, 1996).

—*The Tapestry of Early Christian Discourse: Rhetoric, Society and Ideology* (London and New York: Routledge, 1996).

Rohrbaugh, Richard L., 'The Social Location of the Marcan Audience', *BTB* 23 (1993), pp. 114–27.

—'Introduction' in Rohrbaugh (ed.), *The Social Sciences and New Testament Interpretation'*, pp. 1–15.

Rohrbaugh, Richard L. (ed.), *The Social Sciences and New Testament Interpretation* (Peabody, MA: Hendrickson Publishers, 1996).

Romano, D.G., 'Post-146 B.C. Land Use in Corinth, and Planning of the Roman Colony of 44 B.C.', in Gregory (ed.), *The Corinthia in the Roman Period*, pp. 9–30.

—'A Tale of Two Cities: Roman Colonies at Corinth', in Fentress (ed.) *Romanization and the City*, pp. 81–104.

—'City Planning, Centuriation, and Land Division in Roman Corinth: *Colonia Laus Iulia Corinthiensis & Colonia Iulia Flavia Augusta Corinthiensis'*, in Williams and Bookidis (eds.), *Corinth: Corinth, The Centenary 1896–1996*, pp. 279–301.

Romano, Irene Bald, 'A Hellenistic Deposit from Corinth: Evidence for Interim Period Activity (146 – 44 B.C.)', *Hesp* 63 (1994), pp. 57–104.

Rosner, Brian S. (ed.), *Understanding Paul's Ethics: Twentieth-Century Approaches* (Grand Rapids: Eerdmans; Carlisle: Paternoster, 1995).

Roueché, Charlotte, *Performers and Partisans at Aphrodisias in the Roman and Late Roman Periods* (JRS Monograph, 6; London: Society for the Promotion of Roman Studies, 1993).

Runia, David, 'Review of *Philo and Paul Among the Sophists* by Bruce Winter', *EvQ* 72 (2000), pp. 89–91.

Rutgers, Leonard Victor, 'Archaeological Evidence for the Interaction of Jews and Non-Jews in Late Antiquity', *AJA* 96 (1992), pp. 101–18.

Saller, Richard P., *Patriarchy, Property and Death in the Roman Family* (Cambridge Studies in Population, Economy and Society in Past Time, 25; Cambridge: Cambridge University Press, 1994).

Saller, Richard and Brent Shaw, 'Tombstones and Roman Family Relations in the Principate: Civilians, Soldiers and Slaves', *JRS* 74 (1984), pp. 124–56.

Salmon, J.B., *Wealthy Corinth: A History of the City to 338 BC* (Oxford: Clarendon Press, 1984).

Satlow, Michael L., 'Jewish Constructions of Nakedness in Late Antiquity', *JBL* 116 (1997), pp. 429–54.

Savage, Timothy B., *Power Through Weakness: Paul's Understanding of the Christian Ministry in 2 Corinthians* (SNTSMS, 86; Cambridge: Cambridge University Press, 1996).

Scanlon, Thomas F., '*Virgineum Gymnasium*: Spartan Females and Early Greek Athletics', in Raschke (ed.), *The Archaeology of the Olympics*, pp. 185–216.

Schmithals, Walter, *Gnosticism in Corinth: An Investigation of the Letters to the Corinthians* (trans. John E. Steely; Nashville and New York: Abingdon Press, 3rd edn, 1971).

Schuller, Tom (ed.), *The Changing University?* (Buckingham: SRHE and Open University Press, 1995).

Schüssler Fiorenza, Elisabeth, *In Memory of Her: A Feminist Theological Reconstruction of Christian Origins* (London: SCM Press, 1983).

Scranton, Robert L., *Corinth: Monuments in the Lower Agora and North of the Archaic Temple* (ASCSA, 1.3; Princeton, NJ: The American School of Classical Studies at Athens, 1951).

Segal, Erich, '"To Win or Die": A Taxonomy of Sporting Attitudes', *JSH* 11 (1984), pp. 25–31.

Serwint, Nancy, 'The Female Athletic Costume at the Heraia and Prenuptial Initiation Rites', *AJA* 97 (1993), pp. 403–22.

Sinanoğlu, Ahmet, *Didyma, Miletus, Priene* (trans. Bülent Özgöz; Şti: Hakan Ofset Ltd., 1997).

Smith, Dennis Edwin, 'The Egyptian Cults at Corinth', *HTR* 70 (1977), pp. 201–31.

Snyder, H. Gregory, *Teachers and Texts in the Ancient World: Philosophers, Jews and Christians* (Religion in the First Christian Centuries; London: Routledge, 2000).

Spawforth, Antony J.S., 'The Appaleni of Corinth', *GRBS* 15 (1974), pp. 295–303.

—'Sparta and the Family of Herodes Atticus: A Reconsideration of the Evidence', *ABSA* 75 (1980), pp. 203–20.

—'Agonistic Festivals in Roman Greece', in Walker and Cameron (eds.), *The Greek Renaissance in the Roman Empire*, pp. 193–97.

—'Gymnasiarch', in Hornblower and Spawforth (eds.), *The Oxford Classical Dictionary*, p. 659.

—'Epheboi', in Hornblower and Spawforth (eds.), *The Oxford Classical Dictionary*, pp. 527–28.

—'Roman Corinth: the Formation of a Colonial Elite', in Rizakis (ed.), *Roman Onomastics in the Greek East*, pp. 167–82.

Stanley, Christopher D., '"Neither Jew nor Greek": Ethnic Conflict in Graeco-Roman Society', *JSNT* 64 (1996), pp. 101–24.

Starr, Raymond J., 'Trimalchio's Libraries', *Hermes* 115 (1987), pp. 252–53.

Stoops, R.F., 'Coinage: Jewish', in Evans and Porter (eds.), *Dictionary of New Testament Background*, pp. 222–25.

Stowers, Stanley Kent, *The Diatribe and Paul's Letter to the Romans* (SBLDS, 57; Chico, CA: Scholars Press, 1981).

—'Social Status, Public Speaking and Private Teaching: the Circumstances of Paul's Preaching Activity', *NovT* 26 (1984), pp. 59–82.

Strange, William A., *Children in the Early Church: Children in the Ancient World, the New Testament and the Early Church* (Carlisle: Paternoster Press, 1996).

Stroud, Ronald S., 'Greek Inscriptions at Corinth', *Hesp* 41 (1972), pp. 198–217.

Sturgeon, Mary C., 'The Corinth Amazon: Formation of a Roman Classical Sculpture', *AJA* 99 (1995), pp. 483–505.

Sumney, Jerry L., 'The Place of 1 Corinthians 9:24–27 in Paul's Argument', *JBL* 119 (2000), pp. 329–33.

Swain, Simon, 'Plutarch's Lives of Cicero, Cato, and Brutus', *Hermes* 118 (1990), pp. 192–203.

Talbert, Charles H., *Reading Corinthians: A New Commentary for Preachers* (London: SPCK, 1990).

The Apostolic Fathers, Vol. 1 (trans. Kirsopp Lake; LCL; London: William Heinemann; New York: The Macmillan Co., 1912).

Theissen, Gerd, *The Social Setting of Pauline Christianity* (trans. John H. Schütz; Edinburgh: T. & T. Clark, 1982).

—'The Social Structure of Pauline Communities: Some Critical Remarks on J.J. Meggitt *Paul, Poverty and Survival', JSNT* 84 (2001), pp. 65–84.

—'Social Conflicts in the Corinthian Correspondence: Further Remarks on J.J. Meggitt, *Paul, Poverty and Survival', JSNT* (2003), pp. 371–91.

Thiselton, Anthony C., *The First Epistle to the Corinthians: A Commentary on the Greek Text* (NIGTC; Grand Rapids: Eerdmans; Carlisle: Paternoster, 2000).

Thompson, J.B., *Studies in the Theory of Ideology* (Cambridge: Polity Press, 1984).

— *Ideology and Modern Culture* (Cambridge: Polity Press, 1990).

Tomlin, Graham, 'Christians and Epicureans in 1 Corinthians', *JSNT* 68 (1997), pp. 51–72.

Tomlinson, Richard Allan, 'Palaestra', in Hornblower and Spawforth (eds.), *The Oxford Classical Dictionary*, p. 1099.

Too, Yun Lee, 'Legal Instructions in Classical Athens', in Too (ed.), *Education in Greek and Roman Antiquity*, pp. 111–32.

— *The Pedagogical Contract: The Economies of Teaching and Learning in the Ancient World* (Ann Arbor: The University of Michigan Press, 2000).

—'Introduction: Writing the History of Ancient Education', in Too (ed.), *Education in Greek and Roman Antiquity*, pp. 1–21.

—(ed.), *Education in Greek and Roman Antiquity* (Leiden: E.J. Brill, 2001).

Too, Yun Lee and Niall Livingstone (eds.), *Pedagogy and Power: Rhetorics of Classical Learning* (Ideas in Context, 50; Cambridge: Cambridge University Press, 1998).

Towner, P.H., 'Households and Household Codes', in Hawthorne and Martin (eds.), *Dictionary of Paul and His Letters*', pp. 417–19.

Townsend, John T., 'Ancient Education in the Time of the Early Roman Empire', in Benko and O'Rourke (eds.), *The Catacombs and the Colosseum*, pp. 139–63.

—'Ancient Education in the Time of the Early Roman Empire', in Benko and O'Rourke (eds.), *Early Christianity: The Roman Empire as the Setting of Primitive Christianity*, pp. 139–63.

—'Education (Greco-Roman Period)', in Freedman (ed.), *The Anchor Bible Dictionary*, Vol. 2, pp. 312–17.

Tracey, R., 'Jewish Renovation of an Amphitheatre', in Horsley, *New Documents Illustrating Early Christianity*, 4, no. 111, pp. 202–9.

Tracy, Stephen V., 'Greek Inscriptions from the Athenian Agora: Third to First Centuries B.C.', *Hesp* 51 (1982), pp. 57–64.

Tracy, Stephen V., and Christian Habicht, 'New and Old Panathenaic Victor Lists', *Hesp* 60 (1991), pp. 187–236.

Trebilco, P.R., *Jewish Communities in Asia Minor* (Cambridge: Cambridge University Press, 1991).

Trebilco, P.R. and C.A. Evans, 'Diaspora Judaism', in Evans and Porter (eds.), *Dictionary of New Testament Background*, pp. 281–96.

Tyler, Ronald L., 'First Corinthians 4:6 and Hellenistic Pedagogy', *CBQ* 60 (1998), pp. 97–103.

Tzachou-Alexandri, Olga, 'The Gymnasium. An Institution for Athletics and Education', in Tzachou-Alexandri (ed.), *Mind and Body*, pp. 31–40.

—(ed.), *Mind and Body: Athletic Contests in Ancient Greece* (trans. Judith Binder, Timothy Cullen, *et al.*; Athens: Ministry of Culture – the National Hellenic Committee I.C.O.M., 1989).

Vanderpool, Catherine de Grazia, 'Roman Portraiture: The Many Faces of Corinth', in Williams and Bookidis (eds.), *Corinth: Corinth, The Centenary 1896–1996*, pp. 369–84.

Vanhoye, A. (ed.), *L'Apôtre Paul: Personnalité, Style et Conception du Ministère* (BETL, 73; Leuven: Leuven University Press, 1986).

Wagner, Leslie, 'A Thirty-Year Perspective: From the Sixties to the Nineties', in Schuller (ed.), *The Changing University?*, pp. 15–24.

Wagner, J. Ross, '"Not Beyond the Things which are Written": A Call to Boast Only in the Lord (1 Cor 4.6)', *NTS* 44 (1998), pp. 279–87.

Walbank, F.W., *The Hellenistic World* (Fontana History of the Ancient World; London: Fontana Press, 3rd impression, 1992).

Walbank, M.E.H., 'The Foundation and Planning of Early Roman Corinth' in Fentress (ed.) *Romanization and the City*, pp. 81–104.

Walbank, Mary E. Hoskins, 'What's in a Name? Corinth under the Flavians', *ZPE* 139 (2002), pp. 251–64.

—'Aspects of Corinthian Coinage in the Late 1st and Early 2nd Centuries A.C.', in Williams and Bookidis (eds.), *Corinth: Corinth, The Centenary 1896–1996*, pp. 337–49.

Walker, Susan, and Averil Cameron, *The Greek Renaissance in the Roman Empire: Papers from the Tenth British Museum Classical Colloquium* (Bulletin Supplement, 55; London: Institute of Classical Studies, University of London, 1989).

Wanamaker, Charles A., 'A Rhetoric of Power: Ideology and 1 Corinthians 1–4', in Burke and Elliott (eds.), *Paul and the Corinthians*, pp. 115–37.

Watson, D.F., 'Education: Jewish and Greco-Roman', in Evans and Porter (eds.), *Dictionary of New Testament Background*, pp. 308–13.

—'Roman Social Classes', in Evans and Porter (eds.), *Dictionary of New Testament Background*, pp. 999–1004.

Webb, Ruth, 'The *Progymnasmata* as Practice', in Too (ed.), *Education in Greek and Roman Antiquity*, pp. 289–316.

Weinberg, Saul S., *Corinth: The Southeast Building, The Twin Basilicas, The Mosaic House* (ASCSA, 1.5; Princeton, NJ: The American School of Classical Studies at Athens, 1960).

Welborn, L.L., 'On the Discord in Corinth: 1 Corinthians 1–4 and Ancient Politics', *JBL* 106 (1987), pp. 85–111.

—*Politics and Rhetoric in the Corinthian Epistles* (Macon, GA: Mercer University Press, 1997).

—'Μωρὸς γένεσθω: Paul's Appropriation of the Role of the Fool in 1 Corinthians 1–4', *BibInt* X (2002), pp. 420–35.

West, Allen Brown (ed.), *Corinth: Latin Inscriptions, 1896–1926* (ASCSA, 8.2; Cambridge, MA: Harvard University Press, 1931).

Wilckens, Ulrich, *Weisheit und Torheit* (Tübingen: Mohr, 1959).

White, Eugene E. (ed.), *Rhetoric in Transition: Studies in the Nature and Uses of Rhetoric* (University Park, PA: Pennsylvania State University, 1980).

White, L. Michael, and O. Larry Yarbrough (eds.), *The Social World of the First Christians: Essays in Honor of Wayne A. Meeks* (Minneapolis, MN: Fortress Press, 1995).

Whitmarsh, Tim, 'Reading Power in Roman Greece: the *paideia* of Dio Chrysostom', in Too and Livingstone (eds.), *Pedagogy and Power*, pp. 192–213.

Wiedemann, Thomas, *Adults and Children in the Roman Empire* (London: Routledge, 1989).

Williams II, Charles K., 'Roman Corinth as a Commercial Center', in Gregory (ed.), *The Corinthia in the Roman Period*, pp. 31–46.

Williams II, Charles K., and Nancy Bookidis (eds.), *Corinth: Corinth, The Centenary 1896–1996* (ASCSA, 20; Princeton, NJ: The American School of Classical Studies at Athens, 2003).

Winston, David, 'Response' in Conley, '*General Education*', pp. 18–20.

Winter, Bruce W., 'Civil Litigation in Secular Corinth and the Church: The Forensic Background to 1 Corinthians 6.1–8', *NTS* 37 (1991), pp. 559–72.

—'Civic Litigation: 1 Corinthians 6:1–11', in Winter, *Seek the Welfare of the City*, pp. 105–21.

—'Social Mobility: 1 Corinthians 7:17–24', in Winter, *Seek the Welfare of the City*, pp. 145–64.

—*Seek the Welfare of the City: Christians as Benefactors and Citizens* (First Century Christians in the Graeco-Roman World Series; Grand Rapids: Eerdmans; Carlisle: Paternoster, 1994).

—'Civil Litigation in Secular Corinth and the Church: The Forensic Background to 1 Corinthians 6.1–8', in Rosner (ed.), *Understanding Paul's Ethics*, pp. 85–103.

—*Philo and Paul Among the Sophists* (SNTSMS, 96; Cambridge: Cambridge University Press, 1997).

—'Gallio's Ruling on the Legal Status of Early Christianity', *TynBul* 50 (1999), pp. 213–24.

—*After Paul Left Corinth: The Influence of Secular Ethics and Social Change* (Grand Rapids and Cambridge, UK: Eerdmans, 2001).
—*Philo and Paul Among the Sophists: Alexandrian and Corinthian Responses to a Julio-Claudian Movement* (Grand Rapids and Cambridge, UK: Eerdmans, 2nd edn, 2002).
—'The "Underlays" of Conflict and Compromise in 1 Corinthians', in Burke and Elliott (eds.), *Paul and the Corinthians*, pp. 139–55.
Winterbottom, M., 'Introduction', in *The Elder Seneca: Declamations* (trans. M. Winterbottom, LCL; Cambridge: Harvard University Press, 1974).
Wiseman, James, 'Excavations at Corinth, the Gymnasium Area, 1965', *Hesp* 36 (1967), pp. 13–41.
—'Excavations in Corinth, The Gymnasium Area, 1967–68', *Hesp* 38 (1969), pp. 64–106.
—'The Gymnasium Area at Corinth, 1969–1970', *Hesp* 41 (1972), pp. 1–42.
—'Corinth and Rome I: 228 B.C. – A.D. 267', *ANRW* II 7.1 (1979), pp. 438–548.
Witherington III, Ben, *Conflict and Community in Corinth: A Socio-Rhetorical Commentary on 1 and 2 Corinthians* (Grand Rapids: Eerdmans; Carlisle: Paternoster, 1995).
Witt, R.E., *Isis in the Graeco-Roman World* (N.p.: Thames and Hudson, 1971).
Wolff, C., *Der erste Brief des Paulus an die Korinther* (THKNT, 7; Leipzig: Evangelische Verlagsanstalt, 1996).
Wolfson, H.A., *Philo: Foundations of Religious Philosophy in Judaism, Christianity and Islam* (2 vols.; Cambridge, MA: Harvard University Press, 1948).
Woolf, G., 'Becoming Roman, Staying Greek: Culture, Identity and the Civilising Process in the Roman East', *PCPS* 40 (1994), pp. 116–43.
Wuellner, Wilhelm, 'Paul as Pastor. The Function of Rhetorical Questions in First Corinthians', in. Vanhoye (ed.), *L'Apôtre Paul: Personnalité, Style et Conception du Ministère*, pp. 16–48.
Wycherley, R.E., 'Peripatos: The Athenian Philosophical Scene – I', *GR* 8 (1961), pp. 152–63.
—'Peripatos: The Athenian Philosophical Scene – II', *GR* 9 (1962), pp. 2–21.
Yaghjian, Lucretia B., 'Ancient Reading', in Rohrbaugh (ed.), *The Social Sciences and New Testament Interpretation*, pp. 206–30.
Yamauchi, Edwin M., *The Archaeology of New Testament Cities in Western Asia Minor* (London and Glasgow: Pickering & Inglis, 1980).
Yarbrough, O. Larry, 'Parents and Children in the Letters of Paul', in White and Yarbrough (eds.), *The Social World of the First Christians*, pp. 126–41.
Young, David C., 'Panathenaic Prizes in the Classical Period (*IG* III^2 2311) in Young, *The Olympic Myth*, pp. 115–27.
—*The Olympic Myth of Greek Amateur Athletics* (Chicago: Ares Publishers, Inc., 1985).
—'How the Amateurs Won the Olympics', in Raschke (ed.), *The Archaeology of the Olympics*, pp. 55–75.
Young, Norman H., '*Paidagogos*: the Social Setting of a Pauline Metaphor', *NovT* 29 (1987), pp. 150–76.
—'The Figure of the Paidagogos in Art and Literature', *BA* 53 (1990), pp. 80–86.

Website

http://www.tyndale.cam.ac.uk/Tyndale/staff/Winter/Corinth.htm

This website is identified on the back cover of Bruce W. Winter, *After Paul Left Corinth: The Influence of Secular Ethics and Social Change* (Grand Rapids and Cambridge, UK: Eerdmans, 2001). It provides additional plates of Corinth to support those within his book.

Index of References

Index of Authors